Developing the UN Register of Conventional Arms

Bradford Arms Register Studies

The Bradford Arms Register Studies
(BARS) series is the result of an ongoing
research project based at the Department
of Peace Studies, University of Bradford
and supported by the Ford Foundation.
Studies published so far include:

1. Malcolm Chalmers and Owen Greene,
Implementing and Developing the United
Nations Register of Conventional Arms,
May 1993.

2. Malcolm Chalmers and Owen Greene,
The United Nations Register of
Conventional Arms: An Initial
Examination of the First Report, October
1993.

3. Malcolm Chalmers and Owen Greene,
Background Information: An analysis of
information provided to the UN on
military holdings and procurement through
national production in the first year of the
Register of Conventional Arms, March
1994.

Bradford Arms Register Studies
Department of Peace Studies
University of Bradford
West Yorkshire BD7 1DP
United Kingdom
Telephone: +44 274 385 235
Facsimile: +44 274 385 240

Developing the UN Register of Conventional Arms

Edited by

Malcolm Chalmers Owen Greene Edward J. Laurance Herbert Wulf

Bradford Arms Register Studies No 4

1994

UNIVERSITY OF
BRADFORD

British Library Cataloguing in Publication Data
A catalogue record for this book is available from the British Library

ISSN 0266 0997
ISBN 1-85143-095-4

Typeset by Kim Tay
Cover design by Simon Coley
Printed in Great Britain on acid-free paper
by Redwood Books, Trowbridge, Wiltshire

Contents

Part Four – Implementation and Development

Part Five – Annexes

List of tables, figures and appendices

CHAPTER 1

Introduction

The United Nations Register of Conventional Arms is still very young, having only come into operation in 1993. Yet it is already being reviewed by a UN group of governmental experts which is due to make recommendations on ways to develop and strengthen it in time for consideration by the UN First Committee during autumn 1994. This book aims to examine the implementation and potential development of the Register, and its potential significance for international security. It aims to inform the debates about the priorities for developing the Register amongst governmental policy-makers and the interested public. The chapters have been developed from papers presented at an international workshop on this topic organised by the editors in April 1994, in which most members of the UN Group of Experts participated together with a number of academic and government specialists.

I   The historical development of the Register: a brief overview

The establishment of the UN Register of Conventional Arms took place in a context shaped by two seminal events: the end of the Cold War and the second Gulf War which saw an Iraq armed with imported advanced weapons overrun its neighbour Kuwait, threaten the oil fields of the Gulf, and hold off an international coalition of the major military powers for almost six months. The end of the Cold War saw the disintegration of the Soviet Union and the emergence of a Russia that was working in tandem with the other major powers, in the UN Security Council and elsewhere. The immediate effect was increased attention paid to non-proliferation of weapons systems and transparency.

The increased concern for proliferation gave a huge boost to several non-proliferation efforts such as the stalled Chemical Weapons Convention which was completed in 1993, and the Missile Technology Control Regime (MTCR) whose membership and effectiveness has developed substantially since 1990, during which time Russia, China, South Africa and Israel have also pledged adherence to its guidelines. The Nuclear Suppliers Group (NSG) also responded to the reality uncovered by the Gulf War by strengthening their guidelines for coordinating controls of exports of sensitive nuclear technologies and adding additional dual-use items to its list of restricted items. Having successfully completed the Chemical Weapons Convention, the Geneva-based Conference on Disarmament has turned its attention to negotiating a Comprehensive Test Ban Treaty and, perhaps, a fissile material cut-off agreement.

The international community has also begun to emphasize transparency as a way to promote cooperative security. This is most readily seen in the Conference on Security and Cooperation in Europe (CSCE) where a host of transparency measures were put into effect after 1975 and further developed as the Cold War ended, to include exchanges of information under the CFE and Open Skies Treaties and the more regularized exchange of data on order of battle and inventories of member states. In the United Nations, the UN Disarmament Commission (UNDC) has taken up the question of objective information on military matters. Several regional organizations have begun to take steps to make military information more open.[1] There is even an effort by the international financial organizations to tackle a subject long taboo, making transparent trade statistics on military trade.[2]

Throughout the Cold War the trade in conventional weapons was never a part of the larger non-proliferation agenda, at least at the international and multilateral level. But the end of the Cold War brought about major systemic changes in the arms trade which were relevant to the emergence of the UN Register. Glasnost and subsequent democratisation greatly reduced (ex-) Soviet bloc countries' resistance to increased transparency in this area. Moreover, for a number of reasons, arms exports from the Soviet Union declined radically. This removed one of the major suppliers of the Cold War, leaving the United States as by far the largest arms supplier for some years to come. With the end of the Cold War and its systemic arms race, the demand for advanced high technology weaponry and large conventional forces declined significantly amongst CSCE states, with defense budgets in major military industrial nations declining as a result. Also, the concept of exporting arms for political influence began to be replaced by economic incentives (especially preservation of domestic arms industries and jobs) as the primary motive of supplier states. These factors have led to significant amounts of surplus equipment becoming available at low prices. Major arms producing nations, therefore, have not been able to keep national production up through exports. The above realities resulted in a downward trend in the trade in major conventional weapons that was well underway by August 1990 when Iraq invaded Kuwait with a vast arsenal of imported weapons. After five consecutive years of decline, the downward trend in deliveries of major conventional weapons seems to have stabilized in 1993.[3]

In the wake of the Gulf War there was an unprecedented outpouring of proposals for arms trade control proposals from supplier governments,[4] recipient governments,[5] defense trade publications,[6] the Chief Executive Officer of Daimler-Benz,[7] and European organizations.[8] These proposals called for policies to tighten up export procedures and begin to develop more international controls. On May 29 1991, President Bush announced the "Middle East Arms Control Initiative," calling for the five largest arms supplier nations (the US, USSR, France, the UK and China) to meet in Paris to "establish guidelines for restraints on destabilizing transfers of conventional arms, as well as weapons of mass destruction and associated technology." The proposal also called for expanding the talks to other suppliers and permitting states in the region to "acquire the conventional capabilities they legitimately need to deter and defend against military aggression." To implement the regime, suppliers would commit themselves to "observe a general code of responsible arms transfers, avoid destabilizing transfers, and establish effective domestic export controls on the end-use of arms or other items to be transferred." The proposal also called for a consultative mechanism. Further, it was recommended that a freeze be put on surface-to-surface missiles in the region, with a goal of their eventual elimination.[9] Complementing and sometimes challenging the President's effort were a series of proposals from the US Congress. They ranged from an outright ban on all arms sales to the Middle East, to support for the arms register concept.[10]

Overall, the above developments promoted wide international acceptance of an emerging international principle, that the accumulation of 'excessive or destabilizing' amounts of conventional weaponry by a state is unacceptable. The five permanent members of the UN Security Council began meeting in July 1991 to develop guidelines and procedures for cooperative multilateral restraints on destabilizing arms transfers. They made some progress towards these aims during 1991-2, but the intense competition for arms sales was always going to make it difficult to achieve substantial restraint. In this context, supplier states will always find it difficult to agree that a potential major arms sale, on which jobs and powerful domestic arms industries may depend, would indeed be destabilising. The P5 talks stalled in September 1992, when China suspended its participation in response to the US decision to sell 150 F-16 aircraft to Taiwan, and they have remained stalled since then.

It was in this context that, in parallel with the P5 talks, support developed within the United Nations to promote cooperative transparency arrangements as an alternative approach to confidence-building and the prevention of destabilising accumulations of conventional arms. Proposals to establish a UN register of arms transfers had been considered in the UN since the mid-

1960s.[11] However, no progress was made until the international environment became more favourable towards the end of the 1980s, as the cold war came to an end and as international experience with military transparency arrangements developed (particularly amongst CSCE countries). Moreover, an increasing number of countries began to publish details of their arms exports: the French, Germans, Bulgarians, Czechs and the Soviets all published heretofore secret data on arms exports.[12]

On 7 December 1988, the UN General Assembly passed Resolution 43/75 I, which requested the Secretary-General to undertake, with the assistance of a panel of governmental experts, a "study on ways and means of promoting transparency in international transfers of conventional arms on a universal and non-discriminatory basis."[13] This Expert Study Group was established in 1989 and proceeded to carry out its study, for the most part without attracting much international interest. However, in the aftermath of the expulsion of Iraq from Kuwait, as information about arms exports to Iraq and its neighbours during the 1980s became widely disseminated, proposals to increase the transparency of the international arms trade gained high-level political support in the EC, G7 and P5 states amongst many others. In July 1991, for example, the P5 and G7 summits endorsed proposals to establish a register of arms transfers.[14]

In this context, the report of the Expert Study Group, which was submitted to the UN Secretary-General in September 1991, was well-received. The report included a range of recommendations concerning the role of transparency in promoting restraint in arms transfers, not the least of which being the creation of a universal and non-discriminatory register of arms transfers under the auspices of the United Nations.[15] The EC states and Japan rapidly followed-up this recommendation by circulating a draft resolution to the UN First Committee members. This proposed the immediate establishment of a 'Register of International Arms Transfers', while referring the issue of reporting military holdings and production for discussion at the Conference on Disarmament at Geneva.

However, it soon became clear that this draft proposal would have to be revised if it was to receive wide support, particularly amongst developing, arms importing, countries. Such countries complained that an arms transfers register by itself would discriminate against them, because it would impose more transparency on their arms procurement programmes than on those of countries with substantial arms industries. In response to these concerns, Japan and the EC presented a revised proposal, which was ultimately passed by 150 votes in favour (with Cuba and Iraq abstaining) by the UN General

Assembly on 9 December 1991 (UN General Assembly Resolution 46/36 L, entitled 'Transparency in Armaments'). The resolution established a UN Register of Conventional Arms, its purpose being to enhance transparency in arms transprocurement and military holdings in order to strengthen international security by promoting confidence-building among states and encouraging restraint in the production and transfer of arms.[16] In establishing the Register, the General Assembly hoped it would contribute to the timely identification and prevention of excessive and destabilizing accumulations of arms, while at the same time recognizing the rights of member states to procure and maintain armed forces for the purposes of self-defence.

The Register is thus a transparency arrangement, primarily designed to promote confidence-building and restraint rather than to impose limits or controls on arms transfers and military holdings. Participation is voluntary, and is based on political agreement rather than an international legal convention. As such, it is a relatively modest measure. However, in view of the formidable obstacles to establishing international controls on conventional arms transfers, production or holdings, or even to achieve timely international agreement on the existence and character of destabilising accumulations of arms or regions of tension, it may for the present be the best global arrangement that can be achieved in this area. Certainly, with the stalling of the P5 process, it is now the only such arrangement that we have.

The Register came into effect from January 1992. Member states were requested to submit their first annual report (for 1992) by 30 April, 1993. Initially, states were mainly requested to report imports or exports of seven categories of conventional arms: battle tanks, armoured combat vehicles, large-calibre artillery systems, combat aircraft, attack helicopters, warships, and missiles and missile launchers. However, pending the expansion of the Register to include procurement from national production and military holdings, participating states were also invited to provide background information relating to their military holdings, procurement through national production, and policies and regulations relating to arms transfers. In the meantime, a UN Panel of Experts was established to elaborate and define recommendations for implementing the Register and to report on ways in which it could be developed in the future.

Seventeen countries were represented on the 1992 Panel of Experts, including all P5 states together with Ghana, Japan, Egypt, Brazil, Argentina, Mexico, Switzerland, Malaysia, Canada, India, the Netherlands, and the Czech and Slovak Federal Republic. It was chaired by the Dutch Representative, Ambassador Wagenmakers. The Panel was in some respects a negotiating forum.

Decisions were taken by consensus, in order to achieve wide participation in the Register from the outset. It met four times in the first half of 1992: three times in 'official' session, together with an additional discussion meeting hosted by the government of Japan where the panel members were joined by representatives from many other countries. By making a number of compromises, the Panel was able to produce a consensus report, which was subsequently endorsed by the General Assembly without dissent in December 1992.[17] The report defined the technical procedures and definitions for the operation of the Register, including a standardised reporting form for data on arms imports and exports. Questions relating to enhancing transparency relating to weapons of mass destruction and high technology were referred to the CD in Geneva. A list of issues relating to the early expansion of the scope of the Register were provided for consideration by the 1994 Group of Experts. Meanwhile, some $228,000 per year was allocated for the UN Office of Disarmament Affairs to maintain the Register.

Attention then turned to the task of encouraging states to participate in the Register and providing them with technical guidance on how to fill out the standardised reporting forms. This was a key phase in the establishment of the Register, and one in which the UN Office of Disarmament Affairs (ODA) could play only a limited role. Little UN resources had been allocated for such training. Moreover, a number of states felt sufficiently sensitive about expanding the role of the UN Secretariat that the ODA was instructed that it should play no proactive role in reminding states to submit their returns by the 30 April deadline, and still less in interpreting the reporting requirements. In this context, the process depended on voluntary actions by states. Four regional workshops were held in early 1993 (in Tokyo (Asia-Pacific), Florence (Mediterranean and Middle East), Warsaw (Eastern Europe) and Buenos Aires (Latin America)) to provide relevant government officials with training on guidelines for reporting. Unfortunately, no resources were found to organise a regional workshop for Sub-Saharan Africa. However, those workshops that did take place reportedly had an important confidence-building function as well as a technical one. States that were undecided about whether to participate were often more ready to join the Register once it became clearer that some of their neighbours were also intending to do so. As the deadline for national submissions approached, a number of EC states, together with other countries represented on the Panel such as Japan, Canada, the USA and Brazil, engaged in an organised diplomatic lobbying campaign to encourage countries to participate. In the event, few states met the deadline, but by the time the first report of the Register was published in October, 80 states had responded: an encouraging start to this new transparency arrangement. (Three additional governments replied after the report was published.)

II   The 1994 review process and the Monterey workshop

As part of General Assembly resolution 46/36/L which established the Register in December 1991, it was agreed that a new UN Group of Experts would be set up in 1994 to review the operation of the Register and consider ways in which it could usefully be developed, including the possible addition of further categories of equipment and the elaboration of the Register to include procurement from national production and military holdings . All member states were also invited to submit their views on these issues to the Secretary-General by 30 April 1994, so that these could be taken into account by the Group of Experts. The recommendations of the Group of Experts would then be considered by the UN First Committee and the UN General Assembly during the autumn of 1994.

The 1994 review process was due to take place rather early in the life of the Register. By the time of the first meeting on the Group of Experts, in February 1994, only one annual report would have been issued and evidence of participation in the second year of reporting may still be unclear by the time of its third and last formal meeting timetabled for July and August. As the time approached in the autumn of 1993 to constitute the new Group of Experts, arguments were raised that it might have been better to defer the review process for a year in order to allow the present arrangements to settle down.

However, the process continued according to schedule, in order to maintain the momentum behind the development of the Register. A number of countries were concerned that the Register did not become established in its initial form. Wide agreement amongst UN member states to establish the Register was secured partly on the basis of an understanding that it would be expanded at an early stage to include procurement from national production and military holdings. Egypt wanted an early opportunity to continue to press for transparency measures relating to weapons of mass destruction and high technology items. Moreover, there were many proposals to revise existing weapons categories and include new ones.

There were strong pressures to expand the Group of Experts to include representatives of countries that were not amongst the 17 states represented in the 1992 Panel of Experts. This generated further incentives to participate in the Register in its first year of operation since it was understood that non-participation would undermine a country's chances of being included in the 1994

Group. It was finally agreed to expand the Group of Experts to include repre-
sentatives from 23 countries: Argentina, Australia, Brazil, Canada, China,
Cuba, Egypt, Finland, France, Germany, Ghana, India, Israel, Japan, Jordan,
Mexico, Netherlands, Pakistan, Russia, Singapore, UK, USA, and Zimbabwe.
There was therefore substantial continuity of membership between the 1992
and 1994 panels, enhanced by the fact that most of the individual representatives also remained the same and Ambassador Wagenmakers continued as
Chair of the Group. Of the 23 countries represented on the 1994 Group of
Experts, only Jordan and Zimbabwe provided no report for the Register for
1992. They were included in the group in order to increase participation from
the Middle East and Africa.

The Group of Experts has many issues on its agenda. It met first for the week
beginning 7 February 1994, and has two further two-week-long formal
meetings scheduled to begin on 30 May and 22 July. Some issues are complex
and controversial, and whether or not it will be possible to produce a
consensus on its recommendations may only become clear at the final stages
of its last meeting. In this context, the members of the Group of Experts and
the UN Centre for Disarmament Affairs agreed to a proposal from the editors
of this book to participate in a workshop in which the issues could be informally discussed with a number of academic specialists together with some
additional governmental experts from countries that are not represented in
the Group.

The workshop took place in Monterey, California on 6 – 9 April 1994 in the
hope that this timing - between the first and second of the formal meetings of
the Group - would allow the papers and discussions at the workshop to
contribute most usefully to the review process. The workshop was organised
by the Monterey Institute of International Studies (USA), the Bonn International Center for Conversion (Germany), and the Department of Peace
Studies, Bradford University (UK). It was made possible by the generous and
timely support of the Ford Foundation, Ploughshares Fund and the Volkswagen Foundation.

III   The book

The chapters of this book are edited and revised versions of the papers
presented at the workshop. It is hoped that they will contribute to a deeper
and wider understanding of the issues associated with the implementation and
development of the Register, and its potential contribution to international
confidence-building and security. We hope that it will provide a valuable

resource for governmental experts and officials, analysts and the interested public during the remainder of the 1994 review process and beyond.

Chapter 2 is written by Ambassador Hendrik Wagenmakers, who provides a personal overview of the development and significance of the Register amongst the growing family of confidence-building and transparency measures, together with a discussion of the main issues for the 1994 review process. As the UN representative for the Netherlands during the Dutch Presidency of the EC in the second half of 1991, Ambassador Wagenmakers played a leading role in drafting and promoting agreement on the General Assembly resolution that established the Register. He was subsequently Netherlands representative and chair of the 1992 Panel of Experts and continues in both of these roles in the 1994 Group of Experts, as well as being the Dutch Permanent Representative at the UN in Geneva. He is therefore able to bring unique insight and authority to a review of the process of, and priorities for, developing the Register and also of the related discussions on transparency in armaments at the Conference on Disarmament at Geneva.

High on the agenda for the 1994 review process is the question of whether and how to develop the present register of arms transfers. Part Two of the book therefore comprises four chapters that address and illuminate this question. In Chapter 3, Edward J. Laurance and Herbert Wulf examine the lessons from the first year of the Register's operation. Overall, they judge that the Register had a good start, with 83 governments submitting replies including nearly all of the major arms exporters and most major importers. The great majority of the international arms trade in the seven categories of equipment covered by the Register was reported, in many cases revealing transfers that were not known to independent 'arms watchers' such as SIPRI. However, participation was patchy in several regions of the world, and in the Middle East and Sub-Saharan Africa only a few countries provided information for the Register. Moreover, there were many discrepancies between the information provided by importers and exporters, and countries responded in different ways with some not completing standardised forms or apparently operating according to various understandings of the categories of equipment covered or the definition of a transfer.

There are a range of reasons for these problems, which the authors analyse. However, combined with problems with the categories of arms covered in the Register, they limit the interpretability of the Register and need to be addressed, Laurance and Wulf argue, if the Register is to achieve its objectives in future. The Chapter examines each of these objectives and discusses the extent to which the Register was able to achieve them in its first year. It finishes by examining whether the present seven categories of equipment covered in the Register are adequate to address the major trends in the trade of potentially destabilising weapons, and suggest areas where revisions and extension of these categories should be considered.

The question of whether and how to strengthen, deepen, and widen the present register reporting system is examined in Chapter 4 by Malcolm Chalmers and Owen Greene. Although the Register has, with good reason, started out as a purely voluntary arrangement with little institutional development or resources, the authors argue that it is important that the emerging transparency regime is gradually strengthened and that the rights and obligations of participants are defined and developed. As a first step, they discuss whether definitions of 'participation' should be tightened, whether 'common lists' of equipment covered by the Register should be developed, and whether and how to develop regular review procedures (involving the Secretariat and bodies such as a 'standing panel of governmental experts') to improve the reliability and interpretability of the Register and to address problems and disputes relating to implementation.

In relation to the 'deepening' of the Register, Chapter 4 discusses the possibilities for developing the guidelines to include fuller descriptions of the items reported, drawing partly on the experience with CSCE transparency measures and with the first year of the Register. For example, should information be provided about the designations, types and models of equipment reported? Finally, the authors examine each of the existing seven categories of equipment and discuss whether and how they should be revised, and whether the Register should be extended by expanding categories or adding new ones. They argue that caution is required, but that there are nevertheless a number of areas where a good case can be made for some revision and expansion.

Ian Anthony develops some of these issues in Chapter 5, where he examines the requirements for developing a useful register of arms transfers. He argues that a register of arms transfers is potentially important in its own right, and should not be regarded simply as a stepping stone towards achieving transparency in military holdings. Countries can transform the capabilities of their armed forces relatively rapidly by importing sophisticated equipment that would take years, if not decades, to develop indigenously. Moreover, open information about importers and exporters can encourage restraint and responsibility in ways that a register of military holdings would not achieve so directly.

After a brief introduction to the ways in which SIPRI collect information on arms transfers, Anthony compares these to the approach taken in the Register. In the process, he illuminates the relative strengths and weaknesses of the Register, and raises a number of issues and proposals for improving its usefulness as a source of reliable and interpretable information and as a basis for confidence-building and conflict prevention measures.

The question of whether to extend the Register to include weapons of mass destruction or high-technology with military application has been a controversial one. The Register already covers weapons platforms and delivery vehicles such as missiles, planes and artillery designed to carry weapons of mass destruction, which should be reported alongside purely conventional weapons under the present arrangements. However, the Register covers platforms and delivery systems rather than warheads, whether conventional, chemical or nuclear. Proposals for the Register to cover nuclear warheads, for example, would therefore not only be very controversial but also may raise profound questions about whether also to include conventional munitions. Separate transparency arrangements for nuclear weapons may therefore be preferable to attempts to explicitly include them in the Register.

In Chapter 6, Holger Iburg examines issues associated with developing within the UN system multilateral arms export controls or international arrangements for transparency or control of transfers of high-technology with military application. Partly on the basis of discussions and debates at the Conference of Disarmament, he outlines the problems with arriving at common definitions or understandings of an 'arms transfer', or 'excessive and destabilising' accumulations, or in identifying and defining which 'high-technologies with military applications'. He examines some options and issues that should be addressed by any proposals to develop export control guidelines and institutions in the UN, drawing partly on recent experience relating to Iraq. Finally, Iburg addresses the possibility of extending the Register to include military or dual technology in the Register, coming to the conclusion that the problems with expanding the Register substantially into such areas would be formidable at present.

Perhaps the most important issue for the 1994 review process is the question of whether and how to expand the Register to include procurement from national production and military holdings. The chapters in Part 3 of the book address issues related to this question. It begins with two chapters examining the information that is already available from perhaps the two pre-eminent non-official sources of systematic information on military holdings, arms development and procurement: Jane's Information Group and the International Institute for Strategic Studies (IISS). Chapter 7 is written by Tim Mahon of Jane's Information, and Chapter 8 by Colonel Andrew Duncan from IISS.

In the absence of publicly-available official information, Jane's publications and the IISS's *The Military Balance* are widely used (together with arms transfer data from SIPRI) as sources of authoritative information. As discussed in these chapters, in many cases they have acquired semi-official status. An appreciation of the range and reliability of the information available, and of the ways in which it is collected, is therefore important for discussions relating to the possible expansion of the Register. Such non-official resources can be used to make comparisons with information reported to the Register (as Duncan does, for example, in relation to reported background information on military holdings), to help with the interpretation of data reported to the Register, or to inform the ways in which it could be expanded to include procurement from national production and military holdings. At the simplest level many government officials may be unaware of how much information is already unofficially available, leading to exaggerated concerns about the security implications of releasing such information officially.

Chapter 9 focuses on ways in which the Register itself could be expanded to include procurement from national production and military holdings. Malcolm Chalmers and Owen Greene begin by reviewing the incentives, concerns and potential significance of extending the Register in this way. The incentives and potential significance are very substantial, as are the potential sensitivities. They argue that the success or failure of the 1994 review will probably be judged largely according to the way this issue is addressed. Their chapter examines the experience of reporting on procurement from national production and military holdings in background information in the first year of the Register. Then it discusses possible reporting guidelines for military holdings, such as what categories of equipment should be used and what types of information could be requested. Perhaps the main issue for debates about how to include military holdings in the Register relates to what should be included in the definitions of military holdings. The authors systematically examine the options.

Chalmers and Greene then outline the distinct issues raised by proposals to include procurement from national production in the Register, and discuss ways in which this term could be defined. In principle, two broad approaches can be identified: one focusing on *procurement* by the government of domestically-produced weapons and the other on non-exported arms from *domestic production*. By developing and contrasting the implications of these approaches, the authors illuminate some of the possible loopholes and problems raised by each. They then raise a new proposal for consideration: the establishment of a 'withdrawals' section of the Register. The inclusion of procurement from national production in the Register is mainly motivated by a desire to develop complete coverage of sources of new arms for a country, that is from imports and domestic production. But it may be inconsistent or misleading to focus on this task without also encouraging systematic reporting of withdrawals from service, due for example to accidents, war or obsolescence. Finally, this chapter identifies a number of ways in which guidelines for providing 'background information' for the Register could usefully be developed.

In the final chapter of this section, Ravinder Pal Singh discusses the factors that shape or constrain the transparency of countries' procurement policies, emphasizing that the prospects for establishing an international transparency regime in this area depend greatly on countries' domestic structures and practices. Singh discusses the ways in which the transparency and public accountability of state behaviour may depend on the economic and political characteristics of the states concerned. He suggests that transparency improves efficiency in domestic policy-making, but may depend significantly on levels of economic development. He further suggests that it may be possible to identify clusters of characteristics associated with different types of regime or constitution which will determine overall attitudes towards transparency. Domestic interest groups that are typically for or against domestic transparency are identified.

Singh notes that transparency of policy-making systems, procurement plans, and the procurement budgets are relevant to international confidence-building measures as well as the transparency in numbers and types of arms procured, as might be reported in the Register. In this context, the chapter makes a number of suggestions for international measures that could improve transparency of all of the above dimensions of procurement.

Part 4 of the book is concerned mainly with the relationship between the development of the Register and the development of global or regional confidence-building, cooperative security, or conflict prevention regimes. In Chapter 11, Antonia Chayes and Abram Chayes apply the findings of their recent studies of well-established cooperative security regimes to identify priorities for the development of the Register. The chapter outlines some key characteristics of such cooperative security regimes, including: a strong normative base; an inclusive and non-discriminatory character; transparency; active management; and the availability of recourse to sanctions. In relation to norms, they suggest that an international norm of transparency in arms transfers has begun to develop. The Register is inclusive and non-discriminatory, and is itself a transparency arrangement. Thus, after illuminating the importance and relevance of each of these factors, Chayes and Chayes focus on the significance of active management of the Register. In this context, they argue for the importance of developing institutions and procedures for: policy review and assessment; capacity-building; adaptation and modification of treaty norms; and dispute settlement. The chapter concludes that the development of organisational capacity is a priority for the Register if it is to become an effective cooperative security arrangement.

In Chapter 12, Fred Pearson and Michael Brzoska discuss the potential value of the Register for providing early warning of international conflict. They examine the experience with the India-Pakistan, Middle Eastern, Ogaden, Falklands/Malvinas, and Gulf wars for lessons about the early indicators of emerging conflict. Then, using SIPRI data on annual arms transfers to each of the countries involved in these wars, they ask whether data on arms imports would have provided a reliable early warning indicator of tensions leading to war. They conclude that the relationship between the onset of war and arms build-ups (let alone arms imports) is not sufficiently strong for the information in the Register to be directly used as an instrument for early-warning of conflicts. The onset of war is a complex process in which many factors can be important, and without a detailed knowledge of the situation, information on arms transfers and holdings may be a misleading guide. Nevertheless, exchanges of official information on these matters can provide a basis for the development of regional and global confidence-building and cooperative security regimes, and it is in this way that the Register is likely to make its greatest contribution to international security.

Chapter 13 explores the significance of the Register for a particular region -- Latin America. Augusto Varas begins by outlining the evolution of cooperative security agreements in this region, and examines present trends. He emphasizes the extent to which security perceptions and concerns differ between countries and sub-regions, as does the character of their domestic divisions and alignments and their relationship with the United States. Whereas a range of confidence-building measures and security agreement have developed in relation to weapons of mass destruction, he argues that this is not the case for conventional arms. It is in this context that the Register could contribute substantially to cooperative security-building in the region. However, after reviewing the participation of Latin American states in the Register in its first year of operation, Varas argues that the priority is to promote wider participation and to consolidate and institutionalise the implementation of the Register in the region. Some expansion of the existing categories and the inclusion of procurement from national production and military holdings would be useful, provided that this is done cautiously. However, weapons of mass destruction and high-technology with military applications should be tackled in separate arrangements. Finally, the chapter reviews some opportunities for developing other conflict prevention and transparency mechanisms in the region. Overall, Varas argues that the Register itself should remain a global regime, with regional priorities being to promote full participation in it and to use the Register to stimulate and reinforce a range of regional and sub-regional security mechanisms.

The 'regionalisation' of the Register is often discussed as a possible approach by which it could be made more relevant to the particular concerns and needs of different regions. Following Varas' discussion of Latin America, Joseph DiChiaro III examines the more general issues raised by such proposals in Chapter 14. He outlines the variety of sources of calls for regionalisation, which include the Secretary-General, the General Assembly and the UN Disarmament Commission. However, DiChiaro argues that the intentions and implications of 'regionalisation' proposals has typically been unclear. He concludes that the Register should remain a global instrument, with regional arrangements aiming to complement and reinforce it. A range of ways in which such regional arrangements could be implemented are then discussed, including possible pre-notification and conflict resolution arrangements on a regional level.

Finally, in Part 5 of the book, we provide a number of background documents that we believe will be of value to readers. First, we reproduce or summarise relevant UN documents, including General Assembly resolutions, the 1992 Panel of Experts report, and the current standardized forms for reporting exports and imports. Second, we provide excerpts of the statements made by governments at the 1993 session of the First Committee. This provides more information on current national positions and may provide some useful pointers to the debate within the 1994 Group of Experts. Although the first year's experience suggests that support for the Register in principle has not always been translated into participation in practice, these statements remain in some cases highly significant and may be of value to participants and analysts alike.

We provide a listing of the 83 governments that replied to the request for information in the Register's first year of operation, and then reproduce in a summarised form the information provided on transfers during the first year, together with a comparison of this data with that published in SIPRI Year-book. We are grateful to SIPRI for permission to reproduce this information.

In Annexe 7, in order to illustrate the growing amount of interest in the Register, both in the mass media and in academic work, we provide a bibliography of works referencing the UN Register since January 1993. We hope that this will also be a useful resource for other researchers in the field.

Finally, we list the participants in the Monterey workshop. Although all the discussion at this workshop was on a non-attributable basis, the chapters of this book have all been revised in the light of these discussions, in some cases substantially. We would like to express our genuine thanks, therefore, to all participants for their contribution to the process that made this book possible.

The book thus examines virtually all of the main issues on the agenda for the 1994 review of the implementation and future development of the Register, in some cases from a variety of different perspectives. No attempt has been made to maintain a single consistent position throughout the book on key issues, though we have aimed to ensure that the chapters complement and interrelate with each other and engage with the main counter-arguments when they argue a particular view.

In spite of the diversity of issues and views explored in this book, however, the authors all share a number of concerns and perspectives. Perhaps most importantly, we all believe that transparency measures in general and the United Nations Register of Conventional Arms in particular can make a positive contribution to international security and are worth nurturing and developing. All the chapters share an interest in identifying ways in which the Register can be developed into an enduring, strong and effective transparency regime, but recognise that this can only be achieved gradually. In 1994 and in subsequent years, we need to combine, and if necessary balance, the aim of strengthening, deepening and extending the Register with that of maintaining and increasing participation in it. This means that compromises will be needed and some issues may need to be deferred in order to ensure the success of the 1994 review process. This implies that future reviews will be needed, perhaps on a regular (biannual?) basis, and that priorities need to be established. It also implies that care should be taken that short-term compromises do not threaten to undermine the long-term development of the Register.

Perhaps the biggest issue for the 1994 Group of Experts is whether and how to expand the Register to cover procurement from national production and military holdings. If such an expansion can be achieved in a way that complements and reinforces the arms transfers section of the Register while maintaining wide participation, this would be a prize indeed. A strong and widely supported case can also be made for some early revisions and extensions of the categories of equipment covered by the Register, and for limited expansion of the role of the Secretariat in maintaining and promoting it. Interestingly, discussions at the Monterey workshop seemed to indicate that these measures are more likely to receive wide support amongst governments than measures to strengthen the Register institutionally, such as the development of consultative and review mechanisms and dispute resolution procedures. Even formal declarations to strengthen transparency as an international norm seem likely to be deferred to future reviews. We believe that such developments will ultimately be important to the effectiveness of the Register, but substantial progress may have to be deferred until a future review.

The outcome of the 1994 review process remains unclear, but we hope that this book provides a valuable resource for those who want to contribute to it or follow the debates or interpret its outcome. The book, and the workshop from which it emerged, has benefited greatly from the contributions from a wide range of people. We are most grateful to Ambassador Wagenmakers and his colleagues on the Group of Experts, the UN Centre for Disarmament Affairs, and all of the other workshop participants for their part in making the workshop a success. We thank the Monterey Institute for International Studies for hosting the workshop, in particular its president Robert Gard for his constant support and provision of facilities, and give special thanks to Joseph DiChiaro, Sarah Meek, and Cynthia Miller for all their work in helping to organize it.

The book itself was largely edited in 'real-time', often late at night during the course of the Monterey workshop. We thank all of our authors for responding to editorial suggestions with such grace, intelligence and speed. Kim Tay was indispensable to the success of this editing process, and was largely responsible for preparing the book for publication, seeing it through the printers, and managing its distribution in record time. We are, as so often before, greatly indebted to her. We thank Simon Coley for designing the cover and for his help with the book's production. Thanks are also due to Andrew C. Larkin and Minna Christeller for their help with typesetting. We would also like to thank the Ford Foundation, Volkswagen Foundation and Ploughshares Fund for their generous support for the workshop and for this publication.

Malcolm Chalmers, Owen Greene, Edward J. Laurance, and Herbert Wulf

April 1994

Notes

1. For a summary of these transparency efforts, see for example Hendrik Wagenmakers, "The UN Register of Conventional Arms: A New Instrument for Cooperative Security", *Arms Control Today*, April 1993, pp. 17-19.

2. As part of this effort, the General Agreement of Tariffs and Trade (GATT) is convening a meeting of experts to address the issue.

3. See the forthcoming *SIPRI Yearbook 1994*, Oxford University Press, Oxford, chapter 13.

4. "European Governments Take Steps to Tighten Military Export Controls," *Defense News*, 1 April 1991; "Italians Seek Global Forum on Arms Sales," *Defense News*, 11 March 1991; "France to Urge Export Policy Coordination," *Defense News*, 8 April 1991; "Canada Prods United States on Arms Sales," *Arms Control Today* , June 1991.

5. "Egypt Proposes Regional Arms Control Plan," *The New York Times*, 5 July 1991.

6. "Unify Arms Control," *Defense News*, 22 April 1991.

7. "EC Ponders Single Policy to Regulate Arms Sales," *Defense News*, 1 April 1991.

8. "EC Ponders Single Policy to Regulate Arms Sales," *Defense News*, 1 April 1991; "EC Export Control Scheme Planned," *Jane's Defence Weekly*, 8 June 1991.

9. Middle East Arms Control Initiative. The White House, Office of the Press Secretary, 29 May 1991.

10. For a complete list, see "Congress's Actions on Arms Transfers: From Limits to Loans*,*" *Arms Control Today*, June 1991.

11. For a more detailed history of the development of the United Nations Register of Conventional Arms, see, for example, Herbert Wulf, 'United Nations deliberations on the arms trade', in Ian Anthony (ed.), *Arms Export Regulations*, Oxford University Press, Oxford, 1991; Malcolm Chalmers and Owen Greene, *Implementing and Developing the United Nations Register of Conventional Arms*, Bradford Arms Register Studies Number 1, Department of Peace Studies, University of Bradford, May 1993, pp. 9-30.

12. "Bulgarians to Share Data on Arms Sent to Terrorists," *The New York Times*, 2 August 1990; "Germany's Trade Surplus Down By 20 Per Cent," *The Financial Times*, 15 February 1991; "French to List Export Details," *Jane's Defence Weekly*, 11 May 1991; "Belousov Details 'Diminished' Military Exports," Tass. English translation in FBIS-SOV-91-006, *Foreign Broadcast Information Service*, 9 January 1991. Also see *SIPRI Yearbook 1992*, Oxford University Press, Oxford, 1992.

13. UN General Assembly Resolution 43/75 I "International Arms Transfers," 7 December 1988, para. 5.

Notes *continued*

14. "Kaifu Calls On UN to Monitor Conventional Arms," *Defense News*, 3 June 1991; "Leaders Call for Register on International Arms Sales," *The Financial Times*, 17 July 1991.

15. UN Experts Group report to the Secretary-General, Study on Ways and Means of Promoting Transparency in International Transfers of Conventional Arms, UN Document A/46/301, 9 September, 1991.

16. UN General Assembly Resolution 46/36 L of 9 December, 1991.

17. *Report on the Register on Conventional Arms: Report of the Secretary-General*, UN General Assembly Document A/47/342, 14 August, 1992 (reproduced in Annexe 2 of this book).

CHAPTER 2

Transparency in Armaments

The UN Register of Conventional Arms
as a proud member of a family of efforts

Ambassador Hendrik Wagenmakers
Head of the Netherlands Delegation to the Conference on
Disarmament (Chairman of the UN Secretary-General's 1994 Group
of Governmental Experts on the UN Register of Conventional Arms)

I   Introduction

During the past few years political events have moved at a breathtaking speed and have fundamentally altered the nature of global security concerns. The old East-West confrontation has withered away and the threat of global nuclear war has receded. At present the world situation is in a state of flux and full of uncertainties which make it difficult for states to assess and provide for their legitimate security needs. A major stabilizing factor in this uncertain world is transparency in matters related to military security.

By the adoption of Resolution 46/36 L in 1991 the UN General Assembly has decided to make openness and transparency in armaments its objective. The UN Register of Conventional Arms is the concrete instrument which will make a major contribution towards fulfilling this objective. It must be emphasized that the Register is a confidence building measure. It is a positive, rather than a negative response to threat perceptions felt by states. Transparency is not an end in itself, but rather a means geared to improving security.

In parallel with the development of the Register, the UN General Assembly has requested the Conference on Disarmament to elaborate practical means to increase openness and transparency pertaining to military holdings and pro-

The views expressed in this paper are those of the author.
They do not necessarily reflect the policy of the Netherlands Government.

curement through national production, as well as to weapons of mass destruction and transfer of high technology with military applications.

Together these efforts go beyond lofty ideas to specific measures which create operational instruments of transparency at the global level. I would like to set out my experience and thoughts on the Register and explain why I think that transparency is the key concept for executing the arms control and disarmament agenda of the nineties – transparency can be described as the new code word for enhanced security for all.

II   Birth of the Register

The following remarks are the reflections of an arms control practitioner rather than an academic analysis. However I trust that they complement the comprehensive intellectual thoughts presented in the other chapters of this book.

My involvement in the drive for transparency in the international community dates from 1991. Transparency in Armaments (TIA) fell in my lap by chance. The Netherlands held the Presidency of the European Twelve during the second semester of 1991 when they introduced a draft for a UN General Assembly (UNGA) resolution that provided for the establishment of a UN Register of Transfers of Conventional Arms. The European Twelve worked in conjunction with Japan. As Head of the Netherlands Delegation to the First Committee of the 46th UN General Assembly, I was responsible for mustering support for the draft resolution on behalf of the Twelve.

The negotiations between the Twelve plus Japan on the one hand and the Non-Aligned on the other about the text of the enabling UNGA resolution 46/36 L were complex and tortuous. There was no disagreement about the need of a response by the international community to destabilizing accumulations of conventional weapons as had been witnessed in Iraq. As an instrument to fulfil that objective, the Twelve and Japan had proposed international registration of transfers of seven categories of major conventional weapons with a proven capability for large scale cross-border offensive action and surprise attack. Their view was that transparency could help alleviate unfounded concerns of neighbouring states.

All along, however, the Twelve and Japan were fully aware that openness and transparency did not form a panacea for all security concerns. They recognized that it remained the sovereign right of states to formulate policies to ensure their legitimate self defence (Article 51 of the UN Charter). While maintaining that there was a measure of openness which was essential (reports to legislatures, and other public statements), the Twelve and Japan admitted that there were limits to openness which might vary depending on the security situation in various regions.

Some Non-Aligned countries for their part observed that registration of arms transfers would be insufficient to indicate destabilizing accumulations of arms, since it would discriminate against arms importing states. They argued that a declaration of transfers gave only a partial view of the aggregate military strength of exporting states; whilst arms importing states would reveal not only their imports but also, over time, their holdings. It was therefore finally agreed that the scope of the UN Register should cover military holdings and procurement through national production as well for all participating states.

The task of getting the UN Register of Conventional Arms up and running was entrusted to the UN Secretary-General through a representative selection of governmental experts invited by him (the 1992 Panel of Experts).

At the same time the Geneva Conference on Disarmament was requested to elaborate practical means to increase openness and transparency pertaining to military holdings and procurement through national production. During its 1993 session the Conference on Disarmament (CD) had an active exchange of views. A number of concrete proposals were tabled. The CD is continuing its consideration of these matters in 1994.

During the 46th UN General Assembly a second bone of contention was the desire of certain Non-Aligned countries for application of the transparency concept to holdings and production of weapons of mass destruction as well as to transfer of high technology with military applications. The basic idea here was that the transparency process would in due course yield comprehensive data and information on military capabilities as well as aggregate military force structures and figures. This was not a matter that could be resolved quickly.

The same holds true for the development of means to facilitate the possible transit from denial to conditional access to high technology with military application. The Geneva Conference on Disarmament has been requested to address both these issues and to elaborate practical means to increase openness and transparency in these fields, in accordance with existing legal instruments.

The above summary cannot hide the fact that resolution 46/36 L, entitled "Transparency in Armaments", on which the UN General Assembly finally agreed in 1991, does not qualify for a prize in a beauty contest. The division of labour between New York and Geneva could have been focused more sharply. The explanation is that time constraints were significant. The desire not to lose momentum – to have Transparency in Armaments declared an objective of the UN General Assembly – prevailed in the end.

Whatever the case may be, the establishment of the UN Register of Conventional Arms, a universal and non-discriminatory instrument, is one of the best and most practical things the UN has done recent years. Here, the UN is not launching just verbal attempts at preventing unnecessary and destabilizing accumulations of arms, but rather setting up practical measures to address such issues. One of the strong points of the Register is the relative simplicity of its procedures and definitions, notably its one sheet Standardized Reporting Form. Government-supplied data concerning imports and exports of seven categories of major conventional weapons platforms suitable for large scale cross border offensive action and surprise attack can henceforth be the object of bilateral, regional or even inter-regional consultations. Dangerous misperceptions which fuel fear and mistrust might thus be rectified thanks to transparency. Nations may feel enabled to exercise restraint and plan their security requirements on the basis of better knowledge as a result of the dialogue based on the reports to the Register.

Having described the Register as a major international innovation, it is interesting to note that the debate on this process produced a new use of a word which can now be added to English dictionaries; that is the word "openness".

In 1992 I had the privilege of chairing the Panel of Governmental Technical Experts which produced a consensus report on the technical procedures and adjustments to the Annex of Resolution 46/36 L necessary for the effective operation of the Register. The annex to the Panel's report contains the parameters for reporting and the Standardized Reporting Form. The report of the Panel also contains modalities for its further expansion. Since then, transparency and the Register have become objects of consensus in New York.

III   First activities of the 1994 Group of Governmental Experts

The Register came into effect in 1992. The returns from Member States on transfers that took place during the calendar year 1992 were made available in the consolidated report of the UN Secretary-General of October 1993. Early in 1994 a Governmental Experts Group was set up by the UN Secretary-General to review the operation of the UN Register of Conventional Arms and to examine its further development. The Group held its first session in New York in February 1994. The first Group session went relatively well. Two more Group sessions will follow in June and July.

Clearly, the Group benefited from an element of continuity from the 1992 Panel. There was no desire to stage a general debate. At the first day of the Group's meeting a review of the Register's performance over its first year commenced. The participants expressed their views frankly, and in particular, gave a valuable account of their experience with the first year of reporting. This will form a good basis for further work of the Group.

Consideration of the continuing operation of the Register

In the execution of their mandate concerning the continuing operation of the Register, the Group had a first go at an analysis of the returns from Member States on transfers having taken place during the calendar year 1992. The Group deferred any final judgement on this analysis until the reports for 1993 become available. I outline some highlights of this discussion, and offer some ideas for further developments.

The start of the Register's operation is certainly promising, particularly as it appears that the 83 responses covered the vast majority of the arms delivered in calendar year 1992. Still, the importance of wider participation has to be stressed, also in the form of so-called "nil-returns", since the Register is a political instrument. Submission of a nil report indicates willingness of a Member State to participate in the transparency drive of the international community.

The 1992 reporting showed some inaccuracies and inconsistencies. In view of the considerable differences between the various national administrative procedures of member states, this phenomenon does not come as a surprise. In a way these "mismatches" testify to the genuineness of the Register. Of course, no effort should be spared to do away with these teething problems. It should be noted however, that these are early days and that Governments are still on a learning curve. Some are engaged in the process of introducing legislation enabling them to collect the data from their civilian industry as well as refining their procedures following the first year's experience.

Maintenance of simplicity seemed to be a goal shared by all. The Government branches that have to collect the information and fill out the Standardized Reporting Forms should be enabled to do a clear and simple administrative job. The data must be easily accessible both to administrators and outside users. In particular, some simple procedural fixes might help to make the Standardized Reporting Form even more operational. For instance, on the

Standardized Reporting Form a rubric might be included reminding Governments to explain the national criteria used to define when a transfer becomes effective.

Some suggestions were made concerning adjustments to existing categories. These included for instance, proposals for lowering the ship tonnage threshold from its present level of 750 tonnes.

Another conclusion is that apparently information on the operation of the Register must be more widely disseminated, including to those Government branches not directly involved in arms control and disarmament.

With regard to the improvement of the "user-friendliness" of the Standardized Reporting Form, minor technical changes might help. Mathematical accuracy, however, is subordinate to the purpose of the Register as a political instrument. In this regard the Register is different from, for example, the SIPRI Register or the IISS's *Military Balance*.

The UN Secretariat's Centre for Disarmament Affairs (CDA) has recently been strengthened. In trying to help prevent inaccuracies and discrepancies from occurring, it seems worthwhile to consider whether a further increased role of the Centre is called for.

The Group of Governmental Experts stands to benefit from the willingness of the UN Secretariat to issue a preliminary consolidated report on the returns to the Register for 1993 as early as practicable before the next session of the Group (May 31, 1994).

Further valuable inputs for the work of the Group of Governmental Experts on the continuing operation of the Register would derive from provision by Member States to the UN Secretary-General of the views on the operation of the Register during its two first years, as requested in paragraph 11(a) of Resolution 46/36 L.

Another important element in the Group's discussion was that of regional differences and concerns. It was noted that participation in the Middle East and Africa was low. Our colleagues from those regions helpfully, and in a candid manner, explained their views. Some points related to:

- the scope of the Register, including consideration as to how weapons of mass destruction are being dealt with in the TIA process and elsewhere;

- links with regional organizations, also with a view to using the Register for bilateral, regional or international consultations to address issues of concern;

- the possibility of creating (a) (semi-) permanent consultative mechanism(s);

- the perceived relevance or irrelevance of the arms categories covered by the Register for the particular security concerns of regions.

Initiatives on the above mentioned points could be taken at the regional level. Argentina and Canada have for instance, taken an initiative concerning consultative mechanisms within the framework of the Organization of American States.

The transparency process stands to benefit if mores states provide the Additional Background Information, as well as the data on transfers, as called for in the 1991 UN General Assembly resolution. Only about thirty states did so last year. An important element of this background information relates to military holdings and procurement from national production. It is also expected that information be provided on, *inter alia*, defence policy, legislation and administrative procedures on transfers and the prevention of illicit transfers.

In view of the relative paucity of background information submitted to the Register so far, it is difficult to provide, *rebus sic stantibus*, considered views on this issue. The Group might wish to take into consideration the possibility of the voluntary provision by UN member states of information on military holdings and procurement through national production in the form of data on a standardized reporting format in a similar way as is at present done with transfers.

Consideration also needs to be given to provision of voluntary additional information: particularly as to whether and how this might be encouraged. For instance, declarations, as a complementary confidence building measure, on the size and organization of armed forces or declarations on the closure or conversion of military production facilities, could be devised.

In order to incorporate or consolidate the Register into a cooperative security regime, regular reviews and consultations on its functioning would be important. This could be done either in the form of another group of governmental experts or in some form of consultative mechanism, either regional or international. This would not preclude the bilateral dialogue between states that have concerns. It should be ensured that all parties concerned with any issue raised may participate in such consultations.

In preparation and support of those reviews and consultations, important technical tasks of management of data and information should be mandated to the UN Centre for Disarmament. Even under its present mandate, the UN Centre for Disarmament Affairs could be more proactive in soliciting views of member states.

Consideration of further development of the Register

Given the youth of the Register – sometimes referred to as a baby which cannot yet make big steps – there seems to be little *animus* to add new equipment categories to the Register. Using the same metaphor, it seems appropriate to caution against "rushing". Priority should be given to consolidation and maintenance of the stability of the Register.

On the other hand, the signs for further **development** of the Register in other respects seem to be encouraging. Depending on how the work progresses, the Group of Governmental Experts might well end up, finding consensus on the expansion of the scope of the Register to include data on military holdings and procurement from national production on the same footing as for transfers. If this happens a positive evolution would come about. Technically it is certainly possible. The 1994 Group of Governmental Experts is required to study this aspect and could well elaborate the appropriate procedures.

Thus expanded in scope, the Register would have the following composition:

a) the military holdings of a certain state at a certain point of time;

b) the arms imports of a certain state for a certain calendar year, being part of (a);

c) the procurement through national production of a certain state for a certain calendar year, being part of (a);

d) the arms exports of a certain state for a certain calendar year, being a separate quantity.

Such expansion would be greatly assisted by increasing the responsibilities of the UN Secretariat for management of data and information.

The UN Secretary-General's 1994 Group of Governmental Experts is well aware that they are required to take account of the work of the Geneva Conference on Disarmament (CD). The CD was requested in operative paragraphs 12 to 15 of Resolution 46/36 L to elaborate universal and non-discriminatory practical means to increase openness and transparency related to military holdings and procurement through national production as well as to the transfer of high technology with military applications and to weapons of mass destruction, in accordance with existing legal instruments. In response to the wishes of the members, as Chairman of the 1994 Group of Governmental Experts I have written to the Hungarian Chairman of the CD's Ad Hoc Committee on Transparency in Armaments and asked him to supply the New York group with an up-to-date report of the work of his Ad Hoc Committee, if possible by 31 May, the date at which the New York Group will resume its activities.

IV Parallel efforts of the Geneva Conference on Disarmament

What should the practical outcome be of the Conference on Disarmament's (CD) responsibility for Transparency in Armaments during this year's CD session? In my capacity as Head of the Netherlands delegation to the CD I have offered a number of ideas.

My suggestions for action are largely based on existing proposals, submitted to the Ad Hoc Committee on Transparency in Armaments in 1993. The CD ought to elaborate these proposals with a view to developing confidence building measures. New proposals should of course be encouraged.

Possible action of the CD with regard to conventional arms control

In the conventional field I should like to draw attention to the following confidence building measures (CBMs), which could be implemented as complementary to the Register:

a)   declarations on the size and organisation of armed forces (British proposal);

b)   declarations on the closure or conversion of military production facilities (Italian proposal);

c)   international data exchange of military holdings and procurement through national production (proposals by France, Germany, the Russian Federation and the USA);

d)   complementary regional measures to enhance transparency in armaments (Japanese proposal); for instance regional agreements on visits to military facilities and activities, including overflight regimes;

e)   a code of conduct (suggestion by Poland yet to be elaborated; similar ideas have been brought to the fore by Australia, Ireland, New Zealand and Romania) to bring about voluntary restraint and responsibility in conventional arms transfers.

As I see it, UN member states might , for instance, consider making authorisations for arms transfers dependent on the other contracting party agreeing to have the transfer under reference reported to the Register.

Inspiration for developing criteria can be derived from the sets of guidelines on conventional arms transfers which have already been developed at both the global and regional levels. Here I am referring to those in the London declaration by the Permanent Five Members of the Security Council of October 1991, and those adopted by the CSCE Ministerial Meeting in Rome, December 1993.

f) declarations in advance of major military activities (e.g., exercises).

g) In addition, India is considering, I understand, elaborating some further thoughts on possible CBMs.

h) The Netherlands delegation is in the process of preparing a proposal on provision of information on armed forces personnel by means of a standardized reporting format.

The CD might take into consideration the experience gained in the European region, under the provisions of the Vienna Document 1992 and of the Treaty on Conventional Armed Forces in Europe (CFE). The agreed Treaty ceilings on heavy weaponry (similar to the first five categories of the UN Register of Conventional Arms) have led to the destruction or conversion of 17,000 pieces of equipment by the end of 1993. A lot more will be destroyed over the coming years. More than 1,000 on-site inspections have taken place, including quite a number of challenge inspections. This large number of inspection has contributed considerably to transparency in general between former adversaries.

Such experiences are not confined to the European region. For example the Multilateral Force Organisation (MFO) in the Sinai has been carrying out inspections and observation from the ground and air for many years now, with the full cooperation of the states concerned. This has made a significant contribution to stability in that region.

Steps are being taken in other parts of the world, such as in Latin America and the Asia-Pacific region. Indeed, much can be said in favour of strengthening links between the UN Register and regional organisations, *inter alia* with a view to encouraging participation in the Register.

Regional approaches become all the more important in those areas where the Register's categories are not perceived to be of direct relevance to the security situation of a given region. In that vein, it is possible to envisage regional initiatives, agreed to by all the states concerned, to exchange voluntary information on categories of weapons perceived as destabilising in their geographical area of interest. Such voluntary declarations need not involve supplier states from outside the (sub-) region concerned. These data could be fed into a regional data centre.

Why could confidence building measures (CBMs) not be developed both worldwide and regionally? It is even thinkable to implement certain CBMs, initially at a regional level, before recommending them for universal application.

The CD's Ad Hoc Committee on Transparency in Armaments can certainly do valuable work on the grave problem posed by the present-day misuse of anti-personnel land mines. This question has both political and humanitarian dimensions. The attention of the multilateral arms control community to this issue is certainly warranted. We are all aware of recent initiatives embodied in resolutions adopted by the 48th UN General Assembly last year.

Further efforts are being made in preparation of the forthcoming conference to review the 1980 Convention on Prohibitions or Restrictions on the Use of Certain Conventional Weapons Which May Be Deemed to Be Excessively Injurious or to Have Indiscriminate Effect (the so-called UN Weaponry Convention). Recently, a Group of Governmental Experts discussed this issue when they met in Geneva to start preparations for the review of the operation of the 1980 Convention. This review will probably take place in September 1995. As well as the CD and the UN Weaponry Convention process, the UN Secretary-General's 1994 Group of Governmental Experts on the UN Register of Conventional Arms is also seized of this issue. As a result of all this activity, there is a danger that well-intended efforts might suffer from fragmentation and lack of focus.

It seems to me that the primary field for action on this issue is to improve implementation of existing international law and, equally important, to make essential amendment to this law where needed. Transparency may also play a role in alleviating this problem, but it is not clear that the UN Register is the right instrument. Without prejudice to the ultimate forum to be chosen, what the various fora seized of this issue should do is at least work towards a common view on the best approach to take action.

Possible action of the CD with regard to weapons of mass destruction and transfer of high technology with military applications

The CD's mandate further includes the elaboration of practical means to increase openness and transparency related to weapons of mass destruction. Discussions in the CD on this contentious issue are still in a preliminary phase. It seems useful to make a distinction here between transfers on the one hand and holdings and procurement on the other. As to transfers, I underline that after entry into force of the Chemical Weapons Convention – to be expected in about a year's time – there will exist a set of complementary international agreements prohibiting the transfer of any weapon of mass destruction. As for holdings and procurement of nuclear weapons and other nuclear explosive devices, the Nuclear Non-Proliferation Treaty legitimises the existence of five Nuclear Weapon States. All other holdings and procurement of nuclear weapons are prohibited by international law. The 1925 Geneva Protocol, the Chemical Weapons Convention and the Biological and Toxin Weapons Convention prohibit any development, possession, production and use of chemical and biological weapons. Thus, the basic assignment of the CD seems to be to see to it that the transparency process in due course yields comprehensive data and information on overall military capabilities as well as on aggregate military force structures. This will certainly be a long term process.

It should not be forgotten, however, that a good deal of information on nuclear holdings is already in the public domain. The START treaties, once ratified, represent a signal achievement by the states concerned. Their implementation will require a great deal of transparency; some of which is already apparent. For instance, the full texts of treaties like START and START II are issued as documents of the CD, and are thus widely disseminated. These texts provide information – be it on the basis of specific counting rules – on the size of the strategic nuclear arsenals of the two states concerned. It should be noted of course, that START data as such are note intended to address the question of total stockpile numbers.

Important support for making progress is to be derived from the almost universal adherence to the NPT and the related IAEA safeguards system. Regional arrangements, like the EURATOM Treaty and zones free of nuclear weapons or nuclear-free zones, such as those established by the recently reinforced Treaty of Tlatelolco and the Rarotonga Treaty are further invaluable mechanisms conducive to a general environment of cooperative security and trust. Mention should be made as well of the Argentinian-Brazilian Agency for Accounting and Control of Nuclear Materials accord between Argentina and Brazil on nuclear inspections.

The same holds true, for the brand new Convention on Chemical Weapons (CWC), with its innovative verification provisions. The time is now ripe to capitalise further on what has already been achieved. In this respect I salute respectfully the Mendoza Accord committing Argentina, Brazil and Chile to allow inspections ahead of the CWC coming into force.

As additional practical means to increase openness and transparency in nuclear matters, the Conference on Disarmament could consider:

a) designing confidence building measures under which Nuclear Weapon States might voluntarily supply more information on their nuclear arms holdings and the scale of the reductions of those holdings. Argentina has proposed the establishment of a register which would cover information on the implementation of the relevant provisions of treaties concerning weapons of mass destruction, the so-called log book proposal;

b) designing instruments conducive to make states follow a policy of transparency with regard to plutonium stocks. Such policies could ease the future elaboration of a fissile materials cut-off treaty and would be another step along the way towards nuclear disarmament required by article VI of the NPT;

c) recommendations for advance notification of major military manoeuvres involving nuclear arms.

Resolution 46/36 L further requests the CD to address the issue of **transfers of high technology with military applications**. Obviously, universal adherence to and compliance with effectively verifiable non-proliferation agreements greatly facilitates a dialogue between suppliers and recipients of dual-use technology. It should be recalled that technology is not weaponry, at best it is potential weapons.

Nonetheless, the CD has to address the issue, in view of the request made in Resolution 46/36 L. Here the CD can profit from the ongoing work of the UN Disarmament Commission in New York.

On substance, the point is often made that policies based solely on denial are not sustainable in the long run. No doubt, CD delegations can agree that restrictions on transfers of technology are intended neither to prevent such transfers completely nor to maintain discriminatory control of technology. Rather, while elaborating the practical means requested by the UN General Assembly, the Conference on Disarmament may agree that export controls are a necessary complement to international agreements prohibiting transfers or the acquisition of weapons of mass destruction. States that abide by their international commitments should have no reason to worry about export control regimes.

Here the concept of transparency comes into play as one of the devices which can facilitate the possible transit from denial to conditioned access. I stress, however, that it is my deep conviction that self-denial and restraint will in the long run be the only way to put into practice reasonable international exchange of technology for all states with a view to increasing their development, with due respect for the requirement of non-proliferation and commercial proprietary rights.

V   Reflections on present and future trends

While absorbing the data and information on present-day arms transfers, revealing as the do some rather troubling trends in our post-Cold War world, one is at times tempted to feel some nostalgia for the "good old Cold War" with its clear, bipolar, quasi-Manichean divide. This thought is of course a fallacy.

On a personal note I confess that in relation to the Register I was intrigued by the possible applicability of the maxim that generals tend to prepare themselves to fight the last war, while technological and military developments have continued their relentless advance. It is my conviction that the Register does more than alleviate concerns about the last war's weapons. It will reveal, over time, the patterns of the acquisitions of weapons in an open and transparent way.

Again on a personal note, I would welcome an exchange of views on the significance for the UN Register of force multipliers. Furthermore, in this context one cannot help but think of "smart" weapons. I refer to the so-called "concept of cyberwar", which targets information systems in the modern war-machine. This novel approach to future warfare implies conducting, and preparing to conduct, military operations according to information-related principles. Its techniques include destroying enemy information and communications systems.

I am aware, of course, that addressing command, control and communication systems would introduce major problems of definition, even if the category was restricted to the larger field formation systems. Unfortunate complications for the Register might be the result. Modification programmes would be similarly complicated. On balance, it seems these issues are best dealt with in a regional agreement (for instance as in the Vienna Document) rather than a global confidence building measure.

VI   Conclusion

Among the family of efforts undertaken to promote transparency in armaments, the UN Register of Conventional Arms stands out as a proud member. Its main structure – a relatively simple one – has proved to meet with consensus support. Some minor procedural fixes may have to be applied. Inaccuracies and inconsistencies that have occurred seem not to be of major importance: rather they testify to the Register's genuineness.

The expansion of the Register's scope to cover military holdings and procurement through national production will further enhance the relevance of the Register as a confidence building measure geared to improving security. As a result, states will feel better able to exercise responsibility and self-restraint.

Following a promising start, wider participation, including submissions of nil returns, has to be encouraged. Some institutionalization of consultation mechanisms, including use of existing regional organisations, may be recommended. Future reviews of the Register are certainly warranted. The role of the UN Centre for Disarmament Affairs has to be further strengthened in term of management of data and information. Any comprehensive study of further development of the Register must take account of the work of the Geneva Conference on Disarmament which I believe should produce meaningful complementary initiatives and results. The ideas I have outlined are intended to enhance this work.

Transparency in Armaments brings cooperative security within arms' reach. It integrates arms control and international security in a unique way. At the national level, it holds out the prospect of re-allocation of scarce socio-economic resources, without detriment to security. A secure environment is conducive to investment and economic development. Most of all, transparency can form the basis of a cooperative dialogue on security concerns between countries in different regions of the world. Such dialogue would transcend supplier regimes and complement existing international security treaties and agreements.

Transparency is a process which has a clearly defined pattern of further growth. A "Family of Efforts" consisting of formal and informal approaches, both within and outside the United Nations system, at international, regional, and sub-regional levels is well underway to execute a new, challenging security agenda.

CHAPTER 3

Lessons from the first year

Edward J. Laurance and Herbert Wulf

I   Results from the first year[1]

Introduction

The Register is at the stage in its history where serious consideration is being given to its further development. Although this will involve some specifically mandated considerations, such as the addition of procurement through national production and military holdings, an additional question will be on the minds of those charged with this task. Is the Register process addressing the arms trade trends which have evolved since 1991 and the post-Gulf War environment? To what extent is the Register leading to a mechanism that fails to make transparent or restrain those armaments actually being used in today's conflicts?

Participation

A major aim of the first year of the exercise was to maximize the number of states participating. Eighty-three national replies, over 45 per cent of all member states, were submitted. This was much more than in the older and somewhat parallel exercise of reporting military expenditures to the United Nations.[2] Participation varied significantly by region. In Europe and North America the member states of NATO and most of those of the CSCE went on record as supporting the Register and committed themselves to participation and the sharing of reports. On the other hand, no state in Sub Saharan Africa reported any imports. In the crucial area of the Middle East, no Gulf States reported. The significant number of countries not reporting can partly be explained by the fact that in 1992 they traded no arms in the seven categories of weapons of the UN Register, although they were all asked to report even if it was a nil report. The major weapon importers not reporting included Saudi Arabia, Iran, Thailand, Syria, Taiwan (not a UN member state), Bangladesh and Kuwait.

The 83 states replying generally did so at five different levels. Some states participated at a maximum level, using the forms provided with maximum transparency of data and also submitted background information on their military holdings and procurement through national production. A second group made their returns according to the suggested standardized form for reporting without, however, giving details on transactions such as weapon designations or types of transferred equipment. A third but small group of states announced their unwillingness or inability for some specific reason. In the case of South Africa it was the UN embargo still in place. A fourth group submitted only a *note verbale* covering miscellaneous topics while a fifth group submitted information only on the regulations and policies related to arms exports and imports in their respective states.

The reports also show that exporter participation was greater than that of importers. A total of 194 arms transfers was reported for 1992. Exporters reported 159 transfers while importers reported 109. There were 74 duplicate entries which both exporter and importers reported. The non participation of three key states – the Democratic People's Republic of Korea, Syria and Iran – where public information indicated that significant trade in missiles took place in 1992, creates a major gap in government-produced data.[3]

Of the 33 States submitting Background Information, 15 submitted information on their military holdings and procurement through national production of arms in the seven categories covered by the Register. Nine additional countries reported information on their holdings only.[4] Many of these states reported on their security and/or arms transfer policies.

Quality of reporting

The Register allows for verification through cross-checking, as it asks member states to report both exports and imports. It is possible to determine the extent to which the reports of exporters and importers match, especially when reporting the same transfer. Four types of cases occurred in the reports:

A.   The transfer was reported by both exporter and importer and the number of items matched.

   51 (26%) of the 194 transfers recorded.

B.   The transfer was reported by both exporter and importer but the number of items reported did not match.

   16 (8%) of the 194 transfers recorded.

C.   The transfer was reported by only the exporter or importer, since the other party participated in the Register process but did not report this particular transfer.

70 (36%) of the 194 transfers recorded.

D.   The transfer was reported by only the exporter or importer, since the other party did not participate in the Register process.

57 (30%) of the 194 transfers recorded.

This analysis of matching data, when applied to the seven categories of weapons, reveals that for certain categories, exporter and importer States more readily agreed on the specifics of the transfer, as evidenced by a higher level of matching data. In the table below the percentage indicates the level of agreement among exporter and importer as to the **number of items** transferred.

Table 1.   Agreement among exporter and importer as to number of items transferred

Tanks	82%	N=	1733
ACV	32%	N=	1625
LCA	49%	N=	1682
Combat Aircraft	68%	N=	270
Attack Helicopters	43%	N=	40
Ships	11%	N=	40
Missiles and Missile Launchers	13%	N=	67,878

States which submitted **arms exports data** did so with varying levels of transparency. For example, of the 24 States reporting exports, 17 opted to use the "Remarks" column of the form to provide some description of the weapon system being exported. However, when assessing the use of this column by number of transfers reported, only 64 of the 159 exports reported (40%) contained this type of data. During the elaboration of the 1992 UN Panel of Governmental Experts who prepared the Standardized Reporting Format, it had already become clear that the missile category was most sensitive to security concerns of governments. Because the reporting of weapon designations is not mandatory, many governments chose not to give details on designations and aggregated several transfers into a single figure within the categories. As numerous types of missiles are produced and transferred – probably more than in any other of the UN Register weapon categories – reporting of highly aggregated data in the missile and missile launcher category is particularly dissatisfying. While this complies with the procedures outlined in the *Report on the Register of Conventional Arms: Report of the Secretary-General*,[5] in effect it produced little or no information on the actual transfers which occurred.

Discrepancies and quality of data: patterns and explanations

Lack of confirmed and transparent data

One key to making recommendations for the further development of the Register is to attempt to understand the reasons for the less than expected quality of data in the first year of operation. There are at least six reasons that can be put forward for consideration.

The **first** is basic, namely, the lack of participation by states, especially those with major levels of arms imports in the seven categories in 1992. Data on a transfer cannot be confirmed and thereby have optimum validity when one or the other partner to a deal does not participate in the Register. This suggests that efforts in the UN and other international/ regional forums to increase participation, in addition to reinforcing the norms established in the resolution, could significantly increase the quality of the data.

A **second** reason for the lack of confirmed data is conflicting interpretations of category definitions. For example, Malta reported receiving ships from Germany which did not meet the category definition, i.e., they were below 750 tons and were not armed with missiles. Germany conformed to the procedures and did not report the transfer. So, despite the fact that both countries participated in the Register, this data could not be confirmed. Similar problems occurred with the specific categories of combat aircraft and attack helicopters. A grey area is being created by broad Register definitions for attack helicopters (particularly ship-based helicopters) and combat aircraft (armed trainer aircraft). As a result some governments did not report transfers of systems that were publicly reported in sources such as the Stockholm International Peace Research Institute (SIPRI) arms trade register as meeting UN Register definitions.

A **third** reason for the lack of confirmed data is conflicting interpretations of whether or not a transfer has occurred. Several examples from the first year of reporting make the point. Several states reported receiving ships from the United States, ships that were in fact leased. U.S. national procedures do not define these transfers as a change in control or ownership of the ships and therefore did not report them. A further case of confusion occurred in Europe with co-produced MLRS systems. Some members of the consortium reported them as production, others as transfers.

A **fourth** reason for the lack of confirmed data was conflicting interpretations of when a transfer occurred. In the case of a submarine sold by Germany to the Republic of Korea (ROK) in 1992, Germany reported the export since ownership was assumed by the ROK in 1992. The ROK, however, apparently interpreted a transfer as occurring when the ship was actually under their national control, which they concluded occurred in 1993, and therefore did not report the import of the submarine. A second example occurred between China and Pakistan, who both reported a transfer of tanks from China but differed in the numbers based on differing interpretations as to when Pakistan assumed control of the equipment.

A **fifth** source of lower quality data is due to a poorly defined category, namely Category Seven – missiles and missile launchers. Some states used highly aggregated data in this category, e.g., 109 missiles and missile launchers exported from Country A to Country B. If the "Remarks " column did not break these data out by type and/or model of missile, or disaggregate into missiles and launchers, in effect it produced little or no information on the actual transfers which occurred. While this complies with the procedures outlined in the Report of the 1992 Panel of Governmental Technical Experts (Document A/47/342), it violates the basic purpose of the Register. In this case the results may be more dysfunctional than non participation or non reporting since it may add to misperceptions. Since this was a common occurrence and is ripe for a solution in the current deliberations of the 1994 Group, it is useful to suggest several reasons for this behavior and lack of motivation by states to be transparent about their missile transfers.

It must be remembered that this is a Register created by the Iraq invasion of Kuwait and its aftermath. Despite the tanks and aircraft in the Iraqi arsenal, it was the missiles – air-to-air, surface-to-air, and above all surface-to-surface (e.g., modified SCUDs) which dominated the concern of the allied coalition which fought the Gulf War and the architects of the UN Register. This category, therefore, is the most sensitive since it can have the most impact on regional conflict. On the other hand, these same missiles possessed not by aggressor states but states concerned only with protecting themselves also view their inventory of missiles as critical to that mission. They are expensive and as a result states safeguard them against pre-emptive strikes. It is not surprising, therefore, that some states would not be too enthusiastic about releasing too much information regarding models and types which could then be translated into capabilities to be countered by enemies.

Furthermore, a broad definition of this category adds additional confusion since there are so many types of missiles, especially when compared to weapons systems such as tanks. And these types have widely varying effects when attempting to determine the presence of an "excessive and destabilizing" accumulation.

Another problem arises in this category because not all types are included, for example, ground-to-air missiles and many types of air-to-air and anti-tank missiles. Since the reason for this exclusion is not made clear, it detracts from the credibility of the exercise, at least in this category.

Finally, a critical and perhaps fatal flaw is the lumping together of missiles and missile launchers. Again, this category has its roots in Iraq, where the "SCUD" launchers became as important as the reloads themselves. However, as it stands, the category invites states to mask rather than illuminate their transfers in this category of weapons.

What about cheating and deception? Given the reality of national intelligence services, it is highly likely that there are a number of cases where the reporting has increased suspicion. Where an outside observer might chalk up discrepancies to lack of bureaucratic rigor, in reality deception and cheating cannot be ruled out. While it is highly likely that in the aggregate the Register captured 90–95 per cent of the arms trade in the seven categories, the discrepancies are numerous enough to expect that bilateral diplomatic queries have occurred. One can imagine someone in the various national intelligence services drawing the assignment of comparing the Register returns to the intelligence data. But that is one of the purposes of the Register, to make data transparent and then deal with neighbours or others who have doubts about its validity.

Regional differences

As Table 2 indicates, there was wide variation in reporting and creation of data by region. Part of this was due to the varying regional experience with transparency exercises and the presence of national bureaucracies, such as those in Europe and North America, accustomed to generating military data of this sort. Regions such as Sub Saharan Africa are at a comparatively low level of militarization, at least as concerns these seven categories of major weapons, and have little need to have such a data generation capacity at this point in their young history as a system of independent states. In Latin America and some parts of Asia, a different factor may explain the varying levels of participation, namely civil-military relations. Producing transparent and therefore public data for the United Nations may go against the norm and in some cases the laws in these countries, where the military has used its expertise in such areas to guarantee and in some cases force a political role in the country. Finally, one of the critical realities made clear by the first year of reporting is that in the former Soviet Union, national export control systems were in varying stages of development in the wake of the collapse of the U.S.S.R. This makes it very difficult to assess the first year of the Register in this region, since the public perception was that of a region awash with the continued production and export of arms, but little was reported to the Register.

Table 2.   Regional distribution of member states reporting to the UN Register

	Imports		Exports		
	Data included	Nil report	Data included	Nil report	Background Information
Africa	0	5	0	5	0
Asia	11	7	2	14	4
Middle East	2	1	2	2	2
Latin America	5	3	2	3	4
Western Europe	14	6	9	12	16
CIS and East Europe	4	10	7	6	5
North America	2	0	2	0	2
Total	38	32	24	42	33

Note: Western Europe includes European NATO and neutral countries

Another key factor in explaining the variation in regional participation is indifference, brought about by the fact that many states of the world did not view the Register as a relevant process. In some cases this is a result of irrelevant categories of weapons (e.g., Africa, Central America where hardly any major weapons have been transferred, although small arms supplies do play an important role in the ongoing conflicts). In the case of the Middle East the Register came on line just as the peace process entered a critical stage. This is also a very volatile region and states such as those in the Gulf may simply not find it prudent to participate until more certainty and stability emerges in the region.

Achieving the objectives of the Register – the first year

The development of the Register in the summer and fall of 1991 was a difficult task for the architects, trying to balance the various perspectives of states in an area of international and national security never before attempted. The resolution itself contains various objectives, some of which were added in order to achieve a consensus. The question which now must be asked is how well these various goals and objectives have been achieved in the first year of operations. Such an assessment is another key element in fashioning specific proposals for further developing the Register.

Transparency and openness

An estimate of more than 90% of the actual transfers taking place seems reasonable, although the non participation of some key importers and exporters and the less than adequate control systems in the former Soviet Union cannot allow complete confidence in such an assessment. Deals previously unknown to public specialists and non-governmental organisations (NGOs) were revealed by the Register and the Register confirmed actual numbers of systems and their year of delivery far beyond what was publicly known. In sum, the fact that most of the actual arms trade was made transparent takes this mode of commerce out of the unknown and into the domain of the United Nations where it can be acted on in public. On the other hand the lack of transparency in some transfers, especially missiles and missile launchers, detract from the overall goal of openness.

Confidence building

The fact that 83 states participated in a very new and historic exercise creates an environment of confidence where none existed before on a global scale. States can and will submit transparent military data with little negative effect, either nationally, regionally or universally. The development of a public database of government produced arms trade statistics should give states confidence to continue to submit data and improve the process. One must await the further development of the Register to see the extent of the positive effect of such submissions in regard to confidence building. Detracting from this goal of confidence building was the low level of participation in certain regions and the poor quality of data in the missile and missile launcher category.

Universal participation

The Register was developed as a universal and non-discriminatory process, global in scope. A majority of the key states in the arms trade did participate.

And there is some evidence that there was a chain reaction of sorts, that states became aware of each other's reporting activities and did not want to be seen as being left out of this evolving global process. Regional promotion occurred, both as a result of extant regional organizations (e.g., CSCE, European Union), and the regional workshops conducted by the UN Centre of Disarmament Affairs. Detracting from the achievement of this goal, of course, was the fact that 55% of the member states of the UN did *not* participate. In the case of the Register, participation reinforces the new norms contained in the Register and equates directly with the achievement of this goal.

Prevent excessive and destabilizing accumulation of conventional weapons

As has previously been stated, this is a process designed to prevent an Iraq like situation, by preventing the excessive and destabilizing accumulation (i.e., build-up) of conventional weapons. It must be concluded that during the first year of operation of the Register little progress was made toward achieving this goal, for four basic and understandable reasons. First, the Register as currently constructed contains only data on transfers. An adequate assessment of the destabilizing nature of a military build-up requires a baseline (military holdings) and the acquisitions (imports plus procurement through national production) of each party during the year in question. Secondly, it is highly unlikely that in the case of conventional weapons that one year, particularly 1992 when global arms deliveries were lower than normal, would produce a conclusion of "excessive and destabilizing", especially in light of the proximity in time of the Gulf War experience. Rather the Register can only achieve this goal over time. A third reason that achieving this goal is premature is the lack of any consultative mechanism to assist states in determining the presence of excessive and destabilizing build-ups. And finally, even with such a mechanism, all of the states for whom such a determination is critical and relevant must participate in the exercise. The key to achieving this goal is that the determination must be made in context and it would be folly to attempt to develop a consensus definition of "excessive and destabilizing" which can then be applied to an individual state through traditional diplomatic means.[6] The Register, as has been emphasized by many Governments, is not an intelligence exercise. Rather, the essence of cooperative security is the building on the establishment of a norm such as the prevention of excessive and destabilizing accumulations of arms by developing the structures needed to reinforce the norm and make it operational.

Strengthen regional peace and security

The Register is designed to play a role in bringing about peace and security. As with the previous goal it is clearly premature to talk in such terms. In addition to the points just made, for the Register to succeed it must be integrated into regional and parallel security forums. This must await not only fuller participation but also the further development of the Register.

Promote openness in armaments at the national level

Although not as explicitly developed in the Resolution as the previous goals, the Register process is designed to create and promote openness at the national level through the creation of national control and reporting processes. Some states reporting to the Register had to change their national laws regarding the secrecy of military and proprietary information. Others released data irrespective of existing arrangements, especially in respect to commercial relationships. It must be said, however, that many states, particularly those which did not participate in the first year, have not overcome a very firm tradition of secrecy in military matters.

Restraint

A brief review of the analyses and assessments made public of the first year's operation make clear the disappointment regarding the failure of the Register to bring about any restraint in the arms trade. The point was made by both China and the Democratic People's Republic of Korea in the fall 1993 session of the First Committee of the UN General Assembly. Additionally, critics of U.S. arms export policy also make this point. Given the previous comments on the lack of a consultative mechanism to assist in the determination of an "excessive and destabilizing" arms build-ups, the inability of the Register to bring about restraint is not surprising. No individual state would view its reported imports as anything but defensive and in accordance with Article 51 of the UN Charter. Given this reality, the "restraint" referred to in the resolution is only likely to occur as a result of this prior determination. Restraint for restraint's sake is not a component of the Register process. Rather it is related to a security context that can only be addressed multilaterally.

Early warning

Although this phrase does not appear in the original resolution, UN Secretary-General Boutros-Ghali made it clear in his "New Dimensions" speech in the fall of 1992 that the Register had the potential for achieving such a goal.[7] He continues to stress this function, as late as his opening remarks on disarmament in Geneva in January 1994.[8] As with several other objectives covered in this section of the analysis, its fulfilment awaits the development of some multilateral mechanism or forum in which the data can be addressed. In addition excessive attention on this objective runs the risk of overemphasizing the Register as an intelligence and verification instrument.

II   Does the Register address the current arms trade trends?

Trade in major systems

It is appropriate to ask if the process is addressing the arms trade trends which have evolved since 1991 and the post-Gulf War environment. As mentioned previously, the UN Register is inexorably linked to the role arms build-ups played in the Gulf War. The international arms trade system of the 1980s[9] produced the inventories of not only Iraq but also its neighbours, the end result of which was an unstable military balance highly related to the outbreak, conduct and termination of the Gulf War. This linkage is reflected not only in the terms used in resolution 46/36L but also the seven categories of advanced weapons to be made transparent. "The focus is on weapons indispensable for surprise attacks and large-scale offensive military actions. These weapons systems are relatively easy to identify, define, record and monitor."[10] One needs to be very careful here to not brand the seven categories as offensive weapons. The previous remarks in this report regarding defining "excessive and destabilizing" mean that "offensive" too can only be defined in a certain context. That was one of the reasons the Register was developed, to provide such an opportunity. Nevertheless, these are the categories of systems most likely to cause such situations.

Even if it is assumed that the arms trade system only involves end items in these seven categories (the remainder of this section will question this assumption), the Register falls far short of addressing the trade when it comes to missiles. The inadequacies of this category have been previously addressed. As only one problem, ground to air missiles are not included.[11] In addition the range limitation of 25 kilometers means that several classes of very lethal missiles – e.g., anti-tank, air-to-air – are basically left uncovered by the Register and any subsequent assessments of arms build-ups. Clearly an excessive accumulation of missiles of these types could be destabilizing. Given that the overall trade in major weapons systems (i.e., platforms) has been steadily declining in the post-Cold War era, acquisition of additional missiles is an obvious step to increase one's military capability. There are other major systems not covered by the Register which, if accumulated in certain regions, could contribute to excessive and destabilizing build-ups. Most of these (e.g., electronic warfare systems, remotely delivered mines, etc.) are mentioned in the second part of the 1992 report which served as a menu for the 1994 Group.

New commodities

The Register does not address some of the newer trends in the arms trade, especially those commodities which can significantly effect and alter the build-up of military capability but are not in themselves major stand-alone systems or platforms. For example, given the well-documented shortage of funds which can be used for weapons purchases, recipients are importing upgrades in the form of newer weapons, engines and radars for old platforms already in the inventory. It is not clear how this is to be reflected in the procedures of the Register. Secondly, the Register approach is not well suited for making transparent the early warning and command, control and communication systems which are increasingly being imported as force multipliers. As for trade in the technology itself, in a sense it is being addressed in the Register. Although it is highly unlikely that a military technology register will or can be developed, if the Register does develop into one which makes transparent "procurement through national production," the end result of the technology will be made transparent.

The special case of light weapons

While it is true that increased attention is being paid at the sub national, national and international levels to the negative consequences of unlimited sales of major conventional weapons, especially into areas of regional tension, the opposite is true when it comes to the trade in light weapons. Due to a systemic change in mode of conflict, from major inter-state wars to ethnic and sub national conflict, the demand for light weapons has increased. Combined with the collapse of national export control systems in states possessing a surfeit of such weapons, light weapons, including everything from rifles to land mines to artillery pieces, are now readily available for the host of sub national and ethnic conflicts raging in many parts of the developing world and in particular the former Soviet Union. By all accounts, trade in light weapons – small arms, land mines, mortars, man-portable missiles, etc.- has increased significantly in the post-Cold War era.[12] The end of the Cold War has unleashed ethnic conflicts long dormant and controlled by the logic of the Cold War and the concept of client states. Ironically, this increase in trade, and the accompanying negative consequences, is made increasingly visible due to the greater use of UN peacekeeping and peacemaking operations, which bring along with it mass media coverage. It has always been the case that in armed conflict it is the light weapons which do most of the killing, and there can be no question that an increasing number of such weapons are getting into the hands of an increasing number of soldiers, paramilitary forces, non-state actors and civilians involved in ethnic conflicts which will not be resolved for a long time to come.

III   Conclusion

The expansion and further development of the UN Register of Conventional Arms will depend critically on the experience of the first two years of operation. This assessment of that experience serves to summarize those areas of performance which are logically linked to improvements in the Register which increase the likelihood that its objectives will be accomplished. Hopefully this review of the participation, quality of reporting, and discrepancies in the data submitted to the Register will serve as a guide to those charged with the development of the Register in 1994 and beyond.

Notes

1. The following assessment is excerpted from Edward J. Laurance and Herbert Wulf, *An Evaluation of the First Year of Reporting to the United Nations Register of Conventional Arms*, Research Report, Program for Non-Proliferation Studies, Monterey Institute of International Studies, October 1993. A more detailed analysis is contained in Edward J. Laurance, Siemon Wezeman, and Herbert Wulf, *Arms Watch: SIPRI Report on the First Year of the UN Register of Conventional Arms*, SIPRI Research Report 6, Oxford University Press, Oxford, 1993. Also see Malcolm Chalmers and Owen Greene, *The United Nations Register of Conventional Arms: An Initial Examination of the First Report*, Bradford Arms Register Studies No 2, Department of Peace Studies, Bradford University, October 1993.

2. For more detail on this exercise see Chapter 8, by Andrew Duncan.

3. See Annex 5.

4. Malcolm Chalmers and Owen Greene, *Background Information: an analysis of information provided to the UN on military holdings and procurement through national production in the first year of the Register of Conventional Arms*, Bradford Arms Register Studies No 3, Department of Peace Studies, Bradford University, March 1994, p. 3.

Notes continued

5. *Report on the Register of Conventional Arms: Report of the Secretary-General*, UN Document A/47/342, 14 August 1992.

6. This is exactly what was attempted by key developing states in the Ad Hoc Working Group on Transparency in Armaments of the 1993 Conference on Disarmament session. It was seen by the Western states as a tactic to prevent any serious discussion on transparency, endorsing the point just made in this chapter.

7. Boutros Boutros-Ghali, *New Dimensions of Arms Regulation and Disarmament in the Post-Cold War Era*, UN Document A/C.1/47/7, 23 October 1993.

8. Ibid., UN Document A/C/ 1/47/7, 23 October 1993.

9. For a thorough description and rules of operation of this system, see Edward J. Laurance, *The International Arms Trade*, Lexington Books, New York, 1992.

10. Hendrik Wagenmakers, "The UN Register of Conventional Arms: A New Instrument for Cooperative Security", *Arms Control Today*, April 1993, pp. 17-19.

11. No consensus was possible on this question in the 1992 Panel. For further details see Herbert Wulf, "The UN Arms Register", in *SIPRI Yearbook 1993*, Oxford University Press, Oxford, 1993, p. 539.

12. For two excellent and recent accounts, see Aaron Karp, "Arming Ethnic Conflict," *Arms Control Today*, September 1993, pp. 8-13; and "The Covert Arms Trade," *The Economist*, 12 February 1994, pp. 21-23.

~

CHAPTER 4

Further development of the Register reporting system

Malcolm Chalmers and Owen Greene

I   Introduction

The Group of Experts has been given two tasks by the UN: to look at the Register's "further development" and to examine its "continuing operation." this chapter argues that the success of any proposals for the former are likely to depend crucially on decisions made to improve the latter. Before turning to a discussion of specific ways in which the Register might be 'deepened' or 'widened'' therefore, we suggest some ideas as to how the Register might be 'strengthened'.

After discussing each of these in turn, we then examine a number of proposals being made for expanding the Register. The possible expansion of the Register to include holdings and procurement is left to Chapter 9. Here we focus on, first, the possibilities for expanding, or adding to, the existing seven categories of systems covered by the Register; and, second, proposals that the Register be expanded to include greater information on the types and models of systems reported.

II   Strengthening the Register

Introduction

At present the Register has no definition of what it means to be a 'participant', and obligations are not defined in a treaty or framework convention. Resourcing is modest, and no decisions have been taken as to how to organise development beyond the work of the 1994 Group. There are good reasons for all of this, and it would be premature to attempt to establish the Register in a formal convention at this stage. Nevertheless, if it is hoped that the Register will become a significant and permanent feature in the international system, it is important that it be gradually strengthened as an institution, and that the rights and obligations of participants are defined and developed. Thus, in concentrating on means of extending and developing reporting requirements, measures to improve implementation should not be neglected. The development of implementation review procedures and resources is important, as are other measures to improve the reliability and timeliness of reported data. Mechanisms are needed to provide guidance (and perhaps dispute resolution) where there is confusion or disagreement.

Other chapters will explore such mechanisms further. In this chapter we would like to focus on two examples of areas on which discussion is needed: (i) whether 'participation' should be defined ; (ii) whether there is a need for a regular review procedure for the Register, and if so what forms it should take.

Should participation be defined?

The current Register, on the recommendations of the 1992 Panel, sets out three ways in which data is submitted to the UN:

First, states provide numerical data and countries of origin/destination in **columns A-E of the standardized form**. The character and form of the information to be provided in these forms is relatively clearly set out.

Second, space is provided on the form for information on 'description of item' and 'comments on the transfer'. If provided, this information is published in the annual Report. However, "this column should be filled in at Member States' discretion; no specific pattern is prescribed."[1] It is thus both more voluntary, and less defined, than the main part of the form.

Third, states are invited "in any form they wish" to submit background information on "their military holdings, procurement through national production, and relevant policies". This information is not published in the Secretary-General's report on the Register, but instead is available at the UN Centre for Disarmament Affairs (CDA) for consultation (in line with the 1992 Panel's recommendation that: "the available background information submitted by Member States be open to the public")[2].

A 'common sense' definition of Register participation might be that it involves (at a minimum) satisfying the first of these three requirements (even if this only involves providing a nil return). However, at least 7 of the 80 countries listed in the first report of the Register did not complete the standardised form at all. Because of the understandable desire to maximise the 'headline' figure for participants in Year One, completion of the standardized form was not therefore a condition for being included on this list.

This approach probably makes sense in the first experimental years of the Register, but it could involve growing costs if it is not replaced by a more systematic definition of participation. If some countries can continue to be listed amongst participants by simply writing a brief letter to the Secretary-General, others may be tempted to follow suit. A significant incentive for governments to report data for the Register is the potential political cost (small but real) of being seen not to have participated. If participation is too loosely defined, however, states may be tempted to avoid this cost without actually participating in a meaningful way. In this context, officials in governments making a genuine attempt to respond to the request for information may find it more difficult to overcome resistance within their own government or military to divulging previously confidential data.

Perhaps the Secretary-General's report should therefore in future make a stronger distinction between those states that have filled in the standardized forms and those which have responded in a lesser manner. This might involve the list of replies being divided into subsections: 'full participants' and 'other replies'. To be listed as having fully participated, a country might be required to have filled in columns A-E of the standardized forms (or provided a nil return) for transfers, plus whatever equivalent is agreed for procurement and holdings. As at present no confirmation of the accuracy of the data submitted would be required, no matter how incredible it appeared.

Such a system could increase the incentives for states to follow the guidelines. However, it would have two important implications. First, as the Register expands, there may be several states each year (at least seven in 1993) who respond in some way to the request for reports, but in a way that qualifies them only to be listed as 'other replies', not as 'full participants'. Accordingly, the headline number of 'full participants' would be less than it would otherwise be. Provided that the number of replies continues to rise in the next few years, however, this risk may be relatively low. Moreover, by including all responses in the Report, but with a division between 'full participants' and 'other replies', public damage to the headline figure should be relatively contained, while still increasing pressure on states to participate fully. The Register's success is likely to increasingly be judged by the quality of the returns as well as the number of replies.

Second there would also need to be mechanisms introduced in order to ensure that (a) those clearly not meeting the definition of participation are described as such in the annual report; (b) countries who have reported data in good faith are not excluded from the participation list for essentially technical reasons. One possibility would be to establish a two stage review process.

First, CDA could be empowered to give advice to countries on whether their initial returns appear to meet the requirements of participation. If they do not, countries could then be given the opportunity to resubmit their reports. Although this would require the CDA to exercise some discretion in interpreting the definitions, provided that these are clearly set out this should be an almost entirely technical and administrative task, and thus need not constitute an unacceptable delegation of authority if combined with an appeals procedure. To address cases where an individual country disagrees with the CDA's advisory opinion, procedures would be needed by which a politically authoritative body could decide upon the status of returns before the annual report is finalised and published. Responsibility for examining appeals might be given to either a special committee set up for the purpose (perhaps involving representatives from a cross-section of Member States) or possibly to a Standing Panel (discussed in the next section of this paper).

Improving reliability and implementation review

As the Register expands, the need to have a repository of expertise and advice will also grow. The experience of the first year suggests very clearly the difficulties in seeking to operate the Register without giving the UN a stronger role in reminding and encouraging governments to make appropriate returns, or in providing advice and training to national officials. An expanded role for UN officials is therefore likely to be an important part of successful Register development. Such a role in turn will require some additional resources to be provided.

Given a change in its mandate, much more could be done by CDA officials, especially in promoting wider understanding of Register procedures. It has been suggested, for example, that (with the agreement of the governments concerned) the UN might send small missions to those countries that supported the Register in the General Assembly, but have not yet replied to the request for information. At relatively modest cost, the officials with direct responsibility in this area could be identified and common misapprehensions (especially around the necessity of making nil returns) could be corrected.

Yet some desirable central functions, such as a mechanism for deciding whether or not a state has 'participated', cannot be entirely delegated to UN officials. The CDA can play an initial advisory, monitoring and administrative role. But it may need to be backed up by a body capable of taking political responsibility for the implementation and development of the Register.

One possibility worth considering for this role would be a *Standing Panel of Governmental Experts*, similar in size and composition to the current Group. Such a Panel could meet as often as was necessary to fulfil its functions, which could be both advisory (as at present) and operational. These functions could include:

- Carrying out regular reviews of the operation of, and possibilities for further development of, the Register. Such reviews might, for example, examine proposals for the further evolutionary development of the Register's categories, definitions, and procedures, review the success of each year's returns, and suggest ways in which procedures can be improved. Such a system would mean that the 1994 Group would be seen as only one stage of a continuing review process, and might thus reduce the pressure on it to make 'once-and-for-all' choices. There are many potentially useful proposals on the table which are worthy of serious consideration, but which may need to be deferred in the interests of securing core objectives and improving participation. Agreement to deferrals, however, may depend on there being future opportunities to return to these issues. This in turn suggests that one of the outcomes of the 1994 review should be that it is agreed that future reviews will take place on a regular basis. A Standing Panel would also help to address the widely felt concern that the 1994 Group is meeting a year too soon, and prepare the ground for a more gradual, but consensual, process of regime building.

- Responding to specific requests from the Conference on Disarmament and/or the General Assembly to address specific issues within its remit.

- Acting as a dispute resolution panel where there are doubts or disputes on issues such as whether a state's submission qualifies it to be listed as a 'full participant'.

It has been proposed that the body charged with overseeing the development and operation of the Register should also analyse the data provided, identifying 'destabilising accumulations' of armaments and seeking to provide early warning of conflict. Yet such a role would be fraught with difficulties. The relationship between arms buildups and conflict is unclear.[3] Without a clear definition of 'destabilising accumulation' (itself highly problematic), it would be impossible to reach agreement on when one was taking place. Not least, the very attempt to give a Standing Panel such a role could profoundly undermine its role as custodian of the Register's standards and procedures. The success of the Register will depend in large part on whether and how it can be used in practice. But, whereas the operation and development of the

Register can best be managed at a UN level, its application and use is likely to be a matter, in the first instance, for bilateral and regional discussions.

Some states may not yet be ready to accept the establishment of review mechanisms for the Register such as those discussed above, and thus it may be premature for the 1994 Group of Experts to include these amongst its recommendations. If this is the case, however, such proposals should be high on the agenda for future reviews of the Register.

III   Reporting weapon types

The Register in its current form already includes provision for states to provide further information on the role and model of the weapons which they report. An additional column, divided into two parts, 'description of item' and comments on the transfer', is provided in the standardized reporting form. It has also been agreed that:

> "Since the provision of such information might be affected by security and other relevant concerns of Member States, this column should be filled in at Member States' discretion; no specific patterns are prescribed. To aid the understanding of the international transfers reported, Member States may wish to enter designation, type or model of equipment, or use various descriptive elements contained in the definitions of categories I to VII, which also serve as guides to describe equipment transferred. Member States may also use this column to clarify, for example, that a transfer is of obsolete equipment, the result of co-production, or for other such explanatory remarks as Member States see fit." [4]

One of the items on the agenda of the 1994 Group is whether to revise this formulation. As Table 1 shows, a large number of states did provide further information on the types of weapons transferred in their 1992 replies. In total, 33 states out of a possible 46 states making non-nil returns included such information. By comparison, only 21 out of a possible 83 total respondents included details of military holdings and procurement from national production in 'available background information'. Many states, therefore, appeared to find it easier – in terms of sensitivity and/or data collection – to report types of weapons transferred than to report procurement and holdings.

Table 1. Countries providing details of types in 'description of item' column as of October 1993.

	including details	not including details
OECD	Australia	France
	Austria	Japan
	Belgium	Norway
	Denmark	UK
	Finland	US
	Germany	
	Greece	
	Italy	
	Netherlands	
	New Zealand	
	Portugal	
	Spain	
	Sweden	
	Turkey	
Former Soviet republics		
	Belarus	Russia
	Lithuania	
Other Europe		
	Czech Republic	Bulgaria
	Malta	Poland
	Romania	
	Slovakia	
Asia		
	Nepal	China
	Republic of Korea	India
	Philippines	Pakistan
	Sri Lanka	Singapore
Cenral and South America		
	Argentina	
	Brazil	
	Bolivia	
	Chile	
	Columbia	
	Nicaragua	
	Peru	
Middle East	Egypt	Israel
Africa	Niger	

NB: countries making nil returns are excluded from this table.

There would be a number of advantages from including this information in the Register. Most of all, it would give a more accurate picture of the significance of particular purchases. It would make it easier to make appropriate allowance for the large amount of trade in second-hand systems (for example, a large proportion of German exports last year consisted of former GDR systems surplus to Germany's own requirements). It would help address the concern that a numerical representation of the arms trade ignores the qualitative dimension. It should help to remove the rationale for sub-dividing current categories.

It can also serve as a crosscheck of whether states have understood the Register requirements correctly. If an APC is misclassified as a tank, for example, this can be pointed out to the country concerned. Even if mistakes remain, miscategorisation will matter much less when details of types are included. Finally, it will be easier to crosscheck between independent reports of sales – for which type information is usually available – and the Register data.

Yet, if fuller item descriptions are to be included, the Group will have to overcome the resistance that remains on the part of most major arms exporting nations. NATO and EU members were unable to agree a common position on reporting of types. The US, UK, Japan and France did not give type information, while Germany, Netherlands, Australia and Canada did.[5] By contrast, some other states were more likely to include types data than they were to provide procurement and holdings information. Both Brazil and Italy argued for the inclusion of such data in the 1992 Panel in order to emphasise the relatively low-tech nature of their own exports.[6]

A further part of the explanation for the reticence of major supplier states appears to have been a result of a desire to keep the Register's requirements as simple as possible in its first years. Reluctance on the part of some states to provide descriptions of weapons transferred may, in part, also be a result of concern at the possible reaction of customer states in the Middle East and Far East, many of whom have confidentiality clauses in their contracts, and most of whom did not participate in the Register.

Finally, concerns remain about whether including information on weapon types might compromise security-sensitive material. This concern is particularly felt with regard to missiles, where information on the numbers of a specific type of missile held by another state might be of operational value. Yet it may also be a concern in the case of some systems in the other six categories, either because a state has been able to conceal the existence of a particular system (for example through a secret development programme) or because a state is concerned at the security implications of revealing how many of particular sorts of systems it possesses.

The extent of this problem in the case of the first six categories should not, however, be overstated. In the case of warships, the size of these vessels is such that it is difficult (with the possible exception of small submersibles) to conceal them in any case. And the recent Conference on Cooperation and Security in Europe (CSCE) agreements provide a precedent for states providing detailed descriptions of weapons in the first five categories held in national arsenals. Both through the Conventional Armed Forces in Europe (CFE) Treaty, and subsequently in the March 1992 Vienna Declaration, CSCE members are already providing detailed information on:

(A) Their holdings of conventional weapons, both by model and by location, in eight categories of ground and air systems. These categories[7] are similar to, and in some respects broader than, the first five Register categories.

(B) Detailed information on each type or version of weapon in service in these eight categories, including national nomenclature, details of capabilities such as gun calibre, night vision capability and primary role, together with a series of photographs taken from different angles.

For those states whose territory is entirely covered by CSCE transparency measures, therefore, the additional burden imposed by a requirement to report detailed descriptions of holdings and procurement to the UN Register (at least in Categories I to V) may be rather limited. Indeed, one state (Sweden) provided a copy of its 1992 Vienna Declaration to the UN in its 'background information'.[8]

The Register differs from CSCE data exchange provisions in that the data provided is normally exchanged on a confidential basis between governments. Providing this information to the Register, therefore, does raise the issue of whether there is information which states are willing to allow other states to see, but which it would be unwise to publish more widely. In part, objections to greater public access seem driven by a desire on the part of some governments to frustrate greater public scrutiny of defence programmes. But there is also a genuine concern that some detailed information could be of value to criminal or terrorist organisations. This concern may apply in particular to information on the location of weapons.

If the development of the Register to include descriptions of weapons is to be successful, however, a large number of non-CSCE states will also have to be convinced that the perceived costs of greater transparency do not outweigh its likely confidence-building advantages. This may initially be difficult. But if the

53 states of CSCE – including many in areas of conflict in the former Soviet Union – can agree to such measures, it is possible that others too may find value in similar, if perhaps less radical, measures. The question is: which steps, and how fast?

Central to discussion of this question is the extent to which inclusion of item descriptions should remain more 'voluntary' than the data provided in columns A to E of the standardized form. If item description is encouraged, but is not (for example in the definition of 'full participation') treated as having the same status as the basic numerical data, there may be the risk of further differentiation between countries in the detail of the data they provide. If such a situation persists for some years, one could see different classes of Register participant emerging, perhaps undermining the extent to which governments feel obliged to provide information that they might not otherwise provide.

Despite the problems associated with trying to force the pace on this issue, therefore, the arguments for improving the extent to which states provide item descriptions, perhaps with a view to an eventual universal obligation, are worth considering seriously. Even if it is premature to think of equalising the status given to types data with that given on numbers, some smaller measures could be considered that might encourage the provision of such data:

First, the guidelines for completing the right hand column of the standardized form could be altered so as to clearly encourage the provision of item descriptions. For example, a statement could be included to the effect that states are encouraged to provide such data, except in those particular cases (or categories)[9] where they feel that this might adversely affect their security.

Second, the standardized form itself could be redesigned to increase the status given to item descriptions. For example, the title of 'remarks' could be removed and replaced with two separate columns entitled 'F. Description of Item' and 'G. Comments on the Transfer.'

Third, whichever of these options is adopted, there might be advantages in providing clearer guidelines to governments on how item descriptions should be submitted. The current guidelines state simply that 'Member States may wish to enter designation, type or model of equipment, or use various descriptive elements contained in the definitions of categories I to VII, which also serve as guides to describe equipment transferred.' This could be expanded by specifying more clearly the sort of information that it would be useful to provide, either in column 'F' of the standardized form, or in a separate national list of weapons designations, or in a common international list (see below). Table 2 lists some of the more obvious possibilities for each of the current categories of weapons. The aim of such guidelines would be to encourage states, when they did feel able to provide item descriptions, to do so in as uniform a manner as possible. In this way, it would be hoped, a proliferation of different approaches to transparency under this heading could be avoided. When additional states decide they are able to provide data on this column, they would have clear guidelines as to the form in which such data should be provided.

Table 2. Possible guidelines for descriptions of Register items

Category	Possible information to be provided in list of weapon designations
Battle tanks	name of model, unladen weight, main gun calibre.
Armoured combat vehicles	name of model, unladen weight, gun calibre (if any).
Large calibre artillery pieces	name of model, calibre, number of tubes (in case of MLRS).
Combat aircraft	name of model, integrally mounted armaments (if any), primary role (air defence, strike, etc.)
Attack helicopters	name of model, integrally mounted armaments (if any), primary role (electronic warfare, reconnaissance, etc.)
Warships	name of model, type (aircraft carrier, frigate, minehunter, etc.), standard displacement, integrally mounted armaments.
Missile Launchers and RPVs	name of model, armament, maximum range.
Missiles	name of model, role (air-to-air, air-to-surface, surface-to-surface, etc.), platform(s) on which deployed, maximum range.

Whether or not significant progress is made on the inclusion of item descriptions in the Register will depend, above all, on whether the world's biggest arms producers and military powers – China, France, Japan, Russia, the United Kingdom and the United States – begin to follow states such as Germany, Italy, and Brazil in providing this information voluntarily in their own returns. If they were to do so, they might help create a climate in which a more obligatory formula – or at least a widely accepted reporting norm – is possible in future. The second round of returns (due by 1 May 1994) may give some initial indication of moves in this direction.

Agreeing common lists of systems covered by the Register

An agreed list of those systems which are included in each of the Register categories would make national returns easier to compile for officials, most of whom have no direct knowledge of what the UN means by particular definitions, or what was in the Panel (or Group)'s collective mind when it agreed on a particular definition. Even if there was no requirement to include type/model in returns, such a list would reduce the potential for misinterpretation of what are, in some cases, rather ambiguous guidelines. It might thus help to reduce the costs of adhering to a regime that, if the addition of military holdings and procurement from national production goes ahead, is likely to add a significant administrative burden for national officials.

Compiling such a list could be an evolutionary process. It could begin by asking those states that provide information on their military holdings to attach a list of the systems that they have included in their return for holdings.[10] States could be asked to do so even if the 1994 Group were to decide to leave holdings as part of 'available background information'. For example, the US return for holdings of battle tanks might read:

United States: Military Holdings

Category	Number of items	Systems included
I. Battle tanks	14,832	M48A5, M-60, M-60A1, M-60A3, M-1, M-1A1, M1-A2[11]

For each system, states would be asked to provide enough information to distinguish it from other systems – e.g. gun calibre for battle tanks. But the option would be open for governments to furnish information on which systems they included in their holdings data without stating how many of each system they possess. In some countries, and perhaps in some weapons categories, such an arrangement might provide a useful means of contributing to Register reliability and consistency while meeting the security concerns that might arise where details of numbers of particular systems to be released. In a small number of cases, it is possible that governments may be unwilling even to acknowledge the existence of a particular system. Thus, while the normal expectation would be that the list of 'systems included' should be comprehensive, it may be better if this is not explicitly stated.

Acting on the advice of appropriate experts, perhaps based at the Centre for Disarmament Affairs, an international review body (such as the Standing Panel of Governmental Experts proposed in the previous section) would then examine the lists submitted on an annual basis and seek to agree a common list of systems that definitely fell within each of the Register categories. Where there was a consensus that a system clearly fell within a particular category, it would be included in a published list of systems to be circulated in future years. Where there was no consensus, systems would not be included and the debate would continue in future years (the development of such lists would in any case be an on-going process to keep them up-to-date).[12] But it would be made clear that all systems which governments consider to be within a given category should be included in the aggregate number of systems reported, whether on the list or not. The main function of the lists, therefore, would be to make form-filling easier and to reduce the potential for misunderstanding. The creation of common lists would not be conditional upon a requirement to list transfers and/or procurement and/or holdings by type or model.

Such a system could draw on the experience of CSCE in recent years. In the process of negotiating the CFE Treaty, the problems created by intractably ambiguous category definitions were to some extent circumvented by agreement on lists of systems covered by the Treaty. The Treaty therefore had a protocol listing 24 types of battle tank, 81 types of Armoured Combat Vehicle, 106 types of artillery, 55 types of combat aircraft and 17 types of attack helicopter that are limited by the Treaty. Also included is a list of other systems – 185 types of armoured personnel carrier lookalikes, 18 types of armoured infantry fighting vehicle look-alikes, 17 types of primary trainer aircraft, 25 types of combat support helicopters, 18 types of unarmed transport helicopters, and 13 types of armoured vehicle launched bridges – which are not limited by CFE, but for which data nevertheless has to be provided. In addition, for each new system introduced, states are asked to provide photographs, weight and calibre data. For Register purposes, it might not be appropriate to insist that participants provide such comprehensive data. Yet there is a case to be made for developing an agreed – though not necessarily exhaustive – list of systems that definitely come under each category heading.

A possible final advantage of the creation of common lists is that it may ameliorate the problem of having to change the definitions of the categories every time it is felt that new systems are to be added. It would facilitate a gradualist approach to expansion, and could allow the identification, on a consensual basis, of specific systems whose transfer, procurement or possession should be notified.

IV   Revising and expanding categories

Introduction

Part of the remit of the 1994 Group is to consider "the addition of further categories of equipment". In considering the task of its successor, the 1992 Panel felt that 'a key principle for adding categories should be that of military relevance in terms of the significance of their impact on regional and global security'.[13] It produced a list of possible issues to be considered in this discussion.

In considering the expansion or addition of categories, there is sometimes a temptation to think that more is always better, subject only to security concerns. This attitude should be resisted. Additional coverage involves additional administrative effort. If a substantial amount of time is taken collecting detailed data on systems of only marginal relevance, there may be fewer resources available to deploy on making sure that the correct data are supplied for those systems that do matter. Moreover, every time that definitions are changed, there is bound to be some transition cost. If changes occur too often, it may become difficult to discern trends in transfers, procurement and holdings over time: thus undermining the value of the Register as a measure of 'destabilising build-ups' of weapons. And if too much detail is asked of countries, perhaps particularly those with less well developed bureaucracies, there may be a danger that participation could fail to rise further or even fall. The experience of the UN standardized system for reporting military expenditures suggest that it is not enough to request a mass of detailed information if only a small number of governments (31 in this case in 1993) are prepared to provide it. [14]

Furthermore, in seeking to interpret the returns of those states that do not include item descriptions, there is always a danger that an expansion of the number of models included in any one category will make it more difficult to distinguish the more important systems from the less significant ones. Moreover, it is premature to assume that most states will provide this information for their transfers, military holdings and procurement from national production in the near future.

On the other hand, there could be some cases in which an expansion of the types of weapons covered by the Register can be justified. As we shall discuss, it would be surprising if there were not some anomalies which, as a result of the first two years' experience, it would seem sensible to resolve. If significant changes do seem desirable, in the light of the overall rationale of the Register, it may be better to make them now, before the existing categories become too established.

The value of any extensions, however, will depend very much on the manner in which they are carried out. For each proposed expansion, there are likely to be three options available:

(a)   New categories of weapons could be created, over and above the seven that already exist;

(b)   The scope of one or more of the existing categories could be widened;

(c)   One or more of the existing categories could be divided into sub-categories.

Which of these three possibilities is chosen will depend to some extent on perceptions as to how far we are likely to see an increased level of provision of data on item descriptions. The more that governments provide such data, the less need there will be for new categories or subcategories. The less that they do so, the more that the case for additional categories – or for subcategories – could gain credence. For if additional categories are not created, the addition of new systems to existing categories could threaten to dilute the data provided.

Even if no additional categories are created, and no item descriptions are provided, the addition of extra items can be of value if the items in question are judged to be of a significance comparable to, or greater than, some of those already in the Register.[15] How to apply this criterion will inevitably, however, be a matter of judgement. In each case a trade-off will have to be made between the potential costs and benefits of a proposed expansion.

Having made these general remarks concerning possible additions to the systems covered by the Register, we now proceed to examine a number of specific issues. First, we examine the first five Register categories, covering ground and air systems. Because of the overlap with CFE, these are perhaps the most developed categories. However, we suggest, there are still some important issues worthy of consideration.

We then proceed to examine the issue of Category VI Warships. The 1992 Panel agreed a compromise formula for this category. We examine whether this compromise is satisfactory, or whether there may be a case for a further lowering of the threshold used.

Finally, we discuss in some detail the future of Category VII Missiles and Missile Launchers. Of all the seven categories, this is the one with the most unsatisfactory definition at present. Moreover, it is also the category about which there are the greatest security concerns. We therefore examine possible ways in which to address both these concerns.

Ground and air systems

Adding ground and air systems already subject to CFE

The first five Register categories use some of the same phraseology as the definitions of the weapons *limited* by the CFE Treaty. As a consequence of discussions before and during the 1992 Panel, however, the definitions of armoured combat vehicles, combat aircraft, and attack helicopters were widened in several significant respects.

In addition to *limiting* systems in certain categories, however, the CFE Treaty also defines a wider group of systems which are *subject to the Treaty*. These additional systems are not subject to numerical limitations.[16] But countries are obliged to *exchange information* on them as part of their annual returns, and they are also required to place certain limits on their operations. These are:

> 'primary trainer aircraft, unarmed trainer aircraft, combat [support] helicopters, unarmed transport helicopters, armoured vehicle launch bridges, armoured personnel carrier look-alikes and armoured fighting vehicle look-alikes' [Article II, para 1(Q)][17]

The Register does not include all of these systems, which are also the subject of CSCE-wide information exchange through the Vienna Document of March 1992. Indeed there is no reason in principle why the Register should include all systems subject to CSCE transparency regimes. What is appropriate in Europe may, after all, not be appropriate elsewhere. In considering whether there are potentially destabilising systems which have been missed from the Register, however, it might be useful as part of that process to reflect briefly on those systems which are at present subject to CSCE transparency but are not covered by the Register. We therefore, consider the four main such categories in turn:

I. Primary trainers and unarmed trainer aircraft

The equipment subject to the CFE Treaty (but not limited by it) includes 17 types of primary trainer aircraft:

"which are designed and constructed for primary flying training and which may possess only limited armament capability necessary for basic training in weapon delivery techniques".

By contrast, the Register specifically excludes primary trainer aircraft 'unless designed, equipped or modified' to engage targets 'by employing guided missiles, unguided rockets, bombs, guns, cannons and other weapons of destruction'. The interpretation of this is left to individual states. UK transfers of Hawk trainers have been reported, since this aircraft is (despite its listing in CFE as a primary trainer) clearly capable of being used in combat roles. The SIPRI analysis of 1992 returns reports, however, that neither exporting nor importing state reported the transfer of PC-9 trainers from Switzerland to Thailand, EMB-312 Tucano trainers transferred to Colombia, or Czech L-59 trainers delivered to Egypt, despite the fact that these aircraft are modified to carry bombs and rocket launchers. [18]

At the very least, there is a need to clarify which systems are included in the Register and which are not: here a common list of systems might be of value. The Group might also want to consider whether to widen Register transparency to include all those aircraft subject to the CSCE transparency regime. The number of systems involved is quite small. But trainer aircraft can, in times of conflict, often provide a significant increment to combat capability.

II. Combat support helicopters and unarmed transport helicopters

The Register category 'attack helicopters' is derived from the category of the same name used in CFE. Like the CFE category, it specifies that systems in this category should include 'integrated fire control and aiming systems' for their weapons. Unlike the CFE category, it includes naval attack helicopters and ground-based attack helicopters designed, equipped or modified to carry unguided weapons as well as guided ones.

While attack helicopters are the only helicopters limited by CFE, they are not the only helicopters subject to information exchange. The Vienna Document requires states to provide data on all helicopters in military service, specifying whether their primary role is, for example, "specialized attack, multi-purpose attack, combat support, transport". Only the first two of these roles is included in "attack helicopters." Thus, for example, Sweden's CSCE declaration of December 1992 (also provided to the UN as part of background information) includes its holdings of unarmed transport and combat support helicopters, as well as its holdings of search and rescue and anti-submarine warfare helicopters.[19]

In CFE, a 'combat support helicopter' is defined as a:

> "combat helicopter which does not fulfil the requirements to
> qualify as an attack helicopter and which may be equipped with
> a variety of self-defence and area suppression weapons, such as
> guns, cannons and unguided rockets, bombs or cluster bombs, or
> which may be equipped to perform other military functions"
> (Article IIP)

Unarmed transport helicopters, although subject to the Treaty, do not appear
to be defined. However, the Protocol to the CFE Treaty on Existing Types of
Conventional Armaments and Equipment provides a list of existing types of
both combat support helicopters (25 types) and unarmed transport
helicopters (18 types).

The case for the Register to be expanded to encompass all military
helicopters, as is already the case in CFE and CSCE information exchanges,
appears worth considering seriously. It is not at all clear, for example, why
troop transport helicopters are excluded from the Register while armoured
personnel carriers, even if they do not have any integral weapons, are
included. Because of their greater mobility and versatility, the former is likely
to be able to make at least as significant a contribution to surprise attack and
large scale offensive action as the latter. Similar arguments could be made for
all military helicopters.

An additional, and not incidental, advantage would be that it would reduce
the difficulty that appears to have arisen in some cases because the CFE
definition of 'attack helicopter' differs from that used in the Register. The
recent SIPRI study of the Register suggests that this may have led to the
exclusion of those helicopters armed only with unguided weapons or ASW
weapons, even if they fit within the Register definition.[20] Changing the title of
this Register category to 'Military Helicopters' would remove the problem of
having to distinguish between different sorts of military helicopters, all of
which play important roles.

III. Armoured vehicle launched bridges

Both the CFE Treaty and the 1992 Vienna Document require participant
states to exchange data on the number of armoured vehicle launched bridges
in their inventories. It is generally acknowledged that such systems can play a
crucial role in large scale offensive operations, at least in terrain in which
rivers are an important part of the landscape. Although not limited on a
national level in CFE, therefore, it is recognised that the number and
deployment of these systems is a matter of justified concern. Accordingly, a

Protocol to the CFE Treaty lists a total of 13 types of AVLB's that should be reported. The accession of other countries to transparency in this area, through the Vienna Document, adds further systems to this list (such as Sweden's 17 Brobv-941 armoured bridgelayers).

Should these systems also be added to the Register? In terms of their potential contribution to destabilising build-ups of offence-capable forces, the case is quite convincing. It may also be appropriate to consider extending the definition of such systems to include certain unarmoured bridging equipment to cover wheel-bridging equipment and pontoons designed for military use, that may be equally significant in some regions. Whether it is a priority to include military vehicle-launched bridges in 1994, however, may depend on whether non-CSCE states – for example in the Middle East – share the concern that CSCE states have felt about such systems in the past.

IV. APC lookalikes and AFV lookalikes

In the CSCE regime, the category of Armoured Combat Vehicles (ACVs) has perhaps the most complicated definition, reflecting the wide range of systems encompassed within it. The treaty-limited total is in turn made up of three subcategories, each of which is separately reported: armoured personnel carriers (APCs); armoured infantry fighting vehicles (AIFVs); and Heavy armament combat vehicles (HACVs). In addition to the ACV category, there is also a non-limited category entitled 'APC lookalikes and AIFV lookalikes', such as armoured recovery vehicles, armoured fire direction post vehicles, armoured observation post vehicles, armoured surface-to-air guided missile carriers, and armoured command vehicles.

Despite the identical name, the definition of ACV's in the Register is significantly wider than that in CFE. All treaty-limited ACVs (on the CFE definition) are included in the Register category 'armoured combat vehicle'. But the Register also includes ACV's which are armed with a missile launcher or an integral or organic weapon of between 12.5mm and 75mm, but which cannot carry a combat infantry squad. These might include, for example, APC and AIFV lookalikes armed with a heavy machine gun or a missile launcher.

It would be possible to add all other look-alikes to the Register, thus bringing CSCE and Register transparency in this area closer together. It is less clear that the military justification for such a step is strong enough to make this a priority at this stage. Some useful additional information would be provided on armoured support vehicles. Since these normally operate in close conjunction with armed vehicles, however, the value of this extra data may be rather limited. If one were to prioritise between claims for expansion, therefore, the case may be less strong for look-alikes in this category than for aircraft or helicopters.

Yet even if it were decided that there were no compelling argument for expansion of the existing Register armoured combat vehicle category, the comparison with the CSCE experience may have helped to highlight just how complex the definitional issues are in this area, and how relatively easy, therefore, it is for various governments to interpret the same definition in quite different ways. In CSCE information exchange, the possibility of such misunderstandings is minimised by: (a) the provision of an agreed list of systems under each category against which it is possible to check, and (b) the provision that governments must include in their exchange of information details of the models and types of systems held. If Register participants wish to attain a comparable level of consistency in their returns, they may find it worth reflecting on the desirability of similar measures (as discussed earlier in this paper).

In each of the four cases discussed in this subsection – systems subject to CSCE transparency but presently excluded from the Register – careful judgement is required before deciding whether to add them to the Register. Simply because these systems are in CSCE does not mean that they are appropriate candidates. It does mean, however, that it is worth reviewing these cases seriously.

Adding ground and air systems not already subject to CFE

If it is the case that a system's inclusion in CFE does not necessarily mean that it should be included in the Register, the converse is also true. Simply because a ground or air system is not in CFE, this does not mean that it should not qualify for inclusion in the Register.

The area in which this is perhaps clearest is specialised support aircraft. In the course of the 1992 Panel, there was some considerable discussion about the possibilities for adding such systems to the Register at a later date. Specific mention was made of:

> "(a) aerial refuelling aircraft; (b) reconnaissance aircraft (fixed
> and rotary wing); (c) airborne electronic warfare equipment
> (fixed and rotary wing); (d) airborne early warning and com-
> mand and control systems (fixed and rotary wing)"[21]

Although the number of such aircraft in service is relatively small, some of them could play a critical role in the prosecution of offensive operations, and in some cases are more important in this respect than some of the systems already in the Register. It could be argued that they have been excluded because they are not themselves weapon platforms, although this principle is not used by the 1992 panel. It should be noted, however, that the Register already includes some aircraft and helicopters that are not themselves equipped to engage targets. These are "versions of these aircraft" (i.e. those designed, equipped or modified to engage targets) "which perform specialized electronic warfare, suppression of air defence or reconnaissance missions."[22]

If the criterion of military relevance were the only one used, it would seem hard to justify the exclusion of at least some additional air systems. Refuelling aircraft clearly have an important role in extending the range and capability of both air defence fighters and bombers. Modern AEW aircraft play a role of critical importance in battle management, both in defensive and offensive operations; and the transfer of such systems to a region is often seen as a matter of regional, if not global, concern. Fixed wing transport aircraft, such as the Chinese Y-8 or Lockheed Hercules C-130, although not on the 1992 Panel's list, can play a crucial role in power projection.

The main issue of contention, therefore, is likely to be whether or not to include military aircraft that are not designed to carry weapons. The principle of including systems without integral weapons has already been accepted by the inclusion of armoured personnel carriers. In order for support aircraft to be included, however, it would be important to agree a relatively simple amendment to the description of Category IV that drew a clear line between those systems which are militarily significant and those which are not. All non-combat aircraft in service in the armed forces (including trainers) could be added, or some lower limit in terms of weight or range could be set. Aircraft under the command of civil authorities would be excluded even if, as in the case of air transport aircraft, they might contribute significantly to a state's military potential. This would in turn have implications for definitions of what is meant by 'in service in the armed forces'. Provided that the description used were the same as that used in defining 'military holdings', however, this might be possible to implement without insuperable difficulties.[23]

Weapons for 'low intensity' wars?

It is sometimes argued that categories used in CSCE are too 'Euro-centric', and there may be a degree of truth in this proposition. Yet the most obvious division may be, not between weapons of value in Europe and those relevant to the rest of world, but between those weapons that are 'important for surprise attacks and large scale offensive military operations' against a 'well-armed' opponent and those that can only be of such value against a 'poorly-armed' opponent.

Against a well-armed opponent (such as Iraq, India or Germany), the types of systems covered by the CFE Treaty and the UN Register would indeed form an important part of any ground offensive Highly mobile armoured vehicles would be needed in order to provide adequate protection against defending fire; and offensive action could not hope to succeed without having the capability of at least neutralising an opponent's air power, in turn normally requiring a state to have developed sophisticated air capabilities of its own.

Insofar as the aim of the Register is only to cover those systems which would be of significant offensive value in war between well-armed states, therefore, there may be relatively little need to make significant adjustments to the existing five categories beyond those already discussed. There may, for example, be a case for including additional types of support aircraft when it can be proven that they could be of significant offensive value. But there seems little case, on this criterion, for reducing further (for example) the thresholds for including systems such as artillery and rockets.

Yet two caveats have to be added. Firstly, the categories developed for CFE and the Register are of clearest relevance to **inter-state war** in those parts of the world where states have acquired significant arsenals of major ground and air systems. The latter includes most CSCE states, the Middle East, South Asia, and East Asia: areas of the world that together account for around 97% of total world military spending.[24]

The categories may be less satisfactory in the remaining parts of the world – notably Latin America and sub-Saharan Africa – where levels of military spending per head tend to be lower, but which accounted for 41% of the world's armed conflicts in 1989-92.[25] A significant number of states in both these regions have only small arsenals of Register systems, many of which are often unserviceable. They therefore depend more heavily on lighter weapons than their European and Asian counterparts, both for offensive and defensive purposes. Yet the absence of large stocks of heavy weapons and sophisticated air forces in these regions does not in itself remove the potential for surprise attack. Rather, it means that the possession and deployment of other systems becomes a more important component of that potential. For, against a weak opponent, a surprise attack can be launched, and territory conquered and held, without the weapons that would be necessary for this purpose in regions with more developed arsenals. Mobility can be provided by cross-country civilian vehicles, and firepower by machine guns, mortars and portable missile launchers. Poorly armed opponents, and civilians, can be conquered and intimidated without the need for heavily armoured vehicles or heavy artillery: as indeed experience in a number of recent wars (such as those in Chad and Somalia) illustrates.

Moreover, the concentration on heavy weapons in both CFE and the Register is based on a focus on potential conflict between states. Such a focus may well have been justified in the late 1980s, when the main concern of arms control was to regulate, and make less dangerous, the confrontation between two cohesive military alliances. In the 1990s, when intra-state conflict is much more central to the concerns of the international community (not least in Europe), it is less clear – at least conceptually – that transparency measures should focus exclusively on heavier weapons. While inter-state conflict should remain a central concern of the Register, there is a case for at least considering whether, either in the Register itself or in complementary regional measures, lighter weapons should not also be brought into the picture. It might be particularly appropriate to examine whether enough use is being made of the Register's potential to complement the UN's peacekeeping and peacemaking efforts.

In this context, it might be worthwhile considering a recent example of conventional arms control 'on the ground' in conflict situations in order to learn which weapons are considered as of most relevance in practice. For example the NATO ultimatum to the warring parties in Sarajevo, issued in February, called for the withdrawal, or regrouping and placing under UNPROFOR control, of the:

> 'heavy weapons (including tanks, artillery pieces, mortars, multiple rocket launchers, missiles and anti-aircraft weapons)'[26]

of both the Bosnian Serbs and the Bosnian Government. All weapons with a calibre of 12.5mm or more, including heavy machine guns and all missiles, were considered to be 'heavy weapons' in this ultimatum. Rifles and small arms, by contrast, remained subject to the cease-fire but could be retained by the opposing forces.

The adoption of a similar lower limit in the Category III of the Register would have the effect of bringing in large numbers of additional crew-served weapons (mortars, heavy machine guns, cannon, anti-tank weapons), while still excluding personal weapons, such as rifles and submachine guns. It might help to encourage exporters of such systems to areas of tension, together with their governments, to improve their procedures for monitoring and controlling these exports.

However an expansion of the Register to cover large number of lower-calibre weapons at this time could impose substantial additional reporting burdens at a time when Member States may also have been asked to provide data to the UN on military holdings and procurement from national production. It may be better to postpone a major expansion of this category to a future review, while also seeking to develop other international arrangements to address the legitimate concerns about transfers and accumulations of light weapons.

Land mines

Finally, a case has been made for considering whether the Register should be used as a means for increasing pressure to control the world-wide trade in land mines. On December 16, 1993, the UN General Assembly passed a non-binding resolution calling for a ban on exports. The United States has extended its own moratorium on exports of these weapons, and has called on others to do the same.[27] And the US-based organisation Human Rights Watch has recently called for the inclusion of land mines in the Register.[28]

The case in favour of inclusion is that, if the remaining major suppliers of land mines were obliged to declare their exports of these 'weapons of mass destruction by slow motion', it might contribute to pressure on them to take measures to follow the General Assembly's lead. Moreover, most of the largest producers (including the former Soviet republics, Italy and China) do already participate in the Register.

On the other hand, the proposal to include land mines raises quite important issues of principle. First, on what basis would land mines be judged to meet the criteria for inclusion in the Register? In terms of their contribution to human suffering, the case is clear. Moreover, in some contemporary conflicts they do play a crucial role in hampering the movement of opposing forces and as a weapon of terror against enemy territory. But is this enough to meet the 1992 Panel's suggestion that 'military relevance' should be the key?

Even if it were accepted that mines were militarily relevant, there may be a second argument. It is often argued that central to the Register concept is that it is concerned only with 'legitimate' weapons, i.e. those whose possession is generally judged to be an acceptable part of national self-defence. If it is decided, perhaps through modification of the Inhumane Weapons Convention, that trade in these systems should be ended , they can no longer be seen as part of legitimate trade, and should therefore be a matter for discussion elsewhere.

Insofar as serious progress does take place in the near future towards a global ban on the trade in mines, it would make more sense for transparency measures to take place as part of a regime specifically concerned with mines. Unlike the Register, such measures would be concerned with revealing illegitimate trade, not announcing legitimate transactions. They could also be associated with intrusive verification procedures that would be quite inappropriate for the Register at the present stage of its development. Until and unless the trade in mines is again viewed as legitimate, it might be better to seek other means of monitoring and exposing it.[29] If such measures are not taken, however, there may at some stage be a case for reconsidering the inclusion of these systems in the Register as a second-best alternative.

Warships

The 1992 Panel made significant changes in the definition of this category, lowering the tonnage threshold to 750 tonnes and adding those warships with a tonnage of less than 750 tonnes that are equipped with missiles of a range of at least 25 kilometres. The question for the 1994 Group is whether a further extension of this category is desirable. The threshold as it stands does seem to cover most of the major platforms, and a high proportion of the tonnage, of most major navies. On the other hand, the tonnage threshold does seems to set a much higher threshold for military significance than in the case of air and land systems.

The reporting costs of reducing the threshold do not appear to be very great. A lowering of the threshold to, say, 500 tonnes would bring in such systems as the UK's Hunt class minesweepers/minehunters (displacement 615 tonnes, or 750 tonnes with full load) and its Peacock class large patrol craft currently based in Hong Kong (displacement 690 tonnes with full load).[30] But it would not lead to a quantum leap in the numbers of vessels included. Even a more radical lowering – say to the SIPRI threshold of 100 tonnes – would not overburden the reporting system. For example, Spain (a significant naval power) reported holdings of 32 warships in its Register 'background information' last year. If the threshold had been 100 tonnes, it would have had to report a total of around 70.[31] If comparable proportional increases in reporting requirements were to occur in other countries, as we would expect, the total number of warships reported would increase significantly. But, by excluding the smaller coastal patrol craft, such a threshold would still leave governments with a relatively simple administrative task.[32] It would also be possible to express thresholds in a way that combined tonnage with levels of armament.

As well as examining the possibility of lowering the threshold, the Group may – perhaps in parallel with a similar exercise for helicopters and aircraft – wish to examine whether support ships should be included in the Register. At present, only those ships 'armed *and* equipped for military use' are included, and this appears to exclude unarmed support vessels – such as tankers – even when they perform a specialised military purpose. At the very least, it may be desirable to clarify what exactly is meant by this definition. If, for example, a support vessel above the tonnage threshold is armed only with 12.7mm machine guns, will it still be included? If not, what level of armaments is necessary to be defined as 'armed'? Some definition of 'armed' would appear to be needed in this context.

Alternatively, it could be decided simply to include all those ships "armed *or* equipped for military use". If this had been implemented in the case of Spain, one might have expected the total number of vessels reported to have been around 60 with a 750 tonne threshold. If at the same time the tonnage threshold had been lowered to 100 tonnes, the total reported would have been about 110.[33] Such an extension, however, does raise more fundamental issues concerning the extent to which the Register will cover support systems, and would therefore have to be discussed in the context of a more general discussion.

Missiles and missile launchers

By far the biggest criticism of the current categories relates to the unsatisfactory nature of Category VII: Missiles and Missile Launchers. Moving to a more satisfactory treatment of these systems would remove one of the more obvious anomalies in the current system.

The problems of this category, already recognised by the 1992 Panel, were further highlighted by 1992 Register returns that, at the very least, called into question the value of including information on the current basis. For example, total UK stocks of missiles & missile launchers were estimated to be 23,892: more than half the US holdings of 43,975. By contrast, Germany reported missile stocks of only 40 (excluding classified holdings).[34] In the absence of more detail, these figures are almost meaningless, and cannot contribute significantly to the enhancement of transparency between states.

The inclusion of missile launchers and missiles in the Register is a *fait accompli*. The question for the Group is whether means can be found to develop reporting requirements in such a way that:

i.   Legitimate security concerns regarding the sensitive nature of detailed data on missile stocks (and thus, at least in the medium term, on transfers and procurement) are met.

ii. Constraints on releasing data on missile stocks do not hold back further development of transparency in the other six categories, for example on the issue of type descriptions.

iii. The data that is provided is easier to interpret.

Unlike the other six and a half categories, (including missile launchers), it is sometimes argued that missiles are better classified as 'ammunition' rather than 'platforms'. In fact, they fall somewhere in between these two categories, often themselves capable of delivering a variety of different munitions (as with ballistic missiles). The security concerns relating to the disclosure of missile types can be overstated, and may in part be a result of the fact that it is possible to keep this information confidential, rather than it is necessary. But since the rate at which missile stocks (like stocks of items of ammunition such as tank or artillery shells) are used up can be, at least in principle, related to the duration and intensity of operations, knowledge of an opponent's initial stocks of particular types of missiles through the Register can be of military significance. Those states (including most NATO members) who do not anticipate entering a high-intensity conflict except in alliance with others may feel relatively relaxed about this, since access to new stocks is likely to be relatively easy. The more that states feel they could be obliged to rely on their existing stocks of weapons in future conflicts, however, the more reluctant they are likely to view data on missile stocks as sensitive.

It is important not to overstate the degree of secrecy that exists surrounding missile types. For example, the United States government (which did not provide types data to the Register) regularly provides information to Congress on proposed transfers of defense articles including detailed figures on ammunition and missile numbers. In October-November 1993 alone, requests were sent to Congress for approval of the transfer of the following items:

*   12,000 rounds of 105mm tank ammunition to Egypt.
*   32 Harpoon anti-ship missiles, 64 Mk-46 MOD 5 torpedoes, 40 ASROCs, 40,000 rounds of 20mm ammunition for Phalanx CIWS, 3000 rounds of 5"/54 ammo to Greece.
*   216 MLRS rocket pods to Israel.
*   190 AIM-120 AMRAAM air-to-air missiles, 127 AGM-65 Maverick air-to-ground missiles to South Korea.
*   50 AIM-7M, 36 AIM-9S air-to-air missiles to Singapore.

- 150 Mk-46 MOD 5 torpedoes, 1581 rounds of 5"/54 ammunition, 30,000 rounds of 20mm ammunition for Phalanx CIWS, 18 ASROCs to Taiwan.
- 1772 MLRS rockets to Turkey.[35]

Generally speaking, however, it remains true that many states find it more difficult to be transparent about missiles – especially missile holdings – than about any of the other six categories. This hypothesis is supported by an analysis of the background information on military holdings and procurement from national production provided by states to the UN in 1993. A total of 24 countries provided some data on procurement and holdings, and of these ten countries (Australia, Austria, Brazil, Canada, Chile, Japan, Netherlands, New Zealand, Nicaragua, and Sweden) included item descriptions for their holdings of the first six Register categories. But only one country – Canada – provided item descriptions for its holdings of missiles and missile launchers.[36]

A further explanation of reluctance to agree to openness in this area is that it is more novel than in other categories. The degree of public information available on their numbers is less than in the case of platforms except in the case of strategic and intermediate range systems. Thus, the discussion of sources for the SIPRI Register of trade in major conventional weapons states that 'Exact numbers of weapons ordered and delivered may not always be known and are sometimes estimated – particularly with regard to missiles.'[37] The International Institute for Strategic Studies' *Military Balance* states simply that 'Inventory totals for missile systems (e.g. SSM, SAM, ATGW, etc.) relate to launchers rather than missiles'.[38]

Whatever the explanation, a survey of the background information provided by countries on their military holdings and procurement from national production in 1993 shows that a number of states that have used the first six Register categories to report holdings and/or procurement have not provided comparable data for the seventh category, Missiles and Missile Launchers. Amongst the states not providing such data (in addition to Germany) were Australia, Brazil, Chile, Denmark, France, Hungary, Japan, New Zealand, Poland, and Sweden. It may be surmised that these states are even less likely to be willing to provide full details of the types of missiles that they possess.

Thus the automatic inclusion of all missiles in any 'deepening' proposal may reduce significantly the extent to which states are prepared to accept development on the Register's reporting requirements in other areas. Given the special status which Member States already give to missiles in their returns, therefore, the possibility of formalising this status, through the adoption of a rather different set of requirements for missile transparency than for the other categories, might be considered. For example:

- The existing Category VII could be divided into two separate categories:
  (a) VII Missile Launchers and RPV's.
  (b) VIII Missiles.

- Any additional requirements for transparency in the first seven categories of launchers (including missile launchers & RPV's) – for example for descriptions, procurement and holdings – could be separately debated in the case of the new Category VIII.

This would not necessarily mean that *no* additional data on missiles would be included in the main Register tables. In the case of types information in particular, however, there may be a case for developing transparency for missiles less rapidly than in the case of the first seven categories. The argument for such an approach would be that the first stage should be to seek to maximise the number of countries that release gross figures on missile stocks and procurement. Only when participation has reached some, unspecified, level would the possibility of also releasing types data be considered.

A second way to achieve the same result, which avoids the need to create a new category, would be to accept that types data should be included for Category VII, but then to specify that transfers, holdings and procurement can, if states wish, be categorised simply as either 'missile' or 'missile launcher'!

Longer-range missiles

One of the guiding principles underlying the Register is that there is no general presumption that trade in the weapons that are covered by the Register is illegitimate. It can become so in particular circumstances, for example if a country is subject to a UN embargo. But in many circumstances conventional weapons are a legitimate means of national and collective defence, and the importation of weapons for these purposes can by extension also be acceptable.

There is one possible exception to this general presumption: the Missile Technology Control Regime (MTCR). Although the MTCR guidelines continue to be developed, in essence they state that transfers of missiles that can carry more than 500kg over ranges of more than 300km should take place only in exceptional circumstances and in cases where, in the judgement of MTCR members, there are guarantees that such transfers will not be destabilising and will not exacerbate missile proliferation. This latter provision is often taken to mean that 'core' MTCR members (ones which are close allies or already have well developed missile forces) can still transfer missiles amongst themselves.

MTCR is a selective not a global regime. A number of important missile producers are not members of the regime, and membership is subject to conditions set by existing members. Yet at the same time MTCR principles and guidelines have been widely accepted by most significant non-member states (such as Russia and China), and there may thus be scope for moving towards a more universal regime in future.

The Register might make a modest contribution to the development of MTCR by including a subcategory in the missiles category specifically for those missiles covered by MTCR guidelines (presently those capable of carrying a weapon of mass destruction over a range of more than 300 km). The number of systems reported in this subcategory is likely to be very small, and might be confined to transfers between MTCR states. But it could usefully reinforce the distinction between transfers of short-range missiles and transfers of longer-range missiles. It might also be a useful contribution towards developing a more general transparency regime for longer-range missiles, encompassing military holdings and procurement from national production as well as transfers.

Yet, as in the case of land mines, the argument could be made that the Register should not be used as a means of monitoring trade in those systems where active consideration is being given to a prohibition on use or transfer. Moreover, were it to be suggested that such a proposal should also cover holdings, the nuclear weapon states (particularly those with limited stockpiles) are likely to have substantial objections or concerns. Even if the general case for increased transparency in longer-range missiles is accepted, therefore, it may be that some other forum – such as a Nuclear Weapons Register – is more appropriate for its realisation. [39]

Ground-to-air missiles

The final point worth considering before leaving consideration of Category VII is whether the Group might want to re-examine the decision of the 1992 Panel to agree that the Category "does not include ground-to-air missiles". It is not entirely clear that ground-to-air missile launchers, other than those covered in categories I through VI, are presently excluded, but, for the purposes of this discussion it will be assumed that they are.

One of the arguments put forward in favour of this apparently anomalous exclusion was that GAM's are said to be defensive in nature and thus not 'destabilising'. Yet such a characterisation is open to dispute. The offensive or defensive character of a weapon depends very much on the context in which it is deployed, with 'defensive' tactics and weapons often being a key element of offensive operations. In at least two recent cases, moreover, ground-to-air missile systems have been specifically identified as a source of tension. The NATO ultimatum to forces surrounding Sarajevo specifically mentions the need to withdraw, or place under UNPROFOR control, 'missiles and anti-aircraft weapons'.[40] North Korea has recently complained strongly about the proposed deployment of Patriot missile systems in South Korea. At the very least, therefore, some states view such systems as having an offensive potential.

More generally, however, since the Register is not a control device, the inclusion of any weapon system cannot be taken as an acceptance of the assumption that the systems in question are 'destabilising'. The 1992 Panel itself does not use this criterion, stating only that weapons could be added to the Register if they are 'of military relevance in terms of their impact on regional and global stability' . In view of this, GAM's would appear to be a strong candidate for future inclusion in the Register.

Weapons of mass destruction

The 1992 Panel suggested that the possibility of adding "systems for the delivery of weapons of mass destruction not already covered by the Register " should be included in the work of the 1994 Review. Yet most, if not all, such weapons are already covered in the existing seven categories. 'Combat aircraft' should include strategic and tactical bombers, irrespective of possible payload. 'Warships' should include strategic submarines. 'Missiles and missile launchers' should include (a) independent launchers for all ballistic and cruise missiles with a range of over 25 km; (b) all ballistic and cruise missiles with a range of over 25 km. Despite the Register's title, even a missile exclusively designed and equipped to carry nuclear warheads should still be declared.

As long as the Register's standardised definitions only apply to transfers, this has few practical implications. It implies that transfers of Trident D5 missiles from US ownership to UK ownership should be included in the Register.[41] But we know of no other recent international transfers of delivery systems whose role is primarily nuclear. Indeed an increasingly strong international norm is being developed against such transfers, with the sole exception of the US-UK relationship.

Were the same categories that are currently used for transfers to be used for reporting of military holdings and procurement from national production, virtually all the nuclear-capable missiles of the five recognised nuclear weapon states would have to be included, together with missiles of other states that may be developing nuclear weapons covertly. If, in addition, these countries were to include item descriptions in their holdings and procurement returns, significant additional information on nuclear arsenals and their development would become available.

V   Conclusion

In this chapter we have argued that the prospects for the Register depend on successful blending of two elements: a strengthening of the operation of the Register on the one hand, and a skilful handing of the difficult choices over expansion of coverage on the other. In its first two years of operation, the priority has been to maximise participation. As a result, governments have had considerable latitude to choose how to participate. In future, however, the advantages of loose guidelines will need to be balanced against the risks of a drift away from the principles of universality and non-discrimination upon which the Register is based. There is already a danger that the Register could end up producing high levels of transparency between those states who need it least, and much less between those who need it most. This danger can best be avoided by insisting on clear and universal guidelines for participation, even if as a result the process of 'deepening' is less rapid than some countries would wish.

Yet it is implicit in the deal setting up the Register that there will also need to be serious consideration given to the possibility of expanding the Register's coverage. The possible inclusion of military holdings and procurement from national production is the most important element of such expansion, and we consider this issue in more depth in Chapter 10. But a number of other issues are also significant. On the one hand, there are some gaps in coverage, of which the lack of data on support helicopters and aircraft is perhaps the most apparent. On the other hand, however, there are also instances – notably in the missiles and missile launchers category – in which hopes for increased transparency may need to be tempered by the knowledge of governments' widespread security concerns.

Notes continued

1. *Report on the United Nations Register of Conventional Arms, Report of the Secretary-General,* A/47/342, 14 August 1992, p. 13.

2. This information is now available in Malcolm Chalmers and Owen Greene, *Background Information: An analysis of information provided to the UN on military holdings and procurement from national production in the first year of the Register of Conventional Arms,* Bradford Arms Register Studies No 3 Department of Peace Studies, Bradford, March 1994.

3. As argued persuasively in Chapter 12 by Michael Brzoska and Frederic S. Pearson.

4. *Report on the United Nations Register of Conventional Arms, Report of the Secretary-General,* A/47/342, 14 August 1992.

5. In its letter of transmittal 29 April 1993, the United States stated that it 'considers that it would be useful to provide additional detailed data on type and designation of arms transfers. We are therefore consulting with other interested States regarding what additional data would be useful. We hope to be in a position before the next report is due to provide supplemental data'. *United Nations Register of Conventional Arms: Report of the Secretary-General,* A/48/344, October 1993, p. 109. To our knowledge, supplemental data has not yet been submitted.

6. Herbert Wulf, 'The United Nations Register of Conventional Arms', Appendix 10F, *SIPRI Yearbook 1993,* Oxford University Press, 1993, p. 540.

7. The eight categories of systems which the signatories of the Vienna declaration must declare are:
   - battle tanks,
   - armoured combat vehicles,
   - armoured personnel carrier look-alikes and armoured infantry fighting vehicle look-alikes,
   - anti-tank guided missile launchers permanently/integrally mounted on armoured vehicles,
   - self-propelled and towed artillery pieces, mortars and multiple rocket launchers (100m calibre and above),
   - armoured vehicle launched bridges,
   - combat aircraft,
   - helicopters.

   (Source: *SIPRI Yearbook 1993,* op. cit. ,pp. 637-638.)

8. Malcolm Chalmers and Owen Greene, *Background Information,* op. cit. pp. 64-65.

9. Such as missiles.

10. It would also be possible to request that this information be provided with data on transfers and procurement through national production. However, because it will often be the case that the numbers of items in these returns are typically very

Notes continued

small, this would often be equivalent to a request to reveal the precise type of the items transferred.

11. *Jane's Armour and Artillery* has a list of this sort, but not arranged by Register category. Christopher Foss, *Jane's Armour and Artillery 1993/94*, Jane's, London, 1993, pp. 665-682.

12. Even without a mechanism for agreeing common lists, the publication of national lists might, over time, lead to significant convergence between national approaches. An invitation to governments to provide such lists, therefore, does not depend on either the creation of a Standing Panel or a strengthened role for the Centre for Disarmament Affairs.

13. *Report on the United Nations Register of Conventional Arms, Report of the Secretary-General,* A/47/342, 14 August 1992, pp. 17-18.

14. See Chapter 8 by Andrew Duncan in this book.

15. 'Significance' here is defined as 'their impact on regional and global stability'. *Report on the United Nations Register of Conventional Arms, Report of the Secretary-General,* A/47/342, 14 August 1992, p. 17.

16. With the exception of armoured vehicle launched bridges, which are subject to a limit of 740 held by each group (that is, former alliance) in active service. Individual national limits are not established.

17. Conventional Forces in Europe Treaty as reproduced in *Arms Control Today,* January/February 1991.

18. Edward Laurance, Siemon T. Wezeman and Herbert Wulf, *Arms Watch SIPRI Report on the First Year of the UN Register of Conventional Arms,* Oxford University Press, New York, 1993, *op cit.,* p. 48. Mark Lambert (ed.) *Jane's All the World's Aircraft 1993/94* , Jane's Information Group, Coulsdon, 1993, p. 64 reports that deliveries of the L-59 to Egypt began in January 1993, so this transfer may be reported in 1994.

19. Malcolm Chalmers and Owen Greene, Background Information, op. cit., p. 64.

20. Edward Laurance et al., op cit., p. 48.

21. *Report on the United Nations Register of Conventional Arms, Report of the Secretary-General,* A/47/342, 14 August 1992, p. 17.

22. *Report on the United Nations Register of Conventional Arms, Report of the Secretary-General,* A/47/342, 14 August 1992, p. 11. The Register also includes unarmed armoured personnel carriers in Category II.

23. See Chapter 9, 'Expanding the Register to include procurement through national production and military holdings'– definition of armed forces.

24. International Institute for Strategic Studies, *The Military Balance 1993-1994,* London, Brassey's, 1993, pp. 224-228.

25. Ramses Amer et al., 'Major Armed Conflicts', in *SIPRI Yearbook 1993,* op. cit. Table 3.2.

Notes *continued*

26. NATO communiqué, February 11, 1994, para 6.

27. 'Ban the mine' *Economist*, 7 January 1994, p. 15.

28. Human Rights Watch and Physicians for Human Rights, *Landmines: A Deadly Legacy*, Human Rights Watch, New York, October 1993, pp. 115-116.

29. It should be noted, that the Register includes trade in missiles, including those covered by the Missile Technology Control Regime. In contrast to the case of mines, however, it is not currently being proposed that there be a world-wide ban on trade in such missiles, only a selective one.

30. Captain Richard Sharp (ed.), *Jane's Fighting Ships*, Jane's, London, 1993, pp. 734-739.

31. Ibid., pp. 617-635. We have included in this total all armed vessels of more than 100 tonnes.

32. Even a 100 tonne threshold would exclude midget submarines, which can displace as little as 30 tonnes and can be used to some effect in raids on surface shipping. These small vessels are currently a cause of anxiety to some Gulf states.

33. Ibid.

34. Malcolm Chalmers and Owen Greene, *Background Information,* op. cit.

35. 'Deals in the Works', *Arms Sale Monitor*, 23, Federation of American Scientists, November 1993.

36. Malcolm Chalmers and Owen Greene, *Background Information, op. cit.* p. 38. Canada declared holdings of 845 AIM 7 (Sidewinder) and 784 AIM 9 (Sparrow) air-to-air missiles. Austria made a nil return for 'Missiles/Systems' and Netherlands left blank the space entitled 'Missiles and Missile Launchers' in its holdings declaration.

37. *SIPRI Yearbook 1993*, p. 519.

38. International Institute for Strategic Studies, (IISS), op. cit. p. 6.

39. Malcolm Chalmers, 'Transparency and the existing nuclear weapons states', *memorandum submitted to the House of Commons Foreign Affairs Committee enquiry into weapons proliferation and control*, February 1994.

40. NATO communiqué, February 11, 1994, para 6.

41. If this interpretation was followed by the US and UK in their 1992 returns, it suggests that no Trident sales were completed in calendar year 1992.

~

CHAPTER 5

What is required to have a useful transfers Register?

Ian Anthony

I Introduction

The appropriate test of any data set is whether it meets the objectives that it sets for itself. Ideally these objectives should be simple and clear and data should be collected in a consistent manner over an extended period.

Within the United Nations different people want different things. The UN has to try and meet the objectives of all its members as well those defined by the organization itself. These objectives are rarely defined consistently, articulated clearly and easily reconcilable. Moreover, objectives and national interests can change over time. Equally, in the domestic debate within countries there is no uniform view about the objectives and usefulness of the Register.

The answer to the question of what is required to make the UN Register more useful hinges on the purpose of the Register. If the Register is seen as a predominantly political exercise then enhancing its usefulness means expanding participation beyond the 83 countries which sent returns during the first year of reporting. If the Register is considered to be useful because of the official information it provides to governments about one another, then emphasis would be placed on the structure and content of the returns made to it. The UN Register was opened to all users through the decision to publish a consolidated report as a General Assembly document. In some countries the Register is seen as a public good that raises the accountability of governments before their national parliaments or media.

Finding measures that would be likely to broaden participation and generate a greater level of information is a challenge. It may be that greater participation would be encouraged by further limitations in the volume of information requested by the United Nations. Conversely, a request for more detailed information within the seven existing equipment categories which make up the Register or the addition of new equipment categories may act as a deterrent to countries considering participation. Worse, it might deter countries which chose not to participate in the first year of reporting from joining the Register in its second year.

The overall conclusion of this evaluation is that the basic structure of the transfer-elements of the UN Register is sound even though it does not meet any of the competing objectives noted above perfectly. However, the first year of reports to the Register have revealed several flaws which – while by no means fatal – reduce its value by producing misleading distortions in the data reported. The current group of government experts should take the opportunity to correct these flaws and improve the usefulness of the Register.

The UN Register is presented with little or no explanation of its contents. In the absence of a companion report analysing the returns, governments might usefully seek clarification and elaboration of returns to the UN Register in a consultative body of some kind. Participation might be encouraged if this clarification and elaboration through the consultative body was available only to governments which have submitted a return.

The basis for much of this paper is a comparison of the UN Register with the output of the SIPRI arms transfer data base. It is important to recognize several key differences in the nature of the two bodies reporting on arms transfers, and the value of comparing them should not be over-stated. SIPRI is an independent non-government research institute responsible to a small Governing Board composed of academic researchers. The purpose of its data collection is to deepen understanding of international arms transfers. SIPRI is not a policy planning institute or a 'think tank' and as a result prefers to publish descriptive rather than prescriptive analyses.

SIPRI data and analysis is available to anyone who wishes to use them. While this can include governments they are neither the most important nor most regular consumers of SIPRI products which are more widely used by academic researchers, political interest groups and the electronic and print media.

SIPRI arms transfer data is presented in several forms. One form of presentation is the table contained in each SIPRI Yearbook whose format resembles that of the UN Register. A second form of presentation is statistical, as SIPRI trend indicator values. While expressed in US dollars these trend indicator values are in fact an index of the volume of equipment delivered. This point is explained more fully below. These tables are supplemented in each Yearbook by an extended text which, with its appendices, usually runs to sixty or more pages.

The UN Register, by contrast, is not an academic construction but the result of an inter-governmental agreement. While the information presented in the

UN Register is nothing like as detailed or comprehensive as that provided by SIPRI it carries an authority which SIPRI cannot match. SIPRI data is based on a careful and systematic compilation of information already in the public domain. The UN Register is compiled from returns provided by governments which are, by definition, the primary authority on their national military activities. As a result, the UN Register can provide a basis for dialogue between governments, which SIPRI data never could. If governments which have volunteered information to the UN Register are subsequently questioned about the reasons for any given import or export they must deal with the substantive issues at stake in the case in question. Questioned on the basis of information published by SIPRI, however, governments can avoid issues of substance by challenging the validity of the data.

In spite of these fundamental differences, the structures of the SIPRI and UN data collections are sufficiently similar to permit some comparisons.[1] Both use inter-state transfers as their organizing principle rather than focusing on the defence industry (as a supplier) and the armed forces (as a customer). Both seek to measure the global volume of deliveries of specified items as part of an effort to examine the political and strategic impact of changes in the flow of those items. Neither register is concerned with the financial flows associated with arms transfers or with the economic and industrial impact of the arms trade on suppliers or recipients. Similarly, neither register attempts to track transfers of small arms or dual-use equipment on a comprehensive basis. Both data sets are largely relevant to the discussion of inter-state security and conflict.

II   The SIPRI trend indicator values

The utility of trying to 'measure' trends and developments in the arms trade is often questioned and the contribution which existing data collections can make to resolving analytical problems can be – and frequently is – overstated. The SIPRI philosophy is based on what has recently been labelled 'symbolic analysis'.[2] By translating real event data into symbols it is possible to manipulate the data in ways which sheds more light on the events themselves. The arms trade – composed of many events, no one of which can be regarded as representative of the overall trend – lends itself to this form of analysis.

Data series collected according to a consistent definition and methodology can be of value in helping to identify issues and developments which deserve detailed examination. Series of this type can also be of assistance in evaluating the relative importance and urgency of different analytical issues. If the data can be collected on a continuous basis its utility increases as the time series grows longer. In other words, data collection is a supplement to and not a substitute for analysis.

To perform this analysis it is necessary to transform event data into symbolic data. SIPRI does this by creating an index of trend indicator values which can then be aggregated in a number of different ways. The SIPRI system for evaluating the arms trade was designed as a *trend-measuring device*, to permit the measurement of changes in the total flow of major weapons and its geographic pattern.

Expressing the index in monetary terms reflects both the quantity *and the quality* of the weapons transferred. Aggregate values and shares are based only on actual deliveries during the year or years covered in the relevant tables and figures. It has to be emphasized that the SIPRI values are not actual prices of weapons that have been paid in a particular deal. The purpose of the valuation system is to enable the aggregation of data on physical arms transfers. Similar weapon systems require similar values. The core of the SIPRI index of trend indicator values is based on the average programme unit cost of weapons for which cost data are available. The values for other weapons are estimated on the basis of technical comparisons (of weight, range, speed, year of first production) with weapons for which real costings are available.

The index produced using the SIPRI valuation system is not comparable to official economic statistics such as gross domestic product, public expenditure and export/import figures. The trend indicator values do not correspond to the actual prices paid, which vary considerably – depending on different pricing methods, the length of production runs and the terms involved in individual transactions. For instance, a deal may or may not cover spare parts, training, support equipment, compensation, offset arrangements for the local industries in the buying country, and so on. Furthermore, even if all information on the terms of the deals were available (which is not the case), the use of sale prices would understate the total flow of arms by excluding systems financed through military aid and grants.

Production under licence is included in the arms trade statistics in such a way that it reflects the import share embodied in the weapon. In reality, this share is normally high in the beginning of a programme and gradually decreases over time. However, a single estimate of the import share for each weapon produced under licence is made by SIPRI, and therefore the value of arms produced under licence agreements may be overstated.

Once transformed into the form of an index, data on weapon deliveries can be presented in different ways. The case of Saudi Arabia is used below to illustrate two ways in which the trend indicator values can be presented.

Table 1.   Percentage shares of deliveries of major conventional weapons to Saudi Arabia by supplier

Data are percent

	1988	1989	1990	1991	1992	1993	1988-93
USA	16	7	49	54	77	82	41
UK	22	70	33	17	6	9	30
France	19	20	15	26	4	0	15
China	35	0	0	0	0	0	8
Others	7	2	3	2	12	9	5
Total	100	100	100	100	100	100	100

Source: SIPRI arms trade data base

Looking at the data in Table 1 it is possible to see the replacement of West European suppliers by the United States in the Saudi Arabian market. Whereas Britain and France accounted for 90 per cent of deliveries of major conventional weapons to Saudi Arabia in 1989, by 1993 this figure was less than 10 per cent.

Figure 1 overleaf shows another way in which trend indicator values can highlight developments in Saudi Arabia.

In Figure 1 it is possible to see that, popular perceptions notwithstanding, the volume of deliveries of major conventional weapons to Saudi Arabia has not jumped in the period after the Iraqi invasion of Kuwait. Deliveries remain lower than they were during the late 1980s. A similar figure could be prepared from the SIPRI data base comparing the volume and patterns of Saudi imports with, for example, those of other major regional powers such as Iraq and Iran.

Figure 1.   The trend in deliveries of major conventional weapons to Saudi
              Arabia, 1988–93

Data are SIPRI trend indicator values expressed in billions of (1990) US dollars

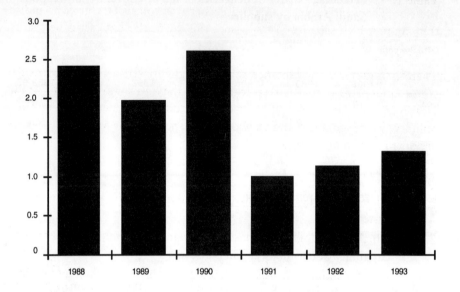

Source: SIPRI arms trade database

It is not being suggested here that these data carry the authority of scriptures,
nor that they can tell us much about how or why events occur. The data
simply assist in the broader process of understanding the dynamics of the
arms trade.

III   The coverage of the UN Register

UN General Assembly Resolution 46/36L of 9 December 1991 included an
extensive catalogue of national, regional and international security problems.
According to the 1992 UN *Report on the Register of Conventional Arms*
tabled by the Secretary General, the Register should be seen as one step in
implementing the resolution. Consequently, the Register does not try to
address all of the issues raised in resolution 46/36L (let alone all of the
challenges facing the international community). The Register has chosen
instead to focus on a narrow coverage limited to the transfer of seven

categories of equipment as well as more general background information on military holdings, procurement through national production and relevant policies.

Instruments of measurement should be as sensitive as possible to the needs of analysis. Clearly those interested in, for example, NATO burden-sharing would need a different data set from those interested in dual-use technology transfer. The way in which the UN Register was constructed gives an indication about which security-related issues this particular data set is best suited to analyse.

There is widespread acceptance that the right to self-defence accorded to states under the UN Charter legitimises the international arms trade. However, there are many different debates currently underway on different military, legal, economic and technological aspects of the arms trade. Several are noted in resolution 46/36L.

The debates include:

1. what constitutes an excessive accumulation of offensive weapon systems?
2. which technologies can most cheaply and effectively enhance the capability of existing weapon platforms?
3 how far should 'dual-use' technologies – that is, technologies with either a civil or a military application – be traded as civil goods?
4. can effective measures to prevent illicit arms transfers be developed and implemented?
5. what are the economic costs and benefits of the arms trade?
6. how is the changing organization of industrial production affecting the nature of the arms trade?

In conditions where governments and researchers alike are trying to come to terms with the security environment that has emerged after the end of the cold war it is natural that the value of a limited approach such as that taken by the UN Register should be questioned. However, it would be unreasonable and counter-productive to ask the UN Register of Conventional Arms to address all of these issues. The question is where the Register can make its greatest contribution in the light of a realistic assessment of what can be achieved both from a political and a technical point of view.

The limited range of items monitored in the UN Register partly reflects the lack of consensus around what is to be monitored outside the narrow categories which were agreed during its preparation. The judgement formed was that most governments would be unwilling to collect and/or release information on a broad spectrum of items. It also reflects a judgement that even if there were no political objections, most governments would be unable to collect detailed information about a wide range of items without increasing the human and financial resources devoted to the task. They would not see sufficient advantages in the Register to make this allocation.

The choice of categories and the judgement about the limits to government participation in an expanded data collection suggest that for the foreseeable future the UN Register can best address itself to the debate about what constitutes an excessive and destabilizing accumulation of weapons. This is where the political will to generate data is greatest and the technical obstacles to data gathering are fewest. The Register should not aim to collect more information than is needed to allow a reasonably informed judgement to be reached on this issue.

Modifying the UN Register

The decision to focus on transfers of equipment in relatively few categories of equipment remains valid and there is no need for a wholesale revision of existing categories or the addition of new ones. However, there are several structural flaws in the UN Register as presently constructed which – while by no means fatal – reduce its effectiveness in meeting its objectives.

These flaws reflect: (a) problems in the definition of the equipment categories; (b) the lack of a clear definition of an arms transfer and (c) the high level of aggregation within each of the weapon categories. Each of these issues was contentious during the drawing up of the parameters of the Register and in the end each was settled with a compromise. The modifications made to UN Register category VII 'missiles and missile launchers' defined in resolution 46/36L have created particular problems and, in the light of the experience with the returns to the UN Register in 1992, this definition needs to be revised.

It would be useful to correct some of the minor flaws as quickly as possible, preferably during the first round of evaluation of the Register by government experts. The Register will become more useful as a time series is developed. Time series need to be consistent and for this reason continuity in the definitions applied is highly desirable. In the worst case, a major change in the Register could invalidate the series and arriving at a set of definitions which can survive for a long period should be a priority goal for the group of government experts.

The definition of the weapon categories

One central problem faced in constructing a register is to isolate categories of items that could serve as reasonable indicators of military capability within the much larger pool of items bought by the military.

In addressing this problem SIPRI and the UN came up with a similar approach of identifying broad categories of equipment.

In spite of their names, therefore, neither the UN nor SIPRI are primarily concerned with covering arms. Arms or armaments can be reasonably clearly defined as munitions – explosives and ordnance. The definition could be extended to include the systems that deliver these arms. In both cases, this narrow definition is linked to unambiguously lethal equipment – weapons of war.

The UN and SIPRI exclude most types of 'arms' from their coverage and focus mainly on the platforms which carry weapons. The inclusion of various kinds of ordnance was considered by the panel of government experts which prepared the 1992 UN *Report on the Register of Conventional Arms*. All of the systems discussed, with one exception, were omitted. This exemption is missiles, which combine some of the characteristics of weapon platforms with those of delivery systems and munitions in the same piece of equipment.

SIPRI includes all guided missiles in its classification of major conventional weapons regardless of range whereas the UN definition is based on range only While the resolution establishing the Register in 1991 refers to a 'guided rocket, ballistic or cruise missile capable of delivering a payload to a range of at least 25 kilometres', the 1992 Panel amended this to also include unguided rockets. This wider definition is the one currently in use (see Table 2).

The modified UN definition created some peculiar distortions during the first year of reporting. For example, the UN definition brings in artillery rockets such as the Brazilian SS-30 and SS-40 – reported as exported to Saudi Arabia. Rockets of this kind are essentially artillery shells with the propellant attached to the warhead rather than separated. The SS-30 has a smaller explosive charge than a 155 millimetre calibre artillery round. As the calibre of the artillery round increases – for example, to 210 millimetres – the distinction between artillery ammunition and unguided rockets grows more and more tenuous. Through participation in the Register a country which chose to build its armed forces around imported rocket artillery would find its ordnance stockpiles revealed. A country which preferred tube artillery would enumerate its artillery pieces but not its ordnance stocks as imports of artillery ammunition are not requested.

Table 2.   Definitions of equipment categories used by SIPRI and the United Nations

SIPRI	United Nations
I. Aircraft All aircraft destined for the armed forces, paramilitary forces or intelligence agencies of another country except: aerobatic aeroplanes, micro-light aircraft and gliders. VIP transport aircraft are included only if they bear military insignia or are otherwise confirmed as military registered.	**IV. Combat aircraft** Fixed-wing or variable-geometry wing aircraft designed, equipped or modified to engage targets by employing guided missiles, unguided rockets, bombs, guns, cannons, or other weapons of destruction, including versions of these aircraft which perform specialized electronic warfare, suppression of air defence or reconnaissance missions. The term "combat aircraft" does not include primary trainer aircraft, unless designed, equipped or modified as described above. **V. Attack helicopters** Rotary-wing aircraft designed, equipped or modified to engage targets by employing guided or unguided anti-armour, air-to-surface, air-to-subsurface, or air-to-air weapons and equipped with an integrated fire control and aiming system for these weapons, including versions of these aircraft which perform specialized reconnaissance or electronic warfare missions.
II. Armoured Vehicles All types of tanks, tank destroyers, armoured cars, armoured personnel carriers, armoured support vehicles and infantry combat vehicles. Military lorries, jeeps and other soft-skinned vehicles are not included.	**I Battle tanks** Tracked or wheeled self-propelled armoured fighting vehicles with high cross-country mobility and a high level of self-protection, weighing at least 16.5 metric tonnes unladen weight, with a high muzzle velocity direct fire main gun of at least 75 millimetres calibre. **II. Armoured combat vehicles** Tracked, semi-tracked or wheeled self-propelled vehicles, with armoured protection and cross-country capability, either: (a) designed and equipped to transport a squad of four or more infantrymen, or (b) armed with an integral or organic weapons of at least 12.5 millimetres calibre or a missile launcher.

SIPRI	United Nations
III. Artillery Multiple rocket launchers, self-propelled and towed guns and howitzers with a calibre equal to or above 100 millimetres.	**III. Large calibre artillery systems** Guns, howitzers, artillery pieces, combining the characteristics of a gun or a howitzer, mortars or multiple-launch rocket systems, capable of engaging surface targets by delivering primarily indirect fire, with a calibre of 100 millimetres and above.
IV. Missiles All guided missiles are included. Unguided artillery rockets and man-portable anti-armour rockets are excluded. Free-fall aerial munitions (such as 'iron bombs') are also excluded. In the naval sphere, anti-submarine rockets and torpedoes are excluded.	**VII. Missiles and missile launchers** Guided or unguided rockets, ballistic or cruise missiles capable of delivering a warhead or weapon of destruction to a range of at least 25 kilometers, and means designed or modified specifically for launching such missiles or rockets, if not covered by categories I through VI. For the purpose of the Register, this category: (a) Also includes remotely-piloted vehicles with the characteristics for missiles as defined above; (b) Does not include ground-to-air missiles.
V. Guidance and Radar Electronic-tracking, target-acquisition, fire-control, launch and guidance systems; shipborne missile-launch or point-defence systems. The values of acquisition, fire-control, launch and guidance systems on aircraft and armoured vehicles are included in the value of the respective platform. The reason for treating shipborne systems separately is that a given type of ship is often equipped with numerous combinations of different surveillance, acquisition, launch and guidance systems.	No comparable category
VI. Ships All ships destined for the armed forces, paramilitary forces or intelligence agencies of another country except: patrol craft with a displacement of less than 100 tonnes unless they carry cannon with a calibre equal to or above 100 millimetres, missiles or torpedoes; research vessels; tugs and ice-breakers.	**VI. Warships** Vessels or submarines armed and equipped for military use with a standard displacement of 750 metric tonnes or above, and those with a standard displacement of less than 750 metric tonnes, equipped for launching missiles with a range of at least 25 kilometers or torpedoes with similar range.

Logically, if the UN Register is to include ordnance of the SS-30 type it should be extended to all kinds of ordnance with similar characteristics. Alternatively, the missile category could be deleted from the Register. As the missile category was one of the more contentious issues in designing the Register, deleting it might clear the way for the further disaggregation of items reported within the remaining 6 weapon categories (discussed further below).

Another alternative would be to return to the definition of missiles used in resolution 46/36L which would improve the comparability between systems reported. If this was not possible then the words 'or unguided' could be deleted from the definition of UN Register Category VII in the Secretary-General's report.

This would make guidance systems an element in determining whether or not a system should be reported and there are good reasons to do this.

In time, the ability to miniaturize electronic components and engineering products – such as flight control systems – will lead to the deployment of more and more 'smart' artillery shells.[3] Rocket artillery is already being used to deliver smart sub-munitions. For example, the MLRS 227 millimetre rocket developed by a consortium of NATO countries originally carried a conventional high-explosive warhead. However, the sub-munitions that have been developed for the rocket are changing the character of the weapon fundamentally.

Apart from missiles, another equipment category which was modified by the 1992 UN *Report on the Register of Conventional Arms* was attack helicopters. The original definition specified helicopters equipped with 'anti-armour, air-to-ground or air-to-air guided weapons'. In the subsequent report this was amended to read 'guided or unguided anti-armour, air-to-surface, *air-to-subsurface*, or air-to-air weapons' (emphasis added). Some countries used the definition in resolution 46/36L as the basis for their report and omitted helicopters configured for anti-submarine warfare – for example, the delivery of SH-60 helicopters to Spain by the United States was not reported by either country.[4]

The focus on the platforms which carry arms and delivery systems to a designated target platforms is partly expedient – transfers of platforms are much easier to monitor – but also substantive. In modern analyses of military trends, this narrow focus of analysis is rare since an effective military force is dependent not only on lethal equipment but also on combat support equipment of various kinds. It has been the development of platforms which has made the battlefield wider and deeper, and also extended it to include the air space above it and the sea space below it. But these changes in the shape of the battlefield would not have been possible without a parallel increase in the capabilities of various types of combat support equipment.[5]

In acknowledgement of the growing importance of target acquisition and fire control systems in particular, the SIPRI data base incorporates guidance and radar systems. These systems are not a proxy for launchers but represent the lowest mix of systems deployable as a single unit. For example, for some surface-to-air missile systems a 'guidance and radar system' could include a mix of several radars, command vehicles and the data links between them.

Even this wider focus on platforms plus target acquisition systems may be being overtaken by new developments. Battlefield success increasingly depends not only on technology incorporated in any given system but on combining several or many different systems to address a single problem. In Russia the term 'reconnaissance-strike complex' has been coined to describe the integrated 'system of systems' considered at the heart of modern advanced military forces. An increasing amount of cost and time is being used to make different systems work together effectively and it may soon be essential to monitor at a minimum transfers of strategic command, control and communications networks in order to grasp the military potential of any given force.[6]

The definition of an arms transfer

Another widely recognized problem with the UN Register is the lack of a clear definition of when an arms transfer takes place.

The decision to focus on deliveries of items in the UN reporting procedure is a significant distinction between the approaches taken by the UN Register and SIPRI. SIPRI records all deals made or ongoing in a given calendar year (though SIPRI trend indicator values are derived only from delivered systems). In its Yearbook SIPRI reports information on all orders, whether or not deliveries have taken place during the reported year. In the SIPRI register the usefulness of information about future deliveries is considered to outweigh the relatively low level of confidence that surrounds many of the figures on future transfers. Many of the transfer agreements which are reported in open sources are not firm contracts but framework agreements which are often modified significantly before they are implemented.

As an illustration of the different approaches, Table 3 compares the information presented for Saudi Arabia in the return to the UN Register for 1992 with the information published by SIPRI.

Table 3.   Arms transfers to Saudi Arabia: a comparison of recent UN and SIPRI data

I. Returns to the UN Register of Conventional Arms for Saudi Arabia in 1992

Exporter	UN Category	No. of items	Description/comments
Brazil	Missiles and missile launchers	50 328	SS30, SS40, SS60 rockets for ASTROS II
Canada	Armoured combat vehicles	262	Wheeled APC
France	Large-calibre artillery systems	175	..
France	Missiles and missile launchers	6	..
UK	Armoured combat vehicles	29	..
UK	Missiles and missile launchers	48	..
USA	Armoured combat vehicles	192	..
USA	Combat aircraft	10	..

II. Data published by SIPRI on major weapons on order or under delivery to Saudi Arabia in 1992

Supplier	No. ordered	Weapon designation	Weapon description	Year of order	Year(s) of deliveries	No. delivered	Comments
Canada	1117	LAV	APC	1990			Deal worth $700 m; 384 LAV-25, 733 other versions
France	3	MM-40 launcher	ShShM launcher	1990			For 3 La Fayette Class frigates
	1200	Mistral	Portable SAM	1989	1991-92	(800)	
	(72)	MM-40 Exocet	ShShM	1990			Arming 3 La Fayette Class frigates
	3	La Fayette Class	Frigate	1992			Part of deal worth $4 b (offsets 30%)
UK	12	BAe-125-800	Transport	1988	1988-92	(12)	Part of 1988 Tornado deal; for VIP use
	20	Hawk-100	Jet trainer aircraft	1988			Part of Tornado deal
	40	Hawk-200	Fighter/ ground attack	1988			Part of Tornado deal
	48	Tornado IDS	Fighterr/ground attack	1988			
	(50)	WS-70	Helicopter	1988			
	461	Piranha	APC	1990	1992	(50)	Deal worth $400 m
	200	ALARM	Anti-radar missile	1986	1991-92	(120)	Arming Tornado IDS fighters
	(480)	Sea Eagle	Anti-ship missile	1985			Arming Tornado IDS fighters
	3	Sandown Class	MCM	1988	1991-92	2	Option on 3 more

Supplier	No. ordered	Weapon designation	Weapon description	Year of order	Year(s) of deliveries	No. delivered	Comments
USA	12	AH-64 Apache	Helicopter	1990	1992	(12)	Deal worth $300 m incl 155 Hellfire missiles; follow-on order for 36 probable
	24	F-15C Eagle	Fighter aircraft	1990	1991-92	22	
	72	F-15XP Eagle	Fighter/ground attack	1992			Deal worth $9 b incl 24 spare engines and 48 navigation lantirn and armament pods
	7	KC-130H Hercules	Tanker/transport	1990			Part of deal worth $750 m incl C-130H Hercules transport aircraft
	8	UH-60 Blackhawk	Helicopter	1990	1991-92	8	Medevac version, deal worth $121 m
	8	UH-60 Blackhawk	Helicopter	1992			Medevac version; deal worth $225 m
	27	M-198 155mm	Towed gun	1990	1991-92	(27)	
	150	M-1-A1 Abrams	Main battle tank	1990			
	315	M-1A2 Abrams	Main battle tank	1990			Deal worth $1.5 b; status uncertain
	207	M-113A2	APC	1990	1991-92	(207)	Part of deal worth $3.1 b
	400	M-2 Bradley	AIFV	1990	1992	(140)	In addition to 220 ordered previously
	50	M-548	APC	1991			Part of deal worth $3.1b
	9	M-577-A2	APC command post	1990			Part of deal worth $3.1b
	43	M-578	ARV	1991			Part of deal worth $3.1b
	12	M-88-A1	ARV	1990	1992	(12)	Deal worth $26 m
	(6)	AN/TPS-43	Surveillance radar	1985	1987-92	(6)	
	8	Patriot SAMS	SAM system	1990			Deal worth $984 m incl 384 missiles, 6 radars and support
	14	Patriot SAMS	SAM system	1991			Deal worth $3.1 b incl 758 missiles
	362	AGM-114A Hellfire	Anti-tank missile	1992			Arming 12 Apache helicopters; deal worth $606 mincl 3500 rockets, 40 trucks and a simulator
	900	AGM-65 D/G Maverick	Air-to-surface missile	1992			Arming 48 F-15XP fighters; mix of D and G versions

Supplier	No. ordered	Weapon designation	Weapon description	Year of order	Year(s) of deliveries	No. delivered	Comments
	770	AIM-7M Sparrow	Air-to-air missile	1991			Part of deal worth $365 m incl laser-guided bombs
	300	AIM-7M Sparrow	Air-to-air missile	1992			Arming 72 F-15XP fighters
	300	AIM-9S Sidewinder	Air-to-air missile	1992			Arming 72 F-15XP fighters
	4460	BGM-71D TOW-2	Anti-tank missile	1988	1989-92	(2000)	
	1750	BGM-71D TOW-2	Anti-tank missile	1990			Deal worth $55 m incl 116 launchers
	384	MIM-104 Patriot PAC-2	SAM	1990			
	758	MIM-104 Patriot PAC-2	SAM	1991			

Source: SIPRI Yearbook 1993

Conventions: ..   Data not available or not applicable

                                    ( )   Uncertain data or SIPRI estimate

There seems little prospect that the UN Register will move to advance notification and this distinction between the UN and SIPRI approaches will remain.

Coverage in the UN Register was confined to deliveries of complete systems – though some countries chose to report kits for assembly by the recipient country. The SIPRI register also includes weapons produced under licence by the recipient country. The volume of licensed production of weapons falling within the UN Register definitions can be quite substantial and for some countries – for example, India and Japan – the purchase of production licenses is more important than direct imports. For SIPRI the utility of introducing this information is therefore considered to outweigh the definitional problems that undoubtedly attend it.

According to the 1992 UN *Report on the Register of Conventional Arms*, international arms transfers involve, in addition to the physical movement of equipment into or from national territory, the transfer of title to and control over the equipment.[7] However, no definition of title to or control over equipment was provided, leading to some differences in interpretation. For SIPRI purposes physical control over an item is sufficient to constitute a transfer. For example, the lease of a warship to Greece by the US Navy constitutes a transfer. However, the governments of the United States (which did not report such transfers) and Greece (which did) took different positions from one another on this.

Under both the UN and SIPRI definitions an international arms transfer may also occur without the movement of equipment across state frontiers if one state grants another title and control over equipment. A transfer of arms to a State would occur when its forces stationed abroad are granted title and control of equipment by the host country or when title and control of such equipment are transferred to the host country.

In 1992 Armenia, Azerbaijan, Kazakhstan, Kyrgyzstan, Moldova, Tajikistan, Turkmenistan and Uzbekistan all emerged as independent states. Russia reported the transfer of 30 unspecified armoured vehicles to Uzbekistan. However, should Russia (as the successor state of the Soviet Union) also have declared any equipment from the Soviet armed forces turned over to these newly independent states as a transfer?[8]

One of the main gains anticipated from the UN Register was that it would clarify the scale and timing of transfers whose broad outline was already known from public sources. One of the perennial problems for the SIPRI register is determining in which year the deliveries of any given system took place and at what intensity.

The Register did go a considerable way to providing this information. Moreover, the Register confirmed some deals which had been reported but at a level considered inadequate for inclusion in the SIPRI register – such as the Italian export of 155 mm guns to Nigeria. The Register also generated some completely new information, especially relating to various land systems. Interesting and previously unreported transfers were reported by Belarus, Bulgaria, China, France and Romania, for example.

Levels of aggregation

The usefulness of the UN Register as a source of information was degraded by the high level of aggregation within each of the seven categories and the lack of differentiation between the systems transferred.

In its publications SIPRI differentiates between individual deals made for the same category or type of weapon system to be delivered to one country, while the UN Register requires that governments state only the total number of items of one category supplied to one country. For example, SIPRI reports the export of M-113-A2 and M-2 Bradley armoured combat vehicles (ACVs) from the USA to Saudi Arabia as two separate entries, while the US return to the UN Register gives only one entry informing that 192 unspecified ACVs have been delivered.

This problem was particularly difficult for those cases where the UN Register added new information to the public domain. For example, according to *The Military Balance 1993–94* produced by the International Institute for Strategic Studies the armed forces of Belarus inherited a variety of different main battle tanks – a mix of T-54, T-55, T-62, T-64, T-72 and T-80. According to their return to the UN Register Belarus transferred 19 tanks to North Korea and 9 to Oman in 1992. However, there is no way of knowing which of these types were transferred. Similarly, Romania reported transfers of 18 122 millimetre calibre howitzers to Moldova. However, these could have been either self-propelled 122 mm howitzers (of which Romania has two types available, the 2S1 and the Model 89) or towed 122 mm howitzers (of which Romania has two types available, the M-30 and the A-19).

IV   Conclusions

After the first year of reporting the UN Register has proved that it is a useful transfer register. However, the Group of Government Experts should consider some modifications of the existing structure before they consider expanding or further developing the Register. They should introduce clarifications in the definitions of equipment categories and the definition of arms transfers. In addition, they should disaggregate the information presented beyond the current level.

The introduction of two sets of definitions of equipment categories – one in resolution 46/36L and one in the 1992 UN *Report on the Register of Conventional Arms* – may well have added to the confusion in the first year of reporting. Therefore, it is not advisable to have frequent changes in the parameters of the Register. Where any changes are made they should be very widely distributed and publicised between governments to ensure that every government is working with the same set of definitions.

Some of the modifications to the equipment categories introduced after the passage of resolution 46/36L have proved to have been unhelpful and should be reversed. The revised definition of missiles in particular introduced an unnecessary distortion which made the value of information reported under the current Category VII at best questionable. This Category should be revised or deleted.

Deletion of the missile category would leave the UN Register as a register of conventional weapon platforms and remove ordnance from its terms of reference. This would further underline the political nature of the exercise being undertaken by the UN through the creation of the Register and allay any suspicions that the Register was contributing useful military intelligence to any power. It might also reduce government reluctance to disaggregate information within the remaining six categories of platform.

Disaggregation of platforms should be by platform name and not by generic type or by roles and missions. Although there is no standard international glossary of platform names, there are sufficient high-quality reference works available to make this a useful and relatively simple procedure.

The group of government experts have considered whether the focus on platforms alone is sufficient to permit a judgement on whether or not an excessive and destabilizing accumulation of weapons is underway in any given location. While undoubtedly a complex undertaking it would be useful to examine the possibility to take a systems approach instead of counting transfers of individual items. In such an approach it would be important to track whether countries are acquiring assets which have a relatively high-visibility in the open sources currently available (and are therefore possible to monitor) and contribute to the development of a reconnaissance-strike complex. These could include telecommunications systems, space-based sensors and the ground stations to process data acquired from them. Trying to identify the elements of such a complex is a direction in which SIPRI reporting is increasingly likely to move. However, arriving at agreement on such an approach is probably beyond the UN Group of Experts at this stage and introducing the idea formally may well be counter-productive.

Notes

1. While individual examples are taken where needed to illustrate a point, there is no general evaluation of the first year of returns to the UN Register as this is dealt with elsewhere in this volume. A detailed evaluation of the data from the *SIPRI Yearbook 1993* compared with the first year of returns to the UN Register is contained in Edward J. Laurance, Siemon T. Wezeman and Herbert Wulf, *Arms Watch: SIPRI Report on the First Year of the UN Register of Conventional Arms*, SIPRI Research Report No. 6, Oxford University Press, Oxford, 1993.

Notes continued

2. The phrase was invented by Robert Reich, now Secretary of Labor in the Clinton Administration, while he was working at the Massachusetts Institute of Technology. Robert Reich, *The Work of Nations*, Simon & Schuster, London, 1991, p. 177.

3. Such shells have already been developed by some countries – e. g. the US M-712 Copperhead 155 millimetre calibre artillery shell. The barrier to widespread deployment of such munitions is partly technological but partly cost. In 1989 a single Copperhead round cost $35,000 whereas a normal high-explosive 155 mm shell cost around $1,000 in 1989.

4. *Jane's All the World's Aircraft 1993–94*, Jane's Information Group, Coulsdon, 1993, p. 565.

5. Echevaria, A. J., and Shaw, J. M., 'The New Military Revolution: Post-Industrial Change', *Parameters*, vol. 22 no. 4, Winter 1992–93.

6. Recent discussions in the United States about the possible transfer of satellites capable of military application or sharing of satellite and other intelligence assets points in this direction.

7. *United Nations Register of Conventional Arms: Report of the Secretary-General*, UN Document A/48/344, October 1993, p. 10

8. The Russian return contains the proviso that 'transfers of arms to Azerbaijan, Armenia, Georgia, Republic of Moldova and Belarus are not included in the standardized reporting form of the Register, since these transfers are effected within the framework of the agreed division of property of the former Armed Forces of the USSR among the successor states of the USSR', *United Nations Register of Conventional Arms: Report of the Secretary-General,* op. cit., p. 91. For the purposes of the UN this is something of a pity as in some of these cases a large amount of major equipment has passed into the sovereign control of new political actors. By taking a more literal interpretation of the definition of an arms transfer governments could have made public extremely useful data.

~

CHAPTER 6

Controlling high-technology with military applications

Holger Iburg

I   Introduction[1]

When the United Nations Register on Conventional Arms was created by General Assembly Resolution 46/36L of December 1991 it was understood that the Register would be expanded in the future.[2] During the preparation of the final document, a group of member states – among them Algeria, Argentina, Brazil, Egypt, Iran, North Korea, Pakistan, Singapore, Syria and Uganda – pointed out that the resolution failed to address the problem of small arms production and transfer, weapons of mass destruction, and the transfer of high-technology with military applications, thus hampering the stated goal of the resolution, namely transparency.[3]

After more discussions about the final draft of the resolution and last-minute changes, Paragraph 7 of General Assembly Resolution 46/36L now invites Member States to provide available information "on military holdings, procurement through national production and relevant policies".

Further, Paragraph 13 directly "requests the Conference on Disarmament to address the problems of, and the elaboration of, practical means to increase openness and transparency related to the transfer of high-technology with military applications and to weapons of mass destruction, in accordance with existing legal documents".[4]

In 1993, the Conference on Disarmament (CD) followed the request stated in Paragraph 13. The representatives of Member States stated their country's positions on the transfer of high-technology with military applications. To no one's surprise, these positions varied even more than those on the term "arms transfer" outlined during the first phase of the development of the Register.

There are basically four arguments:

- technology is in itself neutral, and access to advanced technology (including its underlying scientific knowledge) has to be guaranteed to any country;

- for the purposes of development, the control of high-technology should not constitute an instrument of denial;

- multilateral controls, not unilateral controls should be established as the means to pave the way for transparency;

- dual-use items should be transferred;

Arguments to the contrary run along the following lines:

- technology is not neutral, and there exist certain 'choke-point' technologies that determine whether or not a product could be used militarily;

- the access to high-technology has to be controlled in order to keep an economic advantage over competitors in the international marketplace;

- unilateral controls are easier to impose and could be imposed on a stricter basis than multilateral controls;

- dual-use items should only be transferred if the receiver country shows clearly that high-technology is used only for non-military purposes.

However, the debate showed the existence of a bridging problem. There are two objectives that seem, at times, incompatible – the need to enhance economic development through international cooperation, and the goal of promoting international security.

Both suppliers and recipients of high-technology have their special interests and needs. The problem of defining what high-technology with military applications is, which technologies should be transferred and what transfers should be denied remains unsolved. A solution to these problems seems far away.

This observation is reflected in the existing documents of the discussions of the CD. The issue of high-technology with military applications was not very high on the agenda in 1993.[5]

The bridging problem is best reflected in a working paper submitted by the Disarmament Commission of the General Assembly.[6] Its Paragraph 17 states: "Norms and guidelines for the transfer of high-technology with military applications should take into account legitimate requirements for the maintenance of international peace and security, while ensuring that they do not deny access to high-technology products, services and know-how for peaceful purposes." Again, the problem is that economic and social development could conflict with national, regional, or international security needs.

But, to acknowledge the bridging problem does not mean to condemn the efforts of UN Member States. In fact, the UN Register has embarked on a different course, if not to say a different philosophy compared to existing arms control and arms export agreements and regimes. Instead of concentrating on the trade of weapons before an actual transfer takes place, the Register takes arms transfers as a given fact in the international community and registers the trade after the fact.

What seems to be a rather limited goal, namely transparency in weapons trade and arms build-ups, especially on a regional scale, could, in the long run, prove to be a serious confidence building measure among countries worldwide. Therefore, any discussion of further expansion of the UN Register has to bear in mind the overall goal of transparency. As will be shown, this measure calls for simple definitions that are easy to administer.

Given this goal and while the bridging problem constitutes the background for the problems associated with the expansion of the UN Register of Conventional Arms in the area of high-technology with military applications, I shall, however, focus in this chapter on a more narrow agenda.

First, I concentrate on the difficulties in defining the term "arms transfers" in the UN. These definition problems will be further highlighted when I examine the differences of opinion among Member States of the UN concerning the term "technology transfer" as it was discussed at the CD in 1993.

In the next part of this paper the lack of export regulations within the framework of the UN is discussed. This discussion will be further developed by considering questions related to sanctions and enforcement problems of a regime aiming at the control of high-technology with military applications. In the final section, the discussion will return to the question whether a UN Register for high-technology with military applications makes sense, is practical and could be installed in the foreseeable future.

II   Difficulties

Defining "arms transfers"

The UN Register of Conventional Arms is not a treaty but a confidence building effort. However, defining the term "arms transfer" proved to be a major obstacle before reaching the unanimous vote for the Register at the General Assembly.

General Assembly Resolution 46/36L constituting the UN Register of Conventional Arms lacks a precise definition of what is an actual "arms transfer". Paragraph 2 (a) of the Register's Annex[7] requests Member States "to provide data [...] on the number of items [...] imported into or exported from their territory". No definition of what actually makes up a transfer is given. Also, neither Paragraph 2 (c) nor 2 (f) clearly elaborate the term. While Paragraph 2 (c) only sets up the previous calendar year as the reporting period for imports and exports, Paragraph 2 (f) states: "Arms 'exports and imports' represent in the present resolution, including its annex, all forms of arms transfers under terms of grant, credit, barter or cash".

Intended to be a transparency measure and not an arms control regime, neither Resolution 46/36L nor its Annex provide a detailed set of rules for enforcement. Therefore, no UN body, inter-governmental or national law enforcement agency has to decide when an item from the agreed seven categories of equipment is imported into or exported from a national territory.

Because of the lack of clarity in the original 1991 Resolution, a Panel of Governmental Technical Experts from 17 countries had the task of creating more precise definitions and measurements before the Register reporting started in 1993.[8] The Panel's discussions are reflected in the final report to the Secretary-General.[9] Section B of the report is dedicated to the definition problem. Still, "the Panel did not attempt to define arms transfers" but tried to clarify the issue:

- Paragraph 10 says that arms transfers "involve, in addition to the physical movement of equipment into or from national territory, the transfer of title to and control over the equipment";

- Paragraph 11 specifies the term "transfer of title". A transfer can occur: "without movement of equipment across State frontiers if a State, or its agent, is granted title and control over equipment in the territory of the supplier State." In turn, this could be the case with forces stationed or moved abroad using equipment supplied by the host State, or with equipment, stored or moved abroad and control and title granted to the host country by the owner. If a transfer does not involve control and national title an arms transfer has not occurred under the rules of the Register.

- Paragraph 13 shows that no consensus could be reached as to when a transfer becomes "effective". The Member States are now asked to report the relevant information "in conformity with their respective national criteria used to define when a transfer becomes effective". As SIPRI observed, the lack of consensus is due to "the [existing] variety of national approaches" to the problem.[10]

Since every government has its own definition, consequences are numerous. Ian Anthony has named just a few possibilities involving the reporting process of exporters and importers: "[I]f the exporter reports the export at the moment an item leaves the national territory, air or sea space but the importer reports the import when the item is inducted into the armed forces. This may happen with ships if an exporter includes the delivery when a vessel leaves the territorial waters but an importer includes a delivery when the ship is formally commissioned. It could happen with aircraft if training takes place in the exporting country before items are moved to the recipient. The exporter register an export, feeling that 'title to and control over' an aircraft has passed to the recipient even if the item is still on a training range (the recipient will certainly pay for any damage incurred under training). However, the recipient might register an import only when physical delivery takes place."[11]

The obvious shortcomings of the definition process for the Register showed in the reports that Member States filed for 1992.[12] Looking back on the debate among government experts, Ian Anthony saw no guarantee that the task of finishing the Register could have been accomplished at all if the search for detailed definitions had gone on much longer.[13] In the end the panel of governmental experts came up with a series of definitions that in large parts was developed from the Treaty on Conventional Armed Forces in Europe (CFE).[14]

In doing so, the experts saved the overall goal of the Register, e.g. transparency. Although seldom explicitly stated this goal shines through the 1993 discussions in the Conference on Disarmament (CD), where the debate about clear definitions continued. For example, the related issue of a definition of "excessive and destabilizing accumulation of arms"[15] has been discussed. Reservations concerning a clear definition of the above mentioned terms were more than once based on keen national interest such as a regional conflict or possible or perceived threats. Since these reservations prevail, further discussions in the CD on the subject of excessive and destabilizing accumulation of arms are more than likely. However, in 1993 the debate showed a shift away from discussions about global security towards concern for regional security.[16]

Conclusion

Reflecting on arms export regulations worldwide, Ian Anthony has commented on the "absence of any standard definition of 'arms trade'" as "one of the biggest single obstacles to arms transfer control since it is impossible to have an agreement if the matters to be subject to agreement cannot be specified".[17]

In fact, precise definitions in arms control accords are only found where specific weapons or weapons systems are clearly described. For conventional weapons, this has only been the case with the Treaty on Conventional Forces in Europe.

Again, it has to be emphasized that the UN Register is a new approach. Instead of going after arms exports before they take place the purpose of the Register is to keep track of arms transfers after the fact. In order to make the goal of transparency meaningful and manageable, it was agreed that it should cover seven categories of major weapons systems. However, for the purpose of expanding the UN Register into the area of high-technology with military applications one has to ask whether such a specific topic could be narrowed down to a workable reporting system.

Differences of opinion among UN member states

On 21 January 1993, the Conference on Disarmament decided to establish an Ad hoc Committee on Transparency in Armaments for its 1993 session. Among other topics adopted at its second meeting on 22 March 1993 the Ad hoc Committee planned to address problems related to the transfer of high-technology with military applications. The subsequent discussions in the committee shed some light on the complex issue but fell far short of coming to a common understanding of a workable consensus as to what constitutes the transfer of high-technology with military applications.[18]

While various delegations gave information about their relevant national legislations on export and import controls it was further suggested that there should be:

- a compilation and comparison of existing laws, regulations, and procedures of UN Member States in relation to the transfer of high-technology with military applications (Argentina, Italy, France);

- the establishment of agreed guidelines for the international transfer of such technology as a code for conduct (Argentina, Poland, Rumania, Ireland, Senegal).

China and Nigeria wanted to reduce such an effort to the technically most advanced countries.

The discussion, then, centred around the problem of transfer of high-technology export controls in general.

- It was claimed that existing export control regimes hampered economic and social development of developing countries (India, China).

- This argument was countered mainly by Western Nations – Australia, Canada, France, Germany, the Netherlands, Russia, the United Kingdom, and the United States – which defended such controls on the grounds that controls were necessary to prohibit the transfer of weapons of mass destruction. Russia although part of the team, stressed that the CoCom regime targeted at Russia, should discontinue with this policy and transfer itself towards non-proliferation purposes.

To summarize, compared to other topics on the agenda of the CD in 1993 the discussion about the transfer of high-technology with military applications was rather a background issue. It seems that further discussion of the issue is necessary in order to narrow the field that should actually comprise this topic.[19]

III   The UN Register as an acquisitions Register

UN Resolution 46/36L installing the UN Register of Conventional Arms called for its expansion in the future. Among other issues an expansion effort was called for in the area of the transfer of high-technology with military applications. Such an expansion was meant to enhance the overall goal of transparency as it could produce more information on destabilizing military build-ups.

High-technology with military applications has been and is of concern in a number of control regimes. Such existing control regimes are in place to restrict the flow of relevant technologies before an delivery takes place. However, control, restriction, and embargo measures do not fit the intended goal of the UN Register. The Register is aimed at transparency. The emphasis put on this point again and again reflects the new philosophy in arms control efforts embodied in the Register. This philosophy cannot be underestimated. Compared to control regimes the registering process is an easy one, although the returns for the 1992 report proved that even that kind of reporting is a difficult task. The expanded task of registering high-technologies with military applications would be a major endeavour requiring a very sophisticated reporting system, not to mention a verification process.

Missing export control bodies at the UN and the lack of export control guidelines and regulations

The differences among UN Member States concerning the term "arms transfer" as well as a clear definition of the term "high-technology with military applications" (see part II.) only underscore the point that arms control in general and arms export control in particular are still on shaky ground in the international community when it comes down to hard work, clear definitions, and final consequences in the form of guidelines, regulations, legal agreements, and enforcement procedures.

Although the Second Gulf War has made export control a bigger issue not only on the national level but also on the UN and CD agendas, respectively, there still does not exist an export control institution at the UN level. Rather, export control remains the task of individual nations, groups of nations, or special interest parties, as shown above.

The debate in connection with Resolution 46/36L showed no emphasis on the installation of an export control body within the UN. Instead, in order to reach a working consensus at all, the Register is designed to be a transparency measure. For the more far-reaching task of installing an UN export control agency one has to ask some questions:

• Is an export control body needed within the UN?

• What could such an institution do?

• What would it need in terms of guidelines, personnel, money, enforcement rights and penalties?

First of all, there has to be a consensus among UN Member States as to whether an arms export control regime of any form is deemed necessary. This author doubts that such a consensus is feasible in the near future. Instead, the debate in connection with the UN Register circumvented the point of differing interests, e.g., the problem of controlling the spread of weapons around the globe and at the same time the demand for technology as a means for economic and social development. In the case of dual-use technology this problem becomes evident.

Second, a UN export control body would have to have governing definitions and guidelines as to what is an arms export that should be controlled and restricted. And further still, there would have to be enforcement procedures.

Third, a UN export control body would need money and personnel. If it were a real control and enforcement body this institution could become one of the major bodies within the UN. As the "Ongoing Monitoring and Verification" (OMV) effort in the aftermath of the Second Gulf War has shown, the costs can easily run into millions of dollars.

Without going into further detail it should be mentioned at this point that the UN OMV effort[20] is still the only such effort carried out by the UN. This undertaking supervised by the UN Special Commission (UNSCOM) is meant to evolve into a long-term monitoring regime comparable to any of the existing viable and effective verification regimes.

So far, the UN arms-monitoring effort in Iraq has to be treated as a special case, because there exists a political consensus among UN Member States about this particular country and the items to be controlled – which will consist of items found in the MTCR annexes, the CNS lists, the NSG trigger lists, the IL list of the former CoCom regime. A consensus building measure has been that officials from over 38 UN Member States were present at various inspections, including officials from Iran.[21]

Compared to the Iraq venture, the UN Register is a multilateral effort involving different objectives and interests that guide the definition process of items to be registered. Therefore, at this moment in time the monitoring example does not serve as a starting point for a UN arms export control body, although it may be viewed as such in the future. Rather, it points towards caution when it comes to talk about a UN export control institution. And, again, the Iraq effort is aimed at controlling a certain state and so far, the UN has shown its willingness to impose sanctions on Iraq for non-compliance, while the Register is meant as a transparency measure that relies on the good will of <u>all</u> states involved.

Another solution, the UN-as-a-clearinghouse with enforcement still in the hands of the national enforcement agencies, would be cheaper. But different countries have different governmental cultures. This could lead to totally different outcomes in terms of reports to the UN. This observation is backed by the 1992 reports to the existing Register.[22]

However, at this point and for obvious reasons, an UN export control institution is not feasible in the near future. Everything is missing that could sustain an installation effort for such a control body within the UN. And even a clearinghouse solution seems to have no chance of becoming a major issue because the problems involved are too complex and too complicated to tackle.[23]

Obstacles

Besides of a missing export control body at the UN, the foremost obstacle to an expansion of the UN Register in the area of high-technology with military applications would be to define what is meant by high-technology and which high-technologies should be registered.

As the overview of the debate in connection with the UN Register concerning the term "arms transfer" has demonstrated such definitions do not come easily. Also, the examples of the EU's approach and CoCom's experience have clearly shown that even the existence of an agreed term does not mean that the term means the same to all parties involved.

A definition of the term 'high-technology with military applications' is even more difficult to agree on. Several studies of production and trade have revealed a variety of criteria.[24] Since 1976 the US. has tried to impose its own definition of technology on the control regimes of which it is a member. It embodies the concept of military critical technologies and differentiates between evolutionary and revolutionary.[25] Its inventors believed it would be possible to select the subset of technologies of significant military value and restrict the transfer of these technologies. In fact, the European allies of the US. have always doubted that this is possible.[26]

While the American approach focused rather on the front-end of a product, limiting access to design and manufacturing know-how, a different approach evolved in CoCom, namely concentration on the end-use of a product. Civilian and military trucks are based on the same design and process technology, but their use is different. The same is true for most airplanes. Especially in the fields of electronics and microprocessors, end products are based on similar materials and manufacturing processes whereas, again, they could be used in quite different environments.

With the focus on end-use, one can distinguish three categories of technologies: military, civil, and multiple-use. An example for the first would be a tank, for the second a household appliance such as a mixer, and for the third the computer chip stands out.

Although on paper these categories seem made for easy fit into an arms control regime of any kind, the opposite has been true, mainly in the third category. In fact, the vocabulary used in studies and agreements on technology is rather meagre and weakly defined. In most cases it is not clear what is a product, a technology, a component, a system, a sub-system, a weapon etc. And a technology and a good are not the same. The former refers rather to the knowledge embodied in a good while the latter is the result of the former.[27]

Karp has pointed out that "the diversity of technology makes clear definitions of what is to be restricted extremely difficult".[28] For the purpose of a Register this diversity would pave the way for an endless list-producing process. Not only weapons systems of all kinds, ammunition of all sorts, spare parts and materials, even production assistance and training and maintenance exercises (for example in the case of licensing agreements), would fall into the scope of the Register.

Additionally, dual-use technology and respective goods would pose major problems. Computer technology is but one illustration of the overwhelming effort necessary to keep track of the transfer of goods and knowledge.[29] Hardware that was ten years ago at the edge of the computer science is now readily available off-the-shelf. Software is an even more fluid good. Its production and its producer need little room, its storage absorbs even less space, and its transport seems almost uncontrollable, given the fact that even sophisticated software is now produced off-shore and moved electronically through wires or via satellite links. To say the least, simplicity would not come easy if at all in a Register covering the transfer of high-technology with military applications.

The computer example also points to the speed of change in modern technology development. This high pace makes the review process of control lists not only a permanent one but seems to be most of the time an uphill battle and in the end a lost race. While the industry through worldwide competition is forced to adopt to permanent change faster than ever governments tend to be slow in their adjustment to new developments. To name just one factor, competing bureaucracies within a state have usually long review procedures. Transferred into the international sphere procedural anomalies tend to multiply and slow down the pace of change even more. Within the UN context and the framework of the UN Register of Conventional Arms given its intent to reach a consensus, if ever possible, the goal of registering high-technology with military applications seems to be not realistic.

The speed of technological change has become a problem for the military itself. In some high-tech fields, civil economic interests have already passed the once ruling military. To name but one example, for a long time deep sea explorations were dominated by demands from navies. Now, it seems, civilian interests, for instance mining and fishing, are pushing technological progress faster than the military.[30]

The lack of exact definitions and criteria for the term technology is also recognisable when it comes to assessing the impact of a transfer. There are still no certain criteria and methods to judge when a given transfer is excessive or destabilizing , vis-à-vis a country, in a region, or on an even grander scale. Given the lack in both areas this would have an extreme impact on any registering effort whatsoever.[31]

As has been shown above in this paper, there does not exist a formalized UN control institution. Such a body would be necessary for assessing reports, verifying them, and remarking on the returns, all in all a very costly undertaking. A solution that would use the existing UN Register as a clearinghouse would without doubt run into the definition problems elaborated on before. Governments would interpret rather unclear definitions according to their interest and even the lowest common denominator seems rather impossible.

IV   Conclusion

This chapter aimed to explore the possible expansion of the UN Register of Conventional Arms to cover military and dual-technologies. Two major obstacles exist that make such an expansion unlikely to succeed. First, high-technology with military applications is hard to define. In fact, in certain technology fields it is almost impossible to decide what is a weapons technology or a nearly-weapons technology. Second, high-technology with military applications is even harder to register given the possible disagreements among participants on what is to be registered.

The experience of CoCom and the European export control regimes has demonstrated, time and again, that the before-the-fact approach of catching possible arms exports is very difficult to implement effectively. With this approach controllers, or for that matter future registers, always face the problem of pursuing somebody without ever catching them. This description points to one of the major underlying reasons why CoCom, before its dismantling, had been moving in the direction of becoming a certifying regime for countries outside of CoCom, and the EU is moving towards the control of the possible end-use of a given good.

Given the problems involved in defining, controlling, and registering the transfer of high-technology with military applications, the effort of expanding the UN Register of Conventional Arms in this direction does not seem worthwhile at present. The UN Register would serve the goal of transparency far better by maintaining its focus on transfers, or the national production and military holdings of specific hardward, rather than seeking vague data on technologies that are difficult to measure and even harder to judge.

Notes

1. In writing this paper I have enjoyed the advice and received the help of friends and colleagues. In particular I would like to thank Thomas Horlohe, Edward J. Laurance, Joyce Rosenthal, Mark Schleisner, and Herbert Wulf.

2. General Assembly Resolution 46/36L, UN General Assembly document A/RES/46/36L, 9 Dec. 1991.

3. Statements by Member States in the 46th session of the General Assembly (UN document A/46/PV.66, Agenda Item 60), p.43. Also note that even after the vote several delegates stated their continued reservations. See for an overview Herbert Wulf, "The United Nations Register of Conventional Arms" in Edward J. Laurance, Siemon T. Wezeman, Herbert Wulf, *Arms Watch: SIPRI Report on the First Year of the UN Register of Conventional Arms*, Oxford University Press, Oxford, 1993, p. 130.

4. Note that despite the usual notion of weapons of mass destruction and high-technology with military applications this paper will focus mainly on the latter while the former is dealt with elsewhere.

5. Ambassador Wagenmakers of the Netherlands who also chaired the panel of governmental experts that elaborated on definitions and types of weapons summed up the state of affairs when he said his delegation looked "forward to continuing the exchange of views on these issues both in the Ad hoc Committee and in the United Nations Disarmament Commission". See Statement by Ambassador Wagenmakers (Netherlands) in Conference on Disarmament, document CD/PV.644, 1993, p. 8.

6. Report of the Disarmament Commission, General Assembly Official Records. Forty-eighth Session. Supplement No. 42 (A/48/42), Chairman's working paper on draft guidelines and recommendations on "The role of science and technology in the context of international security, disarmament and other related fields", New York 1993, p. 23-27.

7. General Assembly Resolution 46/36L, as modified in Resolution 47/342 of the UN Secretary-General, Report on the Register of Conventional Arms, UN document A/47/342, 14 Aug. 1992, endorsed by the General Assembly in Resolution 47/52L.

8. Edward J. Laurance et al, op. cit., p. 12.

Notes *continued*

9. The following quotes are taken from *Report on the Register of Conventional Arms, Report of the Secretary-General*, UN General Assembly document A/47/342, 14 Aug. 1992.

10. Edward J. Laurance et al, op. cit., p.12.

11. Ian Anthony, "Transparency in Armaments: Information and International Security in the Post-Cold War World" in Edward J. Laurance et al, op. cit., p. 138.

12. Edward J. Laurance et al, op. cit., p. 43ff, 52.

13. Ian Anthony, "Assessing the UN Register of Conventional Arms" *Survival*, Vol. 35, No, Winter 1993, p. 119.

14. The Treaty on Conventional Armed Forces in Europe was circulated in 1991 as a document of the Conference on Disarmament (CD/1064). The treaty text can be found as Appendix II United Nations, *Disarmament Yearbook*, Vol. 15: 1990, Department of Disarmament Affairs, New York, 1991. There, the Protocol on Existing Types of Conventional Armaments and Equipment is not reproduced. Article II of the CFE Treaty lists definitions of five weapons categories: battle tanks, armoured combat vehicles, artillery, combat aircraft, and attack helicopters.

15. Conference on Disarmament, *Report of the Conference of Disarmament to the General Assembly of the United Nations*, UN document CD/1222, 3 Sept. 1993, pp. 48f.

16. Ian Anthony, op. cit., p. 118.

17. Ian Anthony (ed.), *Arms Export Regulations*, SIPRI/Oxford University Press, Oxford, 1991, pp. 3f. See also Edward J. Laurance, *The International Arms Trade*, Lexington Books, New York 1992, p. 7 and chapter 2.

18. For the following section, if not stated otherwise, I refer to Conference on Disarmament, *Report of the Ad hoc Committee on Transparency in Armaments*, document CD/1218, 24 August 1993, especially pp. 12f, and the various documents submitted by Member States and mentioned in this context.

19. See also the rather limited participation that took place following the invitation of the General Assembly in connection with Resolution 46/38D of 6 December 1991 "to make available [...] information [...] related to international transfer of high technology with military applications", *Review of the Implementation of the Recommendations and Decisions by the General Assembly at its Tenth Special Session: Transfer of High Technology with Military Applications, Report of the Secretary General*, General Assembly document A/47/371 (27 August 1992) and Add. 1 (5 Oct. 1992) and Add. 2 (10 Nov. 1992). Resolution 46/38D, titled The transfer of high technology with military applications, is reprinted in The United Nations, Disarmament Yearbook, Vol. 16, 1991, pp. 358-360.

Notes continued

20. The most relevant documents concerning the monitoring of Iraq are the UN Resolutions 687, 707, 715. Resolution 687 set the formal stage for the monitoring, Resolution 707 required complete disclosure of all activities related to weapons of mass destruction. Resolution 715 required Iraq's acceptance of the OMV plan. See also "UN speeds arms-monitoring effort in Iraq" in *New York Times*, February 13, 1994, p. 6.

21. Information provided by an inspection official who requested to stay un-identified.

22. See for 1992 "The first year of Reporting" in Edward J. Laurance et al, op. cit., pp. 16-37.

23. Note for the complexity the example of the transfer-of-technology negotiations between developing and developed states at the UN Conference on Trade and Development (UNCTAD). During the last 25 years, UNCTAD has produced minimal results on the issue of technology transfer although there have been regular meetings by its Transfer of Technology Committee, six negotiating sessions by its Intergovernmental Group of Experts on the International Code of Conduct for Technology Transfers, and six conferences devoted solely to the issue. See Elizabeth Ridell-Dixon, "Technology and the New International Economic Order in World Politics" in David G. Haglund, Michael K. Hawes (eds.), *Power, Interdependence & Dependence*, Harcourt Brace Jovanovich, Canada, 1990, pp. 361ff.

24. See for instance US Congress, Office of Technology Assessment, *Technology, Innovation, and Regional Economic Development*, OTA-STI-238, Washington, D.C., US G.P.O., 1984; OECD, *Technology Indicators and the Measurement of Performance in International Trade*, Paris, OECD, 1983.

25. The standard American definition holds science as the pursuit of knowledge whereas technology is the systematic application of knowledge to practical purposes. Given this, the transfer of technology concerns the transfer of capability. But such a transfer is hard to measure.

    The definition for the military critical technologies derived from a report prepared for the DoD and came to be known as the Bucy Report: *An Analysis of Export Control of US. Technology – A DoD Perspective*, A Report of the Defense Science Board Task Force on the Export of US. Technology, Washington, D.C., 1976.

26. See Angela Stent, "Technology Transfer to the Soviet Union: a challenge for the cohesiveness of the Western Alliance", *Arbeitspapiere zur internationalen Politik*, Forschunginstitut der Deutschen Gesellschaft für Auswåartige Politik e. V., Bonn, April 1983, p. 5f.

27. See for a discussion William Walker, Mac Graham, Bernard Harbor, "From components to integrated systems: technological diversity and interactions between the military and civilian sector" in Philip Gummett, Judith Reppy (eds.),

Notes continued

The Relations between Defence and Civil Technologies, Kluwer Academic
Publishers, Dordrecht, Boston, London 1988, pp. 17-37.

28. Aaron Karp, "Controlling Weapons Proliferation: The Role of Export Controls"
    The Journal of Strategic Studies, Vol. 16, March 1993, No. 1, p. 36.

29. Here, knowledge refers to written documents. But scientists as individuals may
    hold, at times, even more knowledge of a given technology. How would a
    Register measure their movements?

30. See for a recent example, "Navy Has Long Had Secret Subs For Deep-Sea Spying,
    Experts Say" *New York Times*, 7 February 1994, p. 1, B7.

31. Because existing export control regimes differ there have been proposals for
    combining them. These proposals incorporate more than can practically be
    handled. Normally, regimes are the result of a difficult bargaining process. Their
    outcome embodies usually numerous compromises. A unifying export control
    regime would, at best, result in the lowest common denominator.

CHAPTER 7

Jane's Information Group

Collection, interpretation and dissemination of publicly available information

Tim Mahon

I   Introduction

This paper addresses three principal objectives.

1) To provide an outline of publicly available information.
2) To discuss some of the collection and interpretation methodologies used by Jane's.
3) To provide some thoughts for the future handling of such information.

Jane's Information Group is entering its 97th consecutive year in the business of gathering, interpreting and publishing information on the world's military forces, their equipment, capabilities and doctrine. During that time, significant changes have taken place in the world. Consequently, the information available to us has changed in nature, as have the demands of the professional end user of our information services.

II   What is publicly available information?

Jane's guards jealously its reputation for impartial, accurate and responsible reporting. In doing so, we constantly stress the fact that we deal only with information in the public domain – we do not have access to sensitive or classified information, nor do we seek such access. In some cases, however, the definition of what type of information is in the public domain will vary from country to country.

For example, some years ago we published a work intended to provide defense manufacturers with detailed information on the procurement practices, systems and opportunities in a total of sixteen countries in the Pacific Rim. In fifteen of these countries, our requests for information and assistance in assembling the relevant data met with great enthusiasm. In the sixteenth, however, legal problems existed, since there were significant legislative restrictions on any local media coverage of the armed forces except in the most basic fashion. After considerable discussion, much of which concentrated on the benefits to the defense industry of the country concerned of having foreign companies interested in the development of strategic alliances and joint ventures if they could be persuaded that a significant market opportunity existed, legislative action was taken to relax the pertinent restrictions for the specific purpose of publishing the Jane's work in question.

This raises the question of defining "information in the public domain". This is almost impossible to do in any way that will meet all possible eventualities, since by the very nature of the subject matter, defense-related information is an issue of different sensitivities in different countries and circumstances. For the purposes of collecting information in the varying manners described below, it may be loosely defined as information emanating from unclassified sources. This is not a graceful solution, but serves as a starting point for discussion.

III   What type of information is available?

For the categories of equipment of concern to the Register, vast quantities of technical, commercial and operationally-related information is available. For the 'platform' categories (Battle Tanks, Armored Combat Vehicles, Large Calibre Artillery Systems, Combat Aircraft, Attack Helicopters and Warships) this information includes quantities produced, quantities in service, development histories, technical characteristics, operational capabilities, identification of associated systems, combat experiences and so on. For the Missiles category, the same information is available in many cases, with the notable exception of quantities in service and/or deployed. This is due in large part to the fact that a missile is more of a consumable defense item than a durable one. It is treated increasingly as a round of expendable ammunition rather than a weapon system.

With the exception noted above, it is perhaps worth reflecting in a little more detail on the exact nature of the information available in Jane's major yearbooks. Typically, each individual model or type of platform or missile is treated in detail in a separate report. The information provided will include a development history, a physical description of the platform or weapon system, a technical description of the major subsystems or components. For a main battle tank, for example, these would comprise the main armament or gun system, the armor protection, engine and transmission, sighting devices and major electronic systems.

Additional information will include an identification of the manufacturer, the numbers built and dates delivered, the current operators of the weapon system and an indication of status – whether it is still in production or becoming obsolescent – or indeed whether it is in the process of being upgraded. In terms of performance, most entries indicate the approximate levels of capabilities in the most important areas for the system in question. For instance, for a missile this would include minimum and maximum ranges, warhead types, speed of flight, reload time and so on. Appendices and tabular annexes to some books list, for example, the specific types or models of weapon systems operated by individual countries. This is especially true of such titles as *Jane's Armour & Artillery* and *Jane's Land-Based Air Defence*.

It is worth noting at this point that the list of types of available information given above is not exhaustive – nor is it necessarily true that all types of information are available for every system, piece of equipment or other subject under scrutiny. The list simply represents those areas of information which are typically available in the public domain – if one knows where to look. In addition to purely equipment-related information, Jane's is increasingly developing information services which provide data, analysis and commentary on security, political and intelligence issues. Typical examples of this area of activity include a series of articles written in 1990 on the equipment and warfighting capabilities of the Iraqi armed forces – large numbers of which were reprinted by the US Government for distribution – and an April 1994 special report on developments within North Korea.

Considerable work has been done in recent years in achieving a level of consistency of data entry and reporting. This has meant that a whole system of categorization has been developed, resulting in a series of subdivisions in each book. *Jane's Armour & Artillery*, as an example, has rigid distinctions between Main Battle Tanks, Medium Tanks and Light Tanks – classified in the main by gross weight. In fact, at one point in late 1988, the US and Soviet delegations to the Conventional Forces in Europe (CFE) talks in Vienna, unable to develop a mutually agreeable system of classification for these very vehicles, eventually decided to adopt the categories appearing in the then current edition of *Jane's Armour & Artillery*, essentially agreeing that if a vehicle appeared in the Light Tank section of Jane's, it would be considered as such by both delegations.

It is apposite at this point to note that, while this paper concentrates in large part on the information available concerning equipment falling into the seven categories under the aegis of the Register, there are many more categories of military systems which have a direct effect on the capabilities of military forces to wage war. These include, in the main, systems which are typically referred to as 'force multipliers", reflecting their seminal effect on the operations of those systems which may be included in the Register's consideration. For example, the Airborne Early Warning and Control Aircraft (AWACS) operated by the US, NATO, Japan, France, the United Kingdom and Saudi Arabia, has an extremely beneficial effect on the effectiveness of air operations. It can provide extremely detailed information to assist planners, controllers and pilots in the planning, mounting and conduct of air strikes, air intercept operations or airmobile operations, thus enhancing the effectiveness of the operation, saving needless expense of materiel. There are countless examples of systems and platforms which fulfil this type of role, ranging from ocean patrol vessels through electronic warfare aircraft to combat engineer vehicles. It is possible that consideration of such systems and/or platforms will become necessary or be advisable in the future. If so, it is important to remember that available information is not just limited to the seven categories currently under discussion. Many sources exist with data, commentary and analysis relevant to such systems, Jane's among them. A separate appendix is included of the major Jane's reference books at the end of this paper.

Public information, already available in raw form, exists in a multitude of formats. Andrew Duncan, of the International Institute for Strategic Studies in London, addresses the issue of published information in Chapter 8. This varies in quality and quantity from country to country and in some cases varies from Administration to Administration within the same country over a period of years. Public statements by governments and armed forces, defense and foreign affairs journals, newspapers, manufacturers promotional material, video footage, photographs – the list is practically endless. The availability of published information – what will be termed 'secondary sources' for the purposes of this paper – is undoubtedly an important aid in assembling the raw data from which such publications as those produced by the IISS, Jane's and SIPRI stem. But the question of primary sources – those from which raw, unverified data is drawn – needs to be addressed. In this regard, this paper addresses only those primary sources used typically by Jane's.

IV   Jane's sources of information

This paper does not intend to list the individual sources of information used by Jane's, since to do so would contravene the most basic tenets of responsible editorial and journalistic policies as well as incurring potential commercial and economic damage to the Company. Rather, it will examine some (but by no means all) of the information sources available to and typically used by the Company in the preparation of its various publications.

Perhaps most obviously, the series of publications issued by Jane's depends for origination on the team of editors, correspondents and experts which has been built up over the last twenty years or more. Currently consisting of some 120 individuals in over 50 countries, the editorial team consists of veteran defense and foreign affairs journalists, leading authorities on modern weaponry and technical specialists. Unsurprisingly, perhaps, they have considerable experience in determining the overall impact of the raw information gathered from primary and secondary sources on the particular market or technology areas in which they have expertise. This team comprises a vital resource for the gathering and interpretation of data, as well as the dissemination in some forms – answering some 600 global media requests for information in the first 48 hours of the Gulf War, for example.

Information can arrive at Jane's in a wide variety of forms, with an equally wide variety of provenances. As well as reports of events, forecasts of equipment purchases, technical treatments of operational issues and verbatim interviews with defense-related figures, much information arrives in graphic form. Many of our users prize imagery above almost all other forms of information, relying on their own photo-interpretative skills to provide the degree of analysis and verification they require. Subject matter of the photographs received by Jane's varies widely – typical examples are: unsolicited (and at the time non-attributable) pictures of a then unknown Soviet artillery system, taken through a gap in railway siding sheds in East Germany; photographs of the bow of a damaged submarine in the Mediterranean, revealing considerable detail of the sonar transducer array; photographs of a Royal Naval vessel revealing details of optical systems which had not at that time been openly discussed.

A large number of sketch maps and other graphic forms of data can be used by Jane's as well. For example, when six MiG-29s made a goodwill visit to Finland in July 1986, detailed video footage of the aircraft taken as they landed and taxied was in *Jane's Defence Weekly*'s offices within hours. Analysis of the video made possible conclusions about the technical characteristics and performance of the aircraft which had been the subject of conjecture and intense debate up to that point.

The team of editors and correspondents around the world have developed their own individual (and normally discreet) networks of information sources over the years. Many of these sources lie inside the defense industry, since manufacturing and service companies comprise an extremely well-informed component of the defense community. The question of motivation for the release of information – contact with credible media outlets is encouraged by corporate management since it is viewed as cheap (or free) marketing support and advertising – gives rise to questions about the reliability of data obtained in this way. In response to such questions, it is worth reflecting first on the expertise of the individual and the publication to whom the information is passed – few Public Relations Managers in industry would risk future advantage by passing out blatantly false information – and second on the process of verification and corroboration through which a Jane's article or commentary will pass before publication. In this regard it is appropriate to point out that the individual authors, editors and experts to whom such information is being passed will almost invariably be more familiar with the pertinent technology or system than the Public Relations or Marketing Manager conducting the briefing. Thus any attempt to obfuscate an issue or to wantonly "pad" performance characteristics of a weapon system will be quickly identified and discarded. That such attempts are almost never made speaks volumes of the competence and experience of the individual team members and the strength of their personal networks and relationships with industry. Jane's guards very carefully its reputation for accurate, impartial and above all responsible reporting and takes great pains to ensure that at no time is information published which does not meet severe criteria of corroboration.

Information is a two way street and Jane's has always recognized this. Several of our editors and experts have been involved in equipment and system design and/or development projects in a variety of countries. Such involvement has led to the establishment of enhanced relationships with officials, organizations and informed individuals worldwide – relationships which have led increasingly to enhanced input. For example, *Jane's Fighting Ships* has upwards of 400 contributors for each annual edition. These range from official contributors from national naval authorities, responding to our formal requests for data, to entirely unsolicited input from individuals and organizations with an interest in the subject matter.

Questions often arise as to "how accurate is Jane's?" It would be simplistic (and wrong!) to suggest that we get everything right one hundred per cent of the time, despite the stringent efforts at quality control and editorial veracity. But let us put this in perspective – *Jane's Fighting Ships*, for example, is a book of a quarter of a million facts. Even if we are only 99% accurate, we can expect some 2,500 errors of one sort or another in this one publication. Individuals and organizations have little hesitation in bringing our errors to our attention. We consider this to be a healthy sign of the concern of our users for the accuracy of what is for them a primary information source. It should always be borne in mind that Jane's is a commercial enterprise, which lives or dies by its ability to service a demanding market at a profitable rate. Having been in business doing just that for almost a century would seem to indicate that there are not too many severe problems in the quality of the service provided.

V What does it all mean?

Collection of data is the first step in making available a series of useful information services. But the interpretation and verification of that data is an equally important part of the overall process. Here, once more, our team of editors and experts is an important asset. It is undoubtedly true to say that Jane's works in just about the same way as any national intelligence system, with the obvious difference that Jane's works only in the unclassified, open-sourced domain. Widely different (and often differing) items of information are fed to an analysis team or an individual expert whose responsibility it is to collate, verify, corroborate and validate the data and to provide an assessment of what impact this data has on existing publications. Is it an entirely new development, not seen before? Is it an enhancement or upgrade of existing equipment? Is it an announcement of the disbanding of a unit, necessitating the updating of an order of battle and table of materiel?

In recent years, much work has been done in coordinating the information flow to and from these various teams in an effort to ensure consistency and reliability of data. An additional benefit has been to speed up the analytical and interpretative process within the editorial function. Verification of data begins to take on increasing importance when one considers the vast amounts of information now becoming available and the fact that such information is becoming more uncertain as the pace of political change and technological development increase almost exponentially.

VI Some thoughts for the future

It is difficult to make any predictions, except of the most general nature, when concerning oneself with the world of defense and security issues, since political priorities – the driving force behind defense policy – can change so rapidly. It is doubly difficult to predict what will happen in the world of defense-related information as the twentieth century comes to a close, given the gigantic steps that being made in the information technology world every year.

These changes are making possible the handling, manipulation and analysis of vast amounts of data in ways and at speeds which would have been unthinkable even a few years ago.

In recent years Jane's has devoted considerable effort to developing an electronic product capable of meeting the demands of our professional users. So much information now exists that much of it will be discarded by the user unless he can see a way to shape it and integrate it into his own existing application. The side benefit of having developed a CDROM-based series of publications is that operations can now be performed on Jane's data – in terms of searching for specific items of equipment in service worldwide, for example – which are next to impossible using the traditional hard copy publications unless one is intimately familiar with the structure and historical development of each individual Jane's title. These developments now open up the use of our data to persons and bodies who in the past were not especially concerned with ploughing through hundreds of pages of facts.

This, however, is by no means the end of the line. There are significant moves afoot within the Company at this moment in terms of continued development of electronic product. Though no firm decisions have yet been made, we have already developed "customised" electronic products for certain military customers – principally in the field of recognition training where the swift and efficient electronic handling of digitized images is an important asset – and are now investigating such development channels as CDI (interactive CDROM), "bulletin board" news systems, multimedia products and enhanced image-handling software systems.

As the work of the Register progresses over the next few years, there will undoubtedly be changes in its reporting structure, its coverage and the type of information it requests. At this time it will be necessary to assess the way in which any or all of the sources discussed in the papers delivered today by IISS and Jane's can be harnessed to achieve the Register's objectives and to make the Panel's function easier and more efficient. Consideration of the vast volumes of data already available in the public domain – whether it is The Military Balance, Jane's Intelligence Review or any one of the raw data or 'secondary' sources mentioned above – will be a sine qua non before beginning to assess the impact of reports to the Register from participating countries. Much of the information requested by the Register (probably as much as 90 per cent) already exists in some form or other in the public domain and can be harnessed and put to work on the Register's behalf quickly and effectively.

Appendix A

Jane's Major Yearbooks

Jane's major yearbooks – each published annually (except where otherwise noted), covering global developments within their specific fields.

Jane's Fighting Ships – a detailed listing and physical/technical descriptions of submarines and surface vessels in naval service.

Jane's Naval Weapon Systems (binder – updated three times per year) – naval missiles, guns, torpedoes, anti-submarine weapons and associated control systems.

Jane's All the World's Aircraft – development histories, technical descriptions and performance data for all fixed-wing and rotary-wing aircraft (military and civil) currently in production or under development.

Jane's Civil & Military Aircraft Upgrades – extends the coverage of Jane's All the World's Aircraft to include those aircraft no longer in production but currently being upgraded, refurbished or retro-fitted.

Jane's Air-Launched Weapons (binder – updated three times per year) – technical and performance characteristics of air-launched missiles, bombs "multi-weapon systems" and torpedoes plus aircraft guns cannon and rockets.

Jane's Armour & Artillery – main battle tanks, armoured combat vehicles, reconnaissance vehicles, anti-tank vehicles, self-propelled and towed artillery (excluding anti-aircraft) and ancillary armoured vehicles. Includes holdings by type but not quantity.

Jane's AFV Retrofit Systems – weapon systems, powerpacks, control systems and other components and assemblies used to enhance or modify existing armoured fighting vehicles.

Jane's Military Vehicles and Logistics – military trucks, prime movers, artillery tractors and associated logistic equipment and systems.

Jane's Military Training Systems – equipment used in driving and gunnery training, battlefield simulation systems, pyrotechnics and other training equipment.

Jane's Radar & Electronic Warfare Systems – naval, airborne and ground-based radar systems and electronic warfare equipment used in ESM

(Electronic Support Measures), ECM (Electronic Countermeasures) and ECCM roles (Electronic Counter-Countermeasures).

Jane's Avionics – airborne communications, IFF (Identification Friend or Foe) and sensor equipment.

Jane's Land-Based Air Defence – ground anti-aircraft missile and artillery systems. Includes holdings with some quantitative information.

Jane's Military Communications – voice and data transmission, reception and handling equipment.

Jane's C4I Systems – computers, command, control, communications and intelligence equipment and systems.

Jane's Strategic Weapon Systems (binder, updated three times per year) – offensive and defensive strategic weapon systems, including NBC-capable (Nuclear, Biological, Chemical). Includes texts of major arms control treaties and agreements.

Jane's Space Directory – military and civil satellites, launchers and space programs, including directories of industrial capabilities.

Jane's Infantry Weapons – small arms, mortars, anti-tank weapons, infantry support weapons.

Jane's Security and Counter-Insurgency Equipment – weapons, sensors, surveillance systems and mobility equipment in use by paramilitary and law enforcement authorities.

Jane's Battlefield Surveillance Systems – remotely-piloted vehicles, surveillance radar, proximity sensor and warning system for battlefield deployment.

Jane's Underwater Warfare Systems – sonar, decoys, torpedoes and other systems for anti-submarine warfare activities.

Jane's NBC Protection Equipment – detection, protection and decontamination equipment in service or under development for use in Nuclear, Chemical and Biological warfare situations and training.

Jane's Ammunition Handbook – technical characteristics of ammunition from small arms to heavy-calibre artillery.

CHAPTER 8

The Military Balance and publicly available military information

Andrew Duncan

I Introduction

The United Nations Register of Conventional Arms is the first official global exercise in openness and transparency relating to conventional arms since World War II. Transparency by the provision of military information is a key element in both the Conventional Forces in Europe Treaty (CFE) and the Vienna Document 1992 agreed by the members of the Conference for Security and Cooperation in Europe (CSCE). But these information exchanges only cover weapons in Europe and involve only 53 countries of which five have no armed forces (CSCE has 53 member states of which 29 are also CFE signatories). However there are a number of non-governmental organisations whose publications collate the publicly available information. The best known of these, each of which specialises in different fields of information, are: the Stockholm International Peace Research Institute (SIPRI) (military expenditure, arms production and trade); Jane's Information Services (weapons and equipment manufacture and technical characteristics); and the International Institute for Strategic Studies (IISS) (armed forces strengths, military organisations and weapons holdings).

The Editor of *The Military Balance*, the IISS's annual publication, is responsible for collecting as much information on each nation's armed forces as possible. This chapter will describe the collection process, and the methods and sources of information used by the IISS to compile *The Military Balance*. It will also briefly explain what information can be found in *The Military Balance* and, more importantly, what information can not. Finally it will also examine how much the UN Conventional Arms Register adds to the availability of military information.

II   *The Military Balance* collection process

It is important to stress that compiling *The Military Balance* is a relatively low cost operation. It could undoubtedly be more accurate and more comprehensive if funds were available to employ more staff, to allow them to travel so as to establish both governmental and other contacts, and to purchase more publications. At present only six staff are employed. Apart from the Editor, who coordinates the work, organises the collection of information and is responsible for covering nuclear and chemical weapons, there are four analysts responsible respectively for: ground forces, naval forces, air forces and space, and defence expenditures and industry. There is also one secretary.

It is also important to stress that the IISS seeks only openly available information. It does not employ a string of agents across the world actively collecting military information. Everyone who is asked to provide information knows that what they say will be published and that highly secret information is not being sought.

Although *The Military Balance* is only published once a year, in October, the task of up-dating it is never ending. Adding new information and correcting errors goes on throughout the year. The most important source of information is, of course, the governments of each country listed in *The Military Balance*. Each government is sent, in February or March, the first draft of their country's entry for that year. This is the previous year's entry up-dated and revised with the information which has become available during the previous six months.

Sadly not all governments reply. In some cases this is no doubt because of genuine security concerns. In other cases it is probably because of language difficulties. *The Military Balance* team can only correspond in English; a much larger staff with the relevant language ability could produce drafts in several other languages - Arabic, Russian and Spanish for example - which might generate more response. In some cases it is possibly due to idleness and inefficiency. Some countries prefer it not to be known that they have provided official comment and data; no list of those who regularly reply can therefore be given. However it can be said that for many years the members of the North Atlantic Treaty Organisation and the neutral and non-aligned countries of Europe have replied frankly and fully. Since the end of the Cold War these have been joined by the former non-Soviet members of the Warsaw Pact, and now with the break-up of the Soviet Union the new republics are also increasingly providing information. The main problem here is to find the correct point of contact and the most reliable method (and route) for communicating. Response from the rest of the world is disappointing. A number of Central and Southern American countries reply from time to time. A few Asian countries always respond. Virtually no African states provide assistance and no Middle Eastern ones do.

Other sources and commentators must therefore be found. The IISS has a strict policy of not asking any country to provide information about its neighbours or potential enemies. While to do so might gain valuable extra information it would be counter-productive in that those asked would immediately suspect that similar information on their forces was being sought from their neighbours. Nevertheless many countries value the publication of *The Military Balance* which has over the years acquired a reputation for accuracy and credibility. They often publicly quote *The Military Balance* figures both for their own forces and those of other countries. This avoids giving an official view. It also protects the success or failure of their intelligence services; and it allows a policy of never giving official data on their own forces to be followed.

Many countries realise that it is in their best interests to ensure that *The Military Balance* maintains its reputation and that is why they provide the IISS with information. In some countries where a "no reply" policy is in operation there is no such restriction on non-governmental sources, either individuals or other research institutes, in replying to IISS enquiries. Indeed in some cases information provided had been vetted by the government concerned before it was sent.

Unofficial respondents are therefore the second best source of information for *The Military Balance*. Of course much of what they learn from open sources may well have already been noted by the IISS and, if the original report is incorrect, then false confirmation may be given. Most importantly these respondents greatly increase the Institute's coverage of material in languages which the IISS does not understand and in journals it cannot afford to purchase. All assistance is given freely and the IISS has a policy of never paying for *The Military Balance* information. The respondents come from a wide field of activity and include academics, journalists, business men, retired military officers, members of the Institute as well as staff at other International Affairs and Military Studies organisations.

Much information is acquired purely by reading. Many governments publish data on their armed forces and defence policy as a matter of routine. It is not practical to provide a list of all governments and their publications but as an example of what is available details are set out for the US, Russia and China at Appendix A. Also a good number of armed forces and individual armies, navies and air forces publish their own newspapers and magazines from which careful reading will normally pick up a new fact or two. Such magazines are published even by traditionally security phobic states such as South Africa (Paratus) and Israel (Bamahane).

Arms control treaty data is the most informative of government produced information. The Strategic Arms Reduction Treaty (START) contained a detailed list of the types, numbers and locations of the strategic nuclear weapons of the US and Soviet Union; this list is to be up-dated once the Treaty comes into force. The Intermediate Nuclear Forces Treaty provided similar information for other nuclear forces now all eliminated. The CFE Treaty requires all signatories to exchange extremely detailed military data annually. The information lists all army and air force organisations down to independent battalion level showing each unit's immediate and next higher command headquarters. It gives the location of all units holding Treaty Limited Equipment (TLE) that is: tanks, armoured combat vehicles, artillery, armoured bridge layers, combat aircraft and attack helicopters. The numbers and type of each category of TLE at each location is listed, as is the manpower strength of each unit. The information is not the complete inventory of all the nations concerned as only TLE in the Treaty area (Europe from the Atlantic to the Ural Mountains) is subject to the Treaty. Weaponry elsewhere – in the US and Canada; Russia east of the Urals; French and British overseas garrisons for example – are not listed. Nor are naval forces, surface to air weapons and many other areas of military capability. Similar information is exchanged annually by the members of CSCE which includes all European countries and also the five Central Asian republics of the former Soviet Union. Data exchanges are made on the understanding of confidentiality and so countries may not release others' data but a good number provide the IISS with copies of their own returns. With such widespread distribution treaty data can be counted as publicly available information, but is exchanged by governments on a 'treaty confidential' basis and so cannot be released outside recipient government's officials. However, it is the CFE and CSCE countries which are already the most open about their armed forces.

Virtually all newspapers, magazines and other publications carry military information from time to time. So too do many radio and television broadcasts. The IISS purchases many publications and the *Summary of World Broadcasts* (monitored and published by the BBC). It is the IISS analysts' job to read all these and extract any items for inclusion in the new edition of *The Military Balance*. A number of specialist and regional journals include sections on defence and security; for example *African Affairs*, *Latin American Monitor*, *Flight International*, and *Aviation and Space Technology*. There are numerous defence journals of which the US published *Defense News* and

Armed Forces Journal, the Russian *Military Review* and Jane's Information Services' stable of publications are amongst the most informative examples. There are other publications which specialise on information concerning nuclear weapons, chemical and biological agents and ballistic missiles. Here the *Bulletin of the Atomic Scientists*, *Arms Control Today* and *The Chemical Weapons Convention Bulletin* are the most authoritative. There are many others.

The Military Balance uses all these sources in compiling its inventories of the armed forces of the world, but how informative is it really? Any country when making a threat assessment of a potential enemy must consider two separate elements of that threat. The first is the military capability it poses and secondly its political intentions, in other words the likelihood of that military capability being employed. *The Military Balance* provides only part of the data needed to assess military capability and does not address political intentions. It is therefore necessary to describe what *The Military Balance* sets out to provide and to point out what it does not, and often cannot, provide.

The Military Balance contents

In very general terms *The Military Balance* lists quantity (in terms of finance, manpower and weapon holding) but not quality.

The first part of each country's entry is devoted to economic and demographic data. Economic data (GDP, growth, inflation, etc.) are generally available from official and commercial sources. Whenever possible International Monetary Fund (IMF) and World Bank publications are used. These are supported by a wide range of publications by national and regional official and academic organisations and include for example: *World Debt Tables*, *Key Indicators of Developing Asian and Pacific Countries*, *Marchés Tropicaux et Méditerranéens* and the *Southeastern European Yearbook*.

Details of defence expenditure is less readily available, a list of countries regularly reporting their defence expenditures to the UN standardised Reporting of Military Expenditures schemes is shown at Appendix B. Not all expenditures cover the same items: some countries include the cost of internal security, others exclude items such as pensions and others even research and development (R and D). In the Soviet Union many items of defence expenditure were charged to other ministries' budgets including much R and D and weapon procurement; most analysts believed that Soviet defence expenditure was at least double the officially published figure. The situation in China where the army runs many civil manufacturing companies is even more unclear. A further problem is the question of comparability. This is simpler in, for example, NATO countries as NATO has its own definition of defence expenditure which adjusts the inclusions and exclusions to a common standard, and where countries have convertible currencies and normally stable market exchange rates. But many countries have multiple official and market exchange rates and often these exchange rates alter so dramatically that it is difficult to express GDP and defence expenditure in dollar terms. The situation is further complicated when conditions of chronic inflation or hyperinflation are present. Much work has been done in this area, in particular in the use of the Purchasing Power Parity method (which is a measure of the relative prices of goods and services from different countries valued in a common currency). However it is possible to compare a country's defence expenditure over a number of years both in absolute terms and as a percentage of GDP or total government spending to see whether it is expanding or being reduced.

Demographic data is taken, unless more up-to-date national statistics are available, from *World Population Projections* published by the John Hopkins University Press for the World Bank. In addition to total population figures *The Military Balance* shows the size of three "military cohorts". The age group from 18 to 22 years is that most likely to volunteer or be conscripted for military service; those of 23 to 32 years of age are those which may have most recently had military service and would be the first to be recalled in an emergency; and the 13 to 17 years age group indicates the potential for future years. In future editions *The Military Balance* intends to give more detail on significant ethnic minorities; Serbs and Croats in Bosnia-Herzegovina, Russians in the republics of the former Soviet Union, and Kurds in Turkey, Iran and Iraq for example.

Manpower is an area where quality is vitally important. Obviously volunteer armies are more professional than conscript ones, not just because men serve for longer periods (essential when manning modern weapons and equipments) but also because they will be better motivated being volunteers. Conscript forces are invariably far larger than all-volunteer forces because manpower is so much cheaper and so many men can be employed on menial and labouring tasks which are usually contracted out to civilians in volunteer forces. Reservist manpower must also be examined so as to assess its effectiveness which mainly depends on what refresher training is carried out and how often, and how the reserves are organised. Here volunteer reserves such as the US National Guard will score far more highly than, say, Russian low category divisions dependent on recalled conscripts.

Where countries maintain nuclear forces *The Military Balance* lists these at the start of each entry; only strategic assets are listed separately while dual-capable weapons are listed under their respective service. All nuclear capable weapons are listed again at the end of the book in a table which also gives details such as kilotonnage, circular error probable and range. A new problem in this area is that a number of weapons have been taken off operational status and have been partially de-activated. However until they have been eliminated under the detailed rules laid down in the START Treaty they are still countable, and indeed many could still be restored to operational readiness. With the exception of China, the recognised nuclear powers are reasonably open about the size and shape of their strategic nuclear forces. The published edition of the START treaty includes detailed data, including locations, on US and USSR strategic nuclear weapons. Both France and the UK make annual statements on their nuclear forces. However all restrict their statements to details of delivery means, and do not reveal the size of their nuclear warhead stockpiles.

Under the Strategic Forces heading *The Military Balance* also lists Strategic Defences. Currently only Russia fields an anti-ballistic missile system. All Early Warning systems are listed as are Strategic Reconnaissance assets such as satellites.

The Military Balance listing for ground forces gives the main organisations for each state. Naturally these differ according to the size of the country. For example for Russia and the US divisions, brigades and regiments are listed while at the other end of the scale for Brunei and Côte D'Ivoire battalions and specialist independent companies are shown. The internal organisation for large formations such as divisions is given as the shape and strength of these varies considerably. The numbers of main weapon systems held (tanks, APCs, artillery, anti-tank and anti-aircraft weapons and helicopters) are given by type. However army equipment inventories do not include small arms or weapons such as grenades or mines. Nor does *The Military Balance* list many essential equipments which are not weapons such as: communication systems, surveillance radars, engineer plant and logistic vehicles. This is an omission that should be remedied as their inclusion would give an indication of the sophistication of a force (does it employ satellite communications for instance) and its deployability (does it have tank transporters or fuel bowsers with a multi-refilling capability). At present restrictions on space rule this out.

The technical characteristics of all the weapons and equipments listed in *The Military Balance*, and a large number that are not, are given in the Jane's series of year books such as *"Armour and Artillery"*, *"Fighting Ships"* and

"All The World's Aircraft". From time to time *The Military Balance* does include comparative tables of particular weapon types (tanks, artillery, attack aircraft and helicopters) showing details such as range, speed, weapon fit, armoured protection and whatever else is relevant for that weapon system.

Naval information is a simpler matter. Firstly there are far fewer warships to trace than there are tanks and aircraft. Secondly details of keel-laying, launching and commissioning are very often fully publicly reported. *The Military Balance* lists naval ships by function (submarine, destroyer, minesweeper etc.) and by class and gives the weapon fit of each class including whether a helicopter is embarked or not. Support shipping is essential for any navy that is to have long-range operational reach and these ships are also listed by role (tanker, ammunition or stores re-supply) and whether they have a replenishment at sea capability or not.

For Air Forces *The Military Balance* adopts two formats. For the smaller air forces the number of units (usually squadrons) of each aircraft role (bomber, fighter, transport etc.) together with the total number and class of aircraft which are held is listed. For the larger air forces the number of units for each role is given followed by a full inventory of all aircraft held. Where possible an indication is given of the numbers of aircraft held in reserve (in Military Balance terminology "in store"). Here *The Military Balance* is referring to aircraft above the numbers required to maintain units up to establishment and those which are rotating from units through the maintenance and modification process. Maritime aircraft are shown under either the Navy or Air Force heading dependant on whether air crew are Air Force or Navy personnel. In some countries there is an Air Defence Force comprising both fighter aircraft and ground based air defence weapons (surface to air missiles (SAM) and anti-aircraft artillery (AAA)) and these are shown separately. Often though ground-based air defences form part of the air force. In the case of ground and naval forces where missile launchers are listed, the type of missile (anti-tank, surface to surface, surface to air etc.) is implicit. This is not so for air delivered missiles and so *The Military Balance* lists the types (Sidewinder, Maverick, HARM etc.) of missile in the inventory, distinguishing between air to air and air to ground missiles. All air forces rely on their aircrew skills and *The Military Balance* should (but at present does not) report the annual quota of flying hours budgeted for each pilot (this is a norm often restricted by lack of funds). In future it is hoped to be able to do so.

The Military Balance does not attempt to list the availability or stocks of ammunition whether missiles (of any description), artillery or other natures. Gaining reliable information is not possible, but of course such information forms a vital part of assessing any force's capability, or indeed lack of capability. It is for that reason that the drafters of the United Nations Register of Conventional Arms left the definition of the missile/missile launcher category deliberately vague.

Serviceability is another major factor and here *The Military Balance* attempts to indicate where forces are unable to keep their equipments in an operational state.

For major nations *The Military Balance* next lists their forces' deployment. For Russia and China this is by military district/fleet and for the US by combatant command (Central, Europe, Atlantic etc.). Elsewhere it is sufficient to show the countries in which forces are stationed outside national borders. *The Military Balance* also provides a cross reference by listing Foreign Forces located in each country. This last includes both United Nations and other peace-keeping forces. A separate section details the mandate and composition of each peace-keeping operation.

The Military Balance also lists what it describes as Para-Military Forces. In some countries these can be as powerful as the active army (the Russian Ministry of Interior division stationed near Moscow or the Saudi National Guard for example). In others they are little more than police, but in war have a useful role in rear-area defence which relieves active forces for the battlefield.

Finally *The Military Balance* lists what it calls Opposition Forces. Here only forces which threaten the continuance of the established government of a state are listed. For instance terrorist organisations such as the Irish Republican Army, Euskadi ta Askatasuna (the Basque Separatist Movement in Spain) or the Red Army Faction which are most unlikely ever to overthrow the authorities are not listed. However, organisations such as UNITA in Angola and the Sendero Luminoso in Peru are listed. A new category of Other Forces has had to be introduced to cover former opposition groups such as Umkhonto we Sizwe (the combat arm of the ANC) in South Africa and RENAMO in Mozambique which are being incorporated into the government forces. Acquiring information on Opposition Forces is one of the hardest tasks for the IISS.

III Information *The Military Balance* does not provide

As stated earlier *The Military Balance* does not attempt to judge quality. The main reason for this is that gaining the necessary information is one of the hardest tasks facing professional military intelligence and would be quite beyond the resources of the IISS. To gain some elements of information requires the employment of covert collection means. It would also probably be counter-productive as nations whose forces were slated as inefficient or poorly trained would be unlikely to respond to IISS enquiries.

A number of factors effecting force quality have already been mentioned in previous paragraphs. Weapons and equipment quality is excellently covered by Jane's. Other matters which must be taken into account when judging quality include: training, leadership, tactics, organisation, logistics and electronic warfare.

The combat capability of all forces whether in fighting units or in support or logistic roles depends very much on training; its frequency, its relevance and its realism. But training is expensive and training costs such as flying hours, sea time, track mileage and live ammunition usage are constantly under review and often reduced. Judging the standard of training is hard enough for those supervising it, let alone outsiders.

Good training is dependent on good leadership. While leaders can be taught what to do, there is very much more to good leadership. From good leadership will stem many of the qualities needed by fighting men: morale, motivation and discipline. Judging in what measure these qualities are present is not easy; no-one advertises their absence.

Tactics and organisation go together. Information on both can be acquired but usually only by obtaining training manuals, tables of organisation and doctrine papers, and by studying the course of training exercises. This sort of information is rarely publicly available.

Logistics is obviously a vital factor. This covers not just the provision of ammunition, fuel, food and other stores but also in getting it to the right place at the right time. It includes the ability to repair broken or damaged weapons and equipment close to the front line. It also includes the system for the evacuation and treatment of casualties. Most field training manoeuvres last too short a time to really test the logistic system and so judging its effectiveness is difficult. Even judging the size of stocks of ammunition is hard enough, and it is worth recalling how surprised NATO was to discover the true extent of East German ammunition stocks.

Finally another area of increasing importance which *The Military Balance* cannot begin to address is the question of Electronic Warfare (EW) capability. EW includes both Electronic Counter Measures (ECM), steps taken to degrade an enemy's ability to use the electronic system (whether for communicating, surveillance and target acquisition or air space control) and Electronic Counter Counter Measures, steps taken to defeat the enemy's ECM.

IV   How Accurate is *The Military Balance?*

There is, of course, no way of knowing the answer to this question. Only each country can judge for its own armed forces (and possibly some others it particularly studies) but countries which don't respond to IISS enquiries are unlikely to publicise that *The Military Balance* is inaccurate in their case. Obviously the more open any country is and the more cooperative they are in responding to the IISS requests for information the more accurate *The Military Balance* will be for that country. The IISS is, therefore, reasonably confident that it accurately portrays the armed forces of the North American and European members of CSCE with the exception of Georgia, Armenia and Azerbaijan (although even here some information is available) and of Russia east of the Urals. Elsewhere in the world the IISS is less confident. However, the IISS has been told by a senior retired Indian General that its data is "reasonable accurate, above 80 per cent". In the British parliament a defence minister stated "It is not the Government's practice to publish their assessments of the strengths of the armed forces of other states. The principle public source of such information is *The Military Balance* published by the IISS and widely regarded as authoritative". *The Military Balance* has been quoted by several other governments' officials including those of the former Soviet Union. The IISS is extremely conscious of its reputation and does its utmost to ensure this is justified but it is well aware that in some areas it may be wrong. However, whenever inaccuracies are pointed out, they are always admitted in the next year's edition. In many war torn areas such as Afghanistan, Angola, Ethiopia and Somalia it would be dishonest to pretend to have more than a very basic idea of the strengths of the different parties.

The publication of the United Nations Conventional Arms Register has provided the first opportunity to check *The Military Balance*'s accuracy. The IISS has analysed the country submissions to the Register and found a total of 28 transfers which it had not noted in open sources nor been informed of. A list of these is given at Appendix C. Four export transfers from China were missed, all of significant numbers of weapons, whereas the five transfers from Russia which had not been noted were all of a relatively unimportant nature.

It is hard to analyse accurately the proportion of imports and exports which were not publicly known when there are so many inconsistencies between reports to the UN by importers and exporters. The table below gives an indication of the scale of transparency.

Table 1.   Comparison between exports and imports reported in the Register and IISS

Item	Reported Exports	Not Noted by IISS	Reported Imports	Not Noted by IISS
Battle Tanks	1711	125	1222	113
ACVs	845	454[a]	1296	43[a]
Large Calibre Artillery System	1327	202	1091	114
Combat Aircraft	243	3	194	5
Attack Helicopters	11	–	44	22
Warships	16	–	24	–

Note: a. The export of 262 APC's from Canada to Saudi Arabia accounted for over half this total. IISS was aware of the contract to supply but did not know the delivery date. Similarly the plan to 'cascade' APC's from The Netherlands to Portugal was publicised but again the delivery date was not known.

An examination of the background information provided by just under 30 per cent of those who reported to the UN Conventional Arms Register shows that this data, except in the case of three Latin American countries, added little or nothing to *The Military Balance*'s data base. Only 14 countries provided both information on holdings and procurement through national production and ten more gave data on holdings only. However, of these, only nine countries itemized their holdings by type of tank, artillery piece or aircraft; the other 16 purely gave total figures for each system listed in the Register. Of those credited as reporting national production: four had no national production, one reported only equipment expenditure, one had only procured one frigate and one submarine, six gave total numbers for each system but without giving the types procured, one gave the types of systems without the numbers, and only Japan gave the full details of the systems, types and numbers procured plus the expenditure incurred on each. This cannot be considered a very meaningful set of data. Of the countries providing information on holdings, 13 were members of NATO (Iceland, Luxembourg, and Norway did not report) and three were former members of the Warsaw Pact. All these countries already exchange detailed military information as signatories of the CFE Treaty and, joined by Austria and Sweden as required by the CSCE Vienna Document. Australia, Japan and New Zealand are traditionally extremely open with military information. This leaves Brazil, Chile and Nicaragua, all of which provided data on both types of systems and numbers held.

With Brazil, *The Military Balance* listed the Navy more or less totally accurately missing one nationally built corvette (and misnaming some classes). Naval aviation and marine corps assets were correct. *The Military Balance* listed more aircraft than were reported but probably at least three of these were due to crashes not picked up by the IISS, and the AMX figure published in 1991 had been corrected by the 1992 addition. The Army inventory shows the most inaccuracy: elderly US M-3 tanks were shown as still being held when they had, presumably, been scrapped, and the number of M-41 tanks had been understated by some 40. Brazil reported having 409 EE-9 recce tanks while *The Military Balance* listed 300 EE-9 and 250 EE-3. The number of artillery pieces was also overstated by 50 SP and 150 towed guns, nor was the number of heavy mortars known. The IISS credited Brazil with four instead of only one ASTROS MRL system and believed that other MRL types were in service but had no information on numbers (types which were not reported by Brazil).

The same pattern was repeated with *The Military Balance* listing for Chile. Naval holdings were correct, aircraft holdings were also correct apart from more recent acquisitions which have been overstated by some 7 percent. The majority of discrepancies, again, are in the Army inventory where tank figures are 10 per cent out in overall numbers with some types shown as having more and others less than the reported number. *The Military Balance* has grossly overstated the numbers of armoured combat vehicles. Artillery data is more or less accurate but some older guns listed have, presumably, been scrapped while 12 Israeli 155 mm howitzers were not listed. Chile does not own to holding 120 mm mortars but this may be a reporting misunderstanding.

With Nicaragua, *The Military Balance* is more accurate. Naval data is correct, as are aircraft numbers except that the Air Force is credited with ten helicopters more than reported and with a number of light COIN aircraft which *The Military Balance* lists as probably unserviceable but which Nicaragua does not report and so may have been scrapped. Army weapon holdings are encouragingly accurate, never more than 10 per cent out and usually by no more than five weapons in any one type.

Of course it may not always be *The Military Balance* which is inaccurate. Some reports, because of definitional misunderstanding for instance, may not give the full picture.

There is no doubt *The Military Balance* would be more accurate if more countries, particularly those that are not signatories of arms control treaties, provided the UN Conventional Arms Register with the full details of their weapons holdings as did the nine countries which provided itemized holdings to the 1992 Register.

There is also no doubt that if the UN Register contained comprehensive details of domestic arms procurement *The Military Balance*'s accuracy would be improved. For many years the IISS published details of major contracts signed but found it difficult to monitor how delivery was progressing, particularly when this was stretched over a number of years. Naturally the IISS monitors reports of contracts and uses these as the basis for some of the questions it sends out each year with *The Military Balance* drafts. Quantifying the increased degree of accuracy is not possible.

V   Conclusion

This paper has concentrated on setting out what military information is publicly available in the context of compiling *The Military Balance*, and how easy it is for the IISS to obtain this information. In some countries the availability of military data is way beyond the needs of a directory like *The Military Balance*. In other areas there is virtually no information, but this situation normally occurs where the level of defence spending, and the strength and armament of the armed forces are not significant in global terms though they may be quite threatening for neighbouring states.

Already it can be seen that the publication of the UN Register of Conventional Arms has provided additional information not in the public domain and some of it of a not insignificant nature (Cameroon increasing its artillery by 50 per cent, Nepal its artillery and mortars by 200 per cent and Moldova its APC's by 200 per cent and artillery by nearly 50 per cent). Undoubtedly adding domestic procurement to the Register would provide even more information particularly in respect of major arms producers such as China and Russia. But more important than expanding the scope of the Register is the task of convincing the one hundred members of the UN who did not report to the Register to do so.

Appendix A

Examples of government published military information

The United States (a small sample of available literature)

Department of Defense
Annual Report to The President and The Congress.
Report to the Congress on the Strategic Defense Initiative.
United States Special Forces Posture Statement.
Program Acquisition Costs by Weapon (gives quantity as well as cost).
Report on Allied Contributions to Common Defense.
Worldwide Manpower Distribution by Geographical Area.
Joint Military Net Assessment.
Reserve Components of the United States Armed Forces.
US Army Weapons Systems.
US Army Force Posture Statement.
Army Focus 1993.
Navy Fact File.
(Note: The majority of the above are annual publications)

General Accounting Office
Status of C-17 (strategic transport aircraft) Development Program.
US Military Presence in Europe: Issues related to the Drawdown.
Army Force Structure: Need to ensure ample supply of Ready Support Forces.
1994 Defense Budget: Potential Reduction to Ammunition Programs.

Congressional Budget Office
Structuring US Forces After The Cold War.
Moving the Marine Corps by Sea.
Strategic Defenses: Alternative Missions and Costs.
Rethinking the Trident (SLBM) Force.

Office of Technology Assessment
American Military Power: Future Needs, Future Choices.
Future of Remote Sensing from Space: Civilian Satellite Systems and
Applications.
Technologies Underlying Weapons of Mass Destruction.
New Technology for NATO: Implementing Follow-on Forces Attack.

Arms Control and Disarmament Agency (Fact Sheets)
Missile Technology Control Regime.
START: Data-Base.
CFE: A Reprise of Key Treaty Elements (TLE Holding at 1 Jan 93)

Central Intelligence Agency:
The Russian Security Services: Sorting Out The Pieces.
El Salvador: The Struggle for Rural Control.
Many reports for different countries on: OECD Trade, Directory of Officials,
Economic Profile.

Arms of Congress Publications
Foreign Affairs Committee:
The Crisis in the Former Yugoslavia and US Role.
Future US Arms Control Policy.
Proposed Sale of F-16 Aircraft to Saudi Arabia.
Intelligence Committee:
Future of the Intelligence Community (Director CIA Hearing)
Appropriations Committee:
Military Construction Appropriations for FY 94.
Department of Defense Appropriations.
Armed Services Committee:
Current Military Operations in Somalia.
Use of Force in the Post-Cold War Era.
Intelligence Successes and Failures in Operation Desert Storm.

China

Journals published by the Peoples Liberation Army
PLA Daily: Provides details on unit identification, location, names and
appointments. Information on military exercises and training, weapons and
equipment.
KUN LUN Magazine: Bi-monthly of over 200 pages. Similar items as for the
PLA Daily. Gives detailed information on PLA problems and on PLA senior
officers.
PLA Literature and Art Magazine: Similar information as PLA Daily: Photos
provide naval ship and craft pennant numbers, aircraft tail numbers.
PLA Life Magazine: Monthly. Aimed at battalian and company level
readership. Similar information as for PLA Daily but at the small unit level.
Chinese Naval Dictionary

Russia

Publications Purchased by The Conflict Studies Research Centre, Sandhurst
(Formerly The Soviet Studies Research Centre, Sandhurst)
Armiya (Army).
Aviatsiya I Kosmonavtika (Aviation and Cosmonautics).
Konversiya (Conversion).
Krasnaya Zvezda (Red Star).

Militsiya (Police).
Morskoy Sbornik (Naval Collection).
NA Boevom Postu (At The Military Post).
Na Strazhe Rodiny (On Guard for the Motherland).
Nasha Gazeta (Our Newspaper).
Patriot (Patriot).
Pogranichnik (Border Trooper).
Sobesednik Voyna (Conversationalist of War).
Sovetskiy Voin (Soviet Soldier).
Syn Otechestva (Son of the Fatherland).
Tekhnika I Vooruzhenie (Equipment and Weaponry).
Voennaya Mysl (Military Thought).
Voenno-Istoricheskiy Zhurnal (Military History Journal).
Voenno Znaniya (Military Knowledge).
Voennyy Vestnik (Military Herald).
Zarubezhnoe Voennoe Obozrenie (Foreign Military Review).
Zashchita Otechestva (Defence of the Fatherland).

These are the main Russian military newspapers and journals. Some may have already ceased publication and some are scheduled to do so in the near future. There have been several changes of title: the current title is the one listed.

Appendix B

List of countries which report in the Standardised Reporting of Military Expenditure to the United Nations

Country	1990	1991	1992	1993
Argentina	x	x	x	
Australia		x	x	x
Austria	x	x	x	x
Barbados	x		x	x
Belarus			x	x
Belgium	x		x	x
Brazil		x	x	x
Bulgaria	x	x	x	x
Canada	x	x	x	x
Chile		x	x	x
Colombia		x		
Croatia				x
Cyprus			x	
Czechoslovakia		x	x	
Denmark	x	x	x	
Finland	x	x	x	x
France	x			x
Germany	x	x	x	x
Greece	x	x	x	x
Hungary	x	x	x	x
Ireland				x
Israel	x	x		
Italy		x	x	
Japan		x		
Kazakhstan				x
Luxembourg		x	x	
Malaysia	x			
Malta	x	x	x	
Mauritius				x
Namibia				x
Netherlands	x	x		x

Country	1990	1991	1992	1993
New Zealand	x	x	x	
Niger			x	
Norway	x	x		x
Panama				x
Peru			x	x
Philippines				x
Poland	x	x	x	
Portugal	x	x	x	x
Romania		x	x	x
Spain		x	x	x
Sweden		x	x	
Thailand		x	x	
Togo				x
Turkey			x	x
Ukraine				x
United Kingdom	x	x	x	x
United States	x			
USSR/Russia	x			
Yugoslavia		x	x	x

Appendix C

Weapon movements not noted by *The Military Balance*

EXPORTER	IMPORTER	WEAPONS
Belarus	North Korea (a)	19 Tanks
Belarus	Oman (a)	3 Tanks
China (b)	Bolivia	36 Artillery, 18 AA Gun
Bulgaria (c)	Russia	3 Aircraft (d)
Russia (b)	Bulgaria	5 Aircraft (d)
Canada	Saudi Arabia (a)	262 APC
China	Pakistan	97 Tanks
China	Sudan (a)	18 Artillery
China	Iran (a)	106 Artillery
Czech Republic	Zimbabwe	20 Artillery
Egypt	Algeria (a)	53 APC
Egypt	Rwanda	6 Artillery
France	Morocco (a)	14 ACV
France	Qatar (a)	12 ACV
Israel	Botswana (a)	4 ACV
Italy	Nigeria	9 Artillery
Russia (b)	Lithuania	15 APC
UK (b)	Nepal	8 Artillery
India	Nepal	52 Mortars
Netherlands	Portugal	28 APC
USA (b)	Peru	14 Light Tanks
Nicaragua	Peru	19 Helicopters
Russia (b)	Peru	3 Helicopters
Romania	Cameroon (a)	12 Artillery
Romania	Nigeria (a)	9 Artillery
Romania	Moldova (a)	51 APC, 48 Artillery
Russia	Oman (a)	6 Tanks
Russia	Sierre Leone (a)	4 APC

Notes: (a) Countries which did not provide reports to the Register
(b) Not reported by the Exporter
(c) Not reported by the Importer
(d) Probably aircraft movements to/from overhaul and not true imports/exports.

~

CHAPTER 9

Expanding the Register to include procurement through national production and military holdings

Malcolm Chalmers and Owen Greene

I   Introduction

One of the most important issues for the 1994 Group will be how to fulfil its mandate to examine the modalities of an early expansion of the Register to include Procurement through National Production and Military Holdings. Wide agreement amongst UN member states in 1991 to establish the Register was secured partly on the basis of an understanding that such an expansion would take place.

An important reason why there is wide demand to extend the Register to cover national procurement is that this would complement information on transfers, and thus provide more complete information on trends in military holdings. It would also address the concern that the current Register imposes greater transparency on major arms importers than on countries with substantial domestic arms industries. Moreover, whereas relatively few countries have much to report in any one year on transfers or procurement of major conventional arms, virtually all countries have significant military holdings. Such an extension could therefore help to extend the perceived relevance of the Register as a means of monitoring levels of conventional arms.

Yet expanding the Register to cover both procurement from national production and military holdings would substantially increase international transparency in an area where there has previously been little publicly available official information. There are therefore likely to be many sensitivities raised by such an expansion, and the Group will have to consider how these can be taken into account.

In Section II, we examine the data on military holdings and procurement from national production that has already been provided as 'background information'. While only 24 countries provided such data, this 'trial run' has been of some value. The very fluidity of the method chosen for the submission of information has raised a number of interesting issues which could have implications for the Group's deliberations, and we discuss some of these.

In Sections III and IV of the chapter, we consider in turn the main issues involved in including, on a standardized basis, data on military holdings and procurement from national production. We examine the case for differentiating the reporting of military holdings from that for procurement through national production. We argue that, while both should be included in future development if possible, the speed and detail of their inclusion might well differ.

In Section V, we discuss possible ways to develop 'background information', as a means of providing more useful data on military holdings and procurement from national production and also to promote its value for international transparency in other ways. Such developments may be particularly important if the Group of Experts decided against recommending the extension of the Register to cover military holdings or national production at this stage of its development, but wanted either to prepare for such an extension in the future or at least to make 'background information' more useful. However, even if the Register is expanded to include procurement from national production and military holdings, there is still scope for usefully developing guidelines for background information.

II   Reporting military holdings and procurement through national production through 'Background Information'[1]

For the first years of operation of the Register, participating states were asked to provide, as part of their reply to the Secretary-General, "available background information" regarding their military holdings, procurement through national production and relevant national arms import and export policies, legislation and administrative procedures. However, partly to emphasise that this "background information" had a more 'voluntary' status than data provided on transfers, no guidelines were provided as to how such data should be submitted. Moreover, in order to emphasise the different status of background information, it was not to be published in full. Rather, General Assembly resolution 46/36L of 9 December 1991 (which first established the Register) requested "the Secretary-General to record this material and to make it available for consultation by Member States at their request" (para. 10). In December 1992, the General Assembly then endorsed a Report from the Secretary-General recommending that: "the available background information submitted by Member States be open to the public".[2] We have recently published a report that examines and reproduces the Background Information submitted on procurement from national production and military holdings.[3]

Of the 83 governments that had replied to the Secretary-General's request for information for the 1992 Register by January 1994, 33 provided background information. Of these, however, only 24 states provided data on military holdings, of which 15 governments also provided information on procurement through national production (see Table 1). A further six governments provided some information on holdings and/or procurement in their reply, rather than in 'background information'.

A large proportion of the states providing holdings and/or procurement data are Conference on Security and Cooperation in Europe (CSCE) members, all of whom already have considerable experience in providing relevant data for transparency measures relating to conventional forces. Every member of NATO (with the exception of Luxembourg and Norway) provided data on holdings. In the rest of Europe, however, the response was much more varied. Amongst those traditionally thought to be non-aligned, Sweden and Austria provided data, but Finland, Ireland and Switzerland did not. In former communist Europe, data was provided by Poland, Hungary and Bulgaria, but not by the Czech Republic, Romania, Slovakia or any of the former Yugoslav republics. None of the six former Soviet republics replying to the UN provided background information of any sort.

Outside the CSCE, only a few countries provided data on procurement and/or holdings under background information: Australia, New Zealand, Japan, Brazil, Chile and Nicaragua. In addition, a few other countries provided data on procurement and/or holdings in other ways. In its standardized form for 1992 imports, Colombia appears to have provided a list of all its holdings of imported arms within the categories covered by the Register. Iceland, Mauritius and Paraguay reported nil holdings, and Solomon Islands, Mexico, Iceland and Mauritius reported nil procurement in 1992 (see Table 2).

There was some discussion in the 1992 Panel regarding the possibility of establishing a standardized form for the submission of "background information" on procurement and holdings. In the end, however, it was felt that this should be left to the 1994 Group to consider. Instead, it was agreed that:

> "The reporting of this information is voluntary and Member States may submit this information in any form they wish."[4]

Table 1. Countries submitting background information to the United Nations Register of Conventional Arms 1992

Countries submitting background information on procurement and holdings (15)	
Australia	Italy
Austria	Japan
Belgium	Netherlands
Brazil	Portugal
Bulgaria	Spain
France	UK
Germany	US
Hungary	
Countries submitting background information on holdings only (9)	
Canada	Nicaragua
Chile	Poland
Denmark	Sweden
Greece	Turkey
New Zealand	
Countries submitting background information but providing no data on procurement or holdings (9)	
Czech Republic	Qatar
Finland	South Korea
Israel	Switzerland
Norway	Yugoslavia
Panama	

Table 2.   Countries providing data on holdings and/or procurement in their published reply, but not in 'Background Information'

Colombia[a]	(total holdings of imported weapons appear to be reported as 1992 imports)
Iceland[b]	(nil procurement and holdings)
Mauritius[c]	(nil procurement and holdings)
Mexico[d]	(nil procurement)
Paraguay[e]	(nil holdings)
Solomon Islands[f]	(nil procurement)

Table 2 Notes:

a. For calendar year 1992, Columbia reports imports of 257 armoured combat vehicles, 300 large calibre artillery systems, 68 combat aircraft, 74 attack helicopters, 38 warships, and 32 missiles and missile launchers. All these weapons were imported from countries (including Argentina, Brazil, France, Germany, Italy, Israel, Spain and the US) that made a detailed return of their 1992 exports for the Register. None of these countries reported any exports to Columbia in 1992. *United Nations Register of Conventional Arms: Report of the Secretary-General,* General Assembly document A/48/344, 11 October 1993, pp. 26-27.

b. In its reply to the request for information, Iceland states that "no arms are manufactured in Iceland, nor were any imported or exported, as Iceland is a non-militarized country". Ibid., p. 49.

c. In its reply to the request for information, Mauritius states that "the Republic of Mauritius does not have any armament industry, and is not a dealer in armaments". Ibid, p. 64.

d. Mexico's reply states that "The Department of National Defence did not acquire in 1992 any arms of the kind indicated in the categories defined by the United Nations. With regard to the Mexican Army and Air Force, all available war materiel is considered conventional and represents the minimum indispensable for the accomplishment of their missions". This could be interpreted as a 'nil return' for procurement through national production. No data is provided on military holdings. Ibid, p. 64.

e. The nil holdings report for Paraguay does not accord with data given in the annual Military Balance, published by the International Institute for Strategic Studies. The 1993/94 edition records Paraguay as having 5 main battle tanks, 63 ACV's, 21 high calibre artillery, a variety of small riverine combatants (possibly too small for the Register), and 19 combat aircraft. In its reply to the request for information, Paraguay states that "the Ministry of National Defence of Paraguay has reported that it does not possess the types of arms referred to in the relevant form". Ibid, p. 79.

f. In its reply to the request for information, Solomon Islands states that it "does not manufacture, buy sell or trade in conventional arms". Ibid, p. 98.

As a result, not all of the states providing information on procurement and/or holdings did so using the seven UN categories, and in some cases it is unclear whether or not these categories have been used. Our estimate is, that of the 24 countries providing data on procurement and holdings, only eight states appear to have provided data using all seven existing Register categories. These countries were Austria, Canada, Netherlands, Portugal, Spain, Turkey, the UK and the US. Germany is a special case, as its report of holdings of 40 missiles and missiles launchers explicitly excluded 'classified holdings' (which probably include the vast majority of German missile holdings).

There are a number of possible reasons why other countries did not use the existing Register categories:

•   First, a number of CSCE states (such as Belgium, Bulgaria, Denmark, Greece, Hungary, Italy, Poland and Sweden) seem to have found it more convenient, for the first five categories of systems, to summarise the data provided in December 1992 as part of the CFE and CSCE processes (see Table 3).

•   Second, a number of states that have used the first six Register categories to report holdings and/or procurement have not provided comparable data for the seventh category, missiles and missile launchers. Amongst the states not providing such data (in addition to Germany) were Australia, Brazil, Chile, Denmark, France, Hungary, Japan, New Zealand, Poland, and Sweden. However, both the US and the UK – which possess two of NATO's largest stockpiles of missiles – reported holdings of 43,975 and 23,892 respectively.

•   Third, the six non-CSCE states (Australia, New Zealand, Japan, Nicaragua, Brazil and Chile) provided procurement and holdings data in many different ways, most of which were very detailed but not easily comparable to the existing Register categories[5]. Of all the countries participating in the 1992 Register, Nicaragua has arguably provided the most detailed information. Brazil and Chile provided detailed information on holdings within most of the UN categories, but no data on holdings of missiles and missile launchers.

The lack of clear guidelines for submitting background information has clearly created some confusion, and may thus have deterred some countries from providing any data on procurement and holdings. Nevertheless the 'trial un' has been of value. The method chosen for the submission of available background information in the first year of the Register has raised a number

Table 3.   Categories used in reporting holdings

Country	Uses Register categories for ground and air systems	Uses CFE/CSCE categories for ground & air systems	Reports data on missiles & missile launchers	Reports details of models
Australia				•
Austria	•		• (nil)	•
Belgium		•	• (nil)	
Brazil	•			•
Bulgaria		•	• (86)[a]	
Canada	•		• (1629)	•
Chile	•			•
Denmark		•		
France	•			
Germany	•		• (40)[b]	
Greece		•	• (332)[c]	
Hungary		•		
Italy		•	• (944)	
Japan[d]				•
Netherlands	•		• (nil)	•
New Zealand				•
Nicaragua[e]				•
Poland	•			
Portugal	•		• (29)	
Spain	•		•(373)	
Sweden		•		•
Turkey	•		• (160)	
UK	•		• (23,892)	
US	•		• (43,975)	

Table 3. Notes:

a. Missile launchers only.

b. Germany reported holdings of 40 missiles and missile launchers, adding a footnote that this "does not include classified holdings".

c. Missiles only.

d. Japan includes a number of systems not included in the Register categories.

e. Nicaragua includes a number of systems not included in the Register categories. It also includes extensive data on military personnel and infrastructure.

of interesting issues which could have implications for the 1994 Group's deliberations:

• First, in an interesting innovation, in addition to a table providing data on Military Holdings and Procurement through National Production, Bulgaria provided a table on 'Military Holdings for Export'. Included in this table were 330 battle tanks, 554 large calibre artillery systems and 39 combat aircraft, all of which were presumably not counted in the table on Military Holdings.

• Second, a number of countries provided data on holdings but not on procurement. This may be because such data cannot so easily be derived from CFE or CSCE data, or because countries may have thought it unnecessary to provide nil returns. This may mean that some countries may find it no easier to agree to expand the Register to include data on procurement than on holdings.

• Third, it is noteworthy that ten countries included details of types and models in their procurement and holdings. These included all six non-CSCE states providing data (Australia, New Zealand, Japan, Chile, Brazil and Nicaragua), as well as Canada, Netherlands, Sweden, and Austria. A number of CSCE states that had provided data on models for the transfers Register – such as Germany, Greece and Turkey – did not do so for procurement and holdings.

• Fourth, some countries are clearly particularly reluctant to include data on holdings of missiles and missile launchers, extending even to relatively open states such as Germany. The US and UK have provided data on missile and missile launcher holdings, but only in a form that is difficult to interpret meaningfully because of the lack of information on missile types.

The problems and issues discussed in this section raise useful lessons for the future development of the Register, both in relation to the possible expansion of the Register to include standardised reporting of procurement from national production and military holdings and to the development of guidelines for background information. These issues are the subject of the following sections.

III   Reporting military holdings

The incentives for expanding the Register to include standardised reports of military holdings are well-known. Perhaps most importantly, transparency in military holdings is of most direct relevance for confidence-building measures and for the identification of destabilising accumulations of conventional arms. Moreover, in contrast to transfers and procurement, virtually all countries have significant military holdings so that their inclusion in the Register could extend its perceived relevance to all countries and regions.

Yet there should be no doubt that a decision to ask governments to provide details of their holdings of conventional arms, even if phased in over two or three years, would require considerable political commitment to make it work. For it would constitute a major advance in transparency which some of the world's more secretive states are likely to resist. The data publicly available on stocks of conventional weapons held by many major developing states is accurate only within rather wide margins of error. Even a massive Cold War intelligence effort by NATO came up with estimates for Soviet and East European conventional arsenals that proved – in the light of subsequent CFE declarations – to be not always very accurate. The lack of a comparable NATO intelligence effort vis-à-vis the armies of developing states means that official estimates for these states may in some cases be even sketchier. As a consequence, by revealing their stocks of aircraft and tanks, states might well be telling other states (and, perhaps of greatest concern, potential regional adversaries) facts that were not previously known. How important such data will be in military terms should not be overstated. Equipment numbers are only one component of military power. As the 'conventional balance' debate of the 1980s in Europe showed, however, numbers also have a political significance. States with large arsenals – even if composed largely of obsolete systems – may be reluctant to expose themselves to the propaganda value that returns on military holdings could provide to their critics.

Governments may decide that such transparency is in their security interests to reassure others that they have only 'reasonably sufficient' arsenals. A policy of secrecy in such matters does not stop others making estimates of force sizes. It may simply increase suspicions that countries have 'something to hide'. In the absence of official data, exaggerated unofficial data – often derived in turn from worst case intelligence estimates – carry wide credibility. But few countries will find it easy to break with traditions of military secrecy, and such traditions and sensitivities will need to be taken into account in order to sustain the wide consensus that is necessary in order to build on the Register's initial success.

Reporting requirements for military holdings

In order to ease both operation and interpretation, it will be important that the categories of systems used for holdings returns are compatible with those for transfers. Thus, if it is decided that governments should report their holdings of armoured combat vehicles, they should use the definition of such systems that is also being used for exports and imports. Yet this does not mean that military holdings data needs to be requested for every category subject to the transfers regime. For example:

a) Even amongst the minority of governments that provided military holdings data under 'background information', it is noticeable how few provided data on holdings of missiles and missile launchers. Insisting on the inclusion of missiles and missile launchers in a standardized form for military holdings may, therefore, deter some countries from making military holdings returns at all. In order to prevent this, one possibility might be to remove the category of missiles and missile launchers from the holdings standardised form.[6] Governments could, if they wished, provide information on their holdings of missiles and missile launchers in 'background information'. But there would be less pressure on governments to provide such data than if it were part of the standardised form; and any data that was provided could (like all 'background information') be in a form of the country's own choosing.

The alternative approach would be for the standardized forms for military holdings to include all of the categories covered in the transfers and procurement registers, with an understanding that some countries may choose not to provide information on missile holdings. This would have the advantage of encouraging consistent reporting of holdings in the full range of categories, but would be at the risk of encouraging a perception that countries may legitimately pick and choose which categories of weaponry included in the standardised forms they will report.

b) The status of the remarks column in the standardized form for reporting transfers is also the subject of discussion by the Group of Experts. Whatever proposal is made in this regard for transfers, however, need not necessarily apply to military holdings. A number of governments that provided types data for transfers in 1993 did not do so for their military holdings in their 'background information'. It would be possible to apply a similar system of differential transparency in the design of new standardised forms for transfers and military holdings.

Defining 'military holdings'

If military holdings are to be included in the Register on a standardized basis, it will be necessary to define what is included in this term. This is by no means a straightforward issue. We have already touched on the issue of the definition of the categories of weapons that might be included, and we discuss this in more detail in Chapter 4. Moreover, it is clear from the 1992 Panel's discussion of the definition of transfers that military holdings should exclude systems held by other states on one's own territory but include systems held outside national territory by one's own forces.[7] The remaining definitional issues can broadly be divided into two:

First, should the holdings of armed forces other than regular military forces be included in 'military holdings'? For example, should the Register cover the holdings of paramilitary, coastguard, reserve and/or internal security forces?

Second, should the holdings of bodies other than armed forces be included in 'military holdings'? For example, should the Register cover systems in transit, held by factories, held in historical collections, or awaiting disposal?

Holdings of armed forces other than regular military forces

Not all the armed forces under government control are regular military forces. In the first place, there are reserve forces that operate on reduced manning levels in peacetime, and whose equipment is often kept in various forms of storage ready for mobilisation. It would be possible to confine Register transparency simply to 'active' forces (say of 70% manning or above), on the argument that these forces are particularly suitable for short-warning surprise attack. Quite apart from the difficulties in deciding on a common position on which forces should be considered 'active', however, such an arrangement would ignore the fact that reserve forces play a vital role in many countries' preparations for combat, both defensive and offensive. Moreover, since countries vary greatly in their active/reserve balance, the exclusion of the latter could severely distort comparisons between states. The case for including the holdings of both active and reserve forces, therefore, seems rather clear-cut.

Matters may be rather more difficult when one comes to forces whose role is not primarily military, but who are nevertheless armed. Many governments have border troops, coastguard troops and internal security forces which can possess significant numbers of such systems and which could, in some circumstances, be redeployed for military duties. For example, Russia's 100,000 border troops are reported to possess 1500 armoured combat vehicles, 90 heavy artillery pieces, 70 aircraft, 200 helicopters and 'about' 212 patrol and coastal combatants. Russian internal security troops hold another 1200 armoured personnel carriers.[8] All these systems, if they are located within the CFE area, are subject to information exchange.[9]

Because these forces could be transferred rather easily to an external security role, there seems a strong case for including these too in the definition of 'military holdings'. For if the holdings of these forces were not included in 'military holdings', questions would also have to be raised about the holdings of those regular forces which are used for both internal and external roles. If Russian internal security forces were excluded from Register-reported holdings, the UK could argue that the holdings of its armoured and infantry units based in Northern Ireland should also be excluded since their role – arguably their primary role – is also an internal one. The eventual result would be confusing and confidence-reducing. Since the Register is not a control device, it does not seek to limit governments' decisions on the provision they make for internal security. Because equipment can be shifted from one role to another, however, all items in the Register categories that are in the possession of government armed forces – whether military or paramilitary – should be included in total 'military holdings'. This would include general reserve stocks of weapons held by the armed forces, even if they were not allocated to specific units.

Holdings of bodies other than armed forces

Some weapons, however, are not in the possession of armed forces. The 1992 Panel specified in particular the following as requiring consideration:

> 'equipment in storage or mothballed, awaiting decommissioning or in transit.....in the process of manufacture or manufacture-related testing, used exclusively for research and development or belonging to historical collections.'[10]

In reaching a decision on this matter, it may be useful to take the experience of CFE into account. CFE deals with these different categories as follows:

a) Equipment in storage or mothballed is subject to the overall treaty limits, but exempt from the sub-limits on items in active units.

b) Equipment decommissioned awaiting disposal, awaiting export, or used only for R&D is subject to information exchange but not subject to the overall treaty limits.

c) Equipment in the process of manufacture, in historical collections, or in transit through the CFE area for less than seven days is not subject to either information exchange or limitation.

Were the Register to be based on similar principles, only equipment in c) would be excluded from the count. The greatest impact of this would probably be on items held by arms manufacturers. It would mean that items still in the process of manufacture were excluded. Once completed, however, they would be included even before they were handed over to a client. By providing 'background information' on its holdings of weapons awaiting export, Bulgaria has already demonstrated how such a system could have a significant impact on the number of weapons declared. In seeking to establish a clear definition of military holdings, the Group of Experts will have to consider whether or not this should become a general principle.

The argument in favour of including stocks held awaiting sale or transfer abroad (or awaiting destruction) is that it would close what might otherwise be seen as a loophole in the reporting system. Weapons 'awaiting export' include not only weapons newly produced for sale. It also (as in Bulgaria's case) includes weapons surplus to national requirements that are intended for sale ('second-hand') to foreign customers. On the other hand, if weapons for export were not included, it would increase the possibility that states could follow Bulgaria's example and declare a significant part of its weapons stocks (perhaps most of those in storage) 'ready for export', even if no buyer has yet been identified and the weapons remain available for use in a future conflict. Whether or not governments would in practice take advantage of such a loophole is difficult to predict in advance. But the suspicion that they might do so, and on a scale comparable to that employed openly by Bulgaria, would be likely in any case to undermine the credibility of the Register as an accurate reflection of the number of weapons available to participant states.

Yet if weapons awaiting sale or transfer abroad are included in holdings, every weapon newly produced for a foreign customer by a private company would be included in the holdings of the exporting state from the date of production to the date of transfer. The additional monitoring burdens on the governments concerned might not be too great, since transfer data on the same systems is already being collected. It could, however, add an element of double-counting to the system. The Group may have to consider whether it is worth this price in order to ensure that as high a proportion of systems are covered as is possible. Whatever decision is made will, however, have to be consistent with the definition adopted for 'procurement from national production'.

Systems in the remaining 'grey areas' – in transit or in museums – are unlikely to account for more than a fraction of total holdings, and the potential for evasion accordingly appears limited. In some ways it may be most unambiguous if all such systems were included in the definition of military holdings. However, there are countervailing arguments in favour of adopting the same appraoch as in the CFE treaty (which would exclude equipment in historical collections or in transit through a country for less than seven days). As long as a clear decision is taken as to whether or not to include these systems, it probably does not matter greatly which way the decision goes.

Implementation requirements

One of the main problems that will be encountered if military holdings are added to the Register is that it will generate a demand for large quantities of information that, in many cases, may not be easily available. Given the average lifetime of equipment, the number of items in military holdings could be 30-40 times as great as those bought (domestically and from elsewhere) in a given year. This information has already been compiled and provided by NATO states, and could also be provided by other CSCE participants from existing CSCE information exchange arrangements (with some amendment). Yet some countries may find they have substantial extra data collection requirements. States do not always retain accurate records for stocks of older weapons, especially if weapons are in storage and/or mothballed. However, most states should aspire to maintaining accurate records. Moreover, once states have established a baseline inventory, collection costs would diminish substantially in subsequent years. At least in the first years, however, allowance will have to be made for technical difficulties and genuine error in the compilation of information.

IV   Reporting procurement from national production

In considering an expansion of the Register, some may argue the case for differentiating military holdings from procurement through national production. Both should be included in a future development if possible, but the speed and detail of their inclusion could differ. Crucially, problems in including holdings should not be used as a reason for slowing the inclusion of procurement.

The inclusion of procurement from national production in the Register raises policy, resource and technical issues that are distinct in many ways from those raised by the inclusion of military holdings. First, the data collection requirements are relatively modest. Information is more likely to be centrally available than that for transfers (because the latter often only involve the government at the licensing stage). Moreover, the volume of procurement through national production is typically likely to be of the same order as, or less than, that of transfers. (In the U.S. and U.K., according to their 1992 background information, the total number of combat aircraft procured domestically in 1992 were 183 and 20 respectively, compared with exports of 165 and 19.)[11] In contrast, reports of military holdings will typically cover larger numbers and a greater variety of equipment.

Second, inclusion of procurement from national production will oblige states with a substantial domestic arms industry to reveal the same proportion of their total procurement as do importing states. Indeed this is the very reason why importing states have emphasised the discriminatory nature of a transfers-only Register. For this very reason, some countries that are substantial arms producers may have particular reservations about the extension of the present transfers register to include procurement from national production. They may be reluctant to increase the transparency of their procurement activities to match that of participating arms importers. The same issues do not arise for military holdings.

Finally, there are strong arguments in favour of including data on exactly the same categories of equipment (at the same levels of detail) for procurement from national production as for transfers. A key motivation for extending the Register to include procurement from national production is to develop the Register so that it covers all sources of major conventional arms. Thus data from transfers and procurement from national production is complementary. In combination they should provide reasonably complete information on national procurement and changes in countries' military holdings. There is less need for information on military holdings to be in the same form as for transfers, and (as discussed in the previous section) there may be scope for requiring different (or at least less detailed) reports on holdings.

Defining 'procurement from national production'

There are two broad approaches to extending the Register to include 'procurement through national production'. The first is to include systems only when their ownership has been transferred to government armed forces (as defined above). The second is to include systems at the point that their manufacture has been completed, even if title has not been transferred to the government. If reporting of procurement from national production is introduced simultaneously with that for military holdings, it will be important that the definitions used are compatible with each other. Even if reporting for military holdings is delayed, however, the definition of procurement from national production will have to bear in mind the implications for a later expansion.

In the first approach, definitions and reporting requirements would be designed to ensure that all procurement by government armed forces of the systems covered by the Register should be included in either imports or procurement through national production. In order to be consistent with the definition of transfers, and given the difficulty involved in defining it in terms of change of location (e.g., from shipyard to naval base, or from factory to airfield), procurement through national production would be defined in terms of 'the transfer of title to and control over the equipment'. It therefore follows that systems produced by a factory, but remaining in the ownership of the company, are not 'procured'. This means that, taking this approach, the Register would not have to include weapons produced and awaiting export, or weapons being used for R&D purposes. This leaves some possibility for distortion if state-controlled arms firms hold large stocks of completed systems. This would be inescapable within this approach.

Under this approach, therefore, a definition of procurement through national production might be as follows:

> "procurement through national production takes place when a system in one of the categories of equipment is added to the military holdings of a Member State. When the system has been transferred from another country in the form of a system defined in one of the defined categories, it is an import. Otherwise, procurement is defined as procurement through national production."

This would imply that the crucial point to determine is whether or not a system exists in terms of the defined categories is when a transfer of ownership takes place (whether that transfer be international or firm to state). Egyptian assembly of an M1 tank, therefore, is national production, and becomes procurement through national production when it is transferred to army ownership. Egyptian upgrade of a T-72 tank it already owns is not counted.

It also implies that the creation of a system in one of the defined categories through the import of an extra component – such as a missile launcher for a ship or aircraft – should count as procurement through national production even if no national 'production' has taken place except bolting an imported launcher onto an imported aircraft. This is still assembly work, and thus qualifies. It needs to be included in order to avoid the exclusion of significant parts of the arms trade.

By contrast, the second approach would (as in CFE data exchange requirements for holdings) include all systems awaiting export or destruction, or those being used for R&D purposes. The problem with this more all-inclusive definition is that it may be judged to include too much.

The thrust of this second approach is that, as far as possible, all national production of relevant categories of military equipment should be covered by the Register, irrespective of whether the state has formally taken control of it. It aims to avoid the risk that loopholes in the coverage of the Register will be created. For example, by avoiding defining reporting requirements in terms of formal transfer of title or control, it helps to reduce the possibility of debate as to whether the 'armed forces' of a state have actually taken control or title of arms produced on its territory. In practice, most governments can take control over any major equipment on their territory in private hands if they need to do so, and such equipment should therefore be considered as part of the military resources of the governments in question, even if equipment is stored by arms companies or other non-governmental bodies. Moreover, since transfers of control or title are harder to monitor than the existence of equipment, this approach could, in the longer term, facilitate independent verification of states' reports on national production.

This second approach would also be consistent with the current guidelines on transfers, where states are generally expected to report imports into their territory, irrespective of whether or not they are due to enter into service with its own armed forces. An initial attempt to define procurement from national production using this second approach could be as follows:

> "procurement from national production takes place when a system in one of the categories in the Register is produced within the territorial jurisdiction of a state"

For the purposes of this definition, production would be defined as:

> "any process by which components, systems and equipment items are changed in such a way as to create an item covered by the Register where an item in that same category did not exist before"

This second approach would create an overlap with the data reported in the exports section. Indeed all exports from national production – that is, most exports – would have to be reported twice (unless some sort of extended 'transit' provision was invoked). As in the case of military holdings, however, the case for this approach would be that the modest cost associated with such double-counting is more than offset by the assurance that all production is covered.

A withdrawals section in the Register?

Our discussion of the choices involved in defining procurement from national production and military holdings, however, raises the further question of how to define at what stage a system ceases to be part of military holdings. Systems are taken out of holdings because of accident or war, because of scrapping obsolescent systems, and because of sale to other states. Others are temporarily withdrawn from service when they are returned to a factory or dockyard for refit or upgrading. For the sake of completeness, it appears we may also need a definition of 'withdrawal from holdings'. Such a definition should probably exclude 'temporary' withdrawal of systems from service for refit/upgrading even when systems are temporarily disabled or disarmed (for example refits for frigates). But it should include 'permanent' withdrawal from service, even if the system retains a military role (for example, using tanks for permanently static defence positions, permanently removing missile launchers from patrol boats).

Thus, there is a case for considering whether to include 'withdrawals' in the Register. It may somewhat complicate the data required. The arguments for such a system are, however, quite strong:

a) If and when returns on military holdings are included, it will in any case be possible to deduce a figure for withdrawals from the change in holdings between two years, combined with procurement data for the year in question. Requiring an explicit statement on withdrawals, however, will act as a valuable cross-check (both within governments and publicly) on the consistency of returns.

b) The numbers involved are relatively modest compared with those in Holdings. Data collection may be correspondingly easier.

c) Security concerns would be less than with Holdings. No explanation would have to be given as to the nature or cause of any withdrawal.

d) It may create a modest additional incentive for states to scrap older systems. Some states could present themselves as actually reducing their arsenals even before declaring their holdings.

e) Even before full Holdings returns are made, it will help an assessment of the extent to which countries' procurement programmes are for replacement or for additional weapons. It would still be necessary to report new procurement separately. But the extra data requirement might appeal to those states (such as China) who claim that increased new procurement is dictated by replacement cycles.

If the case for including withdrawals data in the Register were accepted, the first step might be to ask governments to consider supplying this data as part of their 'background information'. After an initial trial period, however, the data could either be used to create a new standardized form or incorporated into those that already exist for transfers and procurement from national production.

V   Developing the 'Background Information' provided on military holdings and procurement from national production

Participating states are presently asked to provide 'available background information' relating to their military holdings, procurement through national production and relevant arms import and export policies. If the Register is expanded to include military holdings and procurement from national production, this guidance will need to be reconsidered. In any case, there may be ways in which the guidelines for background information may usefully be developed. If the Group of Experts were unable to agree to recommend that the Register be expanded to cover military holdings or national production at this stage of its development, it would want to prepare for such an extension in the future. In this case, they may wish to consider ways in which to make the existing 'background information' system more useful, without making the provision of such information any less 'voluntary' than it is at present.

The most obvious measure to facilitate the effective use of any background information that is provided would be to publish it, perhaps as an appendix to the main annual report on transfers. This would be an unwieldy exercise if all background information were included, because 'background information' currently includes details of arms export regulations, copies of defence white papers and any other documentation that governments decide to provide. But if it included only information on military holdings or domestic production, or (potentially) withdrawals from military holdings, it could be carried out without great additional cost. If this was done, the information would be more widely available, and any potential it had to contribute to confidence-building or international security (or to domestic policy making) would be more likely to be realised by governments, parliamentarians, and non-governmental organisations.

As we have discussed in Chapter 4, there is a case for developing formal procedures to review reports on transfers submitted for the Register, to promote comparability and reliability of the data, or to identify potentially destabilising trends in arms transfers or opportunities for confidence-building. If such review procedures are established, background information could also be taken into account in the review process.

If it proved impossible to achieve agreement in 1994 to expand the Register, it might nevertheless be possible to develop clearer guidelines about the form in which 'background information' on military holdings and national production is submitted. The logical conclusion of one approach to this task would be to develop a standardized form for reporting on holdings or national production. Provided that such forms were appropriately conceived and constructed, they could greatly improve the consistency, comparability and interpretability of submitted data. The difference between this approach and the formal extension of the Register to cover military holdings and procurement from national production would be that submission of such data would remain 'voluntary', and countries would have much more discretion in whether or how they provided it.

This approach could be superficially attractive as a compromise between one group of countries that want to develop standardized reporting procedures to cover procurement from national production and/or military holdings and another group who are opposed to providing such information. However, in addressing this short term need, it could risk undermining the long term development of the Register by creating two tiers of participation. Thus it may not be wise to develop agreed standardized forms for reporting background information, although particular groups of countries could of course informally agree to harmonise their reporting practices if they wanted. If (as we hope) standardized forms are developed for reporting procurement from national production and military holdings, the information should not be classified as 'background'.

However, in this context, there may be ways in which minimal guidelines for presenting background information could usefully be developed without undue risk to the Register's main transparency arrangements. For example, countries could be asked always to clarify the definitions they have used and categories of equipment covered in background information, and the period for which the data applies (which year etc). Thus, background information on procurement from national production or military holdings should, for example, clarify whether the categories of equipment used are the same as for the main part of the Register and, if not, to clarify what categories are being used.

If the Register is extended to include reporting on standardized forms on procurement from national production and military holdings, government should still be encouraged to submit supplementary information relevant to these, in order to help appropriate interpretation. For example, such information could relate to force structures, policies relating to military posture and arms production, and also (as suggested in section IV) withdrawals from military holdings.

Moreover, there may be scope to develop the usefulness of background information in other ways. For example, governments could be asked routinely to provide the UN with a copy of all publicly available official documents containing quantitative information on transfers, holdings, and procurement from national production, including defense white papers, public statements, reports to parliaments and relevant official documents deposited in parliamentary or other libraries. At present there is no central repository of such information. Frequently government officials find it hard even to find out what has been publicly released by their own governments, let alone by others. If such information were organised and made available for consultation at a known location, it could not only increase transparency but also encourage governments, non-governmental organisations, and analysts to take more account of government information. Moreover, if governments systematically deposited details of their legislation, regulations and systems of export controls and management of the military sector, the depository of information could facilitate the adoption of best practices and the development of effective international cooperation in these areas.

Thus, if the Register is expanded to include procurement from national production and military holdings, participating states could be encouraged to provide background information on:

- relevant national arms import and export policies, legislation and administrative procedures;
- relevant policies relating to arms production and procurement;
- relevant information relating to military holdings, force structures, and defence and security policies;
- available information on withdrawals from military holdings (specifying definitions used, where appropriate);
- other available quantitative or factual information on holdings, procurement from national production or transfers.

If the Register is not expanded to cover procurement from national production and military holdings, states should continue to be asked to provide background information on these, accompanied with explanations of what definitions and categories are being used.

VI   Conclusion

The 1994 Group of UN Experts will have to make some difficult choices on the expansion of the Register to include military holdings and procurement from national production. The arguments in favour of such an expansion are strong, but the problems involved are considerable and this chapter does not pretend to have provided a solution. Rather we have aimed to clarify the main alternative options for expansion that appear to be available, and to discuss some of the technical issues (for example on the definition of terms) that these might involve.

Notes

1. This section draws substantially from Malcolm Chalmers and Owen Greene, *Background Information: an analysis of information provided to the UN on military holdings and procurement through national production in the first year of the Register of Conventional Arms,* Bradford Arms Register Studies No 3, Bradford University, March 1994.

2. *Report on the Register of Conventional Arms: Report of the Secretary-General,* UN General Assembly Document A/47/342, 14 August 1992, para. 33, endorsed by General Assembly resolution 47/52 L of 15 December 1992.

3. Malcolm Chalmers and Owen Greene, *Background Information,* op. cit.

4. *Report of the Secretary-General,* op. cit., para. 21.

5. See Malcolm Chalmers and Owen Greene, op. cit.

6. In Chapter 4 of the book we suggest the possibility of splitting Category VII into two. If this were done, it might be decided to include missile launchers, but not missiles, in returns for military holdings.

7. *Report on the Register of Conventional Arms: Report of the Secretary-General,* op. cit., p. 10.

8. International Institute for Strategic Studies, *The Military Balance 1993/94,* Brassey's, London, 1993, p. 106.

9. Paramilitary forces are, however, treated slightly differently from military forces in CFE. All holdings of treaty-limited items by paramilitary forces are subject to information exchange. While holdings of several additional items of equipment held in ground, air, and air defence units (combat support helicopters, unarmed transport helicopters, primary trainer aircraft, re-categorised trainer aircraft, AIFV and APC look-alikes) are also subject to information exchange, this *proviso* does not apply to holdings of these systems with paramilitary units.

Notes continued

10. *Report on the Register of Conventional Arms: Report of the Secretary-General,* op. cit., p. 18.

11. Malcolm Chalmers and Owen Greene, *Background Information,* op. cit., pp. 68-70.

CHAPTER 10

Transparency in arms procurement policies and processes

Ravinder Pal Singh

I   Introduction

This chapter aims to map some of the conceptual issues relating to transparency in arms procurement in keeping with the larger objectives and the principles espoused in the UN General Assembly Resolution 46/36 L leading to the establishment of the UN Register of Conventional Arms. It identifies some of the barriers and impediments in developing transparency in arms procurement policies. The chapter also examines the possibilities of augmenting national initiatives supportive of transparency in arms procurement policy making and related processes.

The chapter makes a number of assumptions. Firstly, internally induced transparency has better sustainability in developing arms procurement restraints than externally generated advice. Secondly, as decisions driven exclusively by the needs of military security are more typically concerned with state building and elite control than with the broader priorities of society, lack of transparency and public accountability could adversely affect national, regional and global security equilibrium. Thirdly, public accountability generated through transparency contributes towards harmonising broader objectives of national security, leads to efficiencies in policy making and reduces influences of extra-constitutional interests. In this sense, if public accountability could be deemed as a public good that the governments should be obliged to deliver to their peoples, then the process would add to the objectives of good governance.

II   Analyses of the objectives of transparency

A survey of available literature debating the concerns with lack of transparency in arms procurement actions engaging the UN Arms Register indicates three general clusters of priorities. While the UN General Assembly Resolution 46/36 L is explicit in stating the need to prevent excessive accumulation of destabilising weapon systems, one also finds equally valid arguments for the need to balance the armament programmes with requirements of national economic development.[1] Another set of commentators appear to promote the need for transparency in national arms procurement as an end in itself. A third stream of opinion appears to be more critical of the limited expectations and cautious demands that are being made for transparency. There is also a likelihood of yet another strand of opinion emerging in the future that would be critical of transparency being developed at a pace faster than their systems can absorb.

At the outset, there is a need to restate that amongst the objectives of the UN Register aiming at transparency in arms procurement, a major objective is to encourage restraint and help to prevent excessive or destabilising accumulations of weapon systems. Reiteration of objectives is considered to be essential to reduce possible misinterpretations due to different priorities of interlocutors engaged in developing the UN Arms Register. There is a possibility that transparency may become perceived as the ultimate objective of the exercise, transparency in arms procurement is only an instrument to achieve the broader objective outlined above.

III   The processes of arms procurement

The objectives of the UN Arms Register were inspired by well founded principles: maintenance of international peace and security; the inherent right of self defence; reasonable defence sufficiency for preservation of regional peace, security and stability; undiminished security for all states at the lowest possible level of armaments; and finally, the need to exercise due restraint in arms transfers based on legitimate requirements to meet the security needs of the member states.

These worthy principles have identified a key objective of the Register as serving the need of preventing excessive accumulation of destabilising weapon systems. While criteria for identifying destabilising systems have been developed, the term 'excessive accumulation' still defies acceptable operational definition. Since this objective is defined in the context of terms like reasonable defence sufficiency and legitimate security requirements, the UN Arms Register would also need to develop acceptable definitions of such terms based on the interpretations of different regions and political cultures. To begin with we need to examine the structure of the arms procurement process as it relates to the demands of transparency.

Figure 1.   Arms procurement processes and transparency

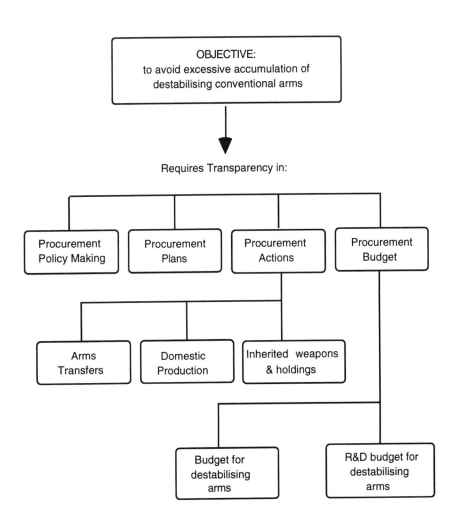

In the context of the model of the components and processes of arms procurement as they relate to transparency described in Figure 1, the UN Arms Register has engaged the transparency problem only within the domain of arms procurement actions. This chapter attempts to present a broader overview of the challenges and issues relating to arms procurement transparency by addressing the following questions:

A. What kinds of problems are involved in promoting transparency in national arms procurement policies and what is the relative influence of the competing interests?

B. What is known of national arms procurement policies and what more should be known to promote or maintain adequate levels of stability?

C. What measures could be used to promote transparency in arms procurements?

IV   Some problem areas in promoting transparency in national arms procurement policies

A major factor that influences the arms procurement process is the regional and national security environment. The industrialised world appears to have come out of the cycle of war, in the sense that there is a wide realisation that possible losses in war could far outweigh the probable gains through conflict. This realisation has led towards developing pluralistic security concepts that are possible in an benign security environment. In contrast, much of the developing world is in the process of emerging from the post-colonisation experience wherein resort to conflict is perceived as a means to redress their notion of deprivation. The end of the cold war has not substantially altered the security environment in different regions of the South. The spectrum of threats in these parts of the world range from potential hostility to situations demanding high states of military mobilisation. In an unstable security environment, the opponents of transparency are naturally more assertive and influential than its supporters. There is a need to design unique strategies to reinforce the influence of supporters of transparency while, at the same time, reduce the effects of its opponents.

Another obstacle to transparency in the arms procurement process is the inherent conflict with the requirements of military technology development. As the demand to monitor transfer of technology and domestic arms production gains momentum, it comes into conflict with interests of weapons-producing states to maintain confidentiality in developing their military-technological competitiveness. This issue might prove to be a major stumbling block in designing broader conventional arms control initiatives.

In most countries, security issues probably still remain more important to the interests of state building than economic questions. These priorities are relatively dominant in the case of developing states, particularly in unstable regions. But as societies develop economically and industrially, economic interests begin to compete with security concerns for public attention. Economic development brings about an accretion in public confidence in the state's policies and decision making structures, which in turn contributes to an increased information flow in the society. As the information environment enhances the element of transparency in public policy making, it gradually broadens its domain to include even the national security issues.

Transparency in state behaviour and public accountability are found to be mutually reinforcing. This relationship in turn may enhance efficiency in government decision making structures as it encourages a more interactive form of administration. Economies of countries that are significantly influenced by their government policies thus find a positive contribution to their development. The relationship between transparency and development also explains the observation that industrialised and developed societies tend to have higher levels of transparency in public policies, including security issues, than others. The relationship of transparency and development is described diagramatically below:

Figure 2. The potential relationship between transparency and national development

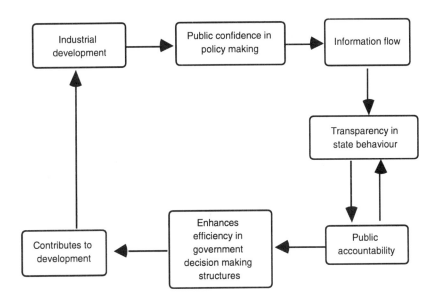

Amongst the major impediments to transparency in arms procurement could be the prevailing political attitudes and culture of the state and the society. In order to get a broader understanding of the behaviour of different political and public actors in their responses to the requirements of transparency, four different constellations of state and public responses are identified as they affect arms procurement policy relations. These constellations of behaviour have not been derived from any empirical study, but can form the basis of such an examination to understand the character, the diverse nature, and relative influence of competing or cooperating interests that impinge upon the arms procurement processes. The design could help in understanding the factional behaviour and the responses of the state and intra state actors to arms procurement policy issues.

For example, the model could be explored in relation to four clusters of political constitutions, namely:

i) states that are governed by the military or military supported elite, totalitarian systems or monarchies that do not have strong democratic processes;

ii) oligarchies with high degree of centralisation;

iii) relatively less centralised structures moving towards democratic administration;

iv) relatively open and democratic structures attempting to develop a more accountable governance.

It is very difficult to capture various shades of political control, as much as it is incorrect to assume that the behaviour of various actors in each of these four constellations would mirror national political constitutions. But to a general extent, these four constellations could reflect broader national attitudes and perspectives related to impediments in transparency.

Table 1 illustrates one of the clusters of possible characteristics of political systems and the behaviour of different social actors, as a basis for further research.

Table 1.   Attitudes of 'cluster (i)' states towards tranparency

• Type of political constitution	– military or military supported governments, authoritarian governments or monarchies which do not have strong democratic processes.
• Organisational behaviour of the decision making structures	– arbitrary, respond to factional interests and reflect inadequate concerns with constitutionality of decisions.
• Legislative oversight and influence	– non existent.
• Relative influence of the military	– political control is exercised through active military support.
• Public accountability of the bureaucracy	– when engaged in politico-security issues: -- public interests are least harmonized with security interests, officials are not accessible to public nor interactive with other government channels; – when engaged in developmental issues: -- limited accessibility.
• Influence of the media in security issues	– avoids objective discussion.
• Structure of military-scientific community	– state sponsored.
• Information flow within arms procurement decision making process	– highly controlled.
• Legal restrictions on debating country's arms procurement policies and issues	– high level of restrictions.
• Levels of public interest	– low.
• Level of arms control expertise to engage the state policies in public debates	– inadequate to perhaps non-existent.

Table 2 illustrates a cluster of possible characteristics of another type of political culture, to indicate the variations and contrasts between the two attitudes towards transparency.

Table 2.   Attitudes of 'Cluster (iv)' states towards transparency

• Type of political constitution	– governments with strong democratic processes;
• Organisational behaviour of the decision making structures	– relatively transparent, equally responsive to broader national interests as they compete with factional or political interests. Noticeable concern with constitutionality of decisions;
• Legislative oversight and influence	– existent and may also be competing for influence with the government;
• Relative influence of the military	– political control does not need military support. The military could be influential should there be strong internationalist interests in national decision making.

• Public accountability of the bureaucracy	– when engaged in politico-security issues:
	  - larger dimensions of public interests are attempted to be harmonized with security interests. Officials are accessible to public and are sufficiently interactive with other government channels.
	– when engaged in developmental issues:
	  - high levels of accessibility.

Influence of the media in security issues	– actively engaged in objective discussion.
• Structure of military-scientific community	– could be in the private sector as well as state supported.
• Information flow within arms procurement decision making process	– developed and in adequate detail.
• Legal restrictions on debating country's arms procurement policies and issues	– constitutional provisions may be available to reduce the negative effects of restrictions.
• Levels of public interest	– high level of awareness.
• Level of arms control expertise to engage the state policies in public debates	– adequately available in terms of quality and range of perspectives.

The descriptions in Tables 1 and 2 are of two typical constellations of behaviour towards transparency in arms procurement. In a similar manner, behaviour of other clusters in different types of political constitution could also be studied. As one examines the barriers in developing transparency in national arms procurement processes, one should also look at possible characteristics which could be supportive of transparency. Such an examination will find a range of actors arrayed with somewhat opposing interests with different levels of influence on transparency in national arms procurement policy making. These groups are neither static nor strictly defined. The components of these interests could be varied in different countries as also their relative influence and cohesiveness. These actors arranged in different interest groups could have conflicting views on transparency and perhaps have a different set of motives for belonging to a specific category, either as the proponents or opponents of transparency.

V   Proponents of transparency

In an environment of positive national growth, development and stability, a liberal perspective is also found to be engaged in the national security issues. Even in relatively less developed countries, one finds such liberal perspective amongst the officials engaged in socio-economic policy making and financial planning; the media and public interest groups; amongst the academia and constitutional experts. Even the government auditors, as a group, could be counted as interested in supporting transparency as far as their official functions are concerned. Amongst the experts specialising in security issues, there could be a diverse range of opinion, but most of them would be interested in accessing information. And to a limited extent, one might find them supportive of transparency. It has also been observed that legislators and politicians, as a group, particularly those in the opposition, would be supportive of transparency until they come to power. In other words, it is the question of public accountability that decides on which side of transparency one's interests are found.

VI   Opponents of transparency

Taking the argument that transparency brings accountability in its train, the interests ranged against transparency often include the politicians in power; the defence and foreign affairs officials engaged in security policy making and planning levels. While the military, in general, is suspicious of the idea of public accountability, it perhaps opposes transparency due to the very nature of responsibilities of the military systems. The consequences of military failure being perceived as either catastrophic or horrendous, the military tends to professionalize caution more than creativity. From the typical military perspective, the nuance-laden value additions to security through regional confidence building that are assumed to be generated by transparency are rather distant and uncertain possibilities, better left to diplomats. Military acculturation is given to dealing with more tangible assets and liabilities. Knowing that it is the nation's last resort in case of a diplomatic failure, the military's resistance to transparency is often concerned with possible dilution in its effectiveness. The scientists in the defence laboratories or the industry engaged in defence contracts also find military security a handy justification to avoid public scrutiny and accountability. The bureaucrats engaged in negotiating such issues, on the other hand, take a even more cautious position as they are not too sure of what kind of package they would be able to sell to their governments back home. As they are more adept at fine tuning their negotiating skills for gaining miles at the costs of not giving more than a foot, in the process, international negotiations on such issues get mired in a progress that grows at the rate of inches. It may well be worth considering whether restructuring the cast and fora of negotiations would help in furthering the aims of transparency?

Convergence of interests of such like-minded groups, either for protecting or enlarging their 'turf', contributes more readily to a conservative opinion on security issues. How far such opinions are representative of larger national interests of the society is indicated by the quality and content of the domestic public debate on security issues in different countries. Scientists investigating organizational behaviour identify such resistance to change as symptoms of groupthink engaged in protection from dissonant information *or opinion* (author's italics), intolerance to deviant opinions, resistance to adoption of new policy and collective attempts at rationalization.[2]

Any analyses of an expansion of transparency in arms procurement would need to examine the influence of the competing interests described above. As these interests address the transparency problem at its grass roots in their respective countries, and if transparency initiatives in arms procurements have to be made self-sustaining, one would need to understand the behaviour of these actors at national level and address the concerns of these interests at regional levels. The chapter goes on to examine what aspects of arms procurements are already in the public domain and what additional aspects should be made transparent in the arms procurement processes.

VII What is known of national arms procurement policies and what more should be known to promote or maintain adequate levels of stability?

The reports on arms procurement policies and processes that are currently in the public domain primarily relate to the developed and industrialised countries. In some developing countries, there could be semi-official publications, and the media are sometimes sufficiently active in generating a public interest in specific procurement actions. The quality of analyses and detail in such cases range from perfunctory to inconsistent. More detailed descriptions on procurement issues are confined to military journals which may not be classified but do not have wide circulation.

At the extreme end of the transparency spectrum are the countries that are being controlled either by authoritarian structures or monarchies in which even the military may not be aware of the procurement plans of the organisations that provide security to the ruling elite and perhaps vice versa. Arms procurement issues in most of the countries neither generate sufficient commercial interest nor political capital, and are therefore not amongst the major concerns of the public. The level of public awareness of security policy making and professional capacities to sustain the public debate consequently ranges from inadequate to indifferent.

In any case, it is not advisable to develop a list of security related actions that can be brought into public domain, as there would be variations between countries as well as between different regions. But a harmonised understanding of acceptable levels of transparency that recognises the legitimate requirements of confidentiality in security issues should be possible to incorporate in a regional security forum. The perceptions of acceptable levels of transparency in different states also vary in accordance with their political culture, constitution and historical experience. The political responses of different societies to the demands of transparency also need to be viewed from the perspective of different civilisations as a system making different political ethos. As security issues tend to arouse a strong sense of vulnerabilities, it is therefore prudent to invest time and effort to develop regional security fora which will be more sensitive to peculiar cultural and political dynamics of the region. Such fora would also build capacities to develop a better understanding of different national security concerns.

In each of the four components of the arms procurement process identified above, that is policy making, planning, actions and budgeting (see Figure 1), there is a need to identify appropriate levels of transparency and related indicators that would be required for alerting the international community to the possible emergence of regional security disequilibrium or instability. Transparency by itself will not serve the objectives of the UN General Assembly Resolution. An entire range of strategic indicators and response mechanisms have to be designed to operate in conjunction with the transparency initiatives of the UN Arms Register in order to stimulate effective international responses.

In the case of procurement policy making, there is a potential for greater transparency which could include issuance of the government white chapters on long term threat assessments, military potential desired, and arms procurement policies. In addition to the defence policies that the governments have been asked to provide the UN, at a minimum official documents should be published relating to arms and technology export regulations and guidelines; arms import and export policies and procedures and guidelines; guidelines and procedures for legislative oversight; and any periodical or extra-ordinary parliamentary reviews of arms procurement decision making procedures.

As regional dialogue is broadened, governmental policy makers could also explain their strategic assessments and financial planning of defence budgets. At national level the procurement policies and processes would balance the military's demands for accretions in its capabilities with that of the larger national priorities including the socio-economic agenda. Such initiatives would induce domestically driven restraints on excessive accumulation of arms.

There is likely to be greater resistance to increasing transparency in procurement plans by the arms-recipient countries than the arms-supplying countries. While the former would be concerned that an early disclosure of procurement intentions could trigger international or regional restraints on the planned purchase, the latter are perhaps concerned with the likelihood of transparency jeopardising the commercial confidentiality of the proposed arms deal. But what needs to be understood is whether an early disclosure of procurement plans could, in any way, adversely affect the recipient's security? It is quite likely that transparency in national procurement plans could contribute towards regional reassurance and acceptance of security needs of the buyer. It is well known that military equipment has replacement requirements on completion of its service life, and, to that extent, disclosure of procurement plans for regional re-assurance does not inhibit or jeopardise security in any way. On the other hand, regional stability could be enhanced through reassurances by the potential buyer through explaining their military's requirements and justifying their procurement plans.

As regards transparency in arms procurement actions, certain levels of transparency in arms transfers have been achieved, as indicated by the responses in the first two years of the UN Arms Register's operation. Despite the governments accepting the UN General Assembly Resolution on the requirements of the expanded register, possibilities of major problems cannot be ruled out when reports of military holdings and procurement through domestic production are requested for the Register. In regard to arms procurement actions, regulations and guidelines for initiating arms procurements should be public knowledge and should explain; the procedures and the methodologies for conducting threat assessments and identifying operational needs; statements of equipment requirements; evaluation and trials of weapon systems; procedures on price negotiations; the regulations on the performance audit of the equipment after it has been introduced into the buyer's military service. If such procedures and so on were publicly known, it would reduce the influence of extra-constitutional methods or incorrect practices creeping into national arms procurement systems without necessarily having any adverse affect on military security.

Transparency of the procurement budgets would be another development that is likely to be resisted by both arms supplying and recipient countries. As arms exporting countries tend to manage their budgets by offsetting the costs of national procurements through export of equipment, they may not like to have costs borne by their military known to the importers of the same equipment. The recipients, on the other hand, would resist the idea of disclosing their procurement budget because of common occurrence of cost overruns in case of licensed produced equipment and possibilities of domestic criticism in case of imported equipment. Transparency in arms procurement budgeting would help in preventing illegal practices creeping in the arms sales.

The need to develop transparency in arms procurement is being felt in two distinct fields of international concerns. One is more concerned with the political and security fall out of excessive accumulation of destabilising arms. The other is more concerned with the effects of excessive investment in arms procurement in diverting national resources from priorities of development to ambiguously defined security requirements of the state or its elite.

A related concern is the serious communication barriers between the decision makers concerned with national security and those concerned with economic development. Assuming internally-induced arms procurement restraints have better acceptance than externally-generated advice, transparency could help in bringing about a dialogue between divergent interests, This is particularly so when general opinion in most of the developing countries have reflexive scepticism to western advice on security issues like transparency. It is essential that the potential of the debate on transparency is carried beyond mere bean counting.

The international financial institutions have developed a focus on national defence budgets to induce restraints in military expenditures that are perceived as undue diversion of scarce national resources from development priorities to security requirements. Consequently, development aid conditionalities have been developed that are linked with military expenditures of the recipient countries. The problems of assessing military expenditures and budgets have been outlined in chapter 8 by Andrew Duncan. In addition, certain components of the defence budget such as expenditure on health, housing, welfare, military assistance to civil administration in backward areas or during natural disasters, can be argued to be important contributors to national welfare. As some of the aid recipients also have major arms procurement programmes, the international efforts to monitor national military expenditures distracts and deflects a coordinated international effort from restraining destabilizing arms acquisitions. A linkage, therefore, needs to be developed between arms procurement budgets and overseas developmental aid as opposed to the general military expenditure and budget. This will also attenuate the criticism by the arms recipients that developmental aid conditionalities are merely dubious initiatives of the governments that are also promoting their arms suppliers.

The Register is reaching the stage where official reports on procurement through national production and military holdings would be expected for its continuation. But should this new transparency regime be allowed to run aground if some states are slow to bring around interest groups opposing transparency to comply with these requirements? Fairly accurate estimates of production and holdings of more visible weapon categories, except for missiles, of the neighbouring countries are available to the intelligence services in the region. What is being desired now is the admission by the governments to that effect, so that an official acknowledgement would allow an international or an regional dialogue to develop. In a number of countries, official publications or government white papers do give details of military holdings, but most of the governments in developing countries could be reluctant to put out such reports for a variety of reasons. This knowledge has to move out of the domain of classified information to become public so as to induce national and international arms procurement restraints.

VIII What could be the suitable methods to promote transparency in arms procurements?

Because of the sensitive nature of the demands of transparency, the different aspects of procurement processes would need to be addressed comprehensively. As these different dimensions of arms procurement tend to reinforce or attenuate each other, this part of the chapter attempts to sketch a few alternatives that could address some of the problems relating to transparency in arms procurement in general.

We need to be clear whether the long term priority objectives of the UN Arms Register are to promote transparency in national defence policies and/or to restraining excessive accumulation of destabilising weapons? In the case of the latter, if the UN Arms Register is to serve as a non- discriminatory and a universal instrument to promote transparency in arms procurement,[3] then transparency has also to be encouraged in the entire chain of actions engaged in promoting the arms trade. In addition to understanding the factors driving the arms trade, the initiatives being taken to manage such factors in the arms exporting countries also need to be understood. In this case, the role of arms export credit and financing practices; incentive structures; national arms or technology export regulations and influence of arms export organisations, and such like should be made transparent to build confidence in the non-discriminatory character of the Arms Register. At present, these issues are relatively marginal in the UN Arms Register, but since such contributory factors have a direct influence in promoting the arms trade. A broader process of transparency would need to examine such processes as well. Transparency in these areas would contribute to the credibility of the international arms control initiatives and understanding of procurement budgets.

As technology develops, the destabilising effects of excessive numbers of weapon systems would be replaced by new systems with upgraded performance. To that extent, the notion of destabilising weapon needs to respond to technological changes. Failure on part of the negotiation process to understand the effects of technological upgrading in the combat capacities of new systems might mean that the UN Arms Register is blind to the replacement of outmoded weapons with more lethal systems. At the same time, we must understand that comparison of qualitative characteristics of armaments poses a complex problem for international negotiations, particularly when this subject has not been adequately studied. The Register could address this issue in two stages. Firstly qualitative parameters of weapon systems that are critical for destabilising capabilities should be determined. For example technologies that contribute towards force multiplier effect. Secondly, transparent measures should be designed to allow the development of destabilising systems through technological improvements to be monitored.

The problem of widespread reluctance to allow arms production to be monitored could be addressed by paring down the broader problem into manageable segments. Currently about fifty countries are known to be either producing or exporting the seven categories of weapon systems, therefore, the problem of monitoring the arms production is not global but needs to focus only on these countries. Of these, only six countries are producers of all the seven categories of weapons that are being monitored by the UN Register. Other countries produce a varying number of weapon categories. [4]

Monitoring arms production may be easier than monitoring research and development, but this may be more of a political problem than a technical one. A possible method for monitoring licensed production could be to identify components that most of the licensed producers have difficulties in developing indigenously. By obligating the producers, the recipients and the suppliers to report production or transfer of the critical and verifiable components, one could monitor arms production through transfer of such components in most of the countries that are assembling weapons from knocked down kits or under license. Instead of controlling a large number of technologies that could have both civil and military applications, it would be better to focus transparency measures on the most critical components that are difficult to fabricate and are verifiable. For example engines, gun barrels and radars could be monitored, instead of controlling every technology, process or component that could go into manufacturing any of the seven categories of arms. Missile technologies are in any case being monitored by the latest stringent requirements of the Missile Technology Control Regime (MTCR).

It might be a productive exercise for the UN Arms Register to address the resistance to transparency in technology transfers by concentrating efforts on ten or twelve major arms exporting countries. To begin with, it would be useful to develop transparency in the costing of major weapon systems. Most of the arms produced in the world are using either West European, American or Russian designs or components. Initially, the five permanent members of the UN Security Council could participate in studies on production cost of weapons. This would go a long way in bringing about transparency in arms procurement budgeting.

One of the major problems to be tackled in promoting the transparency requirements is to have a credible methodology for verification of production and holdings. Unlike the unique self-checking mechanism that was facilitated through independent data supplied by arms supplying and recipient countries, verification of military holdings does not have in-built verification other than the opportunity to compare official reports with military intelligence or independently gathered information from public sources. Generally, rivals in respective region have a relatively accurate idea of major holdings in the neighbour's armed forces. And to that extent, national military confidentiality arguments do not have a strong rationale for withholding information on military holdings. The arguments against revealing such details are that secrecy has possible value in deterrence and military surprise. It is only in the case of missile stocks that intelligence verification may be difficult, but since the objective of the Register is to monitor excessive build up of arms, reports on military holdings of other verifiable categories of weapons would indicate a country's aggressive capabilities. By combining judgement with knowledge, it is possible to arrive at reasonably accurate assessments. The argument that some states have laws against public disclosure of military holdings could be addressed through a legislative amendment authorising exceptions in case of a designated government officer to report to a specific international institution. In this case, this could be the UN Centre for Disarmament Affairs.

IX   Conclusion

Although conventional military threats to most of Western Europe and North America have more or less disappeared, threats to most developing countries still abound in different shapes and levels of intensity. Methods and national capacities to cope with such diverse threats are equally varied. Consequently, there is a problem for these countries in responding to the demands of transparency in a manner which replicates the responses of the North. There is a danger that the UN Register of Conventional Arms might not succeed if adequate attention is not given to unique security concerns in different regions, varied political attitudes and interpretations of the demands of transparency.

At this stage it may be very difficult to design verification methods for military holdings in most of the UN member countries. It is worth examining the advantages of institutionalising regional fora to focus on region specific security issues. For example, the regional interpretation and understanding of terms excessive and destabilising arms could be subjective, depending on different interests and diverse circumstances.

Nevertheless, a common and objective definition needs to be developed that could identify different thresholds of arms acquisition in a region. Arms procurements by a country in excess of such thresholds should trigger engaging it in a co-operative dialogue for restraint. Such a dialogue could also include the specific arms supplier or suppliers. It could be worthwhile to investigate a methodology, that, as its first step, measures the existing level of the seven categories of arms in different countries of the region based on their average holdings in the last ten years. In the second step, commonly acceptable replacement period of the seven categories of arms should be identified, and any procurement earlier than this period and more than the average holdings could be deemed to be excessive enough to engage that specific country in a dialogue for exercising procurement restraints. An additional benefit of the regional fora could be that, with regional arms control framework developing independently, it is quite likely that reluctance in the pace of some of these would be inspired by those regions who are moving faster towards the objectives set by the UN Arms Register.

Notwithstanding the scepticism with which many developing countries view the UN conventional arms control initiatives being promoted by the very countries who, at the same time, are the leading arms exporters, it is important that a parallel process engages with arms procurement restraints at regional levels. It would require encouraging public awareness and accountability in security decision-making that would harmonise broader objectives of national security with the military's demands for enhancing its capability. One of the limitations of the Register is a lack of widespread awareness of its objectives and methods. This shortcoming could be addressed, to an extent, by obligating countries hosting arms shows to also organise workshops or presentations on the UN Register at the same venue. This approach is not dissimilar from the statutory warning the tobacco manufacturers are obliged to print on cigarette packs.

Besides generating arms procurement restraints and security through regional confidence building, transparency would also help in avoiding strategic miscalculations, misapprehensions and mistakes. It would introduce an element of legislative oversight and administrative efficiencies that could reduce the influence of extra-constitutional methods and illicit arms deals.

The UN Arms Register is currently largely engaged in a top down approach to bring about changes in transparency in international arms procurements, in the sense that it is driven from the global level and that there is an absence of initiatives to broaden the debate to engage diverse national and regional perspectives, whether these be either obstructive or supportive of transparency. To make this change self-sustaining, the UN initiative on transparency would have to concurrently engage opinions in different regions and countries that are either major centres of production or engaged in arms transfers. The debate could then be carried to international levels to develop uniform practices. By engaging both supporters and opponents of transparency in weapons producing and exporting countries in specific regions to identify their legitimate security requirements, there is a possibility of reducing their opposition as well as discovering innovative ways of promoting transparency.

Notes

1. *Study on Ways and Means of Promoting Transparency in International Transfers of Conventional Arms*, United Nations Department for Disarmament Affairs; New York, 1991 pp. 34 -36.

2. Vertzberger Yaacov, "Bureaucratic Organisational Politics and Information Processing in a Developing State", *International Studies Quarterly*, No 28, 1984, pp. 73 and 76.

3. Hendrik Wagenmakers, Disarmament Topical Paper 15, *Transparency in Armaments: The Mediterranean Region*, United Nations, New York 1992, p. 22.

4. Stockholm International Peace Research Institute, Arms Trade Project data base.

CHAPTER 11

The UN Register, transparency and cooperative security

Antonia Handler Chayes and Abram Chayes

I   Introduction and framework – the emerging conception of cooperative security

The end of the nuclear confrontation between the two superpowers and their respective alliances implies a radical change in fundamental security policy and philosophy, especially for the major military powers. For forty years, military planning, doctrine and force structure were dominated by the twin perceived threats of massive ground assault in Europe and deliberate, conceivably extended nuclear exchange between the two major nuclear-armed alliances. Whatever may have been the case in the past, neither of these possibilities is any longer sufficiently realistic to provide either a technical or a political basis for decisions on the character and levels of national military forces and budgets.

There is as yet no coherent strategic doctrine to replace the simple verities of the Cold War, and it is by no means clear that one can be devised. But it is already becoming clear that any such doctrine will have to rely heavily on extended cooperation among all or most of the principal military actors, instead of the confrontative measures to deter and repel attack that characterized the Cold War. The scope and characteristics of such a cooperative security doctrine are only beginning to be subjected to systematic analysis. As elaborated in *Global Engagement: Cooperation and Security in the 21st Century*, recently published by the Brookings Institution, cooperative security, though profound in its implications, is nevertheless limited in scope. The focus would be on "preventing the accumulation of the means for mass, deliberate, and organized aggression, such as the seizure of territory by force or the destruction of vital assets by remote bombardment for unilateral gain."[1]

"A fully developed cooperative security arrangement ... would set and enforce appropriate standards for the size, concentration, technical configuration, and operational practices of deployed forces." Although recognizing that such a principle "is now and probably will remain an aspiration only incompletely fulfilled," the Brookings editors argue that in Europe, the area formerly dominated by the Cold War conflict, the elements of a cooperative security regime are already in place:

> The CFE agreement imposes national ceilings on ground force [combat] equipment (tanks. armored personnel carriers, and artillery pieces) and tactical aircraft and [attack] helicopters. These ceilings go a long way toward establishing the principle of defensive postures within recognized sovereign borders.

> The extensive CSBMs established by the Conference on Security and Cooperation in Europe in 1990, which restrict the peacetime movement and concentration of the armies limited by the CFE agreement, also further constrain offensive potential. The Open Skies agreement, together with the inspections that are part of the CFE agreement and their accompanying CSBMs, establish a standard of transparency for military deployments.[2]

In practical terms progress towards cooperative security means building on and strengthening these seemingly unconnected elements, in Europe and elsewhere – arms control agreements, confidence and security building measures (CSBMs), non-proliferation regimes and transparency and verification measures – articulating the implicit linkages and connections among them and making them a more conscious and central objective of international security policy.

Although the UN Register of Conventional Arms could certainly operate as a stand-alone measure, its potential, and its essential nature are best understood as an element in such a cooperative security regime. Indeed, these aspirations are expressed in the preambular clauses and the initial paragraphs of General Assembly Resolution 46/36 L, establishing the Register.[3] This paper therefore accepts the hypothesis of such an emerging regime as the matrix for its analysis of the UN Register.

II   The nature and elements of a cooperative security regime

The central strategic problem for a cooperative security regime is not deterrence, as in the Cold War, but reassurance. For deterrence to be effective, the adversaries must be convinced that any attack will be met by a response sufficient to erase any potential gains to the aggressor. As we have stated elsewhere,[4] in a cooperative security system, by contrast, the actors must have confidence that the other participants are abiding by the applicable restrictions on force structures and capabilities. Unlike deterrence, which relies on strategic interactions between opposed states, the key to reassurance is a reliable normative and institutional structure.[5]

Cooperative security contemplates an expanding network of generally applicable limitations on weapons systems and force structures. The limits will be defined primarily by agreement rather than by unilateral responses to the moves of other actors. Although sanctions have a place in such a system, the absence of any central political authority and the practical limits on resort to force mean that substantial compliance with these strictures cannot be achieved by the threat of military retaliation. It must be induced by the continuing sense that the limits imposed on military capabilities are consistent with the security requirements of the participants and that they are being generally observed. Thus transparency is a central requirement of a cooperative security regime.

In this context, it is important to understand what the UN Register of Conventional Arms is – and what it is not. Its goal is to provide reassurance by offering transparency in the transfer (and in future, perhaps, procurement from national production and military holdings) of conventional arms. But, as has been pointed out in every discussion of the Register, it is not an arms control measure. It does not purport to prohibit or regulate transfers, nor does it limit weapons. Because of what it is *not,* sceptics express concern that it cannot be effective. However, if it is seen as an element of a regime in the process of evolution, the Register holds great promise.

Complex international regulatory regimes can be expected to evolve gradually, over time, as the outcome of an educational and consensus-building process. This has been the pattern of environmental regimes over the last two decades. The framework convention with protocols to follow has been the characteristic format. For example, the Vienna Convention on the Protection of the Ozone Layer, signed in 1985, contained no substantive obligations, but required only that the parties "in accordance with the means at their disposal and their capabilities" cooperate in research and information exchange and in harmonizing domestic policies on activities likely to have an adverse effect on the ozone layer.[6] Two years later, as scientific consensus gelled as to the destructive effect of chlorofluorocarbons (CFCs) on the ozone layer, the Montreal Protocol was negotiated, providing for a 50% reduction from 1986 levels of CFC consumption by the year 2000.[7] In June 1990, the parties agreed to further restrictions: a complete phase out by 2000 and regulation of a number of other ozone-destroying chemical compounds.[8] At Copenhagen two years later, the phase-out date for the main ozone-depleting halons and CFCs was advanced to January 1, 1994 and January 1, 1996 respectively.[9] The reasons for a gradual and not immediately demanding approach are more obvious in the security area, where sensitivity and issues of sovereignty are even more salient than they are in environmental or economic regulation.

In our analysis of the characteristics of a developed cooperative security regime, we have identified five central elements.[10] We review them here to provide a basis for assessing the UN Register, both as an institution on its own and as a part of a relatively long-term evolutionary process.

A strong normative base

The basic conception of cooperative security implies general acceptance of and compliance with commitments as to force levels and deployments. These become the norms of the regime. The key to compliance with such a system of norms is that it be seen as legitimate. Legitimacy, in turn, requires that the norms be promulgated by fair and accepted procedures, applied equally and without invidious discrimination, and reflect minimum substantive standards of fairness and equity. Such norms carry a strong sense of obligation – a sense that they ought to be obeyed. The sense of obligation does not ensure obedience, but in the absence of strong countervailing considerations, the norm will ordinarily prevail. Actions within the domain of the norm are challenged and justified by reference to it. Challenge and justification begin a complex discourse in which the meaning of norm is interpreted and elaborated. The outcome defines the specific performance required of the party in the concrete circumstances of the case.

Inclusiveness and non-discrimination

A cooperative security regime must be broadly inclusive both for legitimacy and effectiveness. But, even though significant hold-outs might undermine the enterprise, the regime cannot be imposed. It must be accepted by the participants, and, when power is relatively diffused among the actors, no system will be acceptable unless its constraints are widely applicable without invidious discrimination. On the other hand, inclusiveness does not necessarily imply a single, overarching integrated structure. There is room, even at an advanced stage, for organizations devoted to specific issues or discrete problems, as are the Register and the Chemical Weapons Convention, and for regional arrangements, such as CSCE confidence-building measures.

Transparency

As already stated, the key to compliance in a cooperative security regime is transparency: the availability and accessibility of information about the regime and the performance of parties under it. The system gains in legitimacy if it is open to scrutiny, for participants can see that it is not being subverted. Transparency induces compliance in a variety of ways. It facilitates coordination, provides reassurance and exercises deterrence. The main source of information will necessarily be the self-reporting by the parties, but party reports are subject to evaluation, checking and independent verification, using all the techniques in the arms control inventory, new types of measures that become available as a result of technological or political developments and the independent action of non-governmental organisations (NGOs).

Active management

Developing norms and establishing transparency do not just happen. They require affirmative effort. The administration of a complex enterprise of international cooperation requires a significant institutional capability. Collection, evaluation, verification and analysis of information is itself a huge organizational task. Using this information stream to reassure the parties that undertakings are being complied with increases the organizational burden. The design of such an organization and the distribution of functions among new and existing institutional components is itself one of the most difficult tasks involved in the construction of a cooperative security regime.

In addition to information management, the chief components of active management include:

Policy review and assessment – One of the most sophisticated tools for managing international regulatory agreements is the systematic review of individual members' past performance and future plans, assessing them in respect to treaty obligations and taking steps to improve performance and plans where they are lagging. In cooperative security regimes, information indicating possible non-compliance with regime requirements must be acted upon promptly and effectively, but responses must be graduated to clarify the issues, to give the party an opportunity to explain and justify its actions, and to correct suspect conduct that is attributable to mistake or misunderstanding. The regime must provide the forum for consultations and the gradual escalation of pressures to move the offender back into compliance. Exposure and disapproval from the other parties, linkage to other economic and political issues and domestic political pressures can all be marshalled to this end. Although these measures are non-coercive in contrast to sanctions, they exert strong pressures upon parties to comply with their obligations. For the most part, they rely on persuasion, but there may be considerable muscle behind the consultations. The threat of exposure or shaming can be a powerful spur to action in an interdependent world where international reputations for reliability matter.

Capacity building – Security regimes have been traditionally directed to state behavior. But many of the components of a cooperative security regime, as is the case, for example with non-proliferation agreements, also require regulation of behavior of private actors – companies producing, exporting and transporting materiel subject to treaty regulation. Assurance that states have the capability and will to perform these internal regulatory function is a crucial part of regime management.

Interpretation and dispute settlement – Ambiguity and differences of interpretation of normative requirements often underlie apparent non-compliance. Binding adjudication of such disputes will likely remain out of reach for a long time, perhaps indefinitely. Nevertheless, other mechanisms for authoritative interpretation and dispute resolution are available to resolve issues of contested behavior and are essential for effective administration of the regime.

Adaptation and flexibility – Any enduring international regime must be able to maintain itself in the face of frequent and often quite disjunctive changes in the technological, economic, political and scientific context. The institutions of the regime should have interpretative and quasi-rule-making authority to be able respond flexibly to changing circumstances.

Sanctions

If the regime is well-constructed, taking adequate account of the legitimate interests of all its members, the likelihood of outright defiance that threatens its viability is very low. Yet as the cases of Iraq and North Korea show, it is not zero. The ultimate prospect of sanctions, however remote, must be available to deter and if necessary redress egregious and obdurate violations. Unilateral military action for this purpose is inconsistent with the postulates of cooperative security. Unilateral economic sanctions are of limited efficacy in a world of increasingly diffuse economic power. The ultimate recourse in such cases is for the UN Security Council or some other legitimate collective organ to authorize concerted economic or military response. Marshaling the necessary consensus for such action will always be difficult, and therefore sanctions cannot be relied upon except for the most regime-threatening crises.

III   Applying the framework

The elements just described are very demanding and, as we stated, look towards a more encompassing and comprehensive regulatory regime. Nevertheless, one way of evaluating the UN Register's promise is to measure it against these criteria, recognizing of course its more limited scope and objectives. How far does it now provide the reassurance necessary to permit states to begin to relax their military posture? And how could it be made more effective to this end?

Norms

The process of norm formation in the UN Register of Conventional Arms is only beginning. The Register was not established by a legally binding treaty. It is elementary that the General Assembly is without power to adopt binding enactments and in any event the resolution establishing the Register is by its terms voluntary. No doubt the sense of obligation to comply gains in power when the norm is embodied in a legally binding arrangement. But all norms are not legal norms. In the first year of reporting, 83 countries – over 40 per cent of UN membership – filed reports. They comprise the world's major arms exporters, including China, although some of the major importers, particularly from Asia and the Middle East, were missing.[11] Thus it is not too much to say that a norm of public disclosure of transfers of major forms of conventional weapons has gained considerable support. It is clear, however, that this norm of disclosure is incomplete. It does not require reporting of the entire range of conventional arms or dual-use weapons; nor of inventories or domestic production; nor of technology transfers that might provide early warning of a threatening arms build up. The Register, at this point, has not gone the next step to proscribe conduct, although one might venture that even the present disclosure requirement is based on an implicit norm against massive conventional build-up without apparent defensive purpose.

Thus the Register is at an early stage of developing a single, modest norm – one that will provide some, but not full reassurance that a nation is not engaging in preparing for conventional attack on its neighbors. Yet even this limited norm of disclosure, if it continues to develop, may, through the processes of transparency discussed below, have a restraining effect on arms sales and acquisitions, even without specific regulation of arms levels. And the acceptance of the importance of disclosure for reassurance may be an important first step in creating more powerful norms that could lead to de-escalation of arms build-up in areas of tension.

Inclusiveness and non-discrimination

A regime is inclusive to the extent that the states affected by it have reasonable opportunity to participate in its processes and it does not unfairly discriminate against any of its members. Formal non-proliferation treaties – the proposed Chemical Weapons Convention (CWC)[12], the Biological Weapons Convention (BWC)[13] and the Nuclear Non-Proliferation Treaty (NPT)[14] – aspire not only to inclusive but to universal membership. The first two are also non-discriminatory. The NPT, however, sets up two classes of members: nuclear weapons states, which manufactured and tested weapons before 1967 and are permitted to keep them, and non-nuclear weapons states, which under the treaty must forego nuclear weapons. This discriminatory feature has plagued the administration of the treaty, at least at the rhetorical level, from the very beginning.

For the Register, inclusiveness remains a goal but is thus far not an actuality. Not every member of the UN has opted in, and some of the more worrisome nations have not participated yet. The Register is by the terms of the General Assembly resolution "non-discriminatory" and therefore can more easily aspire to universality.[15] It will be far easier for the first 40-50 per cent to begin to exert pressure upon non-participating states if all are subject to the same basic requirements.

The non-proliferation treaties are supplemented by informal export restraint agreements among supplier states, backed by the domestic export control regulations of the members.[16] The Missile Technology Control Regime is another suppliers regime, but self-denial is even more difficult in an area where profits appear high for exporters, and military threat looms large for consumers.[17] In all these cases, denial will become increasingly ineffective with the growing diffusion of technology and importance of economic imperatives in national policy. The weaknesses of the denial strategy are intensified by its discriminatory character. Conceptually, supplier controls represent an attempt by a self-selected group of "have" nations, meeting in private, to develop and impose their own views of appropriate security policy by virtue of their technological and economic superiority. They are easy targets for resentment, which contributes to the persistence, and all too often the success of attempts to circumvent them – both by private exporters in supplier states and by recipient governments.[18] Although all the groups are seeking to expand their membership to include new suppliers, to do so will not necessarily cure these defects.[19]

Thus far this has not been even a conceptual problem for the Register, but it is one to be taken into account if any attempt is made to expand the Register at some point into a regulatory regime that tries to set limits on transfers of conventional arms. The experience with other denial efforts suggests that export controls would not be a fruitful strategy to this end.

Transparency

Transparency is the main operational objective of the Register. It is important to understand how it works and how it can be made to work more effectively. Economics, game theory and other disciplines have turned increasing attention to how the availability of information affects action, and particularly to how it helps elicit cooperative action. With transparency – i.e., where the relevant information is available to all participants – we can identify three important functions that work to create a compliance dynamic:

- It permits *coordination* between actors making independent decisions.

- It provides *reassurance* to actors cooperating or complying with the norms of the regime that they are not being taken advantage of.

- It exercises *deterrence* on actors contemplating non-compliance or defection.

These three functions may be treated separately for analytic purposes, but in practice they interact and reinforce each other. In addition, the information revealed provides a basis for using management tools to deal with suspect behavior. The power of transparency in such cases is that deviations from prescribed conduct can be observed by the other members of the regime, who can require that they be accounted for and justified.

In the Register, the uses of transparency are fairly straightforward. The Register is a confidence-building measure. The principal objective is reassurance. Reporting of imports and exports of designated weapons categories is designed to provide reassurance – and if the facts are not reassuring – early warning about intentions. But if we look more theoretically, we see that the Register may have coordination and deterrent functions as well. We examine these three aspects of transparency in greater detail.

Coordination – In the simplest case, transparency reduces transaction costs by providing information that the participating states would otherwise have to assemble with their own resources, often at high or prohibitive cost. The system of reporting on infectious diseases established by the World Health Organization, for example, enables members to adjust their own policies to the epidemiological threat.[20]

Coordination is one of the animating ideas behind the recent proposal for full reporting of nuclear exports, imports and production by International Atomic Energy Agency members. No formal regulation of purchases and sales of nuclear materials is contemplated, but they would be subject to the scrutiny of other interested parties. Since both buyers and sellers are bound by the NPT not to assist non-nuclear weapon states to obtain nuclear weapons, suppliers acting independently will be less likely to sell to a state where the data suggests the possibility of a weapons program. Decisions under conditions of transparency will tend to converge around the norm.

The same conception underlies the Register. If a reliable and public data base on arms transfers had been in existence after the Gulf War, for example, the United States and other arms suppliers would have faced a requirement to account systematically for the divergence between their actions and their declaratory commitments to restraint. Such exposure conceivably could have dampened the escalation of post-Gulf War arms sales to the Middle East. We suggested above that the Register's requirement of disclosure itself rests on an implicit (though inchoate) norm against threatening offensive military establishments. To that extent, the availability of authorized, official information on arms transfers should generate some pressure for the arms sales policies of states to converge around that norm.

The regulatory effect of such coordination can be very powerful. Coordination based on disclosure is the essential element in some of the most important US domestic regulatory regimes. The Securities and Exchange Acts, first enacted in 1933 and 1934, require disclosures of certain business facts to alert unwary investors of the potential pitfalls of specific investments. The details and truth of the disclosures are elaborately policed by the SEC, the body created to implement these laws, but the laws do not regulate or prohibit any form of substantive business activity. The major protection for the public depends not upon regulation of company activity, but upon the disclosures themselves, processed through the complex information and analysis systems of the securities markets. Again, the National Environmental Policy Act requires detailed disclosures of the environmental impact of any federal action or legislation "significantly affecting the quality of the human environment."[21] Although the nature and detail of the disclosure in an impact statement is prescribed, the act does not prohibit actions that threaten harm to the environment of whatever degree nor even require that the least environmentally harmful among potential alternatives be selected. It is left to the public and to the political process, using the information disclosed, to generate pressures to avoid the potential damage, to seek out more benign alternatives or to scrap the project. In each case the substantive norm – against excessive investment risk or environmental degradation – remains implicit. The disclosure requirements have exercised powerful restraining force, without imposing direct restraints.

Reassurance – As we stated above, this is the principal objective of the Register. Even in the absence of an encompassing cooperative security regime, states are under strong budgetary and other pressures to reduce military expenditures.[22] They will be more willing to do so if they can be assured that others are as well. Classically, mutual arms reduction is thought of as a "prisoners dilemma" in which the incentives for defection dominate. But one reason it is a dilemma is the lack of transparency. The conditions of the game specify that the parties cannot communicate with each other.[23] Conversely, if each has reliable information that the others are complying, all can proceed in confidence that the benefits of cooperation will not be expropriated.

Elinor Ostrom, in her path breaking study, *Governing the Commons,* finds that reassurance about compliance is central to the successful management of "common pool resources" like irrigation systems and fishing areas. Such systems, like arms limitation arrangements, are frequently portrayed as prisoners' dilemmas. She argues, however, that participants can pursue a "contingent strategy" and make safe, advantageous and credible commitments to follow the rules so long as most similarly situated individuals adopt the same commitment.[24] But "making a contingent rule-following commitment requires that individuals obtain information about the rates of rule conformance adopted by others."[25] In other words, transparency is critical to the success of the cooperative arrangement.

During the Cold War, the US domestic debates on verification of arms control agreements stressed the need for certainty that the other side was not "cheating," often raising verification requirements to increasingly unattainable levels.[26] The verification systems in the treaties that were actually concluded, however, never achieved this degree of certainty. Their main function, even during the Cold War, was to provide reassurance that the Soviet Union (and after its break up, the successor states having nuclear weapons on their territories) was substantially complying with the obligations it had undertaken so that the United States could continue to adhere to existing treaties and try to negotiate new ones.[27] Although the Cold War arms control agreements did not carry significant affirmative obligations of disclosure, the parties undertook not to deliberately conceal weapons in regulated categories and not to interfere with the other party's national technical means of verification (NTM). More recent arms control treaties, like the Strategic Arms Reduction Talks. The Intermediate-range Nuclear Forces Treaty, and

Conventional Armed Forces in Europe Treaty, contain elaborate provisions for reporting of the size and deployment of forces and for the most far-reaching disclosure measure of all, on-site inspection.

Confidence building and security measures (CSBMs) perform a similar reassurance function by permitting nations to carry out military exercises and other security activities in ways that do not appear threatening to their neighbors. In Europe, during the early 1980s, these CSBMs, negotiated meticulously at Stockholm, helped to moderate severe political tensions.[28] Again, the operative elements were disclosure and transparency – the requirements for advance notification and mutual observation of potentially threatening activities. There is no doubt that in the European theater these measures served an important reassurance function by preventing misunderstanding about deployments and other military activities of neighboring states.

Deterrence – Deterrence is in a sense the obverse of reassurance. Each acts at the opposite end of the transaction. A party disposed to comply with the norm needs reassurance. A party contemplating violation needs to be deterred. Transparency supplies both. The probability that conduct departing from the norm will be discovered operates to reassure the first and to deter the second, and that probability increases with the transparency of the regime.

In the standard analysis, deterrence works if the costs incurred by being caught outweigh the expected gains from the defection. Costs can take various forms. The most obvious is loss of the anticipated benefits of the regime itself. In bilateral treaties or where the impact of the conduct is sharply focused on one state, the aggrieved country may retaliate in kind, and in serious cases, the response may infect other aspects of the relationship between the parties.[29] In a multilateral setting, the delinquent may suffer more diffuse negative reactions from states and other groups with a stake in the regime. Still less tangible, but not to be discounted in a world of increasing interdependence, is the impact on the reputation of the defector as a reliable partner in cooperative enterprises.[30] Finally, at least in democratic states, disclosure may trigger domestic political reaction against the government. As we explain below, regularized procedures within a fully evolved regulatory treaty regime can be structured to mobilize and intensify these negative reactions. The foreknowledge of these processes will itself serve as a deterrent.

The UN Register, like most arms control treaties, operates on the benefit, as well as the cost side of the equation. The main purpose of the Anti-Ballistic Missile treaty (ABM), for example, is to prevent either party from deploying a nationwide ABM system. It accomplishes this goal by prohibiting precursor activities: development and testing of defensive systems and components. If one party discovered that the other was engaged in these activities, it would have ample time for an offsetting response. Thus the treaty creates "a buffer zone so that neither party could come close enough to deployment to be worrisome to the other."[31] Since the prohibited activities were clearly visible to each side's NTM, the likelihood of discovery was high, and the possibility of obtaining a unilateral advantage through deployment of an ABM system was correspondingly low. The high probability of discovery operated to reduce the expected benefits of a contemplated violation in addition to increasing the costs of defection, as in the usual case.[32] Prohibition of testing and other precursor activities in other arms control contexts is designed to have a similar effect.

The Register's deterrent effect is milder and more subtle, and difficult to gauge at this early stage. Since there is no prohibitory norm, but only an implicit concern about massive arms escalation, fear of disclosure may serve somewhat to deter massive conventional arms imports. As with the ABM treaty, the reporting of an unusually high level of arms transfers – or even the failure to participate in the reporting exercise – would give time for an offsetting response, thus vitiating to some extent the expected benefits. Disclosure is more likely to dampen the efforts of suppliers to continued zealous efforts of massive sales into troubled regions. But without more fully developed norms of restraint, the deterrent effect of transparency is not likely to be as great as in more fully developed arms limitation agreements or as it might be in a fully evolved cooperative security regime.

Assembling the data base

The transparency dynamic depends on the effectiveness of the systems used to provide and disseminate information about the regime. Independent data collection by a central organization is costly, intrusive and by no means error-free, as the US experience with the decennial census shows. Military affairs are at the heart of traditional sovereign prerogatives, and secrecy is an almost universal proclivity of military establishments. So in the field of arms limitation, even more than in other international regulatory endeavors, assembling needed information will almost necessarily depend in the first instance on self-reporting by the parties to the arrangements. The precedent for the Register is well established historically, and in fact allows for considerable expansion into the realm of inventories.

Self-reported baseline data has been the starting point for the verification system in all contemporary arms control treaties. Thus, under SALT II, the parties established an "agreed data base," to be updated regularly, on the number of strategic weapons each party deployed in categories covered by the treaty.[33] It consisted of a one page Memorandum of Understanding appended to the Treaty. It is said that when the Soviet negotiator turned over his report disclosing the numbers of Soviet weapons he remarked, "We are repealing four hundred years of Russian history."[34] The agreed data base accompanying the Intermediate-range Nuclear Forces Treaty, concluded less than ten years later, had swelled to 56 printed pages, to be updated every six months.[35] Similarly, states subject to IAEA safeguards are required to declare their peaceful nuclear facilities. It is this declaration that provides the starting point for the IAEA's work.

Two principal issues arise in a system that relies on self-reporting: (1) inaccuracy of reporting and (2) failure to report at all. Why would a state report – or report accurately – information that is to be used in appraising its performance under an arms limitation agreement?

Non-reporting – Only some 40 per cent of the UN membership reported to the Register during its first year. Of course, non-reporting does not violate any international obligation, since participation remains voluntary. As discussed earlier, it is more difficult to establish the norm of disclosure in a voluntary situation than in one where the parties have made binding commitments. Nevertheless, the current participants in the Register represent a substantial minority (including almost all major conventional arms exporters and most of the major arms importers) and can begin to exert pressure on non-reporting nations.

The experience of the International Labor Organization (ILO) illustrates the possibilities for concerted pressure in inducing compliance with reporting requirements. The ILO places high value on reporting, although the obligation is complex and burdensome. Failure to report is reviewed by the ILO Conference Committee on Compliance, and four of the seven offenses for which a party can be blacklisted are reporting failures. In 1979, there was a proposal to end this practice and list delinquencies in reporting separately, since they were likely to be caused by administrative and technical difficulties, personnel changes or the outbreak of armed conflict. The suggestion was rejected. Although the parties agreed to distinguish among reporting failures, it was with the understanding that reporting was essential to the whole compliance process and that it would be unwise to diminish the significance of failures to report.[36] As a result, the record of reporting compliance is good, coming to well over 80% in every year of the Organization's existence, except for the World War II years.[37]

For arms control treaties, as would be expected, the parties insist on strict fulfillment of the reporting obligation. A rare instance of non-reporting under the NPT occurred when North Korea delayed the filing of its initial declaration of peaceful nuclear facilities.[38] Intense pressures, both by the IAEA and important member states, ultimately elicited a lengthy and detailed report.[39] Nevertheless, the IAEA suspected that two sites had not been declared and demanded a special inspection. The action led to North Korea's notice of withdrawal from the NPT on March 12, 1993.[40] Although the operation of this notice was suspended, North Korea has still not permitted inspections sufficient to permit the IAEA to certify that it has not diverted nuclear material from its declared peaceful programs. On March 22, 1994, the IAEA referred the matter to the UN Security Council for appropriate action, the first such instance in IAEA's almost 40-year history. The incident is a serious challenge to the NPT compliance system, and at the present writing, it is not clear how the impasse will be resolved.

Reliability of reporting – Self-reporting is only the beginning, not the end of the data-gathering process. In the bilateral East-West arms control treaties, if a party challenges the accuracy of the data submitted by its treaty partner, the information is not accepted until discrepancies are resolved to the satisfaction of the objecting party. This formal provision simply codifies the formidable incentives to report accurately that already exist in any case. Each side knows that the other has detailed knowledge about its deployments, based on intense and continuous surveillance by NTM and other sources of intelligence. An inaccurate report could sour the whole treaty process.[41] One side cannot be sure what gaps there are, if any, in the other's knowledge. In these circumstances, the incentives for telling the truth are high and the possible gains from misreporting are small.

Verification by NTM has been a staple of arms control from its beginning in the Limited Test Ban Treaty of 1963. In fact satellite capability probably provided the reassurance that permitted the two superpowers to enter into the ABM treaty and the Interim Agreement on Strategic Nuclear Arms in 1972. As treaty limited items have become smaller and more easily concealed, and with the end of the Cold War, verification methods have moved to the more labor-intensive and intrusive on-site inspection. The Chemical Warfare Convention, concluded in January of 1993, contains the most elaborate and intrusive inspection system yet, including the possibility of challenge inspections, initiated by a party that suspects a violation has occurred.

The IAEA/UN Special Commission (UNSCOM) inspections of Iraq pursuant to the 1991 cease-fire resolution of the Security Council show how intrusive and coercive the verification process can become.[42] The resolution, like the typical arms control regime, requires Iraq to declare all of its nuclear, chemical, biological and missile weapons and facilities, providing the starting point for the inspection process. The first Iraqi declarations pursuant to this obligation were checked against information supplied by US and other western intelligence services and found wanting. A series of increasingly intense exchanges with Iraq produced much improved disclosures. Indeed, an iterative process of interchange leading to increasingly complete and detailed Iraqi disclosure has continued throughout the inspection period.[43]

Elaborate verification measures seem unlikely in a voluntary regime such as the Register.[44] But even in the more modest Register process, there are two significant forms of reliability check. First is inherent in the Register. Since all nations are asked to report both exports and imports, accurate reporting should provide a perfect match. A number of regimes that require reports of both imports and exports – for example, commodity agreements and CITES,[45] which prohibits trade in endangered species – use these reports as a cross-check on reliability, though the results are often not available in time to prevent violation of the substantive norms. Laurance, Wezeman and Wulf[46] have pointed out a number of such discrepancies in reports to the UN Register. Some of these, especially among NATO countries, are clearly inadvertent and are most probably based on different understandings of definition and timing. For example, the United States reported sales of 492 tanks to Greece, while the Greek report showed imports of only 347.[47] This cross-checking potential provides an important handle for improving the reliability of the reports and should permit clarification of inadvertent misreporting, while discouraging outright deliberate misreporting.

A second check on the reliability of reporting is provided by NGOs. In the fields of international environment and human rights, concerned NGOs have become increasingly active and effective in verifying national self-reporting. As to conventional arms, the Stockholm International Peace Research Institute (SIPRI) has long kept a data base on transfers. A comparison of the SIPRI figures with the reports to the UN Register already reveal interesting discrepancies, although their significance is hard to judge, because the methodologies differ.[48] SIPRI itself will no doubt begin to clarify these divergencies, and over time, such outside checks are likely to prove invaluable as a management tool for the Register, as it has for the secretariats of international treaty organizations in the environment and human rights fields.

Active management

This is the area that provides perhaps the most important lessons for the Register. In the present initial phase, there has been no attempt at active management. But there is no need to wait for a full-blown treaty regime. As we note below, however, strengthening of the institutional support for the existing reporting system will be essential.

We discuss briefly the four tools of active management identified above: (1) policy review and performance assessment, (2) capacity-building, (3) adaptation and modification of treaty norms and (4) dispute settlement. Our larger work in this area[49] indicates that these instruments are used and useful in bringing about compliance with complex and difficult treaty obligations. Not all of them are to be observed in every compliance process. Some regimes have special advantages in pursuing these strategies. For example, few treaty organizations have the benefits to confer that give the International Monetary Fund (IMF) its clout. Not many yet have even modest funds to help poorer nations develop compliance capacity, as does the Montreal Protocol. But in most cases, regime management can accomplish objectives to a significant extent without resort to costly incentives or coercive measures.

Policy review and assessment – Review and assessment in international regulatory regimes is based in the first instance on national reports, but resort is had to other sources of information, for example NGOs and scholarly studies. All of these sources are available to the Register.

The review is conducted by the parties to the regime, often assisted by a critique and analysis from the secretariat. The state under review begins by presenting and defending its report in terms of the applicable norms of the regime. As in other managerial or administrative settings, the process is not primarily accusatory or adversarial. The premise is that all are engaged in a common enterprise and that the objective of the assessment is to discover how individual and system performance can be improved. In the course of the review, the party's compliance is evaluated. The outcome is often a specification, usually accepted by the party itself, of any corrective actions that need to be taken. There are many variations and degrees of formality – ILO review of members' compliance reports; IMF surveillance of monetary policies and enforcement of conditions on advances to members; OECD harmonization of members' economic and environmental policies. More recently, the GATT initiated a Trade Policy Review Mechanism, which is now embodied in the agreement that emerged from the Uruguay Round establishing the World Trade Organization. In the Framework Convention on Climate Change, program and policy reporting and review by the Conference of the Parties is the principal instrument envisioned to enforce the general obligation of developed countries to adopt measures and policies "with the aim" of reducing emissions to 1990 levels.[50]

When questions about performance emerge, the review and assessment process explores the shortfalls and problems of performance, works with parties to understand the reasons, and develops a strategy for improvement. The dynamics of dialogue and accountability are central. States are given ample opportunity to explain and justify their conduct. Differences about the content and applicability of the governing norms are resolved. Technical and sometimes financial assistance is provided. Promises of improvement contain increasingly concrete, detailed and measurable undertakings. However, in actual regulatory regimes such as the ILO, if resistance persists, the process can assume a more confrontational tone and more explicit pressures for compliance will intensify.

We believe that review and assessment is an essential next step for the Register, even before its status might move from voluntary to regulatory regime.[51] The process of clarification and persuasion and the threat of exposure and shaming can operate without the necessity of binding requirements.

Capacity building – For the Register to work as intended, it may be necessary to provide technical and financial assistance to nations whose bureaucracies are inadequate to meet reporting requirements that are as complex and varied as those that the Register is likely to impose over time, as it becomes more encompassing. The UN has already recognized this problem and conducted regional seminars on the reporting requirements in advance of the first reporting deadline in April 1993. It has also worked to develop a relatively simple reporting form to enable readier compliance. It is possible that some of the discrepancies noted in the first reports of imports and exports reflect lack of capacity to keep records according to prescribed guidelines, as well as the possibility that the guidelines are not sufficiently clear. Moreover, in some developing nations, the military may have considerable independence from the civil government, including substantial control over information about sources and levels of weapons and forces.[52] Technical assistance and training might help solve these problems.

There is ample precedent for capacity building efforts in the experience of other international regimes, both in the security field and elsewhere. Technical assistance is an explicit or implicit objective of many treaty regimes. The IAEA spends half of its budget in technical assistance to developing countries on the peaceful uses of nuclear energy. In the environmental area, technical assistance is increasingly being provided for the express purpose of enabling compliance with treaty obligations. An entire chapter of Agenda 21, adopted at the 1992 Earth Summit at Rio, deals with "National mechanisms and international cooperation for capacity building in developing countries."[53] The Montreal Protocol formally acknowledges that capacity building is central to the compliance process. Despite a ten-year grace period for developing countries to comply with the control provisions, the treaty recognizes that compliance will be impossible for these countries unless they receive technical and financial assistance. The Protocol (as amended in London) establishes a Multilateral Fund, with resources contributed by the developed countries, to "meet all agreed incremental costs of [developing country] Parties in order to enable their compliance with the control measures established by the Protocol."[54] It extends beyond technical assistance to the provision of funds for the incremental compliance costs of actual development projects.

Interpretation and dispute resolution – Numerous discrepancies and anomalies in reporting, some mentioned above, show that the requirements of the Register are not self-defining. Under a treaty, mechanisms to resolve interpretative differences are crucial, but this is also of real importance in a voluntary regime such as the Register. As Ian Anthony points out,[55] there are important ambiguities in all areas of the Register. The moment that a transfer becomes reportable needs to be established – whether at the point of executed contract, delivery or some time in between. Exclusions from any of the defined classes should be spelled out – for example, whether training aircraft are to be counted or not. Some of these ambiguities may account for discrepancies between reports of imports and exports, which, in a perfect world, would match exactly. Elimination of ambiguity will not only clarify and elaborate the norm, but will illuminate misreporting and provide the basis for technical assistance to build capacity, a greater understanding of domestic bureaucratic and political difficulties and if necessary pressures from the international community.

Under the General Assembly resolution, the responsibility for interpretation and clarification was remitted to the two expert committees, convened to advise the Secretary General in 1991 and 1994. But these committees are temporary and, if the Register is to remain vital, there is likely to be need for some continuing forum for resolving differences of interpretations among the participants (such as the Standing Panel discussed in chapter 5 of this book). We would not expect such a mechanism to be formal or legalistic. Even in treaty-based regulatory regimes, disputes are most often settled by informal methods. In regimes managed by international organizations, the preferred alternative to adjudication for the resolution of disputes involving legal issues is authoritative or semi-authoritative interpretation by a designated body of the organization, often the secretariat or a legal committee. Not only is this a far less contentious method for dealing with disputes about the meaning of treaty provisions, but it may help to prevent disputes, and in some situations stem potentially non-compliant behavior before a party has committed itself to an activity that might clash with the goals of the regime. A state is not likely to ignore the answer to a question it has itself submitted, which in the context of the Register could, for example, relate to the definition of a transfer or whether a piece of equipment falls within one of the categories covered by the Register. And the non-adversarial context is conducive to working out the difference or misunderstanding that led to the request for interpretation, either by the parties themselves or with the help of the interpretative body. In addition, the interpretative process provides the continuous clarification and elaboration of the governing legal rules that is performed by the courts or administrative agencies in domestic legal systems. At the extreme, "interpretation" can be a way of adapting the norms to radically changed circumstances.[56]

Adaptation – If a treaty regime is to endure and continue to serve its basic purpose over time, it must be adaptable to inevitable changes in technology, shifts in substantive problems and economic, social and political developments. Part of a management strategy is to foresee and accomplish these necessary changes. It is far easier to adapt a voluntary regime, than to modify a complex multilateral treaty that has to go through national ratification processes, and indeed, the General Assembly Resolution establishing the Register anticipates such an adaptive process. Paragraph 8 requested the Secretary General to report on "the modalities for early expansion of the scope of the Register by the addition of further categories and inclusion of data on military holdings and procurement through national production...". The Secretary General's report on these matters was presented to the 47th Session of the General Assembly in 1992. Before the end of April 1994, UN members are to provide the Secretary General with their views on these subjects and a further report to the 1994 session is to cover "the continuing operation of the Register and its further development."[57]

It may soon be possible, as discussed in several of the chapters of this book, to expand the Register by deepening and widening its categories, adding new categories, or extending it to cover military inventories and procurement from national production. However, in our view, participants in the Register, should now be at least contemplating and discussing a strategy of adaptation towards a legally-binding regime, even if the obligations initially are little more than the "framework" variety, including nothing more demanding than reporting requirements. In that way, it will be possible to move gradually towards a cooperative security regime in which, as envisioned by the General Assembly resolution, the parties begin to reduce threatening military postures reciprocally by agreement, and the mechanisms for active management can be put in place to provide the necessary reassurance that such a regime would require.

III   Conclusion – the need for organizational capacity

In the course of this paper, we have offered and applied to the Register some of the elements we identified for a cooperative security regime, designed to reassure parties about their security so they may reduce their levels of expenditures on arms and readiness in order to turn national attention to development and a better life for their people. We believe that the story of the Register's first year is encouraging and may go far to dispel some of the earlier gloomy prophecies. But the record should be recognized for what it is – a promising beginning. Transparency, in the first instance, supplies considerable reassurance. But the Register has a long way to go in the level of participation and in its depth and reliability before it can fulfil the determination expressed by the General Assembly "to prevent the excessive and destabilizing accumulation of arms, including conventional arms, in order to promote stability and strengthen regional or international peace and security ...". [58]

In our view, the most pressing need for the immediate future is to strengthen the Register's institutional capability. At present, it has no separate organization or secretariat. The Secretary General has been tasked with reporting on the operation of the Register and proposing improvements. The views of Members on these matters are directed to him personally. He has had the assistance and advice of two temporary expert committees, one appointed in 1991 and the other in 1994, but although these two groups have much continuity of membership, there is no arrangement to ensure the continuing existence or institutional memory of this group after it reports in 1994. Administrative duties are performed by the Centre for Disarmament Affairs in the UN Secretariat, but its mission is confined to receiving and compiling the reports and background information supplied by participating governments and maintaining a computerized index of the available background information. These arrangements are both conceptually and practically inadequate to the needs and potential of the Register.

We have emphasized here and elsewhere that regime formation and effectiveness requires active management. The processes of developing norms and inducing compliance are not self-activating. They require continuous attention from an imaginative and dedicated management organization. In our view, without such support, the Register will not be able to proceed very far along the promising path on which it is embarked.

Notes

1. Janne E Nolan (ed.), *Global Engagement: Cooperation and Security in the 21st Century,* Brookings Institution, Washington DC 1994, p. 11.

2. Ibid., p. 12.

3. UN General Assembly (UNGA) Res. 46/36 L, 9 December 1991, Preamble and pp. 1-5.

4. Antonia Handler Chayes and Abram Chayes, "Regime Architecture: Elements and Principles", Janne E Nolan (ed.) in op. cit. at note 1, p. 65.

5. See Amartya K. Sen. "Isolation, Assurance and the Social Rate of Discount," *Quarterly Journal Economics*, vol. 81, 1967, p. 112; Carlisle Ford Runge, "Institutions and the Free Rider: The Assurance Problem in Collective Action," *Journal of Politics*, vol. 46 (1984), p. 54.

6. Vienna Convention for the Protection of the Ozone Layer, Art. 2(2), 26 I.L.M. 1529, 1986, (signed March 22, 1985, EIF September 22, 1988).

7. Montreal Protocol on Substances that Deplete the Ozone Layer, Article 2(4), 26 I.L.M. 1556 (1987).

8. London Adjustment and Amendments to the Montreal Protocol on Substances that Deplete the Ozone Layer, June 29, 1990, Annex I, art. 2A(5), 2B(3), 30 I.L.M. 537 (1991).

9. Montreal Protocol on Substances that Deplete the Ozone Layer, Adjustments and Amendments adopted at Copenhagen, November 23-25, 1992, 32 I.L.M. 874, 1993 A similar sequence marks the Convention on Long Range Transboundary Air Pollution (LRTAP), beginning with a general agreement to cooperate signed in 1979, followed by a protocol imposing limits on SO2 emissions in 1985, and by another in 1988 on nitrogen dioxide (NOx). The global climate change regime has started, like the others, with a Framework Convention on Climate Change containing only a general undertaking for cooperation and no quantitative obligations.

10. Antonia Handler Chayes and Abram Chayes, "Regime Architecture: Elements and Principles," Janne E. Nolan (ed.) in op. cit. pp. 65-130.

11. Edward J. Laurance and Herbert Wulf, *Research Report: An Evaluation of the First Year of Reporting to the United Nations Register of Conventional Arms,* Research Report, Program for Non-proliferation Studies, Monterey Institute of International Studies, October 1993; Malcolm Chalmers and Owen Greene, *The United Nations Register of Conventional Arms: an initial examination of the first report,* Bradford Arms Register Studies No 2, Department of Peace Studies Bradford University, October 1993.

Notes continued

12. Convention on the Prohibition of the Development, Production, Stockpiling ,Use of Chemical Weapons and on Their Destruction, Conference on Disarmament Doc. CD/CW/WP.400/Rev. 2, August 10, 1992.

13. Convention on the Prohibition of the Development, Production and Stockpiling of Bacteriological (Biological) and Toxin Weapons and on Their Destruction, Washington, London and Moscow (April 10, 1972, Entered into force, March 26, 1975), *United Nations Treaty Series*, vol. 1015, United Nations, 1976, p. 163.

14. Treaty on the Non-Proliferation of Nuclear Weapons (July 1, 1968, entered into force March 5, 1970) *United Nations Treaty Series*, vol. 729, United Nations 1970 p. 161, and reproduced in *Arms Control and Disarmament Agreements*, U.S. Arms Control and Disarmament Agency, 1975, p. 98.

15. UNGA Res. 46/36 L, op. cit., p. 7.

16. For the Nuclear Suppliers Group ("NSG"), see Office for Technology Assessment, *Nuclear Proliferation and Safeguards*, 1977, p. 221; for Zangger Committee, see IAEA Docs. INFCIRC/209, 3 September 1974, INFCIRC/209/Mod.1, 1 December 1978, INFCIRC/209/Mod.2, February 1984, INFCIRC/209/Mod.3, August 1985, INFCIRC/209/Mod.4, February 1990, the Australia Group, dealing with chemical weapons, see J. P. Perry Robinson, "The Australia Group: A Description and Assessment," in Hans Günter Brauch Henny van der Graaf, John Grin and Wim A. Smit (eds), *Controlling the Development and Spread of Military Technology: Lessons From the Past and Challenges for the 1990s,* Vu University Press Amsterdam, 1992, pp. 157-176.

17. See US Department of Defense, "Missile Technology Control Regime: Fact Sheet to Accompany Public Announcement", April 16, 1987.

18. Janne E. Nolan, *Trappings of Power: Ballistic Missiles in the Third World*, Brookings Institution, Washington, D.C.,1991, p. 60.

19. Ibid., p. 18.

20. Constitution of the World Health Organization, Articles 2 and 64, *United Nations Treaty Series*, vol. 14, United Nations, 1948) pp. 185-285.

21. The National Environmental Policy Act Pub. Law 91-190 (1969); 42 USC sec. 4331 et seq. See especially Sec. 102(c).

22. Janne E Nolan (ed.) in op. cit. pp. 25-33.

23. For a definition of Prisoner's Dilemma, see Elinor Ostrom, *Governing the Commons: the evolution of institutions for collective action*, Cambridge University Press, Cambridge, pp. 3-5, and see also p. 39, where Ostrom notes that in the true prisoner's dilemma, "acting independently is the result of coercion, not its absence." As to the problem of credible communication, see Thomas C. Schelling, *Strategy of Conflict*, Harvard University Press, 1980, pp. 39, 214.

Notes continued

24. Ostrom, op. cit. p. 186.

25. Ostrom, op. cit. p.187.

26. See Ralph Earle II, "Verification Issues from the Point of View of the Negotiator," in Kosta Tsipis, David W. Hafemeister and Penny Janeway, (eds), *Arms Control Verification: The Technologies That Make it Possible*, Pergamon-Brassey's, Washington, D. C. 1986, pp. 14-19. Both CTBT and SALT 11 were victims of unrealistic verification requirements.

27. See Abram Chayes and Antonia Handler Chayes, "Living Under a Treaty Regime: Compliance, Interpretation, and Adaptation," in Antonia Handler Chayes and Paul Doty eds., *Defending Deterrence: Managing the ABM Treaty Regime Into the 21st Century*, Pergamon-Brassey's, Washington, 1989, pp. 198, 215. Indeed, there was a broader kind of assurance that the overall relationship had not descended to a level of unbounded hostility.

28. Timothy E. Wirth, "Confidence- and Security-Building Measures", and Adam-Daniel Rotfeld "CSBMs in Europe: A Future-Oriented Concept", in Robert E. Blackwill and F. Stephen Larrabee, eds., *Conventional Arms Control and East-West Security*, Duke University Press, 1989, p. 342.

29. Robert O. Keohane, "Reciprocity in International Relations," *International Organization*, vol. 40, Winter, 1986, pp. 1, 19-24.

30. See David Charny, "Nonlegal Sanctions in Commercial Relationships," *Harvard Law Review*, vol. 104, pp. 375, 392 ff., December 1990, for economic literature on reputation effects.

31. Paul Doty and Antonia Handler Chayes, "Introduction and Scope of Study," in Chayes and Doty, *Defending Deterrence*, p. 3; Ashton B. Carter, "Underlying Military Objectives," in ibid., p. 18.

32. Abram Chayes, "An Inquiry into the Working of Arms Control Agreements," *Harvard Law Review*, vol. 85, March 1972, pp. 905, 946.

33. Treaty Between the United States of America and the Union of Soviet Socialist Republics on the Limitation of Strategic Offensive Arms (SALT II), June 18, 1979, Art. XVII(3), and Memorandum of Understanding Between the United States of America and the Union of Soviet Socialist Republics Regarding the Establishment of a Data Base on the Numbers of Strategic Offensive Arms, June 18, 1979, reprinted in *Arms Control and Disarmament Agreements*, U.S. Arms Control and Disarmament Agency, 1990, p. 267.

34. Strobe Talbott, *Endgame*, Harper & Row, New York, 1979, p. 98.

35. Treaty Between the United States of America and the Union of Soviet Socialist Republics on the Elimination of Their Intermediate-Range and Shorter-Range Missiles, June 1, 1988, Art. IX, and Memorandum of Understanding Regarding the Establishment of a Data Base for the Treaty between the USSR and the United States on the Elimination of Their Intermediate-Range and Shorter-Range

Notes continued

Missiles, reprinted in *Arms Control and Disarmament Agreements*, U.S. Arms Control and Disarmament Agency, 1990, p. 350.

36. International Labor Conference, *Record of Proceedings*, ILO, 1980, pp. 37/4-10, 19-22.

37. International Labor Conference, *Report of the Committee of Experts on the Application of Conventions and Recommendations*, Appendix II, ILO, 1992, pp. 530-531.

38. Strictly speaking, the reporting requirement is in the safeguards agreement and does not come into play until the party has signed such an agreement. The IAEA takes the position that all NPT parties should sign safeguards agreements, but a number have yet to do so. Since none of these has any nuclear program, the IAEA does not regard them as in violation of their obligations. In contrast, North Korea did not sign a safeguards agreement until 1992, although it adhered to the NPT in 1985. Since it certainly had some kind of a nuclear program during that period, it was in violation of its treaty obligation. The incident is unique in the history of the NPT. Interview with Dr. Hans Blix, Director-General of the International Atomic Energy Agency, Vienna, Austria, January 22, 1992.

39. David E. Sanger, "North Koreans Reveal Nuclear Sites to Atomic Agency," *New York Times*, May 7, 1992, p. A8(L).

40. David E. Sanger, "North Korea, Fighting Inspection, Renounces Nuclear Arms Treaty," *New York Times,* March 12, 1993, p.1, col.4.

41. In 1990, a dispute over the designation and disposition of Soviet tanks under the CFE threatened the implementation of the agreement. First, the Soviets removed some 20,000 tanks from the areas specified in the treaty before the signing of the agreement, thereby avoiding having to destroy them. Second, they redesignated several army divisions, including tanks, as naval infantry, which they subsequently claimed were exempt from the treaty. Michael R. Gordon, "Soviets Shift Many Tanks to Siberia," *New York Times*, November 15, 1990, p. A3(L); "The Tank War Continues, On Paper," *New York Times*, January 12, 1991, p. 24(L); "U.S. Soviet Accord on Issue of Armies; Obstacle to Cuts in Tanks and Troops in Europe is Lifted," *New York Times*, April 26, 1991, p. A7(L).

42. United Nations Security Council resolution 687, UN Doc. S/RES/687, pp. 4-6. The resolution, according to its terms, did not go into effect until it was "accepted" by Iraq.

43. See Sean Côté, "The Implementation of Section C of United Nations Security Council Resolution 687," *Occasional Paper* (Center for Science and International Affairs, Harvard University, publication forthcoming, 1993). At this writing, Iraq has still not revealed a list of its nuclear technology suppliers. "U.N. Arms Inspectors Expect Iraq To Accept Surveillance by Copter," *New York Times*, February 17, 1993, p. A2. However, Maurizio Zifferero of the IAEA issued a statement on September 4, 1992 that "There is no longer any nuclear activity in

Notes continued

Iraq. [The Iraqis] have no facilities [where they can] carry out this activity." "U.N. Says Iraqi Atom Arms Industry is Gone," *New York Times*, September 4, 1992, p. A2; "John H. Cushman, Jr., "Iraq Accepts Radiation Tests of Water," *New York Times*, September 8, 1992, p. A8.

44. However, if the Register should evolve into a more exacting treaty regime, there are new technical developments in verification of conventional weapons and force limits that may work hand in hand with on-site inspection to verify the accuracy of reports. See John Grin and Henry J. van der Graaf (eds), *Unconventional Approaches to Conventional Arms Control Verification: An Exploratory Assessment*, 1990.

45. Convention on International Trade in Endangered Species of Wild Fauna and Flora.

46. Edward J. Laurance, Siemon T. Wezeman and Herbert Wulf, *Arms Watch: SIPRI Report on the First Year of the UN Register of Conventional Arms*, SIPRI Research Report No. 6, Oxford University Press, Oxford, 1993, pp. 26 ff. See also Malcolm Chalmers and Owen Greene, *The UN Register of Conventional Arms: An Initial Examination of the First Report* in op. cit,. and Edward J. Laurance and Herbert Wulf in Chapter 3 of this book.

47. Edward J. Laurence, Siemon T. Wezeman and Herbert Wulf, op. cit., p. 31.

48. Ibid., p. 39 et seq.

49. Antonia H. Chayes and Abram Chayes, *The New Sovereignty: Compliance with International Regulatory Regimes* (to be published in 1994).

50. Framework Convention on Climate Change.

51. As is also discussed and recommended by Malcolm Chalmers and Owen Greene, *Implementing and Developing the United Nations Register of Conventional Arms*, Bradford Arms Register Studies No 1, Department of Peace Studies, Bradford University, May 1993, pp. 45-53. Some proposals for initial review procedures are discussed in Malcolm Chalmers and Owen Greene, Chapter 9 of this book.

52. Nicole Ball, "Pressing For Peace: Can Aid Induce Reform?", Overseas Development Council, Policy Essay No. 6, Washington, D.C. , 1992, pp. 17-23, 62-63, 115-117.

53. Agenda 21, c. 37, United Nations document A/CONF.151/4 Part I, 22 April 1992.

54. Montreal Protocol on Substances that Deplete the Ozone Layer, Sept. 16, 1987, Art. 10(1), reprinted in 26 I.L.M. 1541, as amended and adjusted by Adjustments to the Montreal Protocol on Substances that Deplete the Ozone Layer & Amendments to the Montreal Protocol on Substances that deplete the Ozone Layer ("London Amendments"), adopted at London, June 29, 1991, U.N. Doc. UNEP/OzL.Pro.2/3, reprinted in 30 I.L.M. 537 (1991).

Notes continued

55. Ian Anthony "Assessing the UN Register of Conventional Arms," *Survival,* vol. 35. Winter 1993, pp. 112, 120-26.

56. This subject is more fully covered in Antonia H. Chayes and Abram Chayes, *The New Sovereignty,* in op. cit., Chapter 11.

57. UNGA Res. 46/36, 9 December 1991, pp. 8, 11.

58. Ibid.

CHAPTER 12

The Register as an early warning system

Case studies and empirical svidence
of the role of conventional arms in conflict

Frederic S. Pearson and Michael Brzoska

I Introduction

From its inception, the UN Register of Conventional Arms was designed to have several potential uses, some of which relate to the issue of tension reduction. For instance, it was to be a measure of increased "security through transparency," through the elimination of misperceptions about arms acquisitions and increased confidence in the good intentions of other states. In addition, some also thought that the Register might be an early warning indicator of decreased security, a revelation of threats and a measure of UN member states' potentially dangerous military acquisitions.

The second approach was not very prominent in the documents establishing the Register. Resolution 46/36L on "Transparency in Armaments" was silent about early warning, though its first paragraph stated that

> "...excessive and destabilizing arms build-ups pose a threat to national, regional and international peace and security, particularly by aggravating tensions and conflict situations, giving rise to serious and urgent concerns".

In a way, the concepts of "early warning" and "excessive and destabilizing arms build-ups" can be treated as equivalent. Are we not seeking warning of excessive and destabilizing arms build-ups? Are not all acquisitions, even if they are minuscule, potentially destabilizing if another state feels threatened by them? "Excessive and destabilizing" determinations can stem either from conflicting parties themselves or from a general consensus among other states that particular acquisitions or acquisition patterns are a problem, because they are relatively large, introduce alarming new technologies, or seem particularly suited to attack strategies. Early warning in a sense goes a step further in identifying the kind of arms configurations deemed highly indicative of impending warfare, whether because of acute imbalances or high threat perception.

Given the relative lack of attention to the question of early warning, it is instructive to determine whether the Register can be useful in assessing conflict potential beyond individual conflicting states' perceptions or claims of excessive and destabilizing arms build-ups. There is certainly the potential for early warning in the Register, at least where accurate data are reported,[1] since governments can obtain detailed information about each other's procurement; but can more precise predictive power about the likelihood of war be gleaned from analysis of the Register as it now stands or might stand in the future? Concomitantly, could or should the Register be changed to provide more and better early warning?

As wars are the most severe form of international crisis, we will focus much of the following analysis on the relationship between arms build-ups and ensuing or ongoing wars (defined as sustained armed combat across national borders between regular armed forces of the conflicting states). Since only one year's data are as yet available from the Register, we will use data from other studies for our purposes, but will try to relate our findings to the Register and possible changes in its format.

First we examine the question of whether available data on arms acquisitions, specifically arms transfers, could have provided early warning of selected wars in the Third World since 1960 (noting that most actual combat in the world has been located in Third World regions since that date). We can reasonably do so because post-facto details are now available on such build-ups and on war-making decisions which at the time might have been obscure or secret. A related question is then posed as to the extent to which arms build-ups themselves generally have ended in wars. On the basis of this empirical analysis, we will evaluate the Register's potential contribution and possible extensions to early warning.

Ideally one would want to know the impact of arms on all forms of warfare – civil and international, among various types of powers, in all regions. Hence, a broadly representative sample of conflicts might be examined to determine whether arms build-ups were closely associated with the outbreak of violence. However, since such a conclusion requires in-depth analysis of action-reaction sequences in arms deliveries, a thorough focused case study approach to nine interstate wars was deemed appropriate at this point. We have, therefore, identified a set of cases of fighting in each region of the world among both long standing regional rivals (such as India and Pakistan or Israel and its Arab neighbors), and relatively unfamiliar opponents (e.g., Britain and Argentina in

1982). In the process we will examine patterns of arms acquisition in both long and short wars, involving balanced or unbalanced forces, and with varying degrees of international arms shipment or sanctions (such as embargoes).[2]

II   Early warning lessons from recent wars

Politicians and generals contemplating attack have to calculate the chances of success, and these are to a considerable extent based on one's level of military capabilities, relative to the opponent or opponents.[3] A prudent military leader will insist on a careful plan, including the acquisition of the weapons necessary for the intended purpose. Of course, the opposing side will do the same, in order to deter or be able to defend. This age-old model of war preparation predicts that arms build-ups, most likely in the form of arms races, precede wars. Is such a simple model at all relevant in the real world? Could arms registers be used for an agreed definition and measurement of the rates of competitive military acquisition among known rivals which would constitute dangerous "arms races?" Do such races indeed result in war or escalated fighting? Must the simple model be modified, by incorporating additional factors shaping the decision to go to war? In order to answer such questions, initially we turn to the case studies of arms acquisition prior to wars.

India-Pakistan wars in the 1960s and 1970s

The major arms build-ups prior to the 1965 Kashmir war took place gradually and in related but contrasting Pakistani and Indian acquisitions during the 1950s and early 60s (see Figure 1). Pakistan's importation of advanced US fighter jets and tanks had taken place in the late 1950s and contributed, along with India's traumatic war with China, to a marked Indian response. At this time, each side was largely dependent on one or two major power suppliers – Britain and the USSR for India, with some older equipment from the US. The US was Pakistan's main arms patron.

Prior arms acquisition affected the conflict, especially since India had considerably improved its forces after 1962. The pace of shipments to India also picked up considerably in 1965 until the outbreak of war in August, coming largely from the Soviet Union and Britain. In comparison, the US slowed its Pakistani shipments during the year, ultimately ending in a joint embargo (with Britain) of both sides once fighting began, an embargo which advantaged India given its Soviet connections.

The Pakistanis were alarmed at India's growing capabilities, including some indigenous arms production, and were not much reassured by Western power efforts to confine Indian capabilities to anti-Chinese mountain warfare, in part by limiting spare parts and ammunition. Equipment and tactics were tested in the spring 1965 skirmishes in the Rann of Kutch, with Kashmir fighting breaking out later in the summer. Pakistan felt capable of challenging Indian constitutional and administrative changes in Kashmir, first by supporting Muslim uprisings, and then in responding to Indian crackdowns. As Pakistan invaded part of Kashmir, India responded by spreading the war generally to West Pakistan. Despite Pakistan's pockets of advanced technology (planes and tanks), India's growing arms imports, and mutual fears, neither side had an overwhelming weapons advantage.

Figure 1.   Imports of major weapons: India and Pakistan

SIPRI trend estimates, in constant 1985$

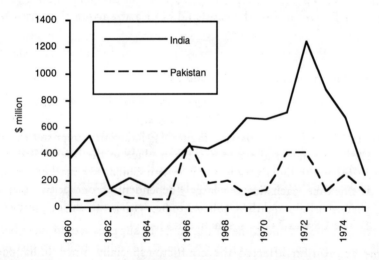

Source: SIPRI

Arms constituted an irritant leading to quicker triggers for this war. Clearly the sporadic build-up was detectable in yearly arms data reports; the specific escalation to war over a quarter-year would have been more apparent in short term data, with specific delivery dates issued, than in yearly compilations.[4] Arms improvements were a background condition for war, but not a tell-tale sign of preparation – since both sides initiated fighting but only one side (India) armed significantly in 1965. The upsurge of Indian deliveries, however, in conjunction with the Indian army's rather mediocre showing in the Rann of Kutch fighting might have signalled a desire to regain the power advantage and initiative on other border questions.

The next round of Indo-Pakistani fighting, in December 1971 over Bengali independence, was pre-planned by the Indira Gandhi government for more than six months. Initial vacillations gave way after the Indian elections of March and resulted in a May plan for a December war.[5] During the interim India launched a diplomatic offensive and built up its weapons, particularly taking advantage of a new Soviet friendship treaty in August to engineer a massive air and sea-lift in November. Again, as seen in Figure 1, the full impact of these weapons shipments would not have been apparent in yearly totals until 1972. India further took advantage of enhanced domestic arms industry capabilities, which of course would not appear in an arms transfer register.

Pakistan suffered a continued arms slowdown during the inter-war period, though as seen in Figure 1, various shipments still got through from China, France, the US, and even the USSR (before the Indian treaty). Pakistan's perceived Bengali human rights violations, however, along with growing Indian strength, tended to discourage arms patrons and to preclude a steady supply of arms.

Despite its disadvantages, and the fact that India was launching cross-border incursions to support Bengali *guerrillas*, Pakistan attacked on a massive scale in December, hoping to divert Indian attentions westward and thereby recon-solidate its hold on East Pakistan, perhaps with the assistance of outside powers pressuring India. The plan failed on all counts, except that the US sought to make sure that at least West Pakistan was salvaged.

Arms acquisitions here signalled hostile intent on India's part probably more clearly than in 1965. While some of the surge in supplies would have been detectable over the year prior to the war, the acute Indian build-up just one month before war would not have afforded time for a Register warning. However, in conjunction with the Soviet treaty, *guerrilla* uprisings, diplomatic overtures to the West, and troop redeployments to the east, there were also ample other signals of Mrs Gandhi's resolve to settle matters in East Pakistan by force if the powers could not bring about Pakistan's submission through diplomacy.

Arms alone were not a conclusive signal, as the side which launched the full scale fighting, Pakistan, had the worse of the pre-war arms build-up, but Indian pressures had boxed it into a corner where it felt it had to attack. We are told that despite India's capabilities, Pakistani leaders continued to express disdain for their foe's fighting ability in pre-war calculations.[6] Thus, governments can delude themselves or dwell on opponents' supposed inabilities to use weapons in order to assess whether arms acquisition in and of itself is excessive and destabilizing.

Middle Eastern Wars in the 1970s and 1980s

The various rounds of Arab-Israeli fighting generally have been preceded by significant arms build-ups, sometimes over a long period of time in steady competition among the parties, and sometimes in hasty supply surges. In repetitive war cycles, such as these or the Indian-Pakistani fighting, some arms acquisitions actually are replacements for previously destroyed equipment, and it can be difficult to determine whether they signal renewed acute hostile intent or just continuing tensions. Generally, though, in the Middle East, the parties kept to a much closer action-reaction sequence in arms acquisitions (see Figure 2) than we saw in the Indian-Pakistani cases.

Arms transfers had not been particularly prominent immediately prior to the 1967 fighting, although a steady multipartite arms race had persisted among Israel and its neighbors during the 1960s.[7] While providing their clients with the wherewithal to maintain a power balance, the superpowers, as in the Indian-Pakistani cases, tried not to inflame passions, limiting the quantity and lethality of weapon deliveries. The USSR, for example, withheld parts and ammunition from Egypt and refused Syria's request for advanced SAM-2 anti-aircraft missiles in the months before the June war. Skirmishes and clashes between Israel and Syria had mounted through the year, and France joined the US, UK, and USSR in tempering or suspending arms deliveries.

How much of this restraint was internationally apparent at the time is not clear. Presumably major power intelligence services knew, but knowledge might not have spread to the region where the USSR actually seemed falsely to alarm their Egyptian clients. Thus, a register that also included arms transfer denials or restrictions could have helped staunch alarmism; indeed in a sense the Israelis themselves tried to do so by inviting Egyptian observers in 1967 to see that rumored Israeli war preparations were untrue. The general arms race, however, which would have been apparent in a register, signalled a potential war in this case.

Both Egypt and Israel substantially replenished and improved their arms positions after 1967, though Syria lagged behind and did not begin to rearm substantially until after 1970 (Figure 2). The Americans and Soviets increasingly transferred battle-tested weapons from the Vietnam theatre to the Middle East, though again with some quantitative and qualitative limits, for example in Moscow's case withholding certain offensive weapon capabilities. Again the powers sought influence over clients' war-making decisions. However, Soviet and US restraint did not preclude Egyptian President Sadat's carefully crafted November 1972 decision to break the stalemate along the Suez Canal with a limited war initiative. Indeed, the USSR was swept up into these plans.

Figure 2.   Imports of major weapons: Israel, Egypt and Syria

SIPRI trend estimates, in constant 1985$

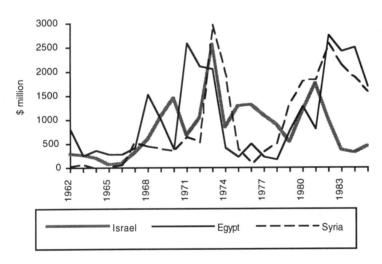

Source: SIPRI

One early warning requirement, therefore, is to distinguish among the types of weapons transferred and their battlefield use potential given developing political scenarios. This is not always easy, since arms can be deceptive as to strategy. As it had done in the Bangladesh war, where it signed a key strategic friendship treaty with India, in 1973 the USSR essentially acquiesced in Egypt's limited war decision and dispatched equipment particularly useful for, though not necessarily indicative of a military attack: special portable bridging equipment to cross the canal, and advanced "defensive" anti-aircraft missiles to shield against superior Israeli air power.

Thus, purportedly defensive arms became crucial to launching an offensive. Even the vaunted Israeli intelligence services were fooled by Egyptian prepa-rations, since it was assumed that an offensive would require types of fighter-bombers which Cairo did not yet possess; the Cairo-Moscow plan to rely instead on Scud surface-to-surface missiles for deterrence and SAM missile shields for attacking aircraft was not foreseen.[8]

The arms supply spigot also had been opened relatively wide to Israel and Syria in the year prior to the Yom Kippur-Ramadan war (see Figure 2), and air skirmishing had developed between these two states as it had prior to previous Arab-Israeli wars. Israel anticipated a continuation of this pattern, but not an early breakout of land warfare, either along the canal or the Syrian border.

Early warning predictions of war through the use of arms supply indicators, therefore, must be made in the context of such mounting tension and hostile political/military interaction, as well as considering the parties' likely assess-ment of their own and opponents' weapon advantages or disadvantages. Specific types of weapons received by or denied to conflicting parties must be carefully reviewed in light of potential scenarios, to determine whether arms seemingly suited for one strategy actually might be used in another way to make up or deficiencies, and whether seemingly destabilizing arms are unlikely to be used given political calculations. In this sense, the old trade-off between a country's military capabilities and its policy intentions is still extremely relevant in assessing threat.[9]

The armament and decision-making pattern seen in 1973 was in many ways repeated prior to the 1982 Israeli-Syrian/PLO war in Lebanon (Figure 2). A Syrian arms build-up had preceded Israel's arms surge in the late 1970s, and, despite Camp David, Egypt renewed military imports in the early 1980s. This time it was Israeli leadership which, in light of the peaceful Egyptian front and an emerging stalemate with Syria, between Autumn 1981 and June 1982 had planned a military attack to disable the PLO and empower a pro-Israeli Phalangist Lebanese government. The occasion of the assassination of the Israeli ambassador in London was seized as the trigger for this offensive.

Weapon technology improvements had been proceeding apace in both Syria and Israel, as well as for the PLO. Syria had moved SAM emplacements into central Lebanon to thwart Israeli raids (Israel and Syria had skirmished in 1981 over Syrian efforts to oust the Phalangists and over Palestinian attacks on Israeli settlements). At this time Syria possessed the most advanced Soviet arsenal seen in the Third World, including varieties of surface-to-surface missiles (limited in quantities since the Soviets still hoped to maintain control of crisis situations) and the latest tanks and fighter jets.

When this level of armament is reached, and especially in light of the destabilizing interpretations attached to surface-to-surface and surface-to-air missiles in a confined region, probabilities of pre-emptive attack appear to increase – especially if the arms technology arrives in the political context of a push or change, such as both Syria and Israel were trying in Lebanon. In addition, in September 1981 the US and Israel had worked out a strategic cooperation agreement, reminiscent of the Soviet-Indian and -Egyptian treaties seen earlier, which reassured the smaller client of continuing basic military support, even if the superpower was circumspect about the extent of such backing in actual warfare.[10]

The overall pattern of Middle Eastern arms acquisition seen in Figure 2 shows that war predictions are possible, though not certain, at peak import points. Some arms replenishment, as for Egypt in the early 1970s, can be designed to make up for prior losses, but can obviously be used for the next war as well. The fighting in 1973 and 1982 was immediately preceded by such noticeable arms peaks that one would want to take notice of arms as a warning in volatile political situations.

Ogaden War 1977/78

For many years, Ethiopia was militarily superior to Somalia and could deny Somali irredentist claims to Ethiopia's Ogaden province, mostly inhabited by ethnic Somalis. But from the late 1960s, Somali armed forces were built up with the help of Soviet and other East bloc military suppliers. Ethiopian military strength, on the other hand, was declining, since relations with Ethiopia's main arms supplier, the United States, began to deteriorate after the military coup of 1974 (see import levels in Figure 3).

The Ethiopian leadership tried, ultimately successfully, to woo the Soviet Union into an arms relationship. After some hesitation, in December 1976 Soviet leaders, hoping to control both sides of the conflict, agreed to Ethiopian requests. Indeed, with Cuban Premier Fidel Castro's help, in early 1977 Moscow sought to persuade the two self-proclaimed socialist states to enter into a union, a tactic somewhat reminiscent of Soviet pressures on Egypt to ally with Syria in 1967.

Somali leader Siad Barre, who had protested in vain against the change in Soviet policy, now saw his chances to bring the Ogaden under his rule dwindling. There would be a "window of opportunity," however, during the rest of 1977, the type that often tempts war initiators: it would take some time for Soviet weapons to arrive in Ethiopia (see the surge in Figure 3), while at the same time the Soviets presumably would continue to supply Somalia.

When Moscow threatened to stop this supply in case of war, Mogadishu also went shopping for alternate weapons suppliers, and though the US hedged, its purported willingness to allow other countries to meet Somali needs contributed to Siad Barre's false sense of confidence in attacking. After providing clandestine support to Ogadeni *guerrillas* from the summer of 1977, Somali forces advanced rapidly against negligible Ethiopian resistance, and occupied almost the whole region by the end of the year.

Figure 3. Imports of major weapons: Ethiopia and Somalia

SIPRI trend estimates, in constant 1985$

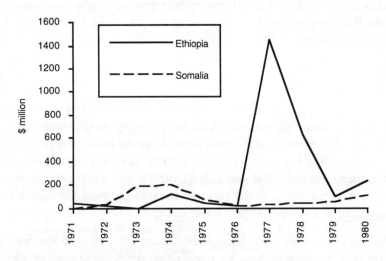

Source: SIPRI

In the meantime, the Soviet Union had completed its reversal of arms supply relationships. Deliveries to Somalia were halted shortly after the invasion, while a massive Ethiopian re-supply operation was initiated. From October 1977, a large number of tanks, armored personnel carriers, and artillery pieces were flown and shipped to Ethiopia, along with masses of Soviet and Cuban advisors. Soon the Ethiopian and allied forces were on the counter-offensive. By February 1978, Somali forces, which lacked spare parts supplies, were driven back over the border.

The large-scale Ethiopian build-up, plus direct Cuban and Soviet involvement in late 1977/early 1978 received great international attention. It was seen as excessive and dangerously destabilizing in the West, even though assurances were given both by the Ethiopian leadership and their Cuban and Soviet backers that Ethiopian troops would not advance into Somalia.[11]

In this case, then, war was preceded not so much by long preplanning and arms build-ups (relatively little armament reached Somalia in 1977-78), but rather by Somali perceptions of present arms advantages and potential future disadvantages. In the context of changing superpower policies and continuing border claims, the opponent's *anticipated* arms build-up hastened war, a situation difficult to fathom merely from raw arms delivery totals. One possible, though admittedly politically controversial improvement in the Register approach, therefore, would be to include some account of arms negotiations and discussions, so that the stabilizing or destabilizing effects of shopping around, witnessed from both sides before this war, could be better monitored as an early warning indicator.

South Atlantic War in 1982

The Falklands/Malvinas fighting is a case where war was preceded by a multi-year general military build-up (see Figure 4). From the late 1960s, Argentina's armed forces had been modernized and successively provided with updated weapon systems.[12] In the early and mid-1970s, the army received most attention; in the late 1970s, large orders were signed by the ruling military *junta* for a substantial modernization and enlargement of the navy as well. The arms build-up was fairly slow and a bit sporadic, though, and since a considerable portion of the weapons were produced under license in Argentina, transfer statistics only showed some of the real increase of military power.

Still, Argentinean arms acquisitions did not go unnoticed. There were worries in the region, for instance in Brazil and Chile, as well as outside, notably in Washington. But these did not stop Argentina's major suppliers, Germany, Britain, and France, from marketing their products up to early 1982. Argentina's conflicts with Chile (over the Beagle Channel), Brazil (over hegemony in the Cono Sur), and Britain (over the Falkland/Malvinas) were apparent, but not even the near outbreak of hostilities with Chile in 1978/79 dissuaded the major arms suppliers.

In January 1982, an anniversary year of British occupation, the Argentine *junta* laid plans for recovery of the Malvinas by October, which would include mounting diplomatic pressure on the UK and military attack if necessary (a pattern reminiscent of India's prior to the 1971 fighting). However, the attack date was moved up to April in light of a landing in the Falklands by Argentine scrap dealers, and British efforts to oust them. Much of the advanced arms on order, therefore, had not yet reached Argentina when hostilities erupted. Thus, again it is apparent that arms registers should ideally account for both orders and deliveries if threat assessment is to be possible, and even then unexpected "windows of opportunity" often complicate the analysis.

Figure 4.   Imports of major weapons: Argentina

SIPRI trend estimates, in constant 1985$

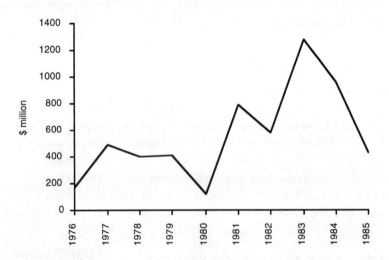

Source: SIPRI

The British government, including intelligence services, were shocked when Argentine troops conquered first South Georgia Island and then East Falkland on April 1-2 1982. Neither repeated warnings that Buenos Aires would not tolerate further British foot-dragging on the decolonization issue, nor the arms build-up had been taken seriously in London. British supplies of components for the Argentine naval industry continued until the very outbreak of hostilities; a British-supplied Argentinean warship had just left Portsmouth, where it had been repaired.

Part of Britain's intelligence problem, similar to that the Israelis faced regarding Egypt in 1973, was that as large as Argentina's arms build-up already had been, it was far from complete (note in Figure 4 the further deliveries peaking in 1983). The long back-list of weapons ordered but undelivered or not fully integrated into Argentine armed forces by March 1982 included: four frigates and six corvettes, four submarines, 24 refurbished Skyhawk fighter aircraft and six Super-Etendard fighter-bombers with their Exocet air-to-ship missiles. Prudent Argentine military planning would have been to wait another two or three years and then strike the Falklands with the best-equipped Navy in the South-West Atlantic. An attack in early 1982 was clearly premature from a military standpoint.

But the *junta* had not considered it likely that Britain, admittedly militarily superior, would resist. As we now know, Argentine leaders were confident that the cost of a UK naval expedition to recapture the Falklands would be too high, given the great distances involved and especially since London had decreased its military presence in the area over the years and had contracted with Argentina for certain services to the islands. The *junta* also counted on the US to come in as a mediator and settle the conflict at an early stage.

Thus, what seems to be a clear case of war preceded by an open, excessive, and destabilizing arms build-up turns out to be more complicated. The still progressing arms accumulation contributed to the March war decision only indirectly, bolstering the *junta*'s self-confidence and the military's desire to use new equipment, if only in an expected easy landing on the islands. War would have been likely in October, when Argentine leaders had planned, but was precipitated by the events of March and April ahead of schedule and ahead of weapon deliveries. Thus, arms supply agreements and deliveries would have afforded indicators of Argentine intentions, but it would have been difficult to pinpoint the exact conflict for which they were intended.

Iraq-Iran War 1980-88 and Iraq-Allied Gulf War 1990-91

Iraq and Iran greatly increased their armaments levels in the late 1960s and 1970s (see Figure 5), importing huge quantities of weaponry from the US, Western Europe, and the Soviet Union. Some major suppliers had shipped arms to both sides, a phenomenon which would be magnified especially by

West Europeans once the fighting began. There is little doubt that a qualitative and quantitative arms race was going on, which Iran generally won during the 1970s with nearly open access to advanced US equipment in the Nixon Doctrine days.

During the Iranian revolution, however, Iraq seized the occasion of the American supply breakdown to redress the power and territorial balances – a calculus somewhat reminiscent of Somalia's in 1977. In the immediate pre-war period, Iraq had much the advantage in weapons acquisition and continued to have it throughout the war (Figure 5). One tell-tale warning sign for war initiation could be the kind of abrupt reversal in arms supply relations among traditionally hostile neighbors seen here in 1979 (and seen less blatantly in the Ethiopia-Somalia totals). Most of Iraq's arms imports from 1977-79 had been tanks and aircraft, including helicopters and transports. While Baghdad sought some supplier diversification, especially in "arms for oil" deals with France, close ties to and a 1972 friendship treaty with the USSR were the mainstays of arms procurement. Again the predictive importance of close major power friendship commitments for subsequent war-making is worth noting, though preplanning for this war did not evidently precede the 1979 Iranian revolution and, as seen below, Moscow did not support Baghdad's initiative as it had in Egypt's and India's cases.

Figure 5.   Imports of major weapons: Iraq and Iran

SIPRI trend estimates, in constant 1985$

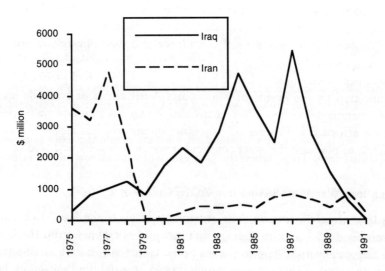

Source: SIPRI

Low-scale fighting and skirmishes had persisted through much of the prior year, but in September 1980 escalated into a large-scale Iraqi invasion of Iran. Obviously, Iraq's leadership believed that Iranian forces would be overrun quickly and that a peace could be dictated to Teheran. This was to prove a glaring miscalculation.

President Saddam Hussein's optimism is indicative that war decisions often are premised on assessments of military advantage and disadvantage which can arise unexpectedly and can seem transitory. Balances of existing forces are not always clearly reflected in arms acquisitions or orders, since it takes time for newly acquired arms to arrive or become operational. Therefore, the calculus for war may dwell primarily on forces, parts, and ammunition supplies in being or in readiness, and additionally on anticipated arms transfers.

In addition to miscalculating Iran's fighting potential, another of Saddam Hussein's important mistaken assumptions was that, given prior close relations, Iraq's main arms supplier, the Soviet Union, would support the Iraqi assault. Instead, given political changes in Teheran and in Iranian-American relations, Moscow denounced the Iraqi invasion, stopped deliveries of large weapons, and decreased supply of ammunition and spare parts. It took some weeks, even months before alternative supplies were organized (not very detectable in the yearly totals of Figure 5), from Western Europe, other Arab states, and, most importantly and probably with Moscow's tacit support, Eastern European states. In the meantime, Iran had regrouped and reinforced its army with large numbers of irregular forces, and was able to stall and then reverse the Iraqi advance.

Between 1982, when the Soviet Union again began to back Iraq with its full power, and 1988, when the war with Iran ended in a UN mediated cease-fire, Iraq imported large quantities of weapons from various suppliers. Few states denounced this as excessive or destabilizing. Instead, both superpowers and most others saw it as necessary to stabilize, even stalemate the front with the more populous Iran. Thus, when the war ended, Iraq had one of the largest and best-equipped armed forces in the world. At the same time, it was in great debt to a number of suppliers.

Satiation and debt seem to have been the major reasons why Iraqi arms imports dropped dramatically after the summer of 1988. Having absorbed all the prior arms deliveries, Baghdad went on to launch a full scale irredentist campaign against Kuwait in early August 1990. Finally, at this point the outside powers reacted with alarm to the Iraqi arms accumulation. The past two years without further arms imports generally were not judged as a time of weakened Iraqi military power, but rather to have allowed Iraq fully to incorporate the available weaponry and reorganize its armed forces. Arms holdings ultimately were seen to be more revealing than arms imports in this case.

To reiterate, between 1988 and August 1990 there had been no general consensus among concerned states that Iraqi conventional weapons were a threat. It was only when more became known about Iraq's production and modification programs for unconventional weapons, such as nuclear, biological, and chemical arms (even the latter had already been documented in Baghdad's anti-Kurdish campaigns), and also surface-to-surface missiles and long-range "super guns," that serious discussion of stopping the Iraqi military machine began. Still, Washington, evidently miscommunicating with Saddam Hussein and misinterpreting Iraqi military planning, continued financial support to Baghdad into 1990,[13] and Western European suppliers were willing to dispatch military technology right up to the Kuwait invasion, provided that Baghdad paid cash. Therefore, both the Argentinean and Iraqi cases show that commercial interests strongly condition assessments of the "excessive and destabilizing" nature of arms acquisition.

Summary

Thus, it appears that for arms registers to be especially useful in early warning they should ideally contain depictions of arms negotiations and domestic arms production rates, as well as the circumstances of lulls in or suspensions of arms deliveries. Such circumstances can include the successful integration and deployment of new weapons in configurations useful for certain offensive or defensive strategies. Clearly the alarm bell rings in circumstances in which political claims, such as territorial irredentism (Iran-Iraq, Iraq-Kuwait, Argentina-Falklands), or abrupt reversals in arms patronage accompany new arms configurations or transitory weapon advantages.

Decisions to go to war are influenced by arms accumulation and build-ups, but in complex ways. These trends generally are available in data compilations, though build-ups undertaken during periods of less than one year might be missed. Yet interpreting the available data in light of evolving political relationships, weapon transfer restrictions or refusals, and risk-taking is quite tricky. Much can be missed when governments decide to use arms in new strategies or to forego further arms imports to strike while the iron is hot.

Wars sometimes are initiated without conspicuous surges in arms acquisition or before arms build-ups are completed, because of perceptions about possible future changes in the balance of military power, because an opponent's level of armaments or capabilities to use them decrease sharply, or because a current level of armament cannot be maintained. One tell-tale sign of war potential may be the acquisition of arms in the context of recent border skirmishing, as seen with India and Pakistan, Somalia and Ethiopia, and Israel and Arab states. Yet some attacks are total surprises, as in the Argentine move in the Malvinas and Egypt's canal crossing.

In addition, arms acquisition can affect war decision-making indirectly, for instance through the strengthening of armed forces and their influence, as well as cost calculations, and presumptions about support from outside powers. Judging *ex post facto*, arms races often have been excessive and destabilizing, and in some instances, anticipated changes in arms balances tempted opportunistic leaders, resulting in war. But these did not always translate into accurate threat assessments at the time, and some destabilizing armaments were ignored by the international, and particularly the supplier community.

Our analysis points to the problem of subjective versus objective interpretations of armament processes: in almost all of the cases, some officials came to view opponents' arms holdings or acquisitions (often the former) as excessive and destabilizing, while others, at minimum the arms suppliers themselves, believed that armament levels were justified by outside threats or good business dealings. The timeliness of arms assessments varied, sometimes coming too late to avert or resist an impending attack.

In addition, given the need to replace arms lost in prior fighting or given the demands of simultaneous conflicts, it is difficult to say that specific arms imports by specific states will lead to violent outbreaks with specific enemies. There is as yet no agreed basis for objective judgements of threat, though we have been able to identify the importance of ongoing or suddenly changed politico-military contexts, ambitious or insecure leaders, and relative real or anticipated changes in military power balances.

III   Hypothetical early warning with arms transfer data

Having examined arms escalations before selected past wars, we now turn the question around, and ask whether past arms build-ups, and specifically arms imports, have been a reliable early warning indicator of tensions ultimately resulting in war.

Obviously, there are some conceptual problems with this proposition. For example, even if an arms build-up were excessive, it might not lead to war. One party might be deterred by the military build-up alone or go broke trying to compete and capitulate before war broke out. Perhaps by definition such outcomes show that arms were "stabilizing" rather than destabilizing, verifying Virgil's dictum, "si vis pacem, para bellum." The suspicion persists, nevertheless, that depending upon various leaders' risk-taking propensities and the timing of arms shipments themselves, a stabilizer in one circumstance could turn into a war precipitant in another. All this means that there can at best be a probabilistic approach to the problem of predicting war from arms shipments.

Observations from arms build-ups

Two forms of arms build-ups, as observed in import data, will be noted here. One is the absolute size of increases, and the other a relative surge in arms imports over the long-year average.

Table 1 ranks the largest arms importers over the past decade, as reported in SIPRI data on major weapons. These rankings entail the total volume of arms imports, rather than percentage changes therein, and therefore give quite a bit of weight to states affording relatively hefty defense expenditures. Does it tell us much about war probabilities, therefore, that India, Saudi Arabia, and Japan have been the world's largest importers? Obviously, war or even crisis involvements cannot be predicted reliably from this alone. Yet both India and Saudi Arabia have seen at least low level fighting during this period, and Japan has been alarmed by political developments in its regions and encouraged to rearm by the US. Furthermore, Iraq's sustained high import position, ended only after the Iran cease-fire and the post-1990 arms embargo, could have alerted observers to its aggressive potential.

Does the fact that some states increased in ranks tell more? Are Greece and Turkey in an arms race that might lead to violence, or are they simply benefiting from NATO military aid that stabilizes the situation in the south-eastern corner of Europe? Iran also has re-emerged in the top ten arms importers, and some have worried about its potential for conflict involvement in the former southern Soviet republics.

Table 1.   The largest importers of major weapons, 1983-92

In rank order, $ billion

Year	'83	'84	'85	'86	'87	'88	'89	'90	'91	'92
India	5th	5th	2th	1st	1st	1st	1st	4th	1st	3rd
Japan	4th	4th	4th	6th	5th	3rd	2nd	3rd	1st	4th
Saudi Arabia	6th	6th	2nd	4th	4th	4th	4th	1st	8th	7th
Afghanistan	1st	*	*	*	*	7th	3rd	2nd	4th	*
Greece	*	*	*	*	*	10th	7th	6th	4th	1st
Turkey	*	11th	13th	*	11th	6th	5th	10th	3rd	2nd
Iraq	1st	1st	3rd	2nd	2nd	2nd	5th	13th	*	*
Egypt	2nd	7th	5th	3rd	*	*	*	6th	*	*
Syria	3rd	3rd	6th	9th	7th	7th	*	*	*	*
Iran	*	*	11th	12th	13th	14th	*	10th	7th	5th

Note: * Not in top 14
Source: SIPRI Yearbooks, Oxford University Press, Oxford.

A bit more may be gleaned by looking at relative surges in arms imports. These are defined here as reported delivery values of more than twice the average over the period 1970-85, for at least two years.[14] The list is quite lengthy, and implies a mixture of possible explanations for the surges (see Table 2). Prominent among them are deliveries of expensive weapons, large rearmament programs, and re-supply during war. Of the 31 cases of arms surge, only five (Afghanistan, Libya, Somalia, Tanzania and Uganda) could be seen as indicative of subsequent war involvements, and in only one case, Afghanistan, of an immediate involvement – in this case in civil war. Response to increasing tensions and preparation or war are factors in about half of the cases.

The criteria and measures chosen here are neither sophisticated nor exhaustive, but they exemplify the basic problems and pitfalls of using armaments data as early warning indicators of crisis and war. Arms build-ups were fairly often connected to increasing tensions, though not in all cases. They can be an indicator of trouble ahead (or behind), but must not be taken as definitive in and of themselves.

Table 2.   **Relative surges in the importation of major weapons, 1970-1985**

State	Years	Possible Explanation
Afghanistan	1977-78	Beginning of war
	1983-84	Resupply during war
Algeria	1977-78	Rising tensions in the area
Angola	1982-84	Resupply during war
Argentina	1983-84	Large rearmament program from late 1970s
Bahrain	1981-82	Deliveries of expensive weapons (ships)
Bangladesh	1982-83	?
Brazil	1976-78	Large rearmament program, rising tensions in the region
Colombia	1980-81	Deliveries of expensive weapons (ships)
Cuba	1981-83	Rising tensions in the region
Ethiopia	1977-78	Resupply during war
Greece	1977-78	?
Hungary	1979-81	?
Indonesia	1979-80	?
Iran	1975-77	Large rearmament program
Iraq	1983-84	Resupply during war
Korea, North	1984-85	Change in supplier alliance
Korea, South	1978-80	Threat of reduced support from major ally
Kuwait	1983-84	Deliveries of expensive weapons (ships)
Libya	1979-80	Large rearmament program, rising tensions in the region
Morocco	1976-78	Resupply during war
Norway	1981-82	Deliveries of expensive weapons (aircraft)
Oman	1983-84	Deliveries of expensive weapons (ships)
Qatar	1982-83	Deliveries of expensive weapons (ships)
El Salvador	1982-83	Resupply during war
Somalia	1972-73	Large rearmament program
Sri Lanka	1978-79	?
Sweden	1978-79	Deliveries of expensive weapons
Switzerland	1979-80	Deliveries of expensive weapons (tanks)
Tanzania	1972-73	Rising tensions in the region
Uganda	1974-76	Rising tensions in the region
Venezuela	1981-82	Deliveries of expensive weapons (ships)

Notes: Criterion: Deliveries valued at more than twice the period average for a minimum of two years

Basic source: SIPRI data as reported in Michael Brzoska & Thomas Ohlson, Arms Transfers to the Third World, Oxford University Press, Oxford, 1987.

Evidence from the arms race/war literature

Probably the most famous authority on arms races, the British meteorologist Lewis Fry Richardson, noted that, "Historians mention arms races only for 10 out of 84 wars between 1820 and 1929."[15] However, he was more interested in distinguishing models of stable and unstable arms races than in examining the historical record in detail. It was only in the 1960s, mostly based on data from the Correlates of War project at the University of Michigan, that systematic quantitative empirical work on the relationship between arms build-ups and wars began.

The starting point has been the hypothesis that "arms-tension spirals" increase the probability of war.[16] A number of empirical tests have failed to produce a statistically conclusive relationship between arms build-ups, or more specifically, arms races and war.[17] Many studies have found weak correlations,[18] but only one major author has found a strong contribution of armaments to war.[19]

Among the complicating problems are data and statistics. What is the relevant independent variable (arms acquisitions, arms imports, holdings, military expenditures) and its time lag (1 year, 3 years, 5 years); what is the best mathematical or statistical procedure? Research also has shifted among levels of analysis, including nation dyads as well as groupings of states in the international system. Analysis has been extended to changes in the balance of power among opposing states. There is some evidence that the effort by one state to catch up militarily with a stronger one is a major predictor of war.[20]

Many factors, some of which have been alluded to earlier, are considered as conditioning the relations between arms and wars.[21] These include the nature of political relations between opposing pairs of states, competitive quantitative arms races between opponents, intentions or motives, size of states, alliance memberships, domestic crises, and the political strength of the military. Generally in this "causes of war" literature, which ranges from the international system to the nature of the human psyche, arms build-ups have a relatively minor place. They are important in some instances and not in others; they seem to add to tension levels while, depending upon relative balances and the availability of spare parts, often diminishing the search for non-violent alternatives.

III   The Register as instrument of early warning of excessive and eestabilizing arms build-ups

The central problem in using the Register as a device for early warning and to detect excessive and destabilizing arms build-ups is the lack of a one-dimensional relation between such build-ups, their excessive and destabilizing nature, and war. Some large arms transfers or acquisitions can be stabilizing, as when they reinforce deterrence, lend defensive credibility, or make up or past deficiencies. Conversely, certain ill-timed or strategically designed small build-ups can be destabilizing, as when they afford the last needed cog in a war machine. Wars also can occur without any noticeable arms build-up (Figure 6).

Figure 6.   Explanations for relationships between arms build-ups and wars

	No War	War
Arms Build-up	• Stable arms build-up • No hostile intentions • Deterrence	• Excessive and destabilizing arms build-up
No Arms Build-up	• Stable peace	• War by surprise attack • Anticipation of future change in military balance • Loss of power by opponent

No definitive criteria yet exist to decide whether specific arms preparations are excessive or destabilizing unless they end in a war or greatly aggravate tensions. Yet individual countries, such as Germany, have written arms regulations to ban sales and transfers to "areas of tension," where transfers might materially irritate a crisis situation, or where destabilizing new technology could be introduced into a region. Thus, on the one hand, warnings through a register might be impractical since conclusive assessments depend on the outbreak of war, when warnings themselves already would be too late. On the other hand, leaders appear to think they can distinguish especially dangerous from routine situations abroad, and regulate arms transfers accordingly (their record on this is not particularly encouraging, as witness the Gulf war sequences). Since, as we have shown, there is often a perceptible, if not necessarily decisive, relationship between quantitative or qualitative arms escalation, crises, and wars, the Register has relevance for early warning, especially if further modified to add more regular accounts of political context, pending transfers, and arms denials.[22] Such accounts ideally should include arms holdings and domestic production, defense doctrines, patronage and friendship treaties (and reversals therein), arms delivery and order dates, new technologies and unconventional weapon categories.

A more comprehensive and annotated register can provide for reassurance as well as alerts. For example, explanations of very large imports in a particular year, which might simply be due to prior delivery schedules, are useful for interpretation to help defuse crisis situations.

Beyond these proposals, the Register would obtain heightened early warning potential through links with other existing or possible data banks on unresolved political problems, such as border and territorial disputes and skirmishes, ethnic disputes, and internal wars. Some such data bases exist, and there is talk of further developing them under UN auspices, especially in the areas of ethnic conflict.[23] Probably the UN Secretariat would be over-whelmed if it opened a "Register of Security Concerns" for all member states, NGOs, or whomever. A less ambitious, though still admittedly untidy idea would be to have, in connection with the conventional arms register, a body of communications about the data it contains, for instance queries about certain transfers, answers by those concerned and so on, conceivably on an electronic bulletin-board. Any technology that could speed arms monitoring, so that quarter year assessments could be made, would be worthwhile. This would combine early warning with confidence building, as it would increase and formalize exchanges about armament processes.

Notes

1. A state pursuing an aggressive course is not very likely openly to report its increased military power. From this, one could deduce that the Register could provide only a crude early warning measure by indicating the lack of a data submission, or, in connection with other data sources, an inaccurate or misleading submission.

2. The information on these cases is derived mainly from Frederic S. Pearson and Michael Brzoska, *Arms and Warfare, Escalation, Deescalation, Negotiation*,

Notes continued

University of South Carolina Press, Columbia, SC, 1994, forthcoming; summaries appear in Pearson, Brzoska, and Christer Crantz, 'Arms Transfers and Recent Wars', *SIPRI Yearbook 1992*, Oxford University Press, Oxford, 1992. SIPRI data were chosen as an authoritative account of arms transfers based on trend estimate values of major arms deliveries. These data also allowed specification of deliveries by month in many cases, thus easing the way in associating arms deliveries with outbreaks of fighting. Given reports already available showing relatively good concurrence between SIPRI accounts of arms transfer volume and the reports in the new UN Register, reliance on SIPRI as a surrogate for the Register in an early warning feasibility study seems highly appropriate. See Ian Anthony, 'What is required for a useful transfers Register?', Chapter 5 in this volume, and Edward J. Laurance, Siemon T. Wezeman and Herbert Wulf, *Arms Watch: SIPRI Report on the First Year of the UN Register of Conventional Arms*, SIPRI Research Report No. 6, Oxford University Press, Oxford, 1993.

3.   On such calculations, see Bruce Bueno de Mesquita, *The War Trap*, New Haven, Yale University Press, 1981, and 'The War Trap Revisited, A Revised Expected Utility Model', *American Political Science Review*, 79, March 1985, pp. 157-76.

4.   In both this study and our larger analysis of *Arms and Warfare*, op. cit., we make every effort to supplement standard yearly sources yearbooks and statistical reports with historical and journalistic accounts by month, as well as details of SIPRI's raw data by monthly dates.

5.   See S. Ganguly, *Origins of War in South Asia, Indo-Pakistani Conflicts Since 1947*, Westview, Boulder, Co, 1986, p. 121; Sallik Siddiq, *Witness to Surrender*, Oxford University Press, Delhi, 1979, pp. 97-98; and Richard Sisson and Leo E. Rose, *War and Secession, Pakistan, India and the Creation of Bangladesh*, University of California Press, Berkeley, 1990, p. 144.

6.   See, for example, Henry Kissinger, *The White House Years*, Weidenfeld and Nicolson, London, 1979, p. 861.

7.   See Nadav Safran, *From War to War, The Arab-Israeli Confrontation, 1948-67*, Pegasus, New York, 1969; Keith Krause, 'Arms Transfers, Conflict Management and the Arab-Israeli Conflict', in David Dewitt and Gabriel Ben-Dor (eds), *Conflict Management in the Middle East*, Lexington Books, Lexington, MA, 1987; and Keith Krause, 'Constructing Regional Security Regimes and the Control of Arms Transfers', *International Journal*, vol. 11, Spring 1990, pp. 398-99.

8.   See Chaim Herzog, *The Arab-Israeli Wars, War and Peace in the Middle East*, Random House, New York, 1982, pp. 227-28.

9.   See J. David Singer, 'Threat Perception and the Armament-Tension Dilemma', *Journal of Conflict Resolution*, vol. 2, March 1958, pp. 90-105.

10.   See Arthur Jay Klinghofer, with Judith Apter, *Israel and the Soviet Union, Alienation or Reconciliation?*, Westview, Boulder, Co, 1985, pp. 191-92.

Notes continued

11. See Zbigniew Brzezinski, *Power and Principle*, Weidenfeld and Nicolson, London, 1983, p. 189.

12. Victor Milan, 'Argentina, Schemes for Glory', in Michael Brzoska and Thomas Ohlson (eds), *Arms Production in the Third World*, Taylor and Francis, London, 1986; Virginia Gamba, *The Falklands/Malvinas War, A Model for North-South Crisis Prevention*, Allen and Unwin, Boston, 1987; and Lawrence Freedman and Virginia Gamba-Stonehouse, *Signals of War*, Faber and Faber, London and Boston, 1990.

13. Jeffrey Record, *Hollow Victory: A Contrary View of the Gulf War*, Brassey's, Washington, D.C., 1993.

14. Very high one year peaks can be found frequently in SIPRI data, and it is useful to look at more longitudinal indicators.

15. Lewis Fry Richardson, *Arms and Insecurity*, Boxwood Press, Pittsburgh, 1960, Chapter 6.

16. J. David Singer, 'Threat Perception and the Armament-Tension Dilemma', *Journal of Conflict Resolution*, vol. 2, no. 1, 1958, pp. 1-18.

17. John C. Lambelet, 'A Dynamic Model of the Arms Race in the Middle East, 1953-1965', *General Systems*, vol. 16, no. 1, 1971, pp. 1-38; John C. Lambelet, 'Do Arms Races Lead to War?', *Journal of Peace Research*, vol. 12, no. 2, 1975, pp. 123-28; Partha Chatterji, 'The Equilibrium Theory of Arms Races: Some Extensions', *Journal of Peace Research*, vol. 11, no. 3, 1974, pp. 203-11; Paul Diehl, 'Arms Races and Escalation: A Closer Look', *Journal of Peace Research*, vol. 20, no. 3, 1983, pp. 202-12; and Paul Diehl, 'Arms Races to War: Testing Some Empirical Linkages', *Sociological Quarterly*, vol. 26, no. 3, 1985, pp. 331-49.

18. Erich Weede, 'Nation-Environment Relations as Determinants of Hostilities Among Nations', *Peace Science Society International Papers*, vol. 24, no. 1, 1973, pp. 67-90; Erich Weede, 'Arms Races and Escalation, Some Persisting Doubts', *Journal of Conflict Resolution*, vol. 24, no. 2, 1980, pp. 285-87; Theresa C. Smith, 'Arms Race Instability and War', *Journal of Conflict Resolution*, vol. 24, no. 2, 1980, pp. 253-84; Rudolph J. Rummel, 'Understanding Conflict and War', *War, Power, Peace*, Vol. 4, Sage, Beverly Hills, 1979; Dina A. Zinnes, 'Why War? Evidence on the Outbreak of International Conflict', in Ted Gurr (ed.), *Handbook of Political Conflict*, Free Press, New York, 1980, pp. 331-60.

19. Michael D. Wallace, *War and Rank Among Nations*, D.C. Heath, Lexington, 1973; Michael D. Wallace, 'Arms Races and Escalation, Some New Evidence', *Journal of Conflict Resolution*, vol. 23, no. 1, 1979, pp. 3-16. Wallace found that 28 of 99 dyadic military confrontations in the Correlates of War list were preceded by what he termed an arms race, of which 23 ended in war, while only three out of the other 71 disputes not preceded by arms races ended in wars. This

Notes *continued*

work has been criticized for its use of data and statistical methodology, for instance by Erich Weede, 1980, op. cit. as well as Hank Houweling and Jan G. Siccama, 'Power Transition as a Cause of War', *Journal of Conflict Resolution*, vol. 32, no. 1, 1988, pp. 87-102; Michael F. Altfeld, 'Arms Races?- and Escalation? A Comment on Wallace', *International Studies Quarterly*, vol. 27, no. 2, 1983, pp. 225-31; and Paul Diehl 1983, op. cit. These critics find only weak relations after correcting for what they see as deficiencies in Wallace's analysis, but the latter has replied to defend his findings; see Michael D. Wallace, 'Some Persistent Findings, A Reply to Professor Weede', *Journal of Conflict Resolution*, vol. 24, no. 2, 1980, pp. 289-92; 'Old Nails in New Coffins The Para Bellum Hypothesis Revisited', *Journal of Peace Research*, vol. 15, no. 2, 1978, pp. 175-92; and 'Armaments and Escalation', *International Studies Quarterly'*, vol. 26, no. 1, 1982, pp. 37-56.

20. See A.F.K. Organski and Jacek Kugler, *The War Ledger*, University of Chicago Press, Chicago, 1980; and Houweling and Siccama, op. cit.

21. See, for example, James E. Dougherty and Robert L. Pfaltzgraff, Jr., *Contending Theories of International Relations, A Comprehensive Survey.* 3rd ed. New York, Harper and Row, 1990, pp. 346-57.

22. The Register allows the responding states to append whatever background information they deem appropriate or relevant in relation to transparency in arms supplies. States have interpreted this variously, ranging from no appendix, to explanation of specific transfers, to whole segments of policy white papers. Thus, there is a place in the Register for context, but it is not mandatory and depends on governments' own descriptions of their situations.

23. See the work of Rudolfo Stavenhagen of the Collegio de Mexico, as well as his cohorts in ethnic studies such as Ted Gurr of the University of Maryland, Valerie Tishkov of the Russian Academy of Sciences, Otto Feinstein and the *Journal of Ethno-Development* at Wayne State University in Detroit, and John Darby in Northern Ireland.

CHAPTER 13

Transparency and military information in Latin America

Augusto Varas

I   Introduction

The UN Register of Conventional Arms is one of the most important post-Cold War initiatives in co-operative security. Its contribution to regional stability could be crucial. Considering its performance in the first year of its initial stage of operation at global and regional levels, there is a basis for a cautious but optimistic view of its future.[1] Nevertheless, to make it a full accomplishment, some additional measures have to be taken.

Two preliminary considerations are important in defining what those should be. First, it has to be recognized that the Register has a double importance. On the one hand, as a global instrument of information gathering it is providing crucial facts which in the long run could prevent regional instabilities. On the other, and equally important, the Register has a strong political meaning. The decision to participate in it is a distinct signal of the governmental willingness to share common security interests and concerns with other regional actors. In this regard, the Register has a definite comparative advantage vis-a-vis other sources of information such as *The Military Balance*, the *SIPRI Yearbook* and other commercial publications. Being complementary with these other publications, the Register is a unique instrument which provides information and at the same time communicates a governmental decision to work collectively in building a regional cooperative security system.

The second consideration is that the Register has to be defined as a new step in the context of a long term process of regional security cooperation. In this regard, the Register co-exists with other global and regional initiatives and instruments. Accordingly, it has to be defined as a long term endeavor which must be developed in conjunction with other security regimes and processes.

Taking into account these preliminary elements, in this chapter I will first analyze the topic of transparency in conventional arms transfers in Latin

America from a dynamic perspective, inserting this initiative in the long term process of regional security cooperation. Second, I will describe the main characteristics of the Latin American background in this respect. Third, I will analyze the Latin American responses to the Register. Finally I will propose a set of additional activities and procedures in order to expand its reception and maximize its usefulness.

II   Security cooperation in Latin America

In order to move forward with security cooperation in Latin America, it is crucial to consider the background and trends which explain the current regional situation.

First, Latin American participation in the *Register* has to be analyzed as part of an actual long term process of regional security cooperation. This process has been difficult, showing moments marked by successes and reversals.

One of the few and fully accomplished initiatives during this century was the 1905 tripartite accord among Argentina, Brazil and Chile on naval disarmament. More recently, the *Esquipulas I Accord* (1985) on peace and demilitarization in Central America proved an important success. Yet several other efforts were less successful. One was the "Costa Rican proposal of arms limitation and reduction in spending on defense measures, coupled with a renunciation of nuclear weapons".[2] Another was the *Ayacucho Declaration* of 1974 which together with its follow up working sessions, unsuccessfully tried to reduce specific types of conventional weaponry.[3] The working groups created to specify the type of offensive and defensive weapon systems did not arrive at any meaningful conclusion due to the different interests of participating countries in including and/or excluding some kind of arms from the lists.

The 1990s have witnessed new disarmament initiatives taking place within the region. Nevertheless, here too there are some positive as well as negative elements co-existing which I will briefly discuss.

Advantages

On the positive side, in Central America, the *Regional Security Agreement* included in the *Panama Declaration* on December 1992, stated the need to follow the Esquipulas I security agreements, including additional measures for enhancing the level of trust; the control of illegal arms trafficking; the establishment of arms, military personnel and security limits; the elimination of foreign military presences; and the enhancement of other transitional sub-regional security mechanisms.

In South America, the *Mendoza Accord* of September 5, 1991, which stated the governmental will of Argentina, Brazil and Chile not to produce and stockpile chemical and biological weapons, followed the *Foz de Iguazú Declaration* of November 28, 1990 by Argentina and Brazil, committing these governments to eliminate and not to manufacture nuclear weapons. These steps would enhance their cooperation in the peaceful uses of nuclear energy and redefine their relations vis-a-vis the International Atomic Energy Agency. The latter accord received the support of Chilean President Patricio Aylwin. The initiative of Peruvian President Fujimori in December 1991, in Cartagena de Indias, Colombia, proposing a regional banning of weapons of mass destruction and a gradual process of arms limitation in the Latin American region, was an additional support to these efforts. At the same line, during 1993 Argentina, Brazil and Chile simultaneously joined the *Tlatelolco Treaty*, an agreement which has now been ratified by their respective congresses. These new regional agreements make it possible to think in terms of the total de-nuclearization of the Latin American region and the elimination of threats regarding chemical, bacteriological, and other weapons of mass destruction.

Finally, in March 1994 the *Expert Meeting on Confidence Building Measures and Security Mechanisms in the Latin American Region*, took notice of the existing regional developments in the field of cooperative security and recommended the pursuit of higher levels of collaboration in this area.[4]

All of these developments in security and cooperation provide a solid ground to engage Latin American countries in supporting the Register. They provide a window of opportunity to increase transparency in arms transfers and to face the development of new arms control regimes in the region with higher possibilities of success than in the recent past.

Obstacles

Nevertheless, there are some negative contextual aspects which have to be considered in order to move forward in a pragmatic way. Several crucial conclusions about security cooperation in Latin America can be drawn from previous regional research.[5]

These conclusions are useful to identify some important black-spots to be analyzed in order to move forward into the area of transparency and peace agreements at a regional level. The first is the dissimilar awareness in each country and sub-region of the effects of global transformations over their security concerns. Thus, the only subregion where the post-cold war was a reality and actually affected security perceptions and policies has been Central America, as it was the subregion most affected by the neo-bipolar confrontation in the 1980s. In the Argentine case, there is a recognition of important global changes and a new long term security policy has been implemented by the Mennem administration. In other cases, like in Brazil, Chile and Peru, global changes are recognized, but main traditional security interests are still important. Thus, Brazil reasserts its independent sub-regional role in the South Atlantic, Sub-Saharan Africa and Latin America; Chile and Peru maintain their traditional border threat perceptions, with new ones, such as narco-terrorism, intervening in the Peruvian case. In the Caribbean, as well as Venezuela, the end of the Cold War did not have the same effect as in Central America since tensions between the United States and Cuba have not yet been resolved. Nevertheless, in the Cuban case, economic and political crises are changing the strategic positioning in the sub-region. Moreover, these continuities coexist with a growing and dramatic interest in economic cooperation which is perceived as blocked by traditional security concerns.

These reactions are, in part, a response to the perceived US security posture in the western hemisphere. The United States government deals with Latin American countries as if all of them were facing the same problems and enacting the same policies. The very conceptualization by the US military of the "Southern Theatre", disregards the variety of national and sub-regional distinctive issues. Latin American governments and elites resent the unilateral definition of the hemispheric security agenda by the United States. Nevertheless, the other side of the coin is that, due to the heterogeneous situation in the region, Latin American countries do not offer a coherent alternative view on hemispheric security.

A second conclusion is that regional security and national defense are not widespread interests in the region. In Central America the new emphasis of the Esquipulas II (1986) Accord on domestic issues has prevented the kind of efforts made in the Contadora meetings and the Esquipulas I Accord towards settling sub-regional security agreements. In Brazil and Peru the concentration of public interest on domestic topics is preventing the development of actual policies for security cooperation. In Chile, the Caribbean, and Venezuela, there is a lack of internal consensus on the definition of the main security interests of these countries and their sub-regions. This situation is also affecting the implementation of cooperative relations at the security level. Thus, no clear common security interests are observed.

Third, the main cleavages inside each country show a variety of internal alignments. In Argentina, entrepreneurs and diplomats differentiate from military circles. In Brazil no clear alignment appears due to the greater importance of current concerns on political regime changes and future political institutions, although a more independent security positioning can be perceived; The same is true in Venezuela due to current turbulence in civil-military relations. In Chile, the alignment opposes diplomats and military views, conservatives and liberals. In Peru, diplomats and military services confront the views of entrepreneurs more interested in cooperation than in confrontation. The same is true in the Caribbean where entrepreneurs are more interested in cooperation, while coping with the remnants of the Cold War. Similarly, in Central America, entrepreneurs are more interested in sub-regional cooperation than their military services which are under intense strains to reshape their institutions in the new democratic frameworks. In sum, traditional security concerns, either typical of the bipolar confrontation or the nineteenth century, are still present. They are combined with new ones such as the Amazonian issue in Brazil, and narco-terrorism in Peru.

Fourth, at the hemispheric level no common approaches vis-à-vis the United States are observed. The Argentine policy is to establish a close relationship with the US, but in Brazil and Chile there is a quest for autonomy. In the Peruvian case there is limited cooperation in the narco-terrorist areas, but not in the military realm. In Venezuela and the Caribbean there is a sense of neglect from the US, a situation which is conceptualized as a "geopolitical vacuum". And in Central America there is a sense of relief at the security level due to the US withdrawal, but also concern due to the negative economic impact resulting from US security detachment. This high level of perceptual and policy heterogeneity makes it more difficult to move toward effective peace agreements and peaceful conflict resolution mechanisms.

However, as a fifth conclusion, these mixed security situations coexist with a variety of formal security agreements. This is the case with confidence building measures,[6] which are highly developed in the cases of Argentina, Brazil, Chile, Central America and Peru. In the cases of Venezuela and the Caribbean, CBMs are out of the picture. Nevertheless, in the Chilean and Venezuelan cases there is a sense that CBMs are not a solution but a pacifier. Due to this definition these governments are prone to increase the number of CBMs in the understanding that they are not going to solve the deeply rooted causes of conflicts and tensions in the sub-regions. This is why CBMs remain low intensity instruments without significant changes in security relations.

Sixth, there is a clear difference among arms control and limitation policies at the conventional level, and the agreements reached at the level of weapons of mass destruction. The latter is a clear and real achievement. The new developments around the Argentine, Brazilian, Cuban and Chilean postures to ratify the Tlatelolco Treaty, the Argentine, Brazilian and Chilean agreements on banning chemical and bacteriological weapons, and the Cartagena declaration banning all weapons of mass destruction in Andean countries, represent the most important successes in disarmament policies at a regional level.

Nevertheless, these achievements are not linked to agreements at the conventional level. On the contrary, all main efforts so far, like the Ayacucho Initiative, have not worked. In this respect there are diverse Latin American postures. In Central America, arms control and disarmament agreements were an integral part of the Contadora accords, but did not play the same role in the Esquipulas II agreements. This is the subregion which shows the greatest level of development of unfulfilled proposals in this respect. In Argentina the Mennem administration has been very active in signing all main arms control and arms limitation agreements, but the Argentine proposals on new security institutions are not fully supported by other Latin American governments due to their perceived pro-American posture and their perception that some old interventionist biases remain. In the Peruvian case, all new administrations are inaugurated with all embracing disarmament and arms control and limitation initiatives, which in the medium and long run, terminate without clear success. In the Brazilian, Chilean, Colombian, Venezuelan and Caribbean cases, there are actual policies to keep their options open to modernize their military services and to cope with their traditional and new security interests.

Finally, at the institutional level, no consensus on the type of multilateral organizations and/or hemispheric security regimes has been observed. Argentina believes that, since Latin American countries are not facing common threats, multilateral security instruments are not necessary. Instead, it prefers to maintain sub-regional balances working through the Rio Group and/or the OAS, although it is proposing a regional center to train Latin American peacekeepers. At the same time Argentina has been active in proposing regional regimes on transparency and ad hoc regional instruments such as a Latin American Conflict Prevention and Management Commission, or a regional initiative similar to the CSCE or the Canadian Cooperative Security Commission. In the case of Brazil there is a different approach – a low profile one – that supports peacekeeping operations under UN control, with an insistence on the OAS as the forum to develop security agreements at a regional level, but which opposes the Zone of Peace initiative. Chile follows similar policies, not endorsing the Zone of Peace initiative and being cautious on multilateral fora. Peru has been very active, promoting a diversity of instruments and institutions, and is an eager supporter of the Zone of Peace initiative. In the case of Venezuela and the Caribbean, there is a different approach, which is to cope with actual conflicts, not to prevent them. Accordingly, they seem to be more interested in ad hoc grouping than in institution building. In Central America, due to previously mentioned reasons, the development of sub-regional security institutions in the framework of the Contadora and Esquipulas processes is in slow motion.

In sum, it is possible to characterize the current Latin American attitude toward security matters around the following elements:

1. The post-cold war international framework is an important variable in the Central American and Argentine cases, linking their posture to US foreign policies. But, in the other cases, the end of the cold war did not affect their security perceptions;

2. There is a low level of interest in national defense and security issues among Latin American societies and elites;

3. Cleavages due to different views among regional elites are widespread, but no clear alignments are observed;

4. Some alignments can be observed as important: ideological issues; the military vs. diplomats and business circles; diplomats and military services vs. entrepreneurs.

5. There is a highly developed bilateral and multilateral regional system of CBMs and disarmament accords on weapons of mass destruction. Nevertheless, these achievements do not comprise – and actually omit – agreements at the level of control and limitation of conventional weapons.

6. Even though entrepreneurs are more prone and interested than the rest of their societies in constructive regional security arrangements, economic crisis could affect their views on these matters, moving them towards a nationalist type of framework.

Explanations

According to these conclusions, the crucial question which has to be answered is: why, in a region with such a variety of CBMs and important disarmament agreements on weapons of mass destruction, have no clear improvements on conventional arms control and limitations been observed? The reasons lie within the peculiar nature of conventional arms control and limitation processes in Latin America.

In the late seventies and early eighties an optimistic view of Latin America as an area of open possibilities for arms control and limitation agreements was disseminated worldwide. This was mainly due to the successful experience of the Tlatelolco Treaty on regional nuclear disarmament. Some authors conceptualized this achievement stating that the region was actually producing a new model for arms control and limitation, the *Tlatelolco Model*. It was indicated that this was possible in areas where some learning experience was available, where an arms race process was in its beginnings, where the level of arms stockpile was low, tranquillity and power equilibrium existed, initiatives could possibly be promoted and agreed upon, and regional maturity existed. Thus, it was perceived that the moment for a "conventional Tlatelolco" had arrived.[7]

Why, after more than a decade, hasn't the moment of a conventional Tlatelolco yet arrived? The answer can be found in the dramatic differences between conventional and nuclear arms control and limitation processes, and the lack of a theoretical understanding on conventional arms negotiations and agreements.

As has been stated, conventional arms control differs from nuclear ones, "it was only in the late 1980s that conventional arms control developed any serious momentum, it has never been well treated in the literature, and is barely mentioned in many books on arms control". Accordingly, "conventional arms never appeared so susceptible to negotiated adjustments. Compared with nuclear negotiations, the participants would always be more numerous, the boundaries more arbitrary, the forces more varied, the theories less coherent".[8] For these reasons,

> "the basic nature of conventional warfare makes it difficult to reconcile the goals of crisis stability and deterrence in the same force structure. Force structures that have been proposed to achieve this reconciliation are politically unattractive; arms control agreements that attempt to impose them on the competitors are inherently quite fragile from a military perspective...Because much of our thinking about arms control has been influenced by efforts to limit nuclear arms, it is useful to contrast conventional forces with nuclear forces to free ourselves of nuclear biases. The huge differences between the two are usually highlighted in order to free thinkers from conventional biases. These two types of forces differ in three ways that have impor-

> tant consequences: first, in destructiveness; second, in organization; and third, in application...To summarize, conventional forces are fragile where nuclear forces are sturdy. Conventional forces depend on secrecy; nuclear forces depend on survivability. Conventional warfare is the realm of military strategy; nuclear warfare is the realm of diplomacy. Conventional forces seek victory; nuclear forces seek a modus vivendi."[9]

In the same vein, other authors indicate that stability at the nuclear and conventional levels depends on a different set of factors.

> "Yet the nuclear theories were inappropriate...In practice --as much was done to address these concerns through confidence-building measures-- which addressed exercises and the movement of forces, as attempts to distinguish between offensive and defensive conventional armaments. An specially inappropriate concept was that of 'balance.' An equality of forces at the nuclear level might symbolize mutual respect based on mutual vulnerability, but at the conventional level such equality could be highly unstable in that it could provide no guide to the outcome of armed conflict. All attempts to construct a formal military balance that would be of any help in negotiations inevitably left out a series of factors – including timing, terrain, reserves, supply lines, training, morale, and so on – that could be decisive in combat...No theory was developed of the relationship between conventional force and crisis. The guidelines area in MBFR reflected negotiating convenience as much as the likely participants in and the boundaries of a European war. The inclusive approach of CFE assumed that warfare would be a set piece confrontation across the length of the East-West divide. The idea of a crisis as a time of stresses and strains in alliance systems, in which military forces would be moved to confirm commitments, issue warnings, demonstrate resolve, did not enter the theory."[10]

The underdeveloped theoretical thinking, the scarcity of successful experiences of multilateral conventional arms control and limitation agreements, and the lack of efficient regional institutions to develop regional security regimes, show that there is the need to create and consolidate stable relationships among hemispheric actors around these issues.

The Latin American reactions and responses to the UN Register of Conventional Arms could be an important opportunity to reinvigorate security cooperation in the western hemisphere.

III   The Latin American response to the Register

Within the recently summarized regional security trends it is possible to contextualize and to evaluate the Latin American response to the Register.

Transparency is one of the most important CBMs for Latin American governments and military institutions. Inasmuch as regional and sub-regional threat perceptions still remain, it is crucial to provide on time information to regional governments about their real military magnitude. The availability of information regarding effective offensive capabilities of potential aggressors could prevent a new long term cycle of competition in arms procurement.

From a comparative perspective, the Latin American quantitative performance has not been different from that observed in other regions of the world. Nevertheless, from a qualitative perspective, the main Latin American importers and exporters are supporting the Register more so than in other areas of the world.

During the first year of the Register, the average proportion of Latin American governmental responses had been relatively the same as the rest of the UN members. That is, out of 186 UN countries to whom the request was sent, 83 (45%) responded. In Latin America, from the 25 countries analyzed[11], 12 responded to the Register (Table I). That is, 48% of regional countries and 14.5% of all world respondents.

An analysis of the 12 Latin American governments which responded reveals that only 7 reported both on arms imports and exports and just 2 of them – Brazil and Chile – that is 8% of Latin American countries, provided a "full report" including background information.[12] The lack of full information from the other 5 countries – Argentina, Bolivia, Cuba, Grenada and Peru- was due to insufficient background information.

Nevertheless, one can conclude from an analysis of the responses by sub-regions and the military importance of these countries, that the main importers in South America (Argentina, Brazil, Chile and Colombia, but also Peru and Venezuela), are supporting the Register by providing all the information requested. Different from other regions, all main Latin American regional exporters (Argentina, Brazil and Chile) are also providing the information requested.

The same is true in the Caribbean case, where Cuba, the main military power in that area, is also providing the information requested. However, the Dominican Republic, another player in this area, has been absent.

Table 1. Latin American responses to the Register

Country	Imports	Exports	Note verbale	Background information
South America				
Argentina*	Nil	Yes		No
Bolivia*	Yes	Nil		No
Brazil*	Yes	Yes		Yes
Chile*	Yes	Nil		Yes
Colombia**	Yes	Nil	Yes	No
Ecuador				
Guyana				
Paraguay**			Yes	No
Peru**	Yes	Blank Form		No
Uruguay				
Venezuela				
Caribbean				
Barbados				
Cuba*	Nil	Nil	Yes	No
Dominican Republic				
Grenada*	Nil	Blank Form		No
Haiti				
Jamaica				
Trinidad & Tobago				
Central America				
Costa Rica				
Guatemala				
El Salvador				
Honduras				
Nicaragua**				Yes
Panama**			Yes	Yes***
North America				
Mexico**			Yes	No

Note: * Full compliance
         ** Partial compliance
        *** Not on holdings

The Central American sub-region has been less involved in complying with the Register. This is especially critical considering that this area has been one of the most conflictual sub-regions in the hemisphere and is currently under a process of pacification.

This brief comparison makes it possible to conclude that even though the regional response to the UN conventional arms Register has not elicited responses from all Latin American countries, there are some key players in the South American and Caribbean sub-regions providing an example which could be followed by the rest of the governments in the region.

Finally, and most surprising, those countries with a more autonomous positioning in security matters (Brazil and Chile) are relatively more supportive of the Register than those more active in security arrangements and achievements (Argentina).

IV   Consolidating the Register

The above summarized regional security context and trends, as well as the Latin American response to the Register are important elements to appraise in implementing policies oriented to consolidate the Register in the hemisphere.

Considering that this newly born initiative is in its first stage of consolidation, it is possible to conclude that the full implementation of the Register could be a regional success if some additional actions are taken to strengthen it.

Improvement of the Register could be based upon two main dimensions: the institutionalization of this emerging international security regime through complementary actions; and the enforcement of domestic measures, including supporting activities, which could make possible a better response of Latin American governments.

Regional institutionalization of Register

The institutionalization of the Register means stabilizing and expanding its coverage with the intent of solving some tensions that have been observed in its first year of operation.

A gradual approach

It should be recalled that this regime is in year one of its first stage of development and that more than half of the UN members did not respond yet to the first call.

In Latin America, and probably in other developing regions, the institutionalization of the Register should be done in the medium term. This consolidation has to be done concentrating efforts on that information more closely related to conventional arms, rather than expanding to areas where there exist other security regimes available to handle these additional dimensions. Accordingly, it would be advisable to define the development of the Register as a gradual process, identifying the following stages:

Promotion – First, it would be important to underline the need of inclusiveness. For this reason, it is urgent to organize an active promotion of the Register through a well designed program of lobbying, showing the benefits of a worldwide participation. This stage could have some targets, such as the inclusion of at least two third of the UN member states.

Clarification – Second, some clarifications are needed. The background information requested has to be defined more clearly. It includes military holdings, procurement through national production and relevant policies.

Regarding military holdings and procurement through national production, a re-evaluation of the performance and methodologies of the previous UN Resolution 33/67 of 14 December 1978 on Military Budgets has to be undertaken as a crucial step towards requiring this type of information.

To legitimize UN initiatives it is important that any modification of previous instruments like this one, has an evaluation of its performance and the reasons of its deficiencies. Doing this, it could be possible to redefine the format of the information requested adapting it to the simple form provided by the Register.

The request of information on relevant policies could be more focused, by indicating precisely the type of policies included, rather than keeping the options to respondents open to "any form they wish."

Limited expansion – Third, expanding the Register to include "further categories of equipment and inclusion of data on military holdings and procurement through national production",[13] should be done separately.

Data on military holdings and procurement through national production could be an integral part of the enforcement of the first stage of the Register, as mentioned above.

Further categories of equipment and the inclusion of new subcategories could be defined as a new step in this regime building process, after an evaluation of the previous ones, a better performance of the instrument in the following years and more discussion before introducing new elements (platforms instead of ammunition, a systemic approach vs. counting weapons).

Simplicity favors transparency. Complexity could be instrumental to prevent it.

Exclusions – Fourth, the inclusion of weapons of mass destruction could be handled by a separate Register constituting a different security regime from the Register. The Argentine proposal of a parallel register makes more sense in Latin America where several agreements, including their verification mechanisms, have banned this type of weapon.

Cooperation – Fifth, the expansion of the Register to include high technology with military application could be handled by other international security regimes, i.e., the MTCR,[14] the NPT, and others. Expanding the Register to include these fields could render institutionalization and full enforcement more difficult. Accordingly, it would be important to establish an active cooperation among several regional and global peace agreements and accords.

Regional participation

The Register, although a global instrument, has to play its most important role contributing to regional stability. That is, this is a global instrument with regional strategic meaning.

The regionalization of the uses of the Register, not its administration, is crucial to increase the regional support for this initiative and to legitimize it among regional governments and local elites and decision makers. To achieve higher levels of legitimation it is necessary to increase the regional participation in the Register. This could be done developing a systemic approach to the uses of the Register and establishing cooperative linkages among regional security initiatives.[15]

A systemic approach – The Register could be defined as an individual and isolated effort of security cooperation or it could be settled into a wider framework of security mechanisms for conflict prevention and control.

Considering that the Register is one of several instruments to prevent conflicts, it has to be linked to other initiatives and regimes created and oriented to the same purposes. This is especially true with regard to defining excessive and destabilizing accumulation of weapons.

The maintenance of regional and sub-regional stability is not necessarily and exclusively linked to the accumulation of conventional weapons. It is also related to and determined by their deployment, military doctrines, grand strategies and other elements. Transparency is the necessary condition for an assessment of potential regional destabilization. A systemic analysis of weapon deployments in specific areas is the sufficient condition. Without a contextual analysis of conventional arms deployments, it would be impossible to assess the level of potential risks in a given region. Accordingly, preventing and controlling certain conflicts implies having permanent, follow-up risk analyses, including examination of the stockpile of certain weapon systems *and* their deployments.

In considering the possibility for a qualified risk analysis of regional conflict potential, it is crucial to move forward in the following directions:

A joint effort – Considering that risk analysis has to be done under a regional and sub-regional basis and expertise, it is important to regionalize the uses of the Register, increasing the participation of regional states.

In the western hemisphere, the regionalization of the uses of the Register would enhance the possibility for cooperation between other UN bodies working in Latin America and other regional organizations.

The following organizations could carry out joint efforts in this regard:

- The UN Regional Center for Peace, Disarmament and Development in Latin America.

Created by Resolution 41/60 J of the General Assembly, on 3 December 1986 and located in Lima, Peru, the Center has been conducting workshops and publications on regional security cooperation. Considering its past work and perspective, the Center could become one of the key actors in maintaining information and promoting the participation of Latin American governments in the Register.

The existence of this Center and its previous works on regional security and cooperation show that with limited resources and an enlightened leadership, it is possible to raise and disseminate important information and to create an arena for regional civil-military interchange on key issues of security and cooperation.

- The Special Committee on Hemispheric Security of the Organization of American States.

The Organization of American States (OAS) has been criticized for its inability to prevent and control regional conflicts. Nevertheless, it has played some important roles in this regard[16] and could play a more significant one in the future.[17] One of the most promising initiatives has been the creation of the *Special Committee on Hemispheric Security* in 1992.

This Committee, attended by governmental representatives and actively engaged in enforcing CBMs in the region, could be an excellent coordinator of regional governmental efforts to consolidate and expand the Register.

Currently, the Committee is involved in organizing the 1995 Santiago conference on CBMs in Latin America. It is also promoting a hemispheric meeting of ministers of defense, and is exploring new ways for interaction with the Inter-American Defense Board and Defense College.

- The Inter-American Defense Board

The Inter-American Defense Board (IADB), created during the World War II period at the Third Meeting of Consultation of Ministers of Foreign Affairs in Rio de Janeiro, January 1942, has evolved in the post-cold war period without a defined relationship with the OAS and without a clear policy orientation.

At this moment it would be possible to redefine its relationship with the OAS,as a OAS Military Staff without operative functions, and headed by a Council nominated by the hemispheric meeting of ministers of defense.

One of the duties of this new body could be to analyze the Register's data and to carry out risk analysis and conflict prevention, among other tasks.

The *Inter-American Defense College (IADC)*, created by the IADB in 1962, could train civilians and military officers in analyzing the Register data and assessing sub-regional situations in order to prevent and control crisis due to excessive weapon procurement and offensive deployments.

The participation of the IADB and the IADC could make possible the active participation of the *Arms Control and Disarmament Agency (ACDA)*, playing an important role in cross-checking exercises. The same is true for Canadian governmental bodies such as the *Cooperative and Regional Security Affairs, International Security and Defence Relations Division* of the Ministry of External Affairs.

- UN Economic Commission for Latin America and the Caribbean (ECLAC)

Considering that ECLAC is the leading multilateral economic institution in Latin America, it is important to include its participation. ECLAC could contribute to standardizing data and analyzing the economic aspects and impacts of conventional arms transfers.

- Regional non-governmental and academic institutions

The integration and participation of regional non-governmental and academic institutions in this institutional pool is of crucial importance to maximize the benefits of the Register at a regional and sub-regional scale.

Regional non-governmental organizations, academic institutions and scholastic networks, such as the Latin American Council of Social Sciences (CLACSO), the Latin American Faculty of Social Science (FLACSO), the Center for International Development (CINDE), and the Latin American Center for Defense and Disarmament (CLADDE), among others, could be engaged in cross-checking studies, in-depth analyses and risk estimations.

This joint effort organization could be managed by a Steering Committee of representatives from the above mentioned bodies and chaired by the UN representative at the Regional Center for Peace, Disarmament and Development in Latin America. This Steering Committee could be advised by a regional standing panel of experts. This model could be replicated in other developing areas.

Expanded governmental participation

All of the above mentioned initiatives would not be possible without a definite commitment by individual governments.

Nevertheless, to make possible a deeper engagement of Latin American governments in sponsoring the Register, some domestic initiatives have to be introduced.

Inter-sectorial coordination – Usually, in Latin America -and probably else-where-governmental policies regarding regional, hemispheric and global security are directly handled by the respective ministries of foreign relations. The relationship between the foreign ministries with their defense counterparts, if there is one, is mainly of consultation on specified issues at critical moments. In addition, cooperative security, CBMs, arms control and limitation and disarmament of weapons of mass destruction are seen by military institutions as conducive to their disappearance or minimization. With this type of perception it would be difficult to find military institutional support to disclose information on arms transfers and domestic procurement.

Accordingly, the limited participation of ministries of defense and their specialized military bodies in these matters precludes a deeper engagement of military institutions in supporting international initiatives on cooperative security.

This inter-sectorial coordination could make possible the participation of military officers in the activities organized to provide information for the Register. From an institutional perspective it would be important to create a special desk in both ministries to work together in these matters.

Parliamentarian participation – Another important sector of Latin American societies usually not considered within the traditional scope of security policies includes members of congress and specialized staffers.

Considering the importance of the surveillance role of parliaments in domestic political life, it is of utmost importance to create ways for their participation either domestically supporting the Register, or the regional level of Inter-Parliamentary Meetings.

The same could be done designing special programs and information to congressional advisory committees on defense and foreign relations, making possible their cooperation in this regard.

NGOs, universities and research centers – To achieve effective transparency and arms control and limitations agreements it is necessary to develop what has been labelled a *pluralistic security community* at the conventional level. Common expectations, governmental policy coordination, value compatibility and a "we feeling", seem to be crucial elements in the development of this pluralistic security community. However, in the Latin American case, these conditions face a complex situation.

On the one hand, compatibility of political values is not that high since regional democratization processes have been recent and are uneven and unstable. On the other hand, policy coordination – the precondition for a "we feeling" – and common expectations, are weak since the current processes of economic structural adjustment and change are producing centrifugal forces diminishing incentives for inter-state cooperation at non-security levels other than commerce.

Due to these reasons, there is the need to develop a set of values and opera-tional concepts which could make possible the development of this pluralistic security community in the Western Hemisphere. This could entail promoting coalitions for security cooperation and empowering societies to influence policy making processes on security issues.

In this process, the participation of NGOs, universities and research centers is crucial. Through their academic activity they will be able to disseminate information, making it available to wide audiences, thus creating a social support for the type of activities in which the Register is one integral part.

V   Conclusion

In sum, the Register presents a good opportunity for Latin American and other developing countries to create a new regional security cooperative regime. The Register appears in a moment of a new wave of security agreements in the region. The complete achievement of transparency through the UN Register has to be made by designing a medium term approach and taking into consideration the main idiosyncratic elements and obstacles. It could be implemented by initiating a promotional campaign or by consolidation through a higher level of gradual institutionalization. However, it needs clarification in some aspects in order to be more focused and less inclusive. In addition, it must be integrated with the efforts of other security regimes and regional institutions and coupled with the implementation of domestic measures to support it.

Notes

1. For some skeptical views on the Register see Andrew Pierre, "Multilateral Restraints on the Proliferation of Conventional Arms: Opportunities and Obstacles", paper prepared for author's workshop on Conventional Arms Proliferation in the 1990s, World Peace Foundation, Carnegie Endowment for International Peace, Washington, D.C., November 12-13, 1992.

2. John Child, *Unequal Alliance: The Inter-American Military System, 1938-1978* , Westview Press, Boulder, 1980, p. 128.

3. María Eliana Castillo, "Control de armamentos: el caso de América Latina", *Documento de Trabajo* , N°31, FLACSO, Santiago, January, 1985.

4. Organización de los Estados Americanos, *Recomendaciones de la Reunión de Expertos sobre Medidas de Fomento de la Confianza y Mecanismos de Seguridad en la Región* OEA/Ser.K/XXIX SEGRE/doc. 41/94, 18 March 1994.

5. *Global Transformations and Peace: Arms Control, Disarmament and the Resolution of Conflicts in the Western Hemisphere in the Post-Cold War Period*, regional research project conducted and coordinated by Augusto Varas FLACSO-Chile and Joseph S. Tulchin, The Wilson Center from 1992 to 1994, supported by the John D. and Catherine T. MacArthur Foundation.

6. On CBMs, see Augusto Varas and Isaac Caro Editors, *Medidas de Confianza Mutua en América Latina* , FLACSO, Santiago,1994.

Notes continued

7. Jacques Huntzinger, "Regional Recipient Restraints", in Anne Hessing et.al., (eds), *Controlling Future Arms Trade* , Council on Foreign Relations, New York, 1977, p. 183-185.

8. Lawrence Freedman, "The End of Formal Arms Control", in Emmanuel Adler (ed.), *The International Practice of Arms Control*, The Johns Hopkins University Press, Baltimore, 1992, p. 77.

9. Barry R. Posen, "Crisis Stability and Conventional Arms Control", in ibid., pp. 233 and 235.

10. Lawrence Freedman, "The End of Formal Arms Control", in op. cit., p. 79. Also see Michael Moodie, "The Conventional Arms Control in Europe", *Disarmament*, Volume XIV, Number 2, 1991.

11. Edward J. Laurance, Siemon T. Wezeman and Herbert Wulf, *Arms Watch: SIPRI Report on the First Year of the UN Register of Conventional Arms*, Oxford University Press, New York, 1993, and Malcolm Chalmers and Owen Greene, *Background Information: An Analysis of Information Provided to the UN on Military Holdings and Procurement through National Production in the First Year of the Register of Conventional Arms*, Bradford Arms Register Studies No 3, Department of Peace Studies, Bradford University, March 1994.

12. Colombia reported holdings instead of imports by mistake and no background information.

13. *Report on the Register of Conventional Arms: Report of The Secretary General,* General Assembly, A/47/342, 14 August 1992, paragraphs 34 to 41.

14. It has been suggested that the MTCR, an informal arrangement, should be transformed into a treaty, adopted by the UN and transformed into one of its international agencies. See, Amy F. Woolf, "Arms Control and Disarmament Activities: A Catalog of Recent Efforts", *CRS Report for Congress*, Congressional Research Service, Washington, D.C., January 17, 1993, p. 45.

15. Robert D. Tomasek, "The Organization of American States and Dispute Settlement From 1948 to 1981: An Assessment", *Revista Inter-Americana de Bibliografía*, Volume XXXIX, N°4, 1989, pp. 461-476.

16. This is the meaning of the statement made by the Secretary General of the UN calling for a "regionalization" of the *Agenda for Peace*.

17. Larman C. Wilson, "The OAS and Promoting Democracy and Resolving Disputes: Reactivation in the 1990s?", in ibid., pp. 477-499; and Viron P. Vaky and Heraldo Muñoz, *The Future of the Organization of America States* , The Twentieth Century Fund Press, New York, 1993.

CHAPTER 14

The UN Register in a regional context: basic concepts

Joseph DiChiaro III

I   Introduction

Throughout the development and into the implementation phase of the United Nations Register of Conventional Arms, the call has often been made for the development and application of regional variations of the Register in order that the aims and goals of the UN system be more manageable and salient to the states submitting information, and to encourage more substantive participation from all parties. It has also been argued by some of those involved in this debate that the expansion of the Register into further categories of armaments, national holdings and procurement through national production may require a region-by-region approach rather than an attempt to reach universal consensus.

However, the substantial gains made by the initial establishment and operation of the Register as a global political instrument should not be disregarded in fashioning more regionally specific measures. Rather, any such approach should serve to complement gradual universal progress towards establishing global standards by addressing particularly local security needs in conjunction with, not in competition with, the UN Register. Just how feasible and desirable such a regional approach would be, in the area of transparency in arms transfers and procurement through national production, is thus the focus of this Chapter.

II   A mandate for cooperative action?

In order to approach the question of regional cooperation in the maintenance of both regional and global peace and security, a review of the call to regional initiative may be necessary.

The call for collaboration between the United Nations and regional and sub-regional bodies in the maintenance of international peace and security has been based on two main points. First, it is argued that local actors are perhaps better equipped to observe and monitor events in their own region and that they may in turn be more attuned to the means of conflict resolution most applicable under local conditions. Second, given the enormous resource constraints on the United Nations, it is argued that other bodies may need to share the financial and personnel burden of effective security management.

United Nations Secretary-General Boutros Boutros-Ghali laid the groundwork for a new, post-Cold War complementary relationship between the Security Council and regional organizations in his June 1992 *Agenda for Peace*. In this report, Boutros-Ghali devoted an entire section to "Cooperation with regional arrangements and organizations" where he underlined the potential for regional bodies to act in concert with the United Nations while tactfully, though understandably, avoiding the difficult questions concerning the nature of the proposed relationship and the ensuing division of labor.[1] This was soon followed in October 1992 by Boutros-Ghali's *New Dimensions of Arms Regulation and Disarmament in the Post-Cold War Era* which explicitly encouraged regional approaches. In it, the Secretary-General noted that "Regional and sub-regional organizations can further the globalization of disarmament, both in cooperation with each other and with the United Nations."[2] While pointing to conventional arms races as an area deserving attention, once again little detail was supplied. Finally, in a potentially significant departure from these broad calls for regional action, the Secretary-General, in an address to the Advisory Board on Disarmament Matters in January 1994, stated that "Regional registers of conventional arms should now be the next step. They have the advantage of allowing the categories of weapons to be registered to reflect the security concerns felt in the region."[3]

Within the General Assembly the call for regional initiatives and cooperation with the United Nations in the field of confidence-building and disarmament has been no less ambitious. Resolution 46/36 H of 6 December 1991 requested that the Secretary-General "assist...in holding meetings and seminars at the national, *regional* and international levels, as pertinent, with a view to...promoting the concept of transparency as a confidence-building measure..." (author's emphasis).[4] Furthermore, under a resolution entitled "Regional Disarmament," the General Assembly declared its support and encouraged efforts aimed at promoting confidence-building measures at regional and sub-regional levels.[5] Finally, within the resolution which established the United Nations Register of Conventional Arms, 46/36 L of 9 December 1991, the General Assembly called "upon all Member States to cooperate at a regional and sub-regional level, taking fully into account the specific conditions prevailing in the region or sub-region, with a view to enhancing and coordinating international efforts aimed at increased openness and transparency in armaments."[6] Subsequently this specific provision has been reiterated in the "Transparency in armaments" resolution of the 48th General Assembly.[7]

Also the Disarmament Commission, the United Nations disarmament machinery's deliberative body, has seriously broached the issue of regional action. During its 1993 substantive session, the Commission enumerated "guidelines and recommendations for regional approaches to disarmament within the context of global security,"[8] which it in turn reported to the 48th session of the General Assembly. While these guidelines are a good start in terms of formulation of ideas, the burden of initiative still appears to lie firmly on the shoulders of regional actors. However, should a strong regional proposal receive United Nations support and technical assistance, it could help to define the possibilities and limits of such an approach, and thus serve as a model for emulation and adaptation elsewhere.

Had regional entities or even individual Member States responded to this call to action with creative and locally specific initiatives for effecting regional stability, the foregoing would be irrelevant. Yet, while a few have called, like the Secretary-General, for region-specific arms registers, none have elaborated what this would actually mean to the region in question. Nor is it certain whether either supporters or detractors of this concept are even working from the same definition.

III   The regional approach to the Register

Despite these general calls for action, however, little work has been done to elaborate what a regional approach to the arms Register might mean in practice. There is concern that the current Register mechanism is unable to take into account the particularities of individual regions or to account for weapons systems which concern some regions but not others. If the Register is to develop much further while simultaneously enhancing its relevance to states' concerns, therefore, there may be a case for the development of regional complements to the global reporting system.

The proponents of a regional approach to conventional arms restraint are a diverse group. Included among its most ardent supporters are Pakistan in South Asia, Argentina in Latin America, and Malaysia in Southeast Asia. The common thread running through the comments of those in favor of a regional approach is that the universal approach embodied in the UN Register fails to account for the history or particular security needs of states in individual regions. By contrast, a regional approach could be tailored to suit the peculiarities of the region in question.

Beyond this simple logic, however, arise some fairly difficult questions regarding the elaboration of such an instrument. Would such a register supplement or supplant the current UN system? Would such an approach contribute or detract from the future expansion of the universal register? What would compel states to become more transparent in a regional context as opposed to on the global level?

Most statements in support of the UN Register make it clear that development on a regional level should serve to complement rather than replace it. States have invested far too much political capital towards building universal consensus on the need to restrain certain types of weapons sales to regions of instability to allow, in turn, for those regions to determine their own standards for transparency in weapons acquisition (which may be watered down to the point of irrelevance). Furthermore, some in the developing world consider the Register too valuable an instrument with which to point out the sources of the weaponry causing difficulties within their region to allow for its dissolution.

As such, fashioning a regional variant could be a delicate process of determining what is universally applicable and what may be unique to a particular region. In terms of defining the legitimate security needs of individual states and what, in fact, constitutes excessive and destabilizing accumulations, the regional level may, in some cases, provide a greater degree of consensus when neighboring states are relatively homogenous in nature. In these cases, of which Europe may be one example, the creation of a regional mechanism may allow for a higher level of transparency between regional participants than would be possible through a global mechanism. However, given the suspicion and mistrust which proximity often engenders, in some other regions this approach may prove more divisive than useful. In these cases, states may be less likely to share information with less than amicable neighboring states than they are to provide data to a universal and non-discriminatory global Register.

A principle which could be useful in the further development of this approach is "subsidiarity." Much maligned within the European Community, which is in a very large part responsible for the term's existence, subsidiarity refers to the idea that the Community should undertake and assume only those tasks and responsibilities that could be better carried out in common than by member states acting separately. Yet, depending on which side of the subsidiarity fence one sits, the principle takes on different meaning. For Eurofederalists, such as Jacques Delors, subsidiarity would enable the Community's organs to focus on key issues, leaving the more mundane issues to the competence of member states. On the other hand, a number of member states see subsidiarity as a means of guarding against Community intrusion into traditionally national and highly sensitive issue areas.

Applying this principle to the further development of the Register to account for regional variations would mean that those elements of security unique to a particular region could be left to the competence of that group of states, while entrusting the international community with the establishment of more generally applicable standards and norms in countering the negative effects of arms transfers and procurement. In the case of the arms trade, as in the case of the Community, however, it is how these responsibilities will be divided which may prove problematic.

IV   Modalities of a regional approach

The components of a regional approach to arms transparency, developed as a complement to the UN Register, could include some or all of the following:

•   If it is to induce compliance among states, a regional approach must not be seen by prospective participants as imposed, either from the 'North' or from a dominant power within the region. Any such perception is likely to hamper participation and negate its usefulness.

•   If it is agreed that there are weapons systems and technologies that are specifically destabilizing when excessively accumulated within a particular region, in addition to those already included in the United Nations Register, these could be identified and included as items to be reported. This may include a decision to expand beyond conventional weapons into weapons of mass destruction, (complementing and strengthening the monitoring provisions of the Biological Weapons Convention, Chemical Weapons Convention and Non-Proliferation Treaty). It could expand the coverage of small arms and support systems not covered in the global Register (for example AWACS aircraft, mortars of less than 100mm calibre, armoured bridges). By recognizing the peculiarities of individual regions, an additional layer of transparency could be added that could enhance regional stability and international security.

•   Even with particularly destabilizing systems properly identified (recognizably no small task), a decision must be reached on the types of transfers to be reported. A major issue will be the determination of whether only intra-regional trade and imports into the region be addressed, with exports of systems not covered by the UN Register being excluded.

• If holdings and procurement from national production are not included in the UN Register, or are only included on a partial basis, then they should be addressed on a regional level. For without the inclusion of national procurement, either on a global or regional basis, reporting of imports and exports may be biased against countries primarily reliant on imports. Without a baseline of holdings from which to judge, the Register's utility as an early warning instrument may be negligible.

• The timeliness of submissions should also be addressed. Certain regions may desire more timely notification of transfers as a means of building trust and instilling confidence. As such, they may opt for a real-time reporting system or even prior notification of weapon acquisitions or transfers.

• A particularly sensitive issue, which may only find resolution on the regional level, is that of inclusion of a verification and/or conflict resolution mechanism to ensure the accuracy of the data submitted and to resolve any disputed figures or allegations of destabilizing build-ups. A promising approach could be to build upon the current UN database-centered system to include a regional mechanism for the mediation of disputes arising from perceived excessive transfers or build-ups.

• States may be willing to participate in such regional mechanisms if they believe that they have been tailored to the specific needs of their region. By being the result of negotiation and compromise among the regional group, claims of inherent discrimination, such as those criticisms levelled at the Non-Proliferation Treaty (NPT) or Missile Technology Control Regime (MTCR), could be avoided. If states not only have an important stake in ensuring the success of the endeavor, but have also invested much time and effort in shaping such an exercise to fit their needs, participation in regional approaches could play a useful complementary role to the global Register.

• In developing a complementary and parallel regional variation, states may wish to restrict submissions of especially sensitive additional material, such as pre-notification of transfers, to only regional government-to-government distribution. Although this would be counter to the idea of openness in armaments, this could be crucial for regional consensus.

V   Strengthening regional organizations

Possibly the greatest obstacle to enhanced security through regional confidence building measures is the weakness of the regional organizations currently in existence. Without delving into the myriad reasons why regional organizations outside of Europe have failed to establish strong responsibilities in the field of regional security, one need merely observe the weakness or lack of security functions within the Organization of African Unity, Organization of American States (OAS), and Association of South East Asian Nations (ASEAN). Yet, it is still early in the post-Cold War era and these organizations may still (in fact they are already looking to) take on increasing responsibility in the maintenance of peace and security within their own sphere.

In a recent article, Jon Lunn proposes the creation of Regional Security Commissions (RSCs) as a means of creating a formal link between the United Nations Security Council and regional organizations.[9] Such a body would be tasked with coordinating the activities of the two groups and working out a division of powers. If created as proposed, such a body would be a good locale for the establishment and maintenance of a regional arms register able to collect data from the region and prepare and submit it to the United Nations. On the other hand, such an arrangement could create a redundant layer of bureaucracy and may be unlikely to attract a more capable staff than existing organizations. With or without such RSCs, the regional organizations themselves must be significantly strengthened in order to sufficiently manage the host of new responsibilities being suggested. One way to do this is to have them take on increasingly important tasks which, if adequately handled, will enhance their viability and the likelihood member states of the region will increasingly delegate further tasks to them.

VI   Possibilities: Latin America & Southeast Asia[10]

Finally, a brief overview of the prospects for implementation of a regional variant of the UN Register system may be useful in fashioning a workable approach. Two states have been particularly vocal in support of such an approach being developed within the framework of existing organizations: Argentina, for application within the OAS; and Malaysia, within ASEAN. The differing circumstances in which each region and regional organization currently finds itself regarding trends in military expenditure, weapons procurement, past history of arms control initiatives, and Register participation, serves to highlight the need for differing approaches and may be an indication of potential success.

Differing trends in military expenditure between the two regions point to, on the one hand, the potential for success in Latin America, and on the other, a growing need for such a mechanism in Southeast Asia as a means of promoting restraint in arms transfers. The end of the Cold War and the conclusion of the Gulf conflict have both directly and indirectly led to a plummeting of defense expenditures on the part of Latin American states and a dwindling of export orders leading nearly to the cessation of national production. By contrast, while virtually every other region of the world has seen a precipitous drop in procurement and expenditures, Southeast Asia has seen an influx of weapons imports and a rise in indigenous production capabilities.

While the history of arms control and disarmament in Latin America is rich with initiatives fostered by the strong political will of states in the region towards promoting stability, these initiatives frequently failed owing to the security environment in which these initiatives were forwarded.[11] The current period may be graced with the convergence of both the requisite political will and favorable security environment necessary for the successful implementation of an effective arms control regime. Southeast Asia, again in contrast, has neither a tradition of arms control initiatives, nor as opportune an environment favoring restraint. Implementation of such a mechanism, therefore, is all the more essential, and yet uncertain of success.

In terms of willingness to participate in such an exercise, results from the first year of the UN Register are the only benchmark we have. In terms of sheer numbers, the much smaller ASEAN had 50 per cent of its members report whereas the OAS only a little over 30 per cent. However, within Latin America, all the major importers and exporters of advanced weaponry – including Argentina, Brazil, Chile and Peru – reported, whereas among ASEAN members Indonesia and Thailand, fairly significant weapons importers, did not participate. As such, participation by the major players in the OAS bodes well for the development of a more effective and perhaps intrusive regime. The same cannot be said for ASEAN, although its members may be more willing to participate should a mechanism be devised which includes the issues more salient to them and vital to their national security.

While the effectiveness and utility of the OAS is often in question, its established structure and permanent council are well positioned to handle additional responsibilities in the field of regional security. In particular, its Special Committee on Hemispheric Security is increasingly being asked to examine possible areas in which the organization can effectively contribute to the security of the region. "Transparency in Armaments" is, interestingly, one issue area it has already been mandated to explore. ASEAN, however, does not share this tradition and may find the task of building meaningful structures difficult. Paradoxically, though, in creating a function which the states of the region find in their best interest to support, the regional body may itself be empowered and expanded.

All of this points, in the case of Latin America and the OAS, to a single fundamental question: Does such a regional initiative matter in a region where interests are converging, tensions lessening, and military expenditures dramatically reduced? My answer is a qualified "yes." Networks of conflict-resolution will be established which will be convenient in the best of times and crucial in the worst; and a standard will be established for emulation in other regions.

VII Conclusions

Much of the criticism to date concerning the United Nations Register of Conventional Arms has focused primarily on the mechanism itself and what it does not do to halt the trade in conventional weapons.[12] Yet, to refer to the Register solely as a technical (and inadequate) means of arms control is taking an overly simplistic view. It betrays a lack of awareness of the two-year process of negotiation leading to its establishment and the unprecedented volume of dialogue on the arms trade it has generated within a variety of international and regional fora. The Register was established as, and continues to function as, merely a first step in a series of measures aimed at promoting transparency in military matters, thus reducing fear and mistrust among states and enhancing regional as well as global peace and security. Only after such a foundation has been established can measures aimed at placing limitations on the transfer of conventional weapons be reasonably expected to succeed.

If developed carefully, and as a complement to the development of the global Register, regional arms registers could lend support to this process of achieving global norms by accounting for local peculiarities and meeting the security needs of the states of a particular region. Such mechanisms would lend an air of immediacy to the issue and encourage broader participation both on the regional and international levels. Such regional initiatives could also serve to answer the increasing call, both within and outside the United Nations, for burden-sharing in the maintenance of global peace and security.

Notes

1. Boutros Boutros-Ghali, *Agenda for Peace: Preventive Diplomacy, Peacemaking and Peace-keeping,* United Nations, New York, 1992. See especially paragraphs 60-65.

2. Boutros Boutros-Ghali, *New Dimensions of Arms Regulation and Disarmament in the Post-Cold War Era,* United Nations, New York, 1992, para. 16.

3. *Address of the Secretary-General, Mr. Boutros Boutros-Ghali, to the Advisory Board on Disarmament Matters,* United Nations Press Release SG/SM/94/3, 12 January 1994.

4 . UN General Assembly resolution 46/36 H, "International arms transfers," 6 December 1991, op. para. 8.

5. UN General Assembly resolution 46/36 I, "Regional disarmament," 6 December 1991, op. para. 5.

6. UN General Assembly resolution 46/36 L, "Transparency in armaments," 9 December 1991, op. para. 17.

7. See UN General Assembly resolution 48/75 E, "Transparency in armaments," 16 December 1993, op. para. 6.

8. *Report of the Disarmament Commission,* UN General Assembly document A/48/42, annex II.

9. Jon Lunn, "The Need for Regional Security Commissions within the UN System," *Security Dialogue,* Vol. 24, No. 4 December 1993, pp. 369-376.

10. Region-specific assessments of the Register concept are currently in progress at the Conventional Arms Proliferation (CAP) project at the Monterey Institute. This brief summary is illustrative of the type of findings to be forthcoming.

11. For a more detailed analysis of arms control and disarmament initiatives in Latin America, see Augusto Varas, "Transparency and Military Information in Latin America," Chapter 13 in this volume.

12. For example, see Jozef Goldblat, "Reservations About UN Arms Register," *Arms Control Today,* July/August 1993, p. 30.

Annexes

Annexe 1 Relevant resolutions of the United Nations General Assembly

General Assembly resolution 46/36 L of 9 December 1991

Transparency in armaments

The General Assembly,

Realizing that excessive and destabilizing arms build-ups pose a threat to national, regional and international peace and security, particularly by aggravating tensions and conflict situations, giving rise to serious and urgent concerns,

Noting with satisfaction that the current international environment and recent agreements and measures in the field of arms limitation and disarmament make it a propitious time to work towards easing tensions and a just resolution of conflict situations, as well as more openness and transparency in military matters,

Recalling the consensus among Member States on implementing confidence-building measures, including transparency and exchange of relevant information on armaments, likely to reduce the occurrence of dangerous misperceptions about the intentions of States and to promote trust among States,

Considering that increased openness and transparency in the field of armaments could enhance confidence, ease tensions, strengthen regional and international peace and security and contribute to restraint in military production and the transfer of arms,

Realizing the urgent need to resolve underlying conflicts, to diminish tensions and to accelerate efforts towards general and complete disarmament under strict and effective international control with a view to maintaining regional and international peace and security in a world free from the scourge of war and the burden of armaments,

Recalling also that in paragraph 85 of the Final Document of the Tenth Special Session of the General Assembly it urged major arms supplier and recipient countries to consult on the limitation of all types of international transfer of conventional arms,

Disturbed by the destabilizing and destructive effects of the illicit arms trade, particularly for the internal situation of affected States and the violation of human rights,

Bearing in mind that, in accordance with the Charter of the United Nations, Member States have undertaken to promote the establishment and maintenance of international peace and security with the least diversion for armaments of the world's human and economic resources, and that the reduction of world military expenditures could have a significant positive impact for the social and economic development of all peoples,

Reaffirming the important role of the United Nations in the field of disarmament and the commitment of Member States to take concrete steps in order to strengthen that role,

Recalling its resolution 43/75 I of 7 December 1988,

Welcoming the study submitted by the Secretary-General, pursuant to paragraph 5 of resolution 43/75 I and prepared with the assistance of governmental experts, on ways and means of promoting transparency in international transfers of conventional arms, as well as the problem of the illicit arms trade, taking into account views of Member States and other relevant information,

Recognizing the major contribution of an enhanced level of transparency in armaments to confidence-building and security among States, and also recognizing the urgent need to establish, under the auspices of the United Nations, as a first step in this direction, a universal and non-discriminatory register to include data on international arms transfers as well as other interrelated information provided to the Secretary-General,

Stressing the importance of greater transparency in the interest of promoting readiness to exercise restraint in accumulation of armaments,

Considering that the standardized reporting of international arms transfers together with the provision of other interrelated information to a United Nations register will constitute further important steps forward in the promotion of transparency in military matters and, as such, will enhance the role and effectiveness of the United Nations in promoting arms limitation and disarmament, as well as in maintaining international peace and security;

Recognizing also the importance of the prevention of the proliferation of nuclear weapons and other weapons of mass destruction,

1. *Recognizes* that an increased level of openness and transparency in the field of armaments would enhance confidence, promote stability, help States to exercise restraint, ease tensions and strengthen regional and international peace and security;

2. *Declares its determination* to prevent the excessive and destabilizing accumulation of arms, including conventional arms, in order to promote stability and strengthen regional or international peace and security, taking into account the legitimate security needs of States and the principle of undiminished security at the lowest possible level of armaments;

3. *Reaffirms* the inherent right to individual or collective self-defence recognized in Article 51 of the Charter of the United Nations, which implies that States also have the right to acquire arms with which to defend themselves;

4. *Reiterates its conviction*, as expressed in its resolution 43/75 I, that arms transfers in all their aspects deserve serious consideration by the international community, inter alia, because of:

(a) Their potential effects in further destabilizing areas where tension and regional conflict threaten international peace and security and national security;

(b) Their potentially negative effects on the progress of the peaceful social and economic development of all peoples;

(c) The danger of increasing illicit and covert arms trafficking;

5. *Calls upon* all Member States to exercise due restraint in exports and imports of conventional arms, particularly in situations of tension or conflict, and to ensure that they have in place an adequate body of laws and administrative procedures regarding the transfer of arms and to adopt strict measures for their enforcement;

6. *Expresses its appreciation* to the Secretary-General for his study on ways and means of promoting transparency in international transfers of conventional arms, which also addressed the problem of the illicit arms trade;

7. *Requests* the Secretary-General to establish and maintain at United Nations Headquarters in New York a universal and non-discriminatory Register of Conventional Arms, to include data on international arms transfers as well as information provided by Member States on military holdings, procurement through national production and relevant policies, as set out in paragraph 10 below and in accordance with procedures and input requirements initially comprising those set out in the annex to the present resolution

and subsequently incorporating any adjustments to the annex decided upon by the General Assembly at its forty-seventh session in the light of the recommendations of the panel referred to in paragraph 8 below;

8. *Also requests* the Secretary-General, with the assistance of a panel of governmental technical experts to be nominated by him on the basis of equitable geographical representation, to elaborate the technical procedures and to make any adjustments to the annex to the present resolution necessary for the effective operation of the Register, and to prepare a report on the modalities for early expansion of the scope of the Register by the addition of further categories of equipment and inclusion of data on military holdings and procurement through national production, and to report to the General Assembly at its forty-seventh session;

9. *Calls upon* all Member States to provide annually for the Register data on imports and exports of arms in accordance with the procedures established by paragraphs 7 and 8 above;

10. *Invites* Member States, pending the expansion of the Register, also to provide to the Secretary-General, with their annual report on imports and exports of arms, available background information regarding their military holdings, procurement through national production and relevant policies, and requests the Secretary-General to record this material and to make it available for consultation by Member States at their request;

11. *Decides*, with a view to future expansion, to keep the scope of and the participation in the Register under review, and, to this end:

(a) *Invites* Member States to provide the Secretary-General with their views, not later than 30 April 1994, on:

(i) The operation of the Register during its first two years;

(ii) The addition of further categories of equipment and the elaboration of the Register to include military holdings and procurement through national production;

(b) *Requests* the Secretary-General, with the assistance of a group of governmental experts convened in 1994 on the basis of equitable geographical representation, to prepare a report on the continuing operation of the Register and its further development, taking into account the work of the Conference on Disarmament as set forth in paragraphs 12 to 15 below and the views expressed by Member States, for submission to the General Assembly with a view to a decision at its forty-ninth session;

12. *Requests* the Conference on Disarmament to address, as soon as possible, the question of the interrelated aspects of the excessive and destabilizing accumulation of arms, including military holdings and procurement through national production, and to elaborate universal and non-discriminatory practical means to increase openness and transparency in this field;

13. *Also requests* the Conference on Disarmament to address the problems of, and the elaboration of practical means to increase, openness and transparency related to the transfer of high technology with military applications and to weapons of mass destruction, in accordance with existing legal instruments;

14. *Invites* the Secretary-General to provide to the Conference on Disarmament all relevant information, including, inter alia, views submitted to him by Member States and information provided under the United Nations system for the standardized reporting of military expenditures, as well as on the work of the Disarmament Commission under its agenda

item entitled "Objective information on military matters";

15. *Further requests* the Conference on Disarmament to include in its annual report to the General Assembly a report on its work on this issue;

16. Invites all Member States, in the meantime, to take measures on a national, regional and global basis, including within the appropriate forums, to promote openness and transparency in armaments;

17. *Calls upon* all Member States to cooperate at a regional and subregional level, taking fully into account the specific conditions prevailing in the region or subregion, with a view to enhancing and coordinating international efforts aimed at increased openness and transparency in armaments;

18. *Also invites* all Member States to inform the Secretary-General of their national arms import and export policies, legislation and administrative procedures, both as regards authorization of arms transfers and prevention of illicit transfers;

19. *Requests* the Secretary-General to report to the General Assembly at its forty-seventh session on progress made in implementing the present resolution, including relevant information provided by Member States;

20. *Notes* that effective implementation of the present resolution will require an up-to-date database system in the Department for Disarmament Affairs of the Secretariat;

21. *Decides* to include in the provisional agenda of its forty-seventh session an item entitled "Transparency in armaments".

ANNEX

Register of Conventional Arms

1. The Register of Conventional Arms ("the Register") shall be established, with effect from 1 January 1992, and maintained at the Headquarters of the United Nations in New York.

2. Concerning international arms transfers:

(a) Member States are requested to provide data for the Register, addressed to the Secretary-General, on the number of items in the following categories of equipment imported into or exported from their territory:

I. Battle tanks

A tracked or wheeled self-propelled armoured fighting vehicle with high cross-country mobility and a high level of self-protection, weighing at least 16.5 metric tonnes unladen weight, with a high muzzle velocity direct fire main gun of at least 75 millimetres calibre.

II. Armoured combat vehicles

A tracked or wheeled self-propelled vehicle, with armoured protection and cross-country capability, either: (a) designed and equipped to transport a squad of four or more infantrymen, or (b) armed with an integral or organic weapon of at least 20 millimetres calibre or an anti-tank missile launcher.

III. Large calibre artillery systems

A gun, howitzer, artillery piece combining the characteristics of a gun and a howitzer, mortar or multiple-launch rocket system, capable of engaging surface targets by delivering primarily indirect fire, with a calibre of 100 millimetres and above.

IV. Combat aircraft

A fixed-wing or variable-geometry wing aircraft armed and equipped to engage targets by employing guided missiles, unguided rockets, bombs, guns, cannons, or other weapons of destruction.

V. Attack helicopters

A rotary-wing aircraft equipped to employ anti-armour, air-to-ground, or air-to-air guided weapons and equipped with an integrated fire control and aiming system for these weapons.

VI. Warships

A vessel or submarine with a standard displacement of 850 metric tonnes or above, armed or equipped for military use.

VII. Missiles or missile systems

A guided rocket, ballistic or cruise missile capable of delivering a payload to a range of at least 25 kilometres, or a vehicle, apparatus or device designed or modified for launching such munitions.

(b) Data on imports provided under the present paragraph shall also specify the supplying State; data on exports shall also specify the recipient State and the State of origin if not the exporting State;

(c) Each Member State is requested to provide data on an annual basis by 30 April each year in respect of imports into and exports from their territory in the previous calendar year;

(d) The first such registration shall take place by 30 April 1993 in respect of the calendar year 1992;

(e) The data so provided shall be recorded in respect of each Member State;

(f) Arms "exports and imports" represent in the present resolution, including its annex, all forms of arms transfers under terms of grant, credit, barter or cash.

3. Concerning other interrelated information:

(a) Member States are invited also to provide to the Secretary-General available background information regarding their military holdings, procurement through national production, and relevant policies;

(b) The information so provided shall be recorded in respect of each Member State.

4. The Register shall be open for consultation by representatives of Member States at any time.

5. In addition, the Secretary-General shall provide annually a consolidated report to the General Assembly of the data registered, together with an index of the other interrelated information.

Resolution 47/52 L of 15 December 1992
Transparency in armaments

The General Assembly

Recalling its resolution 46/36L of 9 December 1991, entitled "Transparency in armaments",

Continuing to take the view that an enhanced level of transparency in armaments contributes greatly to confidence-building and security among States and that the establishment of the United Nations Register of Conventional Arms, contained in the annex to resolution 46/36 L, constitutes an important step forward in the promotion of transparency in military matters,

Welcoming the Secretary-General's report on the technical procedures and adjustments to the annex necessary for the effective operation of the Register and on the modalities for its early expansion,

Welcoming also the guidelines and recommendations for objective information on military matters as adopted by consensus in the Disarmament Commission,

Welcoming further the report of the Conference on Disarmament on its agenda item entitled "Transparency in armaments",

1. *Declares* its determination to ensure the effective operation of the Register of Conventional Arms as provided for in paragraphs 7, 9, and 10 of its resolution 46/36 L;

2. *Endorses* the recommendations contained in the Secretary-General's report on the technical procedures and adjustments to the annex necessary for the effective operation of the Register;

3. *Notes* the suggestions offered in the report as a first step in the consideration of modalities for early expansion of the Register;

4. *Calls* upon all Member States to provide the requested data and information to the Secretary-General by 30 April annually, beginning in 1993;

5. *Encourages* Member States to inform the Secretary-General of their national arms import and export policies, legislation and administrative procedures, both as regards authorization of arms transfers and prevention of illicit transfers, in conformity with paragraph 18 of its resolution 46/36 L;

6. *Reaffirms* its request to the Secretary-General to prepare a report on the continuing operation of the Register and its further development with the assistance of a group of governmental experts convened in 1994 on the basis of equitable geographical representation;

7. *Requests* the Secretary-General to ensure that sufficient resources are made available for the United Nations Secretariat to operate and maintain the Register;

8. *Encourages* the Conference on Disarmament to continue its work undertaken in response to the requests contained in paragraphs 12 to 15 of resolution 46/36 L;

9. *Requests* the Secretary-General to report on progress made in implementing the present resolution to the General Assembly at its forth-eighth session;

10. *Decides* to include in the provisional agenda of its forty-eighth session the item entitled "Transparency in armaments".

General Assembly Resolution 48/35 E of December 1993
Transparency in armaments

The General Assembly

Recalling its resolutions 46/36L of 9 December 1991 and 47/52 L of 15 December 1992, entitled "Transparency in armaments",

Continuing to take the view that an enhanced level of transparency in armaments contributes greatly to confidence-building and security among States and that the establishment of the United Nations Register of Conventional Arms constitutes an important step forward in the promotion of transparency in military matters,

Welcoming the consolidated report of the Secretary-General on the first year of operation of the United Nations Register of Conventional Arms;

Encouraged by the response of Member States pursuant to paragraphs 9 and 10 of its resolution 46/36 L to provide data on imports and exports of arms as well as available background information regarding their military holdings, procurement through national production and relevant policies;

Welcoming the work of the Conference on Disarmament under its agenda item entitled "Transparency in armaments";

Welcoming further the organization by Member States of initiatives and seminars aimed at promoting transparency in military matters through a widespread reporting of data to the United Nations Register of Conventional Arms,

1. *Reaffirms* its determination to ensure the effective operation of the Register of Conventional Arms as provided for in paragraphs 7, 9, and 10 of its resolution 46/36 L;

2. *Calls* upon all Member States to provide the requested data and information to the Secretary-General by 30 April annually;

3. *Reaffirms* its request to the Secretary-General to prepare a report, with the assistance of a group of governmental experts convened in 1994 on the basis of equitable geographical representation, on the continuing operation of the Register and its further development, taking into account the work of the Conference on Disarmament and the views expressed by Member States, with a view to a decision at its forty-ninth session;

4. *Requests* the Secretary-General to ensure that sufficient resources are made available for the United Nations Secretariat to operate and maintain the Register;

5. *Encourages* the Conference on Disarmament to continue its work undertaken in response to the requests contained in paragraphs 12 to 15 of resolution 46/36 L;

6. *Reiterates* its call upon all Member States to cooperate at a regional and subregional level, taking fully into account the specific conditions prevailing in the region or subregion, with a view to enhancing and coordinating international efforts aimed at increased openness and transparency in armaments;

7. *Requests* the Secretary-General to report to the General Assembly at its forty-ninth session on progress made in implementing the present resolution;

8. *Decides* to include in the provisional agenda of its forty-ninth session the agenda item entitled "Transparency in armaments".

*Source: Excerpt from General and Complete Disarmament: Transparency in
Armaments, Report on the Register of Conventional Arms, Report of the Secretary-
General, UN General Assembly document A/47/342, 14 August 1992, pp. 8–29.*

. . .

INTRODUCTION

1. On 9 December 1991, as part of the larger family of international efforts to promote transparency in military matters, the United Nations General Assembly adopted resolution 46/36 L entitled "Transparency in armaments" [for the text of the resolution, see Annexe 1]. That resolution established the Register of Conventional Arms to include data on international arms transfers as well as available background information provided by Member States on military holdings, procurement through national production and relevant policies. The Secretary-General's action to that effect was communicated to all Member States in a note verbale of 1 January 1992. In accordance with that resolution Member States are requested to provide data on an annual basis by 30 April each year in respect of imports into and exports from their territory in the previous calendar year, with the first such registration to take place by 30 April 1993 in respect of the calendar year 1992.

2. In paragraph 8 of the same resolution, the Assembly:

"*Also requests* the Secretary-General, with the assistance of a panel of governmental technical experts to be nominated by him on the basis of equitable geographical representation, to elaborate the technical procedures and to make any adjustments to the annex to the present resolution necessary for the effective operation of the Register, and to prepare a report on the modalities for early expansion of the scope of the Register by the addition of further categories of equipment and inclusion of data on military holdings and procurement through national production, and to report to the General Assembly at its forty-seventh session."

3. In paragraph 11 (*a*) of the same resolution, the Assembly invites Member States to provide the Secretary-General, not later than 30 April 1994, with their views on the "operation of the Register during its first two years" and "the addition of further categories of equipment and the elaboration of the Register to include military holdings and procurement through national production". In addition, in paragraph 11 (*b*) of the resolution, the Assembly requests the Secretary-General, "with the assistance of a group of governmental experts convened in 1994 on the basis of equitable geographical representation, to prepare a report on the continuing operation of the Register and its further development, taking into account the work of the Conference on Disarmament, as set forth in paragraphs 12 to 15 below, and the views expressed by Member States for submission to the General Assembly with a view to a decision at its forty-ninth session".

4. In paragraph 12 of the same resolution, the Assembly:

"*Requests* the Conference on Disarmament to address, as soon as possible, the question of the interrelated aspects of the excessive and destabilizing accumulation of arms, including military holdings and procurement through national production, and to elaborate universal and non-discriminatory practical means to increase openness and transparency in this field."

In paragraph 13 of the resolution, the Assembly also requested the Conference on Disarmament, *inter alia,* to elaborate practical means to increase openness and transparency "related to the transfer of high technology with military applications and to weapons of mass destruction, in accordance with existing legal instruments".

5. Also, in paragraph 14 of the same resolution, the Assembly

"*Invites* the Secretary-General to provide to the Conference on Disarmament all relevant information, including, *inter alia,* views submitted to him by Member States and information provided under the United Nations system for the standardized reporting of military expenditures, as well as the work of the United Nations Disarmament Commission under its agenda item entitled 'Objective information on military matters'."

In paragraph 15 of the resolution, the Assembly "*Further requests* the Conference on Disarmament to include in its annual report to the General Assembly a report on its work on this issue".

6. In addition to the work of the Conference on Disarmament, Member States, in paragraphs 16 and 17 of the resolution, are urged to take measures at the national, regional and subregional levels aimed at increased openness and transparency in armaments.

7. The present report, a step in the implementation of General Assembly resolution 46/36 L, is the result of the work of the Panel of Governmental Technical Experts.

I. TECHNICAL PROCEDURES FOR THE OPERATION OF THE REGISTER

A. *General*

8. Part I of the work of the Panel stems from the mandate contained in paragraph 8 of General Assembly resolution 46/36 L, namely "to elaborate the technical procedures and to make any adjustments to the annex to the present resolution necessary for the effective operation of the Register". It is further based on paragraph 7 of the resolution, in which the Assembly requests the Secretary-General to establish and maintain the Register "in accordance with procedures and input requirements initially comprising those set out in the annex to the present resolution and subsequently incorporating any adjustment to the annex decided upon by the General Assembly at the forty-seventh session in the light of the recommendations of the panel referred to in paragraph 8".

B. *Arms transfers*

9. Paragraph 2 (a) of the annex to General Assembly resolution 46/36 L states that "Member States are requested to provide data for the Register, addressed to the Secretary-General, on the number of items in the following categories of equipment imported into or exported from their territory". The Panel did not attempt to define arms transfers but, for the purpose of the Register, considered that the terms "imported into or exported from their territory" needed some clarification, as stated in paragraphs 12 and 13 below.

10. International arms transfers involve, in addition to the physical movement of equipment into or from national territory, the transfer of title to and control over the equipment.

11. An international arms transfer may also occur without the movement of equipment across State frontiers if a State, or its agent, is granted title and control over the equipment in the terri-

tory of the supplier State. Therefore, a transfer of arms to a State would occur when its forces stationed abroad are granted title and control of equipment by the host country or any third State, or when title and control of such equipment are transferred to the host country or any third State. Additionally, if title and control of equipment temporarily stored or prepositioned on the territory of another State are granted to the host country by the owner, then an international transfer has occurred.

12. Since the supply of equipment by a State to units of its armed forces stationed abroad does not involve transfer of national title and control, such supply is not considered an international transfer. Equipment of a State can be temporarily stored or prepositioned on the territory of another State with no transfer of title and control of this equipment. This is not considered an international arms transfer.

13. In paragraphs 2 (c) and (d) of the annex to the same resolution, Member States are "requested to provide data on an annual basis by 30 April each year in respect of imports into and exports from their territory in the previous calendar year", with the first such registration taking place by 30 April 1993 in respect of the calendar year 1992. To be reported are those transfers considered by States to have been effected during the relevant reporting year, in conformity with their respective national criteria used to define when a transfer becomes effective. Member States are invited to indicate such national criteria with their return.

C. Categories of equipment the transfers of which are to be registered

14. Paragraph 2 (a) of the annex to General Assembly resolution 46/36 L also identifies the following seven categories of equipment on which Member States are requested to supply data to the Register – battle tanks, armoured combat vehicles, large calibre artillery systems, combat aircraft, attack helicopters, warships, and missiles or missile systems. Based on the adjustments to the annex developed by the Panel pursuant to its mandate, the categories and their definitions to be used for reporting to the Register are, as follows:

I. Battle tanks

Tracked or wheeled self-propelled armoured fighting vehicles with high cross-country mobility and a high level of self-protection, weighing at least 16.5 metric tonnes unladen weight, with a high muzzle velocity direct fire main gun of at least 75 millimetres calibre.

II. Armoured combat vehicles

Tracked, semi-tracked or wheeled self-propelled vehicles, with armoured protection and cross-country capability, either: (a) designed and equipped to transport a squad of four or more infantrymen, or (b) armed with an integral or organic weapons of at least 12.5 millimetres calibre or a missile launcher.

III. Large calibre artillery systems

Guns, howitzers, artillery pieces, combining the characteristics of a gun or a howitzer, mortars or multiple-launch rocket systems, capable of engaging surface targets by delivering primarily indirect fire, with a calibre of 100 millimetres and above.

IV. Combat aircraft

Fixed-wing or variable-geometry wing aircraft designed, equipped or modified to engage targets by employing guided missiles, unguided rockets, bombs, guns, cannons, or other weapons of destruction, including versions of these aircraft which perform specialized electronic warfare, suppression of air defence or reconnaissance missions. The term "combat aircraft" does not include primary trainer aircraft, unless designed, equipped or modified as described above.

V. *Attack helicopters*

Rotary-wing aircraft designed, equipped or modified to engage targets by employing guided or unguided anti-armour, air-to-surface, air-to-subsurface, or air-to-air weapons and equipped with an integrated fire control and aiming system for these weapons, including versions of these aircraft which perform specialized reconnaissance or electronic warfare missions.

VI. *Warships*

Vessels or submarines armed and equipped for military use with a standard displacement of 750 metric tonnes or above, and those with a standard displacement of less than 750 metric tonnes, equipped for launching missiles with a range of at least 25 kilometers or torpedoes with similar range.

VII. *Missiles and missile launchers*

Guided or unguided rockets, ballistic or cruise missiles capable of delivering a warhead or weapon of destruction to a range of at least 25 kilometers, and means designed or modified specifically for launching such missiles or rockets, if not covered by categories I through VI. For the purpose of the Register, this category:

(a) Also includes remotely-piloted vehicles with the characteristics for missiles as defined above;

(b) Does not include ground-to-air missiles.

D. *Standardized form for reporting international transfers*

15. In paragraph 9 of General Assembly resolution 46/36 L, the Assembly "calls upon all Member States to provide annually for the Register data on imports and exports of arms". Also, in the fourteenth preambular paragraph of the resolution, the Assembly refers to the utility of "the standardized reporting of international arms transfers" for the promotion of transparency in military matters. Pursuant to its mandate, the Panel developed the standardized reporting form (see appendix B to the present report) to be used by Member States when providing data for the Register on the number of items exported and imported in each of the seven categories of equipment defined in paragraph 14 above.

16. Pending the review of the operation of the Register in 1994, data on missiles and missile launchers are to be submitted as a single entry in terms of an aggregate number:

(a) For missiles associated with other launchers covered under categories I to VI, the number 606 will be entered. If, in a given year, a country exports to a specific country 50 missiles of one type and 80 of another type, the number 130 will be entered in column B.

(b) Missiles that are launched from equipment in categories I to VI will be reported in category VII. Missile launchers integral to equipment in categories I to VI are considered a component of that equipment and are not to be reported in category VII missile launchers. For example, air-to-air missiles for combat aircraft are reported in category VII, but the missile launcher is considered to be the aircraft and its transfer is to be reported in category IV.

17. Column A in the form lists the seven categories as defined above. In column B the exporter State(s) (in the import form) and the importer State(s) (in the export form) are to be entered. In addition, column B includes a serial number, identifying the different exporter and importer State(s) as appropriate. Column C in the form includes the number of items of equipment the transfer of which was effected during the relevant reporting year. Transfers, as described in paragraphs 12 and 13 to be reported, are those that have been effected during the relevant reporting year.

18. Columns D and E on the form are included to accommodate data on countries which are not the countries of export or import. In the case of an international transfer involving an export of equipment by a State other than the State of origin, the name of the country of origin should be entered in column D. In the case of an international arms transfer involving transport of equipment to an intermediate location, or involving retention of equipment at an intermediate location for the purpose of the integration of equipment of one category within the Register with equipment of another category, the name of the intermediate location should be entered in column E (e.g. the export of missiles to an intermediate location for integration there with a combat aircraft manufactured at the intermediate location, or vice versa).

19. The right hand column on the form, divided into two parts, "description of item" and "comments on the transfer", is designed to accommodate additional information on the transfers. Since the provision of such information might be affected by security and other relevant concerns of Member States, this column should be filled in at Member States" discretion; no specific patterns are prescribed. To aid the understanding of the international transfers reported, Member States may wish to enter designation, type or model of equipment, or use various descriptive elements contained in the definitions of categories I to VII, which also serve as guides to describe equipment transferred. Member States may also use this column to clarify, for example, that a transfer is of obsolete equipment, the result of co-production, or for other such explanatory remarks as Member States see fit.

E. Available background information regarding military holdings, procurement through national production and relevant policies

20. Pursuant to paragraph 7 of General Assembly resolution 46/36 L, the Register is to include "information provided by Member States on military holdings, procurement through national production and relevant policies". Pursuant to paragraph 3 (a) of the annex to that resolution, "Member States are invited also to provide to the Secretary-General available background information regarding their military holdings, procurement through national production, and relevant policies".

21. The reporting of this information is voluntary and Member States may submit this information in any form they wish.

F. Operation of the Register

1. Submission of data on transfers

22. According to paragraph 2 (c) of the annex to General Assembly resolution 46/36 L, "each Member State is requested to provide data on an annual basis by 30 April each year in respect of imports into and exports from their territory in the previous calendar year". Paragraph 2 (d) of the annex to the resolution states that "the first such registration shall take place by 30 April 1993 in respect of the calendar year 1992".

23. Data should be submitted on the form (see appendix B below) taking account of the present report, by 30 April annually to United Nations Headquarters in New York.

24. Member States that do not have anything to report should file a "nil report", clearly stating that no exports or imports have taken place in any of the seven categories during the reporting period.

25. The Office for Disarmament Affairs in the United Nations Secretariat should receive and compile for the Secretary-General's annual report data sheets submitted by Member States and establish a computerized database which will store the reported data.

2. *Submission of available background information*

26. Available background information to be included in the index (as envisaged in paragraph 5 of the annex to General Assembly resolution 46/36 L) of the annual report of the Secretary-General should be submitted by 30 April of each year.

27. The Office for Disarmament Affairs will maintain in its computerized database a running index of the background information submitted, by country, date and title. Member States should assign titles to their submissions.

G. *Annual consolidated report by the Secretary-General*

28. According to paragraph 5 of the annex to General Assembly resolution 46/36 L, "the Secretary-General shall provide annually a consolidated report to the General Assembly of the data registered, together with an index of the other interrelated information".

29. Section I of the annual report will be a compilation of the reports submitted by Member States on the standardized reporting form (see appendix B below), as they are received by the Secretary-General.

30. Section II of the report will be an index of the background information submitted by Member States.

H. *Access to the Register*

31. According to paragraph 4 of the annex to General Assembly resolution 46/36 L, "the Register shall be open for consultation by representatives of Member States at any time". The Office for Disarmament Affairs should therefore make available the data and information received to any requesting Member State.

32. Member States should have access to the computerized data contained in the Register of Conventional Arms, either on-line (electronically) or by physical transfer of disks.

33. As well as the Secretary-General's consolidated annual report to the United Nations General Assembly, it is recommended that the available background information submitted by Member States be open to the public.

II. MODALITIES FOR EARLY EXPANSION OF THE SCOPE OF THE REGISTER

A. *General*

34. In paragraph 8 of General Assembly resolution 46/36 L, the Assembly requests the Secretary-General to prepare, with the assistance of a panel of governmental technical experts, "a report on the modalities for early expansion of the scope of the Register by the addition of further categories of equipment and inclusion of data on military holdings and procurement through national production and to report to the General Assembly at its forty-seventh session".

35. According to paragraph 11 (*a*) of the same resolution, the Assembly "*invites* Member States to provide the Secretary-General with their views on: (i) the operation of the Register during its first two years; (ii) the addition of further categories of equipment and the elaboration of the Register to include military holdings and procurement through national production". In paragraph 11 (*b*) of the resolution, the Assembly

"*Requests* the Secretary-General, with the assistance of a group of governmental experts convened in 1994 on the basis of equitable geographical representation, to prepare a report on the continuing operation of the Register and its further development."

In addition, in paragraph 12 of the resolution, the Assembly

"*Requests* the Conference on Disarmament to address, as soon as possible, the question of the interrelated aspects of the excessive and destabilizing accumulation of arms, including military holdings and procurement through national production, and to elaborate universal and non-discriminatory practical means to increase openness and transparency in this field."

In paragraph 13 of the resolution, the Assembly *"also requests* the Conference on Disarmament to address the problem of, and the elaboration of practical means to increase, openness and transparency related to the transfer of high technology with military applications and to weapons of mass destruction, in accordance with existing legal instruments".

36. The issues identified below are offered as a first step in the consideration of modalities for expansion of the Register. The future development of the Register should take into consideration other efforts designed to enhance transparency in armaments and thus contribute to the enhancement of confidence among States.

B. *Review of the operation of the Register*

37. Since the group of governmental experts to be convened in 1994 is requested in paragraph 11 (b) of the resolution to "prepare a report on the continuing operation of the Register and its further development", it should assess the first two years of the operation of the Register addressing, *inter alia*, the following:

(a) The description of international arms transfers as contained in paragraphs 12 and 13 of the present report;

(b) The standardized reporting form as contained in appendix B to the present report;

(c) The extent of participation by Member States in the Register.

C. *Modalities for the addition of further categories of equipment*

38. To assist in the future deliberations on the addition of further categories

of equipment, the Panel felt that the following might be taken into account:

(a) The possibility of expanding the existing categories by modifying their existing parameters (e.g. tonnage, range, calibre, roles, capabilities and characteristics); or by introducing new parameters or by including subcategories;

(b) The possibility of including new categories:

(i) To take account of significant technical developments relating to the weapons within the existing categories;

(ii) To include weapons not covered by existing categories which should be considered because of their destabilizing potential. In addition to the points above, future deliberations should draw upon the experience of the operation of the Register.

39. While no decisions are required to be taken regarding the expansion of the scope of the Register until 1994, the Panel considered the possibility of additional categories of equipment that could be reported. It was considered that possible additional categories should be based on substantial agreement so as to ensure the widest possible participation in the Register. A key principle for adding categories should be that of military relevance in terms of the significance of their impact on regional and global stability. The objective should be to enhance transparency, without prejudice to the security of Member States, and help avoid destabilizing accumulations of arms.

40. In the Panel's discussions of the scope of certain categories of equipment, as defined in part I of the present report, issues were raised which, without prejudice to how the forums concerned organize their work, are listed below for their benefit:

(a) Aerial refuelling aircraft;

(b) Reconnaissance aircraft (fixed and rotary wing);

(c) Airborne electronic warfare equipment (fixed and rotary wing);

(d) Airborne early warning and command and control systems (fixed and rotary wing);

(e) Warships: the possibility of lowering or removing the tonnage threshold;

(f) Missiles:

(i) Ground to air missiles;

(ii) Range of missiles;

(iii) Unmanned air-breathing vehicles;

(iv) Close-in anti-missile defence system;

(v) Disaggregation of missiles and launchers for the purpose of reporting;

(g) Ammunition, *inter alia*:

(i) Precision-guided;

(ii) Cluster bombs;

(iii) Fuel-air explosives;

(iv) Remotely delivered mines;

(h) Systems for the delivery of weapons of mass destruction not already covered by the Register.

D. *Modalities for inclusion of data on military holdings and procurement through national production*

41. To assist in the future deliberations on the subject of including data on military holdings and procurement through national production in the Register, the Panel felt that a common understanding is required of what constitutes military holdings and procurement through national production. The terms military holdings and procurement through national production need to be defined for the purpose of the Register. With these considerations in mind the following questions were raised by the Panel:

(a) What constitutes armed forces for the purpose of reporting military hold-ings? In addition to holdings of regular forces, are those of paramilitary, coast-guard, reserve and other types of forces, such as organizations designed and structured to perform peacetime internal security functions, to be included?

(b) Should a legal approach be adopted, defining armed forces as those which take on combatant status in time of war?

(c) Should military holdings be reported on the basis of the same categories of equipment as for arms transfers?

(d) Should equipment in storage or mothballed, awaiting decommissioning or in transit be considered as military holdings and be included?

(e) Should equipment in the process of manufacture or manufacturing-related testing, used exclusively for research and development or belonging to historical collections be included?

(f) Regarding data on procurement through national production:

(i) Should data be reported in values and/or in the number of items procured?

(ii) Should procurement be regarded as procurement from any national production facility, whatever the arrangement may be, for example, international collaborative production, licence, and so forth?

(iii) Should equipment procured externally in separate parts and later assembled be considered procurement through national production or reported as imported equipment?

(iv) Should data on procurement through national production relate to equipment ordered by or only that actually delivered to the armed forces (however defined)?

(v) Should data on the upgrading of equipment be included?

III. RESOURCE IMPLICATIONS FOR THE MAINTENANCE OF THE REGISTER

42. At the Panel's request, the following estimates of resources required for the operation of the Register were provided by the United Nations Secretariat.

43. As currently envisaged, the initial operation and storage of the data of the Register can be accommodated through the projected hardware and software system within the Office for Disarmament Affairs. Incremental start-up costs would be limited to computer hardware and software required for system development, and testing at an estimated cost of $50,000.

44. However, the subsequent operation of the system, that is, installation of the data concerning arms transfers, as well as "background information regarding military holdings, procurement through national production and relevant policies", as Member States were invited to do so by the resolution, will considerably increase the operational complexity of the system and the workload of the Secretariat.

45. Moreover, for the database of the Register to be electronically accessible by Member States, an initial estimated amount of $75,000 would be required to develop the system, support it and distribute related instructional and training material.

46. The development, upgrading and maintenance of the Register would require staff from the Office for Disarmament Affairs with politico-military expertise, especially in the area of arms transfers, in combination with a highly specialized knowledge in the field of database management and systems analysis. Such expertise is currently not available within the Office for Disarmament Affairs. In addition, the day-to-day operation of the Register requires one General Service staff experienced in the basics of programming.

47. Based on available information as well as the experience gained in the maintenance of the United Nations system for the standardized reporting of military expenditures, it is estimated that the Office for Disarmament Affairs would require three additional posts at a total cost of $228,000 per year. The breakdown is divided as follows: one post at the P-5 level – $115,700; one post at the P-2 level – $67,500; and one post at the G-5 level – $45,400 per annum.

48. These estimates are approximations, since it would be impossible to forecast accurately the volume of the work involved in the operation of the Register.

49. The Panel of Governmental Technical Experts recommends that the issue be reviewed by the appropriate United Nations bodies to ensure the most cost-effective use of resources.

APPENDIX B
Standardized forms for reporting international transfers of conventional arms

EXPORTS
Report of international conventional arms transfers
(according to United Nations General Assembly resolution 46/36 L)
Reporting country: _____
Calendar year: 1992

A	B	C	D*	E*	REMARKS**	
Category (I–VII)	Final importer State(s)	Number of items	State of origin (if not exporter)	Intermediate location (if any)	Description of item	Comments on the transfer
I. Battle tanks	1) 2) 3)					
II. Armoured combat vehicles	1) 2) 3)					
III. Large calibre artillery systems	1) 2) 3)					
IV. Combat aircraft	1) 2) 3)					
V. Attack helicopters	1) 2) 3)					
VI. Warships	1) 2) 3)					
VII. Missiles and missile launchers	1) 2) 3)					

Background information provided: yes/no

* See para. 18 of the present report.
** See para. 19 of the present report.

APPENDIX B (concluded)
Standardized forms for reporting international transfers of conventional arms

IMPORTS
Report of international conventional arms transfers
(according to United Nations General Assembly resolution 46/36 L)
Reporting country: _____
Calendar year: 1992

A	B	C	D*	E*	REMARKS**	
Category (I–VII)	Final exporter State(s)	Number of items	State of origin (if not exporter)	Intermediate location (if any)	Description of item	Comments on the transfer
I. Battle tanks	1) 2) 3)					
II. Armoured combat vehicles	1) 2) 3)					
III. Large calibre artillery systems	1) 2) 3)					
IV. Combat aircraft	1) 2) 3)					
V. Attack helicopters	1) 2) 3)					
VI. Warships	1) 2) 3)					
VII. Missiles and missile launchers	1) 2) 3)					

Background information provided: yes/no

* See para. 18 of the present report.
** See para. 19 of the present report.

Annexe 3 Excerpts from Statements made at the 48th Session of the First Committee regarding Transparency and the Register of Conventional Arms

Compiled by Eduardo Fuiji of the Monterey Institute of International Studies from the official summaries of the First Committee published by the United Nations.

"...The establishment of the new United Nations Register of Conventional Arms was an important step in creating greater openness and transparency in military matters... In order to respond to these opportunities and challenges, the Secretary-General had decided to rename the Office for Disarmament Affairs the "Centre for Disarmament Affairs" and to keep it in New York as an integral part of the Department of Political Affairs. With the agreement of the General Assembly, the staff would be brought back to its earlier strength with the proposed addition of three posts, primarily in connection with the work on the Register of Conventional Arms... Finally, the United Nations Register of Conventional Arms – while not a substitute for arms reductions – had introduced a new transparency in that area and could prove to be a valuable instrument of preventive diplomacy. Already some 80 countries had submitted data to the Register, and ultimately it would contribute to stability in the world..." (A/C.1/48/SR.3)

Mr. Marrack Goulding, Under-Secretary-General for Political Affairs

Afghanistan

"...As to the question of military transparency, he stressed the usefulness of the United Nations Register of Conventional Arms and urged countries in his region to submit their reports without delay..." (A/C.1/48/SR.10)

Argentina

"...Together with other Latin American countries, Argentina was doing its utmost to ensure that transparency in military matters became a general principle in the activities of all countries in the region. In that connection, it endorsed the proposal for the convening of a meeting of government experts, under the auspices of the Organization of American States (OAS), during which confidence-building measures would be examined..." (A/C.1/48/SR.13)

Australia

"...As to military transparency particularly in regard to armaments, he noted with satisfaction that many countries had already sent their replies to the United Nations Register of Conventional Arms. He looked forward to participating actively during the General Assembly and the Conference on Disarmament in the future development of global transparency mechanisms and arms acquisition guidelines..." (A/C.1/48/SR.3)

Austria

"...The issue of transparency in armaments had occupied a central place in the Committee's deliberations during previous sessions and the United Nations Register of Conventional Arms had been set up in the hope that transparency might lead to future restraint in arms transfers. Austria shared the positive assessment of the Register by the Secretary-General in his report on the work of the Organization. Confidence could be further increased by the expansion of the scope of the Register and consideration of problems related to the transfer of high technology with military applications and to weapons of mass destruction..." (A/C.1/48/SR.6)

Bangladesh

"...In the case of conventional arms control it was essential to focus attention on the interrelated aspects of the excessive and destabilizing accumulation of arms and to elaborate universal and non-discriminatory means of enhancing openness in the matter. Transparency, restraint, responsible policies and good-neighbourly behaviour were essential elements of the consolidation of regional and global stability, security and peace..." (A/C.1/48/SR.6)

Belarus

"...Belarus agreed on the importance for confidence-building of the United Nations Register of Conventional Arms, and had already submitted information to the Register..." (A/C.1/48/SR.8)

Belgium (speaking on behalf of the European Community and its member States)
"...The Community and its member States were convinced that transparency in armaments could contribute very substantially to the creation of a climate of trust. A first step towards enhanced transparency and restraint in conventional arms transfers should be the full implementation of General Assembly resolutions 46/36 L of 9 December 1991 and 47/52 L of 15 December 1992. They were gratified to note that the Register of Conventional Arms had been in operation since the beginning of the year and that 80 countries had submitted the requested data to the Secretary-General. In addition, they appealed to all States which had not yet contributed information to the Register, including States which were not involved in arms exports or imports, to do so as soon as possible. The Community and its member States actively supported the work of the Conference on Disarmament, pursuant to resolution 46/36 L, on the question of transparency in armaments. In their opinion, the work of the Conference on the question of the modalities for the expansion of the Register to cover military inventories and purchases related to national production was an important contribution to the work of the group of governmental experts which would convene in 1994... (A/C.1/48/SR.5)

Brazil

"... The work of the Committee had been oriented towards covering the widest possible range of disarmament subjects, while concentrating on issues on which progress was more visibly within reach. However, the international community had not yet fulfilled the expectations of general and complete disarmament under effective international control. On the other hand, the Committee had been able to adapt to new situations, as was shown by the adoption of the Chemical Weapons Convention and the establishment of the Register of Conventional Arms, and in its negotiations on disarmament had always maintained the priorities and followed the guidelines, principles and main objectives of the United Nations on that subject..."
(A/C.1/48/SR.17)

Bulgaria

"...Bulgaria shared the view that increased openness and transparency in armaments could strengthen peace and stability. The Register of Conventional Arms, which the Organization had established in 1993, would be an effective international instrument for preventing excessive stockpiling of offensive conventional weapons. The Government of Bulgaria had submitted for inclusion in the Register all the necessary data on arms transfers and other available background information, as provided in General Assembly resolution 46/36 L of 9 December 1991 and 47/52 L of 15 December 1992. It hoped that all Member States would be equally willing to support the effective functioning of the Register. The inclusion in the reports of information relating to national production was an important element of the future evolution of the Register..." (A/C.1/48/SR.7)

Canada

"...Canada welcomes the Secretary-General's decision that the United Nations Register "become a priority task" for the Centre for Disarmament Affairs. Canada also cited the historic significance of the establishment of the Register and is gratified that 80 Member States have complied with the Register, but noted that universal adherence must be ensured. The confidence-building goal of the Register will be achieved only with both universal adherence to the Register and its further expansion. Canada called for the early expansion of the Register to include military holdings and procurement through national production..."

Cape Verde

"...He welcomed the progress made with regard to non-proliferation and disarmament in Europe with the conclusion of the Treaty on Open Skies, in Latin America along the lines of the Treaty of Tlatelolco, and in Asia. It must be admitted, however, that there was still much to be done before all the obstacles would be overcome and that there were a number of inconsistencies which, in the view of Cape Verde, were quite unacceptable and which must be resolved. For instance, it was extremely important that the international community should be able to guarantee the practical implementation of the Convention on Chemical Weapons. Because of the number of difficulties that had arisen in the process of the ratification of the Lisbon Protocol, the START-II Treaty, the vital importance of which was generally recognized, had still not entered into force. His delegation hoped that such difficulties would soon be overcome. As the Gulf War and other relatively recent events had shown, the difficulties in ensuring effective monitoring of compliance with the NPT remained a matter of serious concern to the international community. It was important to adopt all measures aimed at

strengthening the legal regime of the Treaty and ensuring compliance with it. Despite the progress made, which was reflected in the establishment by the General Assembly of the Register of Conventional Arms, much work still had to be done to ensure greater transparency in connection with that category of weapons..."
(A/C.1/48/SR.9)

Chile

"...The large number of replies received by the Centre for Disarmament Affairs in connection with the Register of Conventional Arms was encouraging. It was important to improve the Register with a view to making it a real means of promoting confidence at bilateral, regional and global levels. To that end his Government had not only reported on transfers but also on its stocks and indicated its willingness to participate in forthcoming meetings of governmental experts on the subject..." (A/C.1/48/SR.3)

China

"...With regard to conventional weapons transfers, China had always exercised restraint and responsibility, and favoured the adoption of appropriate and practical transparency measures. At the same time, it maintained that such measures should not undermine the security of any country and should be formulated jointly by all States on the basis of equality..."
(A/C.1/48/SR.8)

Colombia

"...The Register of Conventional Arms was an expression of the international solidarity and cooperation required for such a study, as well as a means of building the confidence required for general and complete disarmament..."
(A/C.1/48/SR.8)

Congo

"...His delegation also welcomed the establishment of the United Nations Register of Conventional Arms...His delegation believed that peace and security were

linked not only with development, but also with confidence-building and friendly relations among peoples. On that basis, the Congo and 10 other States of the subregion were implementing the programme of action of the Standing Advisory Committee on Security Questions in Central Africa. That Committee had held two meetings at the ministerial level in Bujumbura, Burundi, from 8 to 12 March 1993, and in Libreville, Gabon, from 30 August to 3 September 1993, which had achieved positive results, namely: a draft non-aggression pact which would soon be offered for signature by the heads of State and Government of the countries of the subregion; research on the question of restructuring armed forces and conversion; a decision to provide information on arms transfers to the United Nations Register of Conventional Arms; and the establishment of a permanent inter-governmental committee for crisis management. The Congo hoped that, as in the previous year, the draft resolution on that question which would be submitted by States of the subregion would be supported by the international community, since that would enable the Standing Advisory Committee to achieve its noble goals..."
(A/C.1/48/SR.13)

Costa Rica

"...The United Nations Register of Conventional Arms was an important disarmament mechanism at the international level, as it was aimed at ensuring greater access to objective and transparent information and promoting restraint where armaments were concerned. The Register could be expanded to include new measures that might regulate the production, sale, stockpiling, distribution, reduction, conversion and balance of arms and armed forces and also prevent illegal traffic in arms. It was essential to promote greater openness and transparency in relations between States by including in the Register objective information on States' policies, procedures and agreements at the national and regional levels in the aforementioned areas. Those elements could provide the basis for establishing a new model of international security which would promote a reasonable balance of armed forces and armaments and their reduction to a minimal level..."
(A/C.1/48/SR.9)

Czech Republic

"...The importance of conventional disarmament should not be overlooked. To that end, his country was committed to the further improvement of the United Nations Register of Conventional Arms and urged all Member States to submit their national reports without delay..."
(A/C.1/48/SR.8)

Democratic People's Republic of Korea

"...Control and reduction of conventional weapons, including weapons of mass destruction, was a critical issue. His delegation was concerned over the fact that even after the establishment of the Register of Conventional Weapons the export of arms to the developing countries had not decreased, while the technologies of sophisticated weapons continued to be transferred, and that the Register, rather than strengthening confidence, was further encouraging the arms race. In order to make it conducive to confidence-building it should provide for the prohibition of arms exports and the registration and phased withdrawal of arms and equipment in other countries..."
(A/C.1/48/SR.9)

"...explaining his delegation's position on draft resolution A/C.1/48/L.18 entitled "Transparency in armaments" before the Committee took a decision, said that despite its reservations and doubts about the credibility and effectiveness of the text his delegation was ready to accept it in a spirit of consensus. The establishment of the United Nations Register

of Conventional Arms had not helped to halt the export of arms from the industrialized countries to the developing countries or the transfer of sophisticated weapons technology and had seemed to be encouraging the arms race instead of building confidence...
(A/C.1/48/SR.24)

Egypt

"...On the important issue of transparency in armaments, Egypt believed that its scope should be widened to include all types of arms, including weapons of mass destruction and high technology with military applications. It therefore welcomed the United Nations Register of Conventional Arms as a positive step in the area of arms control but had reservations concerning the current form of the Register and believed it should be developed in accordance with the proposals submitted by Egypt and contained in document A/48/344...
(A/C.1/48/SR.8)

Fiji

"...On the question of transparency in armaments, Fiji supported the proposals to extend the scope of the United Nations Register of Conventional Arms to include the transfer of high technology with military applications and weapons of mass destruction. The Register, being low-key, incremental and long-term, had the potential to be an effective instrument of preventive diplomacy..."
(A/C.1/48/SR.10)

Finland

"...With regard to the need to step up efforts to prevent the excessive accumulation of conventional weapons, he appealed to countries which had not yet done so to make their national data available to the United Nations Register of Conventional Arms..."
(A/C.1/48/SR.5)

Gabon

"...Gabon supported all the transparency measures introduced by the United Na-

tions to achieve better control of the transfer of conventional weapons, and saw the United Nations Register of Conventional Arms as an important development. The steps taken by certain States to establish an effective system to control exports of conventional weapons offered a significant means of stopping the illicit trade in such weapons and their proliferation. The international community must go further and draw up binding regulations for the transfer and production of conventional weapons, which were a constant threat to security at the regional and subregional levels..."
(A/C.1/48/SR.14)

Ghana

"...The General Assembly had been expected at its forty-seventh session to extend the scope of the Register of Conventional Arms, established by General Assembly resolution 467/36. However, in General Assembly resolution 47/52, it had merely taken note of the suggestions made by the Secretary-General. In that connection it should be stressed that the continued operation of the Register beyond the forty-ninth session of the General Assembly would be determined by the efforts of Member States, through a General Assembly resolution, to extend the scope of the Register..."
(A/C.1/48/SR.7)

Germany

"...It was widely accepted that transparency in military matters was a means of contributing to international peace and security, as was demonstrated by the participation of Member States in providing information to the Register of Conventional Arms..." (A/C.1/48/SR.19)

Hungary

"...He welcomed the growing interest in and recognition of the benefits of transparency in armaments through the success of initiatives including the United Nations Register of Conventional Arms. Although the Secretary-General's initial report on the Register had indicated that reports had been received from less than half of the Member States, it was worthwhile noting that the information they provided, for instance on arms exports, covered more than 90 per cent of the global aggregate. In order to make the Register more representative, any geographical imbalances in reporting should be remedied and States whose statistics were likely to be of regional significance should be encouraged to submit their reports. Further contributions to the Register would enhance confidence-building not only worldwide, but also at the regional level. Moreover, while transparency in armaments should essentially be a cooperative undertaking, it should not preclude the possibility of unilateral action...

...The reliability of the information provided was also an important aspect. To that end, he suggested looking into the possibility of establishing a monitoring or review mechanism along the lines of those set up for the purposes of other non-binding international instruments. One of the main objectives of transparency in armaments was to prevent any further deterioration in global security; however, international action for that purpose could not be taken until a criterion for judging whether the amount of arms accumulated posed a serious threat had been established..." (A/C.1/48/SR.10)

India

"...India was concerned that transparency in arms transfers was becoming an end in itself. Transparency should be reflected in the reduction of defence expenditures in per capita terms and as a proportion of gross domestic product (GDP). Over the period 1987-1992 India's defence expenditure had declined by 4.68 per cent and in 1992 had amounted to 2.75 per cent of its GDP. India had always stood for curbing excess military expenditures which fuelled the arms race. The aim

should be general reduction of conventional arms across the globe to levels dictated by minimum defence needs. An important dimension of transparency in armaments was the illicit arms trade, which was most dangerous because of its destabilizing and destructive effects in fuelling State-sponsored terrorism directed against other countries, subversion and drug trafficking..." (A/C.1/48/SR.11)

Iran (Islamic Republic of)

"...The reckless build-up of conventional weapons had not only devoured much-needed resources but reinforced the atmosphere of mistrust and anxiety. The decision of the General Assembly to establish a Register of Conventional Arms constituted a positive first step for the resolution of that problem. To become effective, the Register should expand to include all categories and types of arms..." However, it was evident that transparency in armaments could not by itself control the accumulation of conventional arms in various regions. What was really needed, globally and particularly in the Middle East, was international cooperation for the comprehensive, non-selective, non-discriminatory, balanced and effective reduction of conventional weapons, which could be realized through reduction of military budgets and weapons procurement and the withdrawal of foreign forces from various regions..." (A/C.1/48/SR.13)

Ireland

"...The establishment of the United Nations Register of Conventional Arms had provided a global instrument for promoting greater transparency in conventional arms transfers. However, transparency did not in itself ensure security; simply reporting information on arms transfers could not absolve States from the responsibility to ensure that their arms imports and exports did not endanger the security of neighbouring States or regions. Ireland envisaged that the proposed code of conduct for conventional arms transfers would be a voluntary instrument which would not limit the right of States to acquire arms for their national security under the United Nations Charter; instead, States would undertake to subscribe voluntarily to a set of principles and criteria in deciding on their arms imports and exports. Since the code would not be a legally binding instrument, it would not need formal verification procedures. However, it should incorporate a mechanism to encourage States to interpret and apply its provisions in a uniform manner. With regard to participation in the code, while arms-producing States had a special responsibility to ensure that their arms exports did not contribute to instability or conflict in other countries or regions, arms-importing countries also had a responsibility to exercise restraint in their arms procurement policies. The dangers posed by excessive accumulations of conventional weapons were not confined to any one region, and the code of conduct should therefore be open to all States..." (A/C.1/48/SR.23)

Israel

"...It had become clear in the wake of the Gulf War that excessive accumulation of weapons arsenals was a major source of instability in the region and that conventional weapons often caused no less destruction than non-conventional weapons. A special effort thus needed to be made to curb arms supplies to the Middle East. In that context, Israel supported General Assembly resolution 47/52 L concerning "Transparency in armaments", and had submitted information to the Register of Conventional Arms..." (A/C.1/48/SR.10)

"... explaining his delegation's position on the resolution [A/C.1/48/L.18 entitled Transparency in Armaments], said that although it had joined in the consensus it did not support the suggested further development of the Register because the existing mechanism must first be given an

opportunity to show that it worked. In any event, the decision to develop the Register ought to be taken first at the regional level by consensus, in order to protect the national security of all the parties concerned..." (A/C.1/48/SR.24)

Jamaica (speaking on behalf of the 12 States members of the Caribbean Community (CARICOM))

"...The Secretary-General's report on the work of the Organization recorded the establishment of the United Nations Register of Conventional Arms, designed to ensure greater transparency in armaments. The members of CARICOM hoped that the Register's scope would be expanded to include other categories of arms..." (A/C.1/48/SR.13)

Japan

"...As had been demonstrated in the Gulf war, the uncontrolled transfer of conventional weapons could destabilize a region and thus give rise to armed conflict. Self-restraint by arms suppliers was essential. It was also the responsibility of the international community to take effective measures to stop the unregulated and unprincipled transfer of weapons. The United Nations Register of Conventional Arms was an important element in that endeavour; Japan hoped that a substantially larger number of States would join its regime. Japan would continue to cooperate with other nations to achieve broader participation and to improve and develop the Register. It felt that there was also a need to promote regional cooperation and to devise supplementary measures on transparency adjusted to the specific characteristics of each region..." (A/C.1/48/SR.4)

...his delegation endorsed the view expressed by the representative of the Netherlands concerning draft resolution A/C.1/48/L.18 on transparency in armaments that to ensure that the United Nations Register of Conventional Arms was effective it was essential to have the widest possible participation by Member States. Efforts must be pursued to increase the understanding and cooperation among States in each region, particularly in regions which still had few participating countries, and the activities of the United Nations regional disarmament centres must contribute to those efforts...

...A conference was to be held at the beginning of 1994 under the auspices of the United Nations Regional Disarmament Centre in Kathmandu; Japan hoped that transparency in armaments and the United Nations Register would be among the main items taken up by the conference..." (A/C.1/48/SR.22)

Kazakhstan

"...Kazakhstan attached great importance to the United Nations Register of Conventional Arms as a further step in strengthening trust, greater openness and transparency in military matters. It had provided the appropriate information to the Register, which, while it could not be a substitute for arms reduction could contribute to confidence-building measures, especially at the regional and subregional levels..." (A/C.1/48/SR.12)

Kenya

"...While the recently introduced United Nations Register of Conventional Arms represented an important first step towards a new era in arms control and should be linked with United Nations work in preventive diplomacy and peace-making, it should aim to achieve transparency and confidence-building while taking into account the specific features of each region..." (A/C.1/48/SR.8)

Latvia

"...Latvia considered transparency in armaments to be an extremely important confidence-building measure. In that regard, it welcomed the establishment of the Register of Conventional Arms, and believed that its gradual expansion would help to promote greater trust among countries..." (A/C.1/48/SR.9)

Lebanon

"... His country reiterated its support for General Assembly resolutions 47/52 L on transparency in armaments and 46/36 L establishing the Register of Conventional Arms. The data provided for the Register should also include information on national arms production..." (A/C.1/48/SR.12)

Madagascar

"...It was encouraging to note that following the first year of operation of the United Nations Register of Conventional Arms, all the major suppliers and purchasers of weapons were among the 88 Member States which had transmitted information in reports covering 90 per cent of world arms exports. The Register's scope should be extended to include other categories of arms, transfers of military high technology and the stockpiling and procurement of arms through national production. By allowing greater transparency in armaments, the Register would help decrease the likelihood that States' intentions would be misinterpreted and would encourage confidence among States. The success of the Register made it clear that disarmament and international security issues did not necessarily have to be solved through formal treaties. In that connection, the Disarmament Commission was making a very valuable contribution to the concerted efforts of the international community to reduce arms to the lowest possible level. Although its recommendations were not binding, they carried the moral authority of an international consensus. His delegation welcomed the adoption at the Commission's substantive session of 1993 of the guidelines and recommendations for regional approaches to disarmament in the context of world security..."
(A/C.1/48/SR.14)

Malaysia

"...An important focus of confidence-building measures was transparency in armaments. International security and stability would be enhanced by increased openness and transparency in the military field, particularly in the area of arms transfers. There was therefore an urgent need to ensure the success of the Register of Conventional Arms and to expand its scope by including further categories of equipment and data relating to military holdings and procurement, as well as detailed information on research and development, arms storage conditions and military budgets..." (A/C.1/48/SR.7)

Maldives

"...His Government supported the recently-concluded Chemical Weapons Convention, as well as the Biological Weapons Convention, to which it had acceded early in 1993. It was alarmed by the continued acquisition and stockpiling of conventional armaments, and believed that the establishment of the United Nations Register of Conventional Arms was a useful first step towards controlling them..." (A/C.1/48/SR.8)

Malta

"...In view of its strategic position in the Mediterranean, Malta was firmly committed to enhancing security and cooperation between Europe and the countries of the Mediterranean region under the auspices of the Conference on Security and Cooperation in Europe (CSCE). The adoption at the Helsinki summit meeting of Malta's proposal that CSCE should declare itself a regional arrangement in conformity with Chapter VIII of the United Nations Charter had been the first step towards more structured cooperation between the United Nations and CSCE countries. Further efforts were required to improve on that relationship and render it more effective in eliminating conflicts and building peace in the region. The current conflicts on the territories of the former Yugoslavia and the Soviet Union highlighted the need to promote greater transparency and accountability with regard to conventional arms transfers, and that should be one of the issues to be taken up in the framework of cooperation between the United Nations and CSCE..." (A/C.1/48/SR.14)

Mongolia

"...In connection with the establishment of the United Nations Register of Conventional Arms and the adoption by the Disarmament Commission of Guidelines and recommendations for objective information on military matters (A/47/42, Annex 1), his country noted with satisfaction that the Conference on Disarmament had established an ad hoc committee on transparency in armaments. The 1993 substantive session of the Commission had adopted guidelines and recommendations for a regional approach to disarmament within the context of global security. Although it had fallen short of reaching agreement on another important item on its agenda - the role of science and technology in the context of international security, disarmament and other related fields - his country hoped that the Commission would be able to finalize its work on the matter at its next session. His delegation deemed it necessary that agreement should be reached as soon as possible on the inclusion of that new item in the agenda of the Commission's next session..." (A/C.1/48/SR.7)

Nepal

"...His delegation appreciated the valuable assistance of the disarmament fellowship programme in training qualified diplomats and expressed satisfaction with the performance of the recently created United Nations Register of Conventional Arms..." (A/C.1/48/SR.9)

Netherlands

"Mr. WAGENMAKERS, speaking as Chairman of the Panel of Governmental Technical Experts on the United Nations Register of Conventional Arms, introduced the Secretary-General's report on the United Nations Register of Conventional Arms (A/48/344). In the aftermath of the Gulf War, there had been consensus in the international community that the world must avoid excessive and destabilizing accumulations of conventional weapons and that greater transparency would help to rectify misconceptions and enable nations to exercise restraint. The United Nations Register of Conventional Arms was the instrument for fulfilling that objective. The Register was not designed to assess the overall capabilities of States nor a measure for controlling arms transfers, but expressed the political determination of Member States to enhance confidence among themselves.

...The Panel of Governmental Experts established in 1992 to elaborate the technical procedures and make any adjustments to the Annex to General Assembly resolution 46/36 L necessary for the effective operation of the Register, and to prepare a report on the modalities for early expansion of the scope of the Register, had submitted a first report (A/47/342) to the General Assembly setting out a clear set of technical procedures for the operation of the Register and a standardized reporting form, and exploring possible further development of the Register. The Secretary-General's current report on the Register (A/48/344) had been compiled on the basis of the information on pertinent transactions relating to 1992 provided by Member States and summarized the replies of 80 Member States, including all the major arms suppliers. Eight more returns had been received since its preparation. The returns covered some 200 arms transfers, amounting to a significant part of the total number of legal arms transfers for 1992 in the categories covered by

the Register. That could be considered a good and promising start.

...The data available through the Register created transparency on conventional arms transfers and thus contributed to building confidence among States. Moreover, being Government-supplied, the data had official status. Information had been provided on arms transfers in each of the seven categories of the Register, and almost half of the returns included background information. The same proportion of States had submitted data on military holdings and procurement through national production, and many States had provided an insight into their national arms import and export policies, legislation and administrative procedures. It was another beneficial consequence of reporting to the Register that it might well cause some nations to do the necessary amount of internal soul-searching.

...The returns to the Register so far, including the "nil" returns, were an expression of firm support for the concept embodied in the Register. They also provided highly relevant data. In that connection, he appealed for timely returns, as, in order to provide the maximum amount of transparency and confidence, the Register should be up to date.

...Apart from their number, the quality of the returns required attention. There was, for instance, the matter of discrepancies evidenced by cross-checking the reported exports and imports of Member States. However, that aspect was not purely negative, as such mismatches indicated at least that returns were genuine, rather than preconcerted. Moreover, solutions to individual discrepancies could be found through consultations between the Member States concerned.

...The initial performance of the Register was impressive. However, if it was to become a powerful factor for building confidence and trust among Member States, maximum participation in the form of returns, including "nil" returns, was a political sine qua non. Member States which had not yet participated in the Register should do so without further delay. Participation in the Register stimulated cooperation at regional and subregional levels, thereby contributing to stability in all regions of the world, as was evidenced by the important regional and subregional initiatives that had already been taken.

...The contents of the returns indicated that the functioning of the Register warranted qualitative examination, particularly with regard to the categories of arms transfers. Not all the returns conformed fully with the seven categories established for arms transfers, although for the Register to be objective and non-discriminatory its contents should be in full conformity with those categories and their definitions. In some cases, definitions might need further adjustment, for example, those of combat aircraft and attack helicopters, the threshold in the definition of warships and the definition of missiles and missile launchers.

...Another more technical question was whether the standardized form for the reporting of arms transfers needed modification. For example, some Member States had anticipated the future development of the Register by using the standardized reporting form to submit information on their military holdings and on procurement through national production. The 1994 Experts Group might usefully address the phenomenon of discrepancies between returns, exploring whether means could be found to help reduce their number, for instance by the gradual harmonization of national administrative procedures. To that end, the experts might develop greater agreement on what constituted an arms transfer in terms of the Register. Attention should be given to those technical aspects of the Register in order to reduce inaccuracies and inconsis-

tencies, the accumulation of which might undermine confidence and reinforce suspicions about intentions. Apart from these aspects, which concerned the operation of the Register in its present form, the 1994 Experts Group should consider the further development of the Register, for example, the possibility of reporting on additional weapons not currently registered or including more details on particular arms transfers. Of course, overloading of the Register should be avoided. Requiring less detailed reports in the first years of its operation might induce additional States to participate. It should also be borne in mind, however, that there was wide support among Member States for including in the Register relevant data on holdings and arms procurement through national production. Certainly, the Register could gradually be developed along such more ambitious lines, and might in due course evolve into the unique early-warning mechanism it had the potential of becoming.

...A number of interesting thoughts and proposals on the present and future functioning of the Register had been put forward in 1993, for example, that States should begin exchanging information on military holdings and procurement through national production and that they should make an annual declaration to the United Nations on the size and organization of their military forces. The discussions within the Conference on Disarmament on that subject were quite promising..." (A/C.1/48/SR.10)

...Summing up, he said that the United Nations Register of Conventional Arms was well on its way to becoming the effective instrument for the strengthening of international security Member States had hoped to create. What was needed to bring it to its full capacity as such an instrument was the cooperation of all Member States in living up to their commitments." (A/C.1/48/SR.10)

New Zealand

"...While the potential for destruction posed by nuclear, chemical and biological weapons was vast, it should not be overlooked that almost all death and destruction in war had been caused by conventional weapons, which consumed the bulk of the world's excessive military expenditure. In 1991, a concrete step had been taken to increase mutual confidence and security through measures to increase transparency in armaments and openness in conventional arms transfers. New Zealand was among the 80 States which had provided information for the United Nations Register of Conventional Arms..." (A/C.1/48/SR.7)

Nicaragua

"...With regard to General Assembly resolution 47/52 L, he noted that two Central American countries had already provided information for the Register of Conventional Arms, acting in the spirit of a policy of full transparency and striving to attain such goals as the demilitarization of Central America and the promotion of general and complete disarmament..." (A/C.1/48/SR.6)

Pakistan

"...At the current time, the arms race in various parts of the world was fuelled not by global disputes but by regional differences. For that reason, conventional arms control measures must be pursued at the regional and subregional levels and be guided by the following considerations: first, the practice of evaluating defence expenditures in gross national product (GNP) terms should be abandoned; second, the argument that a larger country should maintain a larger army was completely unfounded; third, the concept of "defensive sufficiency" should be transformed into practical policy designed to meet the actual threats posed to each State in various regions of the world; fourth, greater transparency in armaments could undoubtedly help curb the arms race; and fifth, the caveats invariably attached to current regional arms control proposals, for example, that the arrangements must originate with the agreement of all parties concerned, were evidence of a built-in bias against the concept of regional arms control..." (A/C.1/48/SR.13)

Peru

"...In recent meetings at the regional level, the President of Peru had reaffirmed his commitment to a significant reduction in military expenditure. Peru believed that the participation of various countries of the region, including Peru, in the United Nations Register of Conventional Arms was useful, and that the enhancement and broader use of that tool would be a significant step towards general and complete disarmament under effective international control..." (A/C.1/48/SR.23)

Philippines

"...The Philippines also welcomed initiatives such as the United Nations Register of Conventional Arms which promoted openness and transparency - prerequisites for the rational reduction of armaments..." (A/C.1/48/SR.4)

Poland

"...Poland welcomed the establishment, within the framework of the Conference on Disarmament, of an Ad Hoc Committee on the establishment of Transparency in Armaments. The regional workshop organized earlier in 1993 in Poland by the United Nations Centre for Disarmament Affairs had facilitated participation by States from the region in the United Nations Register of Conventional Arms, to which Poland attached great importance..." (A/C.1/48/SR.3)

...Poland attached great importance to the issue of transparency in armaments. Openness and transparency in the military area were a prerequisite for achieving a high level of confidence. The numerous practical proposals made in that respect deserved careful considera-

tion. They ranged from possible guide-lines which would serve as an international "code of conduct" in order to help control arms transfers to suggestions regarding an international exchange of military data on subjects not yet covered by the United Nations Register of Conventional Arms. His delegation could not subscribe to an interpretation of General Assembly resolution 46/36 L as setting clear boundaries on the time-frame and scope of the mandate of the Ad Hoc Committee on Transparency in Armaments..."
(A/C.1/48/SR.13)

Republic of Korea

"...The registration of conventional-arms transfers with the United Nations, a process which had begun in 1993 in accordance with General Assembly resolution 46/36 L on transparency in armaments, contributed greatly to confidence-building at both global and regional level. He welcomed the fact that almost 80 countries had registered their arms transfers, including the five permanent members of the Security Council. Universal participation in the Register of Conventional Arms was the key to its success. At the same time he looked forward to further discussions at global and regional level on the implementation and development of the registration system..."
(A/C.1/48/SR.11)

Romania

"...welcomed the measures introduced by the Secretary-General with the aim of strengthening the Centre for Disarmament as well as the initial reaction by States to the establishment of the Arms Register...

...It would be unrealistic to hope for total transparency on all aspects of arma-ments. Arms control and disarmament, including transparency, was bound to be a gradual process leading to the establishment of a comprehensive information system on conventional

weapons and, perhaps, on armaments in general. In fact, there should be no limit to military confidence-building, as a process which would bring greater security and enhance the prospects for international peace. In the meantime, such confidence-building measures should lead to the adoption of agreements on arms limitation and disar-mament. His delegation was therefore greatly concerned by the continuing transfers of sophisticated weapon sys-tems, particularly in areas of tension or conflict...

...Transparency in armaments was one of the new priority issues in the Geneva Conference on Disarmament, which was the most appropriate forum to deal with the matter. Romania was ready to partic-ipate actively in the work aimed at con-solidating the Register and expanding its scope. It was clear that the excessive ac-cumulation of armaments posed a threat to peace and security at all levels and ex-acerbated tensions and situations of con-flict. He therefore supported the propos-als by France and the United States to es-tablish an international data exchange on the seven main categories of military holdings and procurement through na-tional production. The general aspects re-lating to transparency in armaments could be regulated by setting standards and procedures and by establishing an appropriate mechanism for their imple-mentation. In that regard, Romania advo-cated the drafting of agreed guidelines that would serve as an international code of conduct and constitute a first step in that direction..." (A/C.1/48/SR.20)

Russian Federation

"...Commending the establishment by the United Nations of the Register of Con-ventional Arms, the Russian Federation confirmed its intention to continue to provide data to the Register on a yearly basis, supported further consideration of the issue of transparency in armaments at the Conference on Disarmament and in other international forums and had no objection to the inclusion of that item in the agenda of the Disarmament Commission. His delegation also reaffirmed the intention of the Russian Federation to continue to provide data to the United Nations in accordance with the standardized reporting system on military expenditures..." (A/C.1/48/SR.7)

Senegal

"...Despite progress in the reduction and control of certain categories of weapons of mass destruction, the precarious political, economic and social equilibrium in the world was increasingly threatened by the growing build-up of conventional arms in certain vulnerable regions. His delegation therefore welcomed the establishment of the Register of Conventional Arms, and hoped that current discussions would lead to greater transparency in that area...

...Efforts by the Organization to promote disarmament and arms regulation could only succeed with the support of all Member States, particularly the major Powers with their formidable military arsenals. Efforts to build a world of peace and security also necessitated combating hunger, poverty and sickness, which were capable, if left unattended, of becoming more serious threats to international peace and security than those posed by military arsenals..." (A/C.1/48/SR.3)

Sierra Leone

"...The proliferation of conventional arms was of primary importance to many developing countries, and in his delegation's view, attention should be focused on the question of the excessive and destabilizing accumulation of arms, including military arsenals and procurement through national production, and on the enhancement of openness and transparency in that field, especially through the use of the Register of Conventional Arms. While transparency, restraint, responsible policies and good-

neighbourly behaviour were essential elements in increasing regional and global security and peace, it had clearly become imperative for the international community to address seriously the issue of conventional arms transfers, as well as the question of land-mines..." (A/C.1/48/SR.12)

Slovenia

"...Transparency in armaments was an essential element of confidence- and security-building measures, and the Register of Conventional Arms represented an important achievement which created a solid basis for future work, possibly on transparency with respect to non-conventional weapons as well. His delegation hoped that next year a majority of States would exchange the information included in the Register. It also welcomed the organizational efforts of the Secretariat to prepare for the implementation of the Register and the establishment of the Ad Hoc Committee on Transparency in Armaments created by the Conference on Disarmament..." (A/C.1/48/SR.8)

Sri Lanka

"...Transparency in armaments could serve as an effective confidence-building measure only if it guaranteed equal and balanced rights and responsibilities of all States participating in the regime. At present, Sri Lanka was preparing its response to the questionnaire that had been circulated in connection with the preparation of the United Nations Register of Conventional Arms. His delegation believed that the Register should be gradually expanded to include all categories and types of destabilizing arms, including weapons of mass destruction..." (A/C.1/48/SR.11)

Sweden

"...The international community must strengthen its ability to respond to the problem of the spread of conventional weapons, and his Government welcomed the fact that the disarmament and arms control agenda was now increasingly focused on such weapons. Much, however, remained to be done. In 1993 national reports had been submitted to the United Nations Register of Conventional Arms for the first time. For that instrument to acquire a universal character, however, it was essential for all Member States to provide information. Nevertheless, expanding the scope of the Register too rapidly could increase the difficulties of compiling data, and it should therefore be expanded in a careful and gradual manner..." (A/C.1/48/SR.4)

Switzerland
"...The establishment of the United Nations Register of Conventional Arms was a major step forward, in terms both of promoting transparency and of furthering a multilateral approach to arms transfers..." (A/C.1/48/SR.4)

Tanzania (United Republic of)
"...Unexpected conflicts which had emerged since the demise of super-Power rivalry had resulted in the use of arms and the expenditure of enormous resources for the destruction of human life and property. The objectives of the United Nations Register of Conventional Arms would be defeated if the major producers of armaments did not curb the temptation to export conventional arms. It was thus an appropriate time to re-examine the arms control and disarmament machinery and to update it to the realities of the post-cold-war era..." (A/C.1/48/SR.9)

Thailand
"...With reference to transparency in armaments, the subject of General Assembly resolution 47/52 L, Thailand considered that such transparency could never be a substitute for genuine arms reduction. The universal and non-discriminatory application of transparency would, however, enhance the ability of the international community to monitor arms transfers throughout the globe. The goals

of the United Nations Register of Conventional Arms should be clear to all. The security of States would not be compromised by their participation in the process..." (A/C.1/48/SR.11)

Togo
"...Transparency in armaments was the best means of building confidence among States at the subregional, regional and international levels. In that regard the establishment of the Register of Conventional Arms deserved commendation..." (A/C.1/48/SR.13)

Tunisia
"...The United Nations Register of Conventional Arms would encourage greater transparency regarding arms transfers, but could not bring a halt to the manufacture and sales of weapons. The question of extending the scope of the Register, so as to ensure that it served its purpose better, should be taken up at the meeting of the Group of Experts scheduled for 1994. Another related issue requiring urgent attention was the unlawful sale of weapons to terrorist groups and other armed factions whose activities constituted a threat to national and even international security, for a concerted effort on the part of the international community was called for to put a stop to such illicit trafficking, and States should cooperate and exchange information to that end..." (A/C.1/48/SR.14)

Turkey
"...Clandestine transfers of conventional arms, as well as military equipment and technology constituted a serious problem. Such transfers were carried out for lucrative purposes and had a direct bearing on international peace and security, particularly in regions where tensions still existed. In that connection he attached great importance to the work of the CSCE Forum for Security Cooperation in drafting principles governing conventional arms transfers as well as the CSCE

code of conduct. The United Nations Register of Conventional Arms was a further means of building confidence at the regional and international levels..." (A/C.1/48/SR.13)

Ukraine

"...The Centre for Disarmament Affairs fulfilled an increasingly important function. One example of that was the establishment of the Register of Conventional Arms. His delegation supported the request made by other delegations that the Centre should be given the resources to carry out its work effectively... (A/C.1/48/SR.17)

United States

"...In the view of the United States, the 80 replies submitted to the United Nations Register of Conventional Arms established under General Assembly resolution 46/36 L on transparency in armaments, represented a good response - but not good enough. The Register could clearly be strengthened and the United States called for efforts to increase the participa tion of member States and to improve the quality of the information submitted. In addition to its proposals on enhancing transparency and openness, in particular that States should exchange information on military holdings and procurement through national production, the United States had given its consent to ratification of the Treaty on Open Skies. That Treaty would also contribute to greater openness and transparency in military matters in Europe..." (A/C.1/48/SR.5)"...

His Government likewise rejected the expansion of the United Nations register of Conventional Arms to include illicit arms traffic; that was inappropriate and unfeasible, since such transfers were by nature secret and not reportable in a register format..." (A/C.1/48/SR.28)

Annexe 4 Composite table of replies of Governments

Reproduced from *United Nations Register of Conventional Arms, Report of the Secretary-General*, October 1993, General Assembly Document A/48/344, pp. 5–7.

State	Data on imports	Data on exports	Explanation submitted in note verbale	Background information
Argentina	nil	yes		no
Australia	yes	nil		yes
Austria		yes		yes
Belarus	nil	yes		no
Belgium	yes	nil	yes	yes
Bolivia	yes			no
Brazil	yes	yes		yes
Bulgaria	yes	yes		yes
Canada	yes	yes		yes
Chile	yes	nil		yes
China	yes	yes		no
Colombia	yes	nil	yes	no
Croatia	nil	nil	yes	no
Cuba	nil	nil	yes	no
Czech Republic	nil	yes		yes
Denmark	yes	nil		yes
Egypt	yes	yes	yes	no
Fiji	nil	nil	yes	no
Finland	yes	yes		yes
France	nil	yes		yes
Georgia	nil	nil	yes	no
Germany	yes	yes		yes
Greece	yes	yes	yes	yes
Grenada	nil	blank form		no
Hungary	nil	nil		yes
Iceland	nil	nil	yes	no
India	yes	yes		no
Ireland	nil	nil		no
Israel	yes	yes		yes
Italy	yes	yes		yes
Japan	yes	nil		yes

State	Data on imports	Data on exports	Explanation submitted in note verbale	Background information
Kazakhstan	nil	nil	yes	no
Lesotho	nil	nil	yes	no
Libyan Arab Jamahiriya	nil	nil	yes	no
Liechtenstein	nil	nil	yes	no
Lithuania	yes			no
Luxembourg	nil	nil		no
Malaysia	nil	nil	yes	no
Maldives	nil	nil		no
Malta	yes	nil		no
Mauritius		nil	yes	no
Mexico			yes	no
Mongolia	nil	nil	yes	no
Namibia	nil	nil		no
Nepal	yes			no
Netherlands	yes	yes	yes	yes
New Zealand	yes	nil		yes
Nicaragua			yes	no
Niger	see note verbale	nil	yes	no
Nigeria			yes	no
Norway	yes	nil		yes
Oman			yes	no
Pakistan	yes	nil		no
Panama			yes	yes
Papua New Guinea	nil	nil		no
Paraguay			yes	no
Peru	yes	blank form		no
Philippines	yes	nil	yes	no
Poland	yes	yes		yes
Portugal	yes	nil		yes
Qatar				yes
Republic of Korea	yes	nil		yes
Romania	yes	yes		no
Russian Federation	nil	yes		no
Senegal	nil	nil	yes	no
Seychelles	nil	nil		no
Singapore	yes	nil		no

State	Data on imports	Data on exports	Explanation submitted in note verbale	Background information
Slovakia	nil	nil	yes	no
Slovenia	nil	nil	yes	no
Solomon Islands	nil	nil	yes	no
South Africa			yes	no
Spain	yes	nil		yes
Sweden	yes	yes		yes
Switzerland	nil	nil		yes
Tunisia			yes	no
Turkey	yes	nil		yes
United Kingdom of Great Britain and Northern Ireland	yes	yes		yes
United States of America	yes	yes	yes	yes
Vanuatu	nil	nil	yes	no
Yugoslavia	nil	nil	yes	yes

Additional replied received since October 1993

State	Data on imports	Data on exports	Explanation submitted in note verbale	Background information
Lebanon	yes		yes	no
Sri Lanka	nil	nil	yes	no
Ukraine	nil	nil	yes	no

Annexe 5 Returns to the UN Register of Conventional Arms for arms transfers in 1992 compared with SIPRI data

Re-printed with the kind permission of SIPRI, from: Edward J. Laurance, Siemon T. Wezeman and Herbert Wulf, *Arms Watch: SIPRI Report on the First Year of the UN Register of Conventional Arms*, SIPRI Research Report No. 6, Oxford University Press, Oxford, 1993, pp. 58 - 69.

Country	Form	Category[a]	Second country[b]	No. of items	State of origin	SIPRI status[c]	Description/comments[d]
Argentina	Exports	Cbt Acft	Sri Lanka	4	Argentina	Conf.	IA-58 Pucara aircraft/For use as advanced training aircraft by Sri Lankan AF
Austria	Exports	LCA	Thailand	18	..	NR	155mm
Belarus	Exports	Tank	North Korea	19	Russia	NR	870
Belarus	Exports	Tank	Oman	5	Russia	NR	870
Brazil	Exports	M/MI[e]	Qatar	384	..	NC	SS30, SS60 rockets for ASTROS II
Brazil	Exports	M/MI[e]	Saudi Arabia	50 328	..	NC	SS30, SS40, SS60 rockets for ASTROS II
Bulgaria	Exports	LCA	Syria	210	..	NR	..
Bulgaria	Exports	Cbt Acft	Russia	3	..	NR	..
Canada	Exports	ACV	Saudi Arabia	262	..	Diff.	Wheeled APC
Canada	Exports	LCA	Italy	2	Italy	NC	OTO Melara 127/54 ship-mounted gun/Originally imported from Italy; returned as partial payment for overhaul of 7 105mm howitzers
China	Exports	Tank	Pakistan	97	..	NV	..
China	Exports	ACV	Sri Lanka	2	..	NR	..
China	Exports	LCA	Bangladesh	42	..	NR	..
China	Exports	LCA	Iran	106	..	NR	..
China	Exports	LCA	Sudan	18	..	NR	..
China	Exports	Ship	Thailand	2	..	Conf.	..

Country	Form	Category[a]	Second country[b]	No. of items	State of origin	SIPRI status[c]	Description/comments[d]
China	Exports	M/MI	Thailand	24	:	Diff.	:
Czech Republic	Exports	LCA	Zimbabwe	20	:	NR	122mm MRL on wheel chassis Type RM-70
Egypt	Exports	ACV	Algeria	53	:	NR	Wheeled APC with no additional equipment and without armaments
Egypt	Exports	LCA	Rwanda	6	:	NR	122mm howitzer
Finland	Exports	ACV	Sweden	2	:	NR	XA-180
France	Exports	ACV	Morocco	14	:	NR	:
France	Exports	ACV	Oman	4	:	NR	:
France	Exports	ACV	Qatar	12	:	NR	:
France	Exports	ACV	UAE	6	:	NR	:
France	Exports	LCA	Saudi Arabia	175	:	NR	:
France	Exports	LCA	Singapore	26	:	Diff.	:
France	Exports	Cbt Acft	Greece	12	:	Conf.	:
France	Exports	Cbt Acft	Venezuela	4	:	Diff.	:
France	Exports	Atk Helo	Chile	1	:	Diff.	:
France	Exports	M/MI	Brazil	12	:	NR	:
France	Exports	M/MI	Greece	8	:	NV	:
France	Exports	M/MI	Saudi Arabia	6	:	NV	:
Germany	Exports	Tank	Belgium	2	:	NR	T-55, T-72
Germany	Exports	Tank	Canada	8	:	NR	T-72
Germany	Exports	Tank	Finland	97	:	Conf.	T-72
Germany	Exports	Tank	Norway	16	:	Diff.	Leo-1
Germany	Exports	Tank	Sweden	6	:	NR	1 Leo-2, 5 T-72
Germany	Exports	Tank	Turkey	11	:	Diff.	Leo-1
Germany	Exports	ACV	Belgium	2	:	NR	BTR-70, BMP-1
Germany	Exports	ACV	Finland	3	:	NR	MT-LB
Germany	Exports	ACV	Greece	3	:	NR	BMP, MT-LB
Germany	Exports	ACV	Sweden	5	:	NR	MT-LB

Germany	Exports	ACV	Turkey	..	105	Conf.	BTR-60
Germany	Exports	ACV	USA	..	18	Conf.	APC Fuchs
Germany	Exports	LCA	Belgium	..	2	NR	Armoured howitzer 122mm
Germany	Exports	LCA	Finland	..	447	Diff.	Armoured howitzer 122mm, 152mm
Germany	Exports	Cbt Acft	Belgium	..	2	NR	MiG-21, MiG-23
Germany	Exports	Cbt Acft	Turkey	..	11	Diff.	Phantom/RF-4E
Germany	Exports	Atk Helo	USA	..	1	NR	Mi-24
Germany	Exports	Ship	Greece	..	8	Conf.	Landing craft
Germany	Exports	Ship	India	..	1	Diff.	Submarine (kit)
Germany	Exports	Ship	South Korea	..	1	Diff.	Submarine
Germany	Exports	M/MI	France	..	3 852	NC	Missiles RP/C M-26
Germany	Exports	M/MI	France	..	522	NC	Missiles RP/C M-28 (test missiles)
Germany	Exports	M/MI	Italy	..	960	NC	Missiles RP/C M-26
Germany	Exports	M/MI	Italy	..	240	NC	Missiles RP/C M-28 (test missiles)
Germany	Exports	M/MI	Sweden	..	8	NC	A/S missiles S-5
Germany	Exports	M/MI	UK	..	6 888	NC	Missiles RP/C M-26
Germany	Exports	M/MI	UK	..	888	NC	Missiles RP/C M-28 (test missiles)
Germany	Exports	M/MI	USA	..	182	Conf.	Guided missiles
Greece	Exports	ACV	Cyprus	..	49	Diff.	Leonidas
India	Exports	ACV	Maldives	UK	2	NR	..
India	Exports	ACV	Maldives	USSR	2	NR	..
Israel	Exports	ACV	Botswana	..	4	NR	..
Israel	Exports	ACV	USA	..	1	NR	..
Israel	Exports	LCA	USA	USA	1	NR	..
Israel	Exports	M/MI	USA	..	40	Diff.	..
Italy	Exports	LCA	Nigeria	..	9	NR	Self-propelled guns 155mm, 39 calibre
Italy	Exports	Cbt Acft	New Zealand	..	6	Conf.	MB-339C
Italy	Exports	Cbt Acft	UAE	..	1	NR	MB-339C/Replacement
Italy	Exports	Atk Helo	Belgium	..	10	Diff.	A-109 MKII Scout
Italy	Exports	M/MI	USA	..	2	NR	S.S. OTOMAT MKII (improved version)

Country	Form	Category[a]	Second country[b]	No. of items	State of origin	SIPRI status[c]	Description/comments[d]
Italy	Exports	M/Ml	Venezuela	6	..	NR	S.S. OTOMAT MKII
Netherlands	Exports	Tank	Greece	100	Germany	Diff.	Leopard 1-V/CFE Treaty cascade
Netherlands	Exports	ACV	Greece	53	USA	NR	M-106
Netherlands	Exports	ACV	Portugal	6	..	Diff.	YP-408 APCCO/NATO Defence Assistance
Netherlands	Exports	ACV	Portugal	22	..	Diff.	YP-408 ACPI/CFE Treaty cascade/NATO Defence Assistance
Netherlands	Exports	LCA	Greece	171	USA	Diff.	M-30 (4.2" mortar)/CFE Treaty cascade
Poland	Exports	ACV	Latvia	2	..	NR	..
Romania	Exports	LCA	Cameroon	12	..	NR	130mm gun
Romania	Exports	LCA	Moldova	51	..	NR	Amphibious armoured carrier
Romania	Exports	LCA	Moldova	30	..	NR	120mm launcher
Romania	Exports	LCA	Moldova	18	..	NR	122mm howitzer
Romania	Exports	LCA	Nigeria	5	..	NR	122mm/40 MLRS
Romania	Exports	LCA	Nigeria	4	..	NR	130mm gun
Romania	Exports	LCA	Oman	6	..	NR	..
Russia	Exports	Tank	UK	1	..	NR	..
Russia	Exports	Tank	Finland	84	..	NR	..
Russia	Exports	ACV	Sierra Leone	4	..	NR	..
Russia	Exports	ACV	UAE	80	..	Diff.	..
Russia	Exports	ACV	Uzbekistan	30	..	NR	..
Russia	Exports	Cbt Acft	China	20	..	Diff.	..
Russia	Exports	Cbt Acft	China	6	..	Diff.	/Training aircraft
Russia	Exports	Ship	Iran	1	..	Conf.	..
Russia	Exports	Ship	Finland	1	..	NR	/Leased without arms as a museum piece
Russia	Exports	Ship	Poland	3	..	NR	/Payment for warship leased to Poland in 1991
Russia	Exports	M/Ml	China	144	..	Diff.	Tanks T-72/Contract from 1991
Slovakia	Exports	Tank	Syria	81	Slovakia	Diff.	..
Sweden	Exports	Ship	Australia	..	..	Diff.	Submarine sections

Supplier		Category	Recipient	Number	Source	Status	Comment
Sweden	Exports	M/MI	Finland	5	..	Diff.	RBS-15 system
UK	Exports	Tank	Nigeria	25	..	Conf.	
UK	Exports	Tank	Switzerland	6		NR	/Obsolete equipment for museums
UK	Exports	ACV	Australia	8	Czechosl.	NR	/Obsolete equipment for museums
UK	Exports	ACV	Brunei Darussalam	6	Brunei Dar.	NR	/Return of equipment after refurbishment
UK	Exports	ACV	Papua New Guinea	1	..	NR	..
UK	Exports	ACV	Saudi Arabia	29	..	Diff.	..
UK	Exports	ACV	Switzerland	1	..	NR	/Obsolete equipment for museums
UK	Exports	ACV	USA	1	USA	NR	/Obsolete equipment for museums
UK	Exports	LCA	Brazil	4	..	Conf.	..
UK	Exports	LCA	Switzerland	1	..	NR	/Obsolete equipment for museums
UK	Exports	Cbt Acft	India	3	..	Diff.	..
UK	Exports	Cbt Acft	South Korea	10	..	NR	..
UK	Exports	Cbt Acft	Saudi Arabia	1	..	Diff.	..
UK	Exports	Cbt Acft	Zimbabwe	5	..	Diff.	..
UK	Exports	Ship	Chile	1	..	Conf.	..
UK	Exports	M/MI	Saudi Arabia	48	..	Diff.	..
UK	Exports	M/MI	UAE	398	..	NR	..
USA	Exports	Tank	Egypt	75	..	Diff.	..
USA	Exports	Tank	Greece	492	..	NR	..
USA	Exports	Tank	Singapore	1	..	Diff.	..
USA	Exports	Tank	Spain	96	..	Diff.	..
USA	Exports	Tank	Turkey	577	..	Diff.	..
USA	Exports	ACV	Bahrain	101	..	NR	..
USA	Exports	ACV	Canada	21	..	NR	..
USA	Exports	ACV	Denmark	2	..	Diff.	..
USA	Exports	ACV	Greece	150	..	NR	..
USA	Exports	ACV	Oman	2	..	NR	..
USA	Exports	ACV	Saudi Arabia	192	..	Diff.	..
USA	Exports	ACV	Thailand	18	..	NR	..

Country	Form	Category[a]	Second country[b]	No. of items	State of origin	SIPRI status[c]	Description/comments[d]
USA	Exports	ACV	Turkey	220	...	Diff.	...
USA	Exports	LCA	Bahrain	19	...	Diff.	...
USA	Exports	LCA	Greece	72	...	Conf.	...
USA	Exports	LCA	Turkey	75	...	Diff.	...
USA	Exports	Cbt Acft	Chile	10	...	Conf.	...
USA	Exports	Cbt Acft	Ecuador	4	...	NR	...
USA	Exports	Cbt Acft	Egypt	21	...	Diff.	...
USA	Exports	Cbt Acft	Greece	16	...	NV	...
USA	Exports	Cbt Acft	Israel	40	...	Diff.	...
USA	Exports	Cbt Acft	South Korea	1	...	Diff.	...
USA	Exports	Cbt Acft	Kuwait	23	...	Diff.	...
USA	Exports	Cbt Acft	Netherlands	2	...	Diff.	...
USA	Exports	Cbt Acft	Philippines	9	...	Diff.	...
USA	Exports	Cbt Acft	Saudi Arabia	10	...	Conf.	...
USA	Exports	Cbt Acft	Turkey	29	...	NR	...
USA	Exports	Atk Helo	Turkey	6	...	Diff.	...
USA	Exports	Ship	Greece	1	...	Diff.	...
USA	Exports	M/MI	Australia	26	...	NV	...
USA	Exports	M/MI	Bahrain	1 212	...	NV	...
USA	Exports	M/MI	Canada	88	...	NV	...
USA	Exports	M/MI	Egypt	3	...	NV	...
USA	Exports	M/MI	Germany	50	...	NV	...
USA	Exports	M/MI	Greece	120	...	NV	...
USA	Exports	M/MI	Italy	8	...	NV	...
USA	Exports	M/MI	Japan	109	...	NV	...
USA	Exports	M/MI	Netherlands	80	...	NV	...
USA	Exports	M/MI	Portugal	19	...	NR	...
USA	Exports	M/MI	Spain	9	...	NV	...

						NV	
USA	Exports	M/MI	Turkey	1 164	..	..	..
Australia	Imports	M/MI	USA	29	..	Diff.	/Includes Harpoon, Sparrow and Standard missiles and also 2 MK-13 launchers for fitting to Australian frigates *Melbourne* and *Newcastle*; 2 of the missiles were delivered in a telemetry (training) configuration
Belgium	Imports	Tank	Germany	1	GDR	NR	T-55/Already provided in the global figures contained in the UN Register
Belgium	Imports	Tank	Germany	1	GDR	NR	T-72/Already provided in the global figures contained in the UN Register
Belgium	Imports	ACV	Germany	1	GDR	NR	BMP/Already provided in the global figures contained in the UN Register
Belgium	Imports	ACV	Germany	1	GDR	NR	BTR-70/Already provided in the global figures contained in the UN Register
Belgium	Imports	LCA	Germany	1	GDR	NR	2S1/Already provided in the global figures contained in the UN Register
Belgium	Imports	LCA	Germany	1	GDR	NR	D-30/Already provided in the global figures contained in the UN Register
Belgium	Imports	Cbt Acft	Germany	1	GDR	NR	MiG-21/Already provided in the global figures contained in the UN Register
Belgium	Imports	Cbt Acft	Germany	1	GDR	NR	MiG-23/Already provided in the global figures contained in the UN Register
Belgium	Imports	Atk Helo	Italy	10	..	Diff.	A-109
Bolivia	Imports	LCA	China	36	China	NR	T-54-1/Credit agreement between the governments
Bolivia	Imports	LCA	China	18	China	NR	T-65/Credit agreement between the governments
Brazil	Imports	LCA	UK	4	..	Conf.	105mm light gun
Bulgaria	Imports	Cbt Acft	Russia	5	..	NR	..
Canada	Imports	ACV	USA	22	..	NR	Fully tracked APC
Canada	Imports	M/MI	USA	5	..	Diff.	Harpoon ship-launched SSMs

Country	Form	Category[a]	Second country[b]	No. of items	State of origin	SIPRI status[c]	Description/comments[d]
Canada	Imports	M/MI	USA	75	...	Diff.	Sea Sparrow ship-launched SAMs
Chile	Imports	Cbt Acft	USA	10	...	Conf.	Training aircraft designed for counter-insurgency operations/Reported by Chilean AF
Chile	Imports	Ship	UK	1	...	Conf.	Leander Class frigate formerly *HMS Ariadne*/Reported by Chilean Navy
China	Imports	Cbt Acft	Russia	26	...	Diff.	...
China	Imports	M/MI	Russia	144	...	Diff.	...
Denmark	Imports	ACV	USA	25	...	NR	M-113 A2 MK1 being modified with turret
Denmark	Imports	M/MI	USA	2	...	NV	...
Egypt	Imports	Tanks	USA	26	...	Diff.	/Compartments of battle tanks
Egypt	Imports	Cbt Acft	USA	26	...	Diff.	...
Finland	Imports	Tank	Germany	97	Russia	Conf.	T-72 M1
Finland	Imports	ACV	Hungary	1	Russia	NR	SU-57
Finland	Imports	ACV	Russia	84	Russia	NR	BMP-2
Finland	Imports	LCA	Germany	447	Russia	Diff.	...
Finland	Imports	M/MI	Sweden	5	...	Diff.	RBS-15 System
Germany	Imports	M/MI	USA	4	...	NR	Missile launcher
Greece	Imports	Tank	Netherlands	100	...	Diff.	Leo-1V/Imported to replace equal no. of older equipment to be destroyed under CFE Treaty TLE transfer and destruction project
Greece	Imports	Tank	USA	214	...	Diff.	M-60A1
Greece	Imports	Tank	USA	133	...	Diff.	M-60A3
Greece	Imports	ACV	Germany	1	...	NR	BMP-1
Greece	Imports	ACV	Greece	68	...	Diff.	Leonidas/68 ACVs Leonidas procured through national production
Greece	Imports	ACV	USA	150	...	Diff.	M-113

Country	Trade	Category	Supplier	No.		Status	Description
Greece	Imports	LCA	Netherlands	171	..	Diff.	M-30 (4.2")/Imported to replace equal no. of older equipment to be destroyed under CFE Treaty TLE transfer and destruction project
Greece	Imports	LCA	USA	6	..	NR	54 MK-42 (5") gun/Carried by DDG-2 and F-1052 ships (lease)
Greece	Imports	LCA	USA	72	..	Conf.	M-110 A2/Imported to replace equal no. of older equipment to be destroyed under CFE Treaty TLE transfer and destruction project
Greece	Imports	Cbt Acft	France	11	..	Conf.	M-2000
Greece	Imports	Cbt Acft	Germany	5	..	Diff.	RF-4
Greece	Imports	Ship	Germany	4	..	Conf.	Corvettes/Aid
Greece	Imports	Ship	USA	7	..	Diff.	Frigates and DDG/Leasing
Greece	Imports	M/MI	USA	18	..	Diff.	Harpoon missiles/Carried by DDG-2 and F-1052 ships (lease)
Greece	Imports	M/MI	USA	3	..	Conf.	MK-18 launchers
India	Imports	Cbt Acft	UK	3	UK	NR	..
Israel	Imports	Cbt Acft	USA	40	..	Diff.	..
Italy	Imports	LCA	Canada	2	..	NR	Ship-guns OTO 127mm, 54 calibre/Partial repayment for new purchase
Italy	Imports	M/MI	USA	8	..	Diff.	AA type SM-1 -E. R.
Japan	Imports	M/MI	USA	76	..	NV	Hawk 60/For training purposes only
South Korea	Imports	Cbt Acft	UK	10	..	Diff.	F-16
South Korea	Imports	Cbt Acft	USA	4	..	Conf.	F-16
Lithuania	Imports	ACV	Russia	15	..	NR	Type BTR-60 PA
Lithuania	Imports	Ship	Russia	2	..	Conf.	Light frigate Project-1124
Malta	Imports	Ship	Germany	2	GDR	NC	Bremse patrol boats/Bought for a nominal sum
Malta	Imports	Ship	Germany	2	GDR	NR	Kondor patrol boats/Bought for a nominal sum
Malta	Imports	Ship	Italy	3	..	NC	Ex-Guardia di Finanza patrol boats/Donation
Nepal	Imports	LCA	UK	8	..	NR	105mm field guns
Nepal	Imports	LCA	India	52	..	NR	120mm mortars

Country	Form	Category[a]	Second country[b]	No. of items	State of origin	SIPRI status[c]	Description/comments[d]
Netherlands	Imports	Cbt Acft	USA	2	..	Diff.	F-16 A/C FMS
New Zealand	Imports	Cbt Acft	Italy	6	..	Conf.	Aermacchi MB-339C/New training aircraft but capable of modification
Norway	Imports	Tank	Germany	16	Germany	Diff.	..
Pakistan	Imports	Tank	China	97	..	Diff.	/64 tanks received in 1992, 33 tanks in beginning of 1993
Peru	Imports	Tank	USA	14	..	NR	M-501 light amphibian troop carrier, low mileage/Im-ported by Peruvian Navy
Peru	Imports	ACV	USA	12	..	NR	/Imported by Peruvian AF
Peru	Imports	ACV	South Africa	4	..	NR	Mine-resistant armoured troop carrier, CADOPLA MKIII REPONTEC (personnel carrier for use in jungle areas in anti-terrorist and anti-narcotics traffic opera-tions)/Imported by Peruvian Navy
Peru	Imports	Atk Helo	Nicaragua	7	..	NR	Attack helicopter for use in anti-terrorist and anti-narcotics traffic operations/Imported by Peruvian AF
Peru	Imports	Atk Helo	Nicaragua	12	..	NR	/Imported by Peruvian AF
Peru	Imports	Atk Helo	Russia	3	..	Diff.	M5T transport helicopter (helicopter for personnel trans- port and support for national socio- economic develop- ment/Standard version; imported by Peruvian Navy
Philippines	Imports	Cbt Acft	Russia	19	USA	Diff.	OV-10A
Poland	Imports	Ship	..	3	..	NR	Payment for previously leased warships
Portugal	Imports	ACV	Netherlands	26	..	Diff.	YP-408/Military aid
Portugal	Imports	M/M1	USA	5	..	NR	Harpoon AGM-84-A
Portugal	Imports	M/M1	USA	8	..	NR	Harpoon RGM-84-3
Romania	Imports	Cbt Acft	Moldova	1	..	NR	Fighter MiG-29
Singapore	Imports	ACV	USA	1	..	NR	..

Country							
Singapore	Imports	LCA	France	24	..	Diff.	..
Singapore	Imports	M/Ml	USA	1	..	NV	Missile
Spain	Imports	Tank	Germany	96	USA	Diff.	M-60/CFE Treaty
Spain	Imports	M/Ml	USA	11	..	Diff.	2 MK-13 launchers, 9 Standard Block V missiles/SAM
Sweden	Imports	Tank	Germany	5	..	NR	T-72
Sweden	Imports	ACV	Finland	2	..	NR	XA-180
Sweden	Imports	ACV	Germany	5	..	NR	MT-LB
Turkey	Imports	Tank	Germany	11	..	Diff.	Leopard 1A3/Harmonization
Turkey	Imports	Tank	USA	25	..	Diff.	M-60A1/South Region Aid
Turkey	Imports	Tank	USA	391	..	Diff.	M-60A3/Harmonization
Turkey	Imports	ACV	USA	119	..	Diff.	M-113A2/Harmonization
Turkey	Imports	LCA	USA	69	..	Diff.	M-110 203mm howitzer/Harmonization
Turkey	Imports	Cbt Acft	Germany	11	..	Diff.	RF-4E/Harmonization
Turkey	Imports	Cbt Acft	Netherlands	6	..	NR	NF-5A/Netherlands aid
Turkey	Imports	Cbt Acft	USA	9	..	NR	F-4E/South Region Aid
Turkey	Imports	Atk Helo	USA	6	..	Diff.	AH-1P attack helicopters/South Region Aid
Turkey	Imports	M/Ml	USA	24	..	NR	Sea Sparrow guided missiles/FMS
UK	Imports	Tank	Russia	1	..	NR	..
UK	Imports	ACV	Brunei Darussalam	2	..	NR	/Equipment imported on a temporary basis for repair and return to country of origin
UK	Imports	ACV	Canada	1	..	NR	..
UK	Imports	ACV	Venezuela	7	..	NR	/Equipment imported on a temporary basis for repair and return to country of origin
UK	Imports	LCA	Brazil	2	..	NR	/Obsolete equipment for museums
UK	Imports	LCA	France	14	..	NV	/Obsolete equipment for museums
UK	Imports	LCA	Indonesia	1	..	NR	:
UK	Imports	LCA	USA	1	..	NV	/Obsolete equipment for museums
UK	Imports	M/Ml	Czechoslovakia	2	..	NR	/Obsolete equipment for museums
UK	Imports	M/Ml	Germany	6 888	..	NC	/Obsolete equipment for museums

Country	Form	Category[a]	Second country[b]	No. of items	State of origin	SIPRI status[c]	Description/comments[d]
USA	Imports	Atk Helo	Germany	1	..	NR	..
USA	Imports	Ship	Germany	1	..	NR	..
USA	Imports	M/Ml	Germany	187	..	Conf.	..
USA	Imports	M/Ml	Israel	40	..	Diff.	..
USA	Imports	M/Ml	Italy	2	..	NR	..

[a] *Abbreviation:*   *UN Register weapon category:*

Tank	I. Battle tanks
ACV	II. Armoured combat vehicles
LCA	III. Large-calibre artillery systems
Cbt Acft	IV. Combat aircraft
Atk Helo	V. Attack helicopters
Ship	VI. Warships
M/Ml	VII. Missiles and missile launchers

[b] On the exports forms, 'second country' refers to the importer; on the imports forms, it refers to the exporter.

[c] Abbreviations in column for SIPRI status:

Conf.   Confirming the transfer: the entry in the SIPRI register for 1992 is the same or similar to the entry in the UN Register.

Diff.   Different from SIPRI: the transfer is reported in the SIPRI register for 1992 and in the UN Register, but the number of items, the exact designations and/or the delivery years are different, or it is considered as licensed production by SIPRI.

NC   Not counted by SIPRI since it does not fit the SIPRI weapon categories

NR   Not reported in the SIPRI register for 1992 as a delivery or as on order.

NV   Not verifiable because of lack of precise description of equipment in the return to the UN Register.

[d] The wording in the last column is as close as possible to the original text given by governments in their returns to the UN Register.

[e] These were reported to the UN Register as 'large-calibre artillery systems', but for the purpose of this report they are entered as rockets, falling under the UN Register category 'Missiles and missile launchers'.

Annexe 6 Bibliography

Listing of books, newspaper, journal and magazine articles and wire reports referencing the UN Register of Conventional Arms since January 1993. Compiled by Joseph DiChiaro III, Monterey Institute of International Studies.

Anthony, Ian, "Assessing the UN Register of Conventional Arms", *Survival*, Vol. 35, No. 4, Winter 1993, pp. 112-129.

"ASEAN Considers Inviting DPRK to Security Talks", *Pacific Rim Intelligence Report*, 28 May 1993.

"ASEAN Proposes New Venue for Asia-Pacific Dialogue", *Asian Political News*, 22 February 1993.

"At Least 70 States Have Submitted...", *Wall Street Journal*, 30 July 1993, p. 1.

"Attempts Made To Buy Russian Aircraft Carrier", *China Intelligence Report*, 8 February 1993.

Ball, Desmond, "Arms and Affluence: Military Acquisitions in the Asia-Pacific Region", *International Security*, Winter 1993/94, 18, 3, pp. 106-108.

"Bulgaria, Greece, Turkey Form Barrier Against Spread of Yugoslav War", *Associated Press*, London, 28 October 1993, 09:35 EDT.

Burton, Sandra, "What Kind of Defense? As the U.S. presence declines, Southeast Asia rethinks its posture", *Time International*, Hong Kong, 17 May 1993, p. 30.

Campaign Against the Arms Trade, "The UN Register", *CAAT News*, February 1994, p. 7.

Chalmers, Malcolm and Owen Greene, *Implementing and Developing the United Nations Register of Conventional Arms*, Bradford Arms Register Studies No. 1, Department of Peace Studies, University of Bradford, Bradford, May 1993.

Chalmers, Malcolm and Owen Greene, "The UN Register: Development and Implementation", *Council for Arms Control Bulletin*, London, May 1993.

Chalmers, Malcolm and Owen Greene, *The United Nations Register of Conventional Arms: An Initial Examination of the First Report*t, Bradford Arms Register Studies No. 2, Department of Peace Studies, University of Bradford, Bradford, October 1993.

Chalmers, Malcolm and Owen Greene, *Background Information: An Analysis of Information Provided to the UN on Military Holdings and Procurement Through National Production in the First Year of the Register of Conventional Arms*, Bradford Arms Register Studies No. 3, Department of Peace Studies, University of Bradford, Bradford, March 1994.

Chalmers, Malcolm and Owen Greene, "The United Nations Register of Conventional Arms: the first year of operation," in *Verification 1994: Peacekeeping, Arms Control, and the Environment*", Brassey's/VERTIC, London, (forthcoming, 1994).

Chalmers, Malcolm and Owen Greene, "Developing International Transparency: Successes for the United Nations Register of Conventional Arms", *International Defense Review*, 5/94.

Chalmers, Malcolm and Owen Greene, "Preventing Destabilising Build-Ups of Conventional Arms: Transparency, Restraint, and the United Nations Register of Conventional Arms", memorandum submitted to the Foreign Affairs Committee inquiry into weapons proliferation and control, (forthcoming 1994).

Chalmers, Malcolm and Owen Greene, "The United Nations Register of Conventional Arms and the Asia-Pacific region," in Malcolm Chalmers , Owen Greene, and Xie Zhiqiong (eds), *The United Nations and the Asia-Pacific*, Department of Peace Studies, University of Bradford, Bradford, (forthcoming 1994).

Cornish, Paul, "The UN Register of Conventional Arms", *World Today*, February 1994, pp. 24-25.

"Defense Industry Conversion, Diversification Noted", *West Europe Intelligence Report*, 1 October 1993.

"Deutschland ist auf Platz zwei der Waffenlieferanten aufgerückt", *Frankfurter Rundschau*, 25 October 1993, p. 12.

"Development: OECD Official Says Aid Policies in State of Flux", *Inter Press Service*, 11 May 1993.

"Digest Briefs", *Associated Press* , Jerusalem, 29 July 1993, 04:56 EDT.

"Digest Briefs", *Associated Press* , Washington, 25 October 1993, 19:40 EDT.

"Disarmament: More Than 80 States Bare Their Arms at U.N", *Inter Press Service*, 27 October 1993.

"Disarmament: U.N. Head is Rethinking Plan to Relocate Office", *Inter Press Service*, 9 March 1993.

"Disarmament: U.N. Hopes Nations Will Bare Military Secrets", *Inter Press Service*, 14 May 1993.

"Draft Text of Summit Political Statement", *Associated Press* Tokyo, 7 July 1993, 21:16 EDT.

"Factfile: UN Register of Conventional Arms", *Arms Control Today*, Vol. 23, No. 7, September 1993, p. 33.

Federation of American Scientists, "The United Nations Register of Conventional Arms", *Arms Sale Monitor,* Number 24, 15 March 1994, p. 6.

Federation of American Scientists, "Annual Report on Military Expenditure and Arms Control", *Arms Sale Monitor,* Number 24, 30 November 1993, p. 9.

Feinstein, Lee, "52 Countries Volunteer Reports to New UN Arms Register", *Arms Control Today*, Vol. 23, No. 5, June 1993, p. 30.

"Final Text of Summit Political Statement", *Associated Press*, Tokyo, 7 July 1993, 23:54 EDT.

"First Global Account of Arms Transfers Successful", *Defense Marketing International*, Vol. 5, No. 16, 6 August 1993.

"Full Text of G-7 Political Declaration", *Japan Policy & Politics*, 12 July 1993.

"G-7 to Seek Tighter Control of Arms Technology Exports", *Japan Weekly Monitor*, 28 June 1993.

Goldblatt, Josef, "Reservations about UN Arms Register", *Arms Control Today,* July/August 1993, p. 30.

Goldring, Natalie J., "Deadline for UN Arms Register Approaches", *Basic Reports*, No. 29, 16 April 1993, pp. 1-3.

Goldring, Natalie J., "Register Progresses, Key Recipients Missing", *Basic Reports*, No. 32, 9 July 1993, p. 4.

Goldring, Natalie J., "UN Arms Register Apparent Success: Plans for Expansion and Evaluation Begin", *Basic Reports*, No. 33, 17 September 1993, pp. 1, 3.

Goldring, Natalie J., *Moving Toward Transparency: An Evaluation of the United Nations Register of Conventional Armaments* , British American Security Information Council, Washington, DC, October 1993.

Goodman, Anthony, "U.N. Lists Big Tank Imports by Greece and Turkey", *Reuters*, 20 October 1993, 20:30 EDT.

Graham, Victoria, "U.S. Top Seller in U.N.'s First Arms Register", *Associated Press*, 20 October 1993, 21:35 EDT.

Hanley, Charles J., "Arms Deals Unveiled", *Associated Press*, 29 July 1993, 00:15 EDT.

Hanley, Charles J., "Arms Sales on World Market Recorded by U.N. in Register", *Washington Times*, 30 July 1993, p. A9.

Hanley, Charles J., "Bottom Line: Arms Flow Tops $50 Billion in 3 Years Since Invasion", *Associated Press*, 11 August 1993, 23:51 EDT.

Hanley, Charles J., "Governments Check In With First Global Accounting of Arms Trade", *Associated Press*, 29 July 1993, 13:10 EDT.

Human Rights Watch, *Landmines: A Deadly Legacy*, Human Rights Watch, New York, October 1993, pp. 107-116.

"India: World Parliament Group Meets, Arms Control on Agenda", *Inter Press Service*, 12 April 1993.

International Institute for Strategic Studies, *The Military Balance 1993-1994*, Brassey's, London, October 1993, pp. 247-249.

"Israel to Detail Arms Deals", *Interavia Air Letter*, 3 August 1993, p. 5.

"Japan and Russia to Cooperate to Restrict Weapons", *Japan Policy & Politics*, 18 October 1993.

"Japan: Stepping Up Nuclear Arms Control Efforts", *Inter Press Service*, 12 February 1993.

"Japan Taking Reserved Stance in Regional Security Debate", *Japan Policy & Politics*, 4 January 1993.

"Japan to Host Confab on Arms Trade Transparency", *Japan Weekly Monitor*, 25 January 1993.

"Key Points of G-7 Political Declaration", *Japan Policy & Politics*, 12 July 1993.

Laurance, Edward J., "The UN Register of Conventional Arms: Rationales and Prospects for Compliance and Effectiveness", *Washington Quarterly*, Vol.16, No. 2, Spring 1993, pp. 163-72.

Laurance, Edward J. and Herbert Wulf, "The Continued Quest for Transparency in Armaments: Quantity versus Utility of Information", in *Transparency in Armaments: The Mediterranean Region*, Disarmament Topical Paper No. 15, UN Office for Disarmament Affairs, New York, 1993.

Laurance, Edward J. and Herbert Wulf, *An Evaluation of the First Year of Reporting to the United Nations Register of Conventional Arms*, Research Report, Program for Nonproliferation Studies, Monterey Institute of International Studies, October 1993.

Laurance, Edward J., Siemon T. Wezeman and Herbert Wulf, *Arms Watch: SIPRI Report on the First Year of the UN Register of Conventional Arms*, Oxford University Press, Oxford, 1993.

"Lawmakers Press Clinton for an Arms Sales Policy", *Defense Week*, Vol. 14, No. 30, 26 July 1993.

Lederer, Edith M., "United Nations Register Reveals Undisclosed Arms Sales, But Secrets Remain", *Associated Press*, London, 25 October 1993, 14:05 EDT .

"Malaysia Calls for Int'l Confab on U.N. Peacekeeping", *Asian Political News*, 19 July 1993.

"Malaysia Wants Regional Arms Register in Southeast Asia", *Asian Political News*, 14 June 1993.

McKibbin, Warwick J., "A New Military Equilibrium? Preventing Regional Conflicts in the Developing World", *Brookings Review*, Vol. 11, No. 4, Fall 1993, pp. 42-45.

Mussington, David, "Defense exports seek new framework", *International Defense Review*, 3/1994, pp. 23-25.

"Myanmar Navy Chief Visits Japan", *Asian Political News*, 1 November 1993.

"Nations Report to UN Arms List", *Jane's Defence Weekly*, 22 May 1993, p. 5.

Navias, Martin, "Towards a new South African Arms Trade Policy", *South African Defence Review*, 13, November 1993, pp. 38-49.

"New Bills Would Place Limitations on Arms Sales", *Defense Marketing International*, Vol. 5, No. 23, 12 November 1993.

Nolan, Janne E. (ed.), *Global Engagement: Cooperation and Security in the 21st century*, Brookings Institute, Washington DC, 1994, pp. 7, 49, 76-77, 79, 82, 89, 208, 211, 216, 249, 255-257.

"North-South: Britain's Secret Arms Sales Under Fire", *Inter Press Service*, 24 May 1993.

Pallister, David, "UK Fails Terms of Arms Register", *Guardian*, 10 July 1993, p. 8.

Passent, Daniel, "Auditing a Deadly Trade", *World Paper*, July 1993, p. 4.

Pick, Hella, "Brisk Business at the Arms Bazaar", *Guardian*, 30 January 1993, pp. 1, 22.

"Proposes Russia-ASEAN Committee", *Russia-CIS Intelligence Report*, 28 July 1993.

Regehr, Ernie, "The United Nations Arms Register", in Roger Williamson (ed.), *The Arms Trade Today*, January 1993, Commission of the Churches on International Affairs, Geneva, pp. 143-158.

"Rich Nations' Declaration: A Commitment to Democracy and Human Rights", *New York Times*, 9 July 1993.

"Russia Loses the Arms Market", *Moscow News*, 16 July 1993, p. 5.

Smith, R. Jeffrey, "U.S. Leads in Weapons Sales: U.N. Issues Its First Report on Arms Exports", *Washington Post*, 21 October 1993, p. A20.

Sternman, Mark S., "UN Arms Registry: A Good Start", *Arms Control Today*, Vol. 23, No. 7, September 1993, p. 30.

"Tanks, Combat Planes Make U.S. Top Exporter", *Defense News*, 25 October 1993, p. 2.

Taylor, Terence, "Understanding the United Nations Conventional Arms Register", *The Fletcher Forum*, Winter/Spring 1994, pp. 111-119.

Taylor, Trevor and Ryukichi Imai, (ed.), *The Defence Trade: Demand, Supply, and Control*, Royal Institute for International Affairs, London, 1994, pp. 96, 97, 124-126, 128, 135, 168

"Text of Japanese-Russian Document on Nuclear Weapons", *Japan Policy & Politics*, 18 October 1993.

"Undisclosed Arms Sales Documented in UN Report", *Boston Globe*, 26 October 1993, p. 72.

"UN Ambassador: Disarmament, Security Issues Concern Caricom", *Latin America Intelligence Report*, 4 November 1993.

"UN Arms List", *Associated Press*, 20 October 1993, 21:07 EDT.

"UN Arms Register", *Trust and Verify*, No. 35, January/February 1993.

"UN Arms Transfers Register", *Trust and Verify*, May 1993.

"United Nations: Boutros-Ghali to Propose Some Offices Relocate", *Inter Press Service*, 3 March 1993.

"UN Lists Germany and U.S. As Top Missile Exporters", *BMD Monitor*, Vol. 8, No. 22, 5 November 1993.

"UN Panel Calls for Naval Reforms", *Navy News & Undersea Technology*, Vol. 10, No. 16, 26 April 1993.

"U.N. Publishes Arms Register", *Arms Trade News*, November 1993, p. 3.

"U.N. Releases First Arms Register Results", *Defense Marketing International*, Vol. 5, No. 22, 29 October 1993.

"US Hit In Delhi Forum", *APS Diplomat Recorder*, Vol. 38, No. 16, 17 April 1993.

Usui, Naoaki, "Germany to Seek Increased Exports", *Defense News*, 8 November 1993, p. 4.

Wagenmakers, Hendrik, "The UN Register of Conventional Arms: A New Instrument for Cooperative Security", *Arms Control Today*, Vol. 23, No. 3, April 1993, pp. 16-21.

"What U.S. Reported to U.N. Arms Register", *Associated Press*, 29 July 1993, 13:10 EDT.

"White House To Review Conventional Arms Policy", *Defense Week*, Vol. 14, No. 35, 7 September 1993.

Wright, Robin, "Shifting Battle Lines in Arms Race", *Los Angeles Times*, 17 August 1993, pp. 1, 5.

Wulf, Herbert, "The United Nations Register of Conventional Arms", in *SIPRI Yearbook 1993: World Armaments and Disarmament*, Oxford University Press, Oxford, 1993, pp. 533-544.

Annexe 7 List of Workshop Participants

Members of the Group of Governmental Experts

Alexander Akalovsky (United States), Bureau of Multilateral Affairs, Arms Control & Disarmament Agency.

Jean-Paul Credeville (France), Deputy Director of Arms Export Control, Ministry of Defense.

Mitsuro Donowaki (Japan), Ambassador to Mexico.

Zadalinda Gonzalez y Reynero (Mexico), Minister, Alternate Representative to UNESCO.

Paul Hatt (United Kingdom), Director, Proliferation and Arms Control Secretariat, Ministry of Defence.

Pauli Järvenpää (Finland), Minister-Counsellor, Embassy to the United States.

Piotr Litavrin (Russian Federation), Head of Division, Department on Disarmament and Export Control, Ministry of Foreign Affairs.

Antonino Lisboa Mena Gonçalves (Brazil), Minister Counsellor to the US.

Mansur Raza (Pakistan), Second Secretary, Permanent Mission to the UN.

Lt. Col. Mike Sango (Zimbabwe), Counsellor, Military Advisor, Permanent Mission to the UN.

Jonathan Shimshoni (Israel), Brigadier General (ret.).

Donald Sinclair (Canada), Deputy Director, Arms Control and Disarmament Division, Department of Foreign Affairs and International Trade.

Hendrik Wagenmakers (The Netherlands), Ambassador, Permanent Mission to the United Nations at Geneva.

Lt. Col. Yeo Kok Phuang (Singapore), Ministry of Defense, Resource Planning Office.

Other Governmental Representatives

Behrooz Moradi (Islamic Republic of Iran), Second Secretary, Permanent Mission to the UN.

Hajime Sasaki (Japan), Senior Assistant, Arms Control and Disarmament Division, Foreign Policy Bureau, Ministry of Foreign Affairss.

Lt. Col. R.H.M. ten Eikelder (Netherlands), Directorate-General for Materiel, Plans & Process Coordination, Ministry of Defence.

United Nations Personnel

Hannelore Hoppe, UN Centre for Disarmament Affairs.

Presenters

Ian Anthony (United Kingdom), Stockholm International Peace Research Institute (SIPRI).

Malcolm Chalmers (United Kingdom), University of Bradford.

Joseph DiChiaro III (United States), Monterey Institute of International Studies.

Andrew Duncan (United Kingdom), International Institute for Strategic Studies (IISS).

Tim Mahon (United Kingdom), Jane's Information Group.

Owen Greene (United Kingdom), University of Bradford.

Edward J. Laurance (United States), Monterey Institute of International Studies.

Frederic S. Pearson (United States), Center for Peace & Conflict Studies, Wayne State University.

Ravinder Pal Singh (India), Stockholm International Peace Research Institute (SIPRI).

Augusto Varas (Chile), Facultad Latinoamericana de Ciencias Sociales (FLACSO).

Herbert Wulf (Germany), Bonn International Conversion Center (BICC).

Others

Valentin Alexandrov (Republic of Belarus), Ministry of Foreign Affairs.

Natalie J. Goldring (United States), British-American Security Information Council (BASIC).

Tim McCarthy (United States), Monterey Institute of International Studies.

William C. Potter (United States), Monterey Institute of International Studies.

Col. Terence Taylor (United Kingdom), Visiting Fellow, Center for International Security & Arms Control (CISAC), Stanford University.

Ambassador Roland Timerbaev (Russian Federation), Monterey Institute of International Studies.

Lt. Col. Ihor Tymofeyev (Ukraine), First Secretary, Department of Non-Proliferation & Export Controls, Ministry of Foreign Affairs.

About the Contributors

The editors

Malcolm Chalmers is a Senior Lecturer in the Department of Peace Studies, University of Bradford, UK. Together with Owen Greene he is working on a project on the implementation and development of the UN Arms Register, which includes the writing of the *Bradford Arms Register Studies*. He has also written on production control regimes for *Arms Control Today*, and has published articles in *International Security*, *Journal of Peace Research* and *World Policy Journal*.

Owen Greene is in the Department of Peace Studies, University of Bradford, UK. Together with Malcolm Chalmers he is working on a project on the implementation and development of the UN Arms Register, which includes the writing of the *Bradford Arms Register Studies*. He has written widely on international security issues, including *Verifying the Non-Proliferation Treaty: challenges for the 1990s* (VERTIC, London, 1992), and co-authored *Arms Control and Dual-Use Exports from the EC: a common policy for regulation and control* (Saferworld, Bristol, 1992).

Edward J. Laurance is Professor and Associate Director of the Program for Nonproliferation Studies at the Monterey Institute of International Studies, US. He is the author of *The International Arms Trade* (1992) and co-author of *Arms Watch: SIPRI Report on the First Year of the UN Register of Conventional Arms* (Oxford University Press, Oxford, 1993). He has served as a consultant to the United Nations Centre for Disarmament Affairs in regard to the UN Register of Conventional Arms since January 1992.

Herbert Wulf is Director of the Bonn International Center for Conversion (BICC), Germany. From 1989 to 1992 he was the leader of the research project on arms transfers and arms production at the Stockholm International Peace Research Institute (SIPRI). He is the editor of *Arms Industry Limited* (Oxford University Press, 1993), and co-author of *Arms Watch: SIPRI Report on the First Year of the UN Register of Conventional Arms* (Oxford University Press, 1993). He has served as a consultant to the United Nations Centre for Disarmament Affairs in regard to the UN Register of Conventional Arms since January 1992.

The authors

Ian Anthony is the Project Leader of the SIPRI Arms Production and Arms Transfer Project. His most recent publications include: *The Future of the Defence Industries in Central and Eastern Europe*, (Oxford University Press, 1994); *Arms Export Regulations* (ed.), (Oxford University Press, 1991).

Michael Brzoska is a Researcher at the Unit for the Study of Wars, Armaments and Development at the University of Hamburg, Germany, and

Lecturer in the Political Science Department. He was the Co-director of the SIPRI arms trade and arms production project from 1983 to 1986. His recent publications include: *Militarisierungs und Entwicklungsdynamik* (Lit-Verlag, Månster, 1994) and *Armaments and Warfare* (with Frederic S. Pearson, University of South Carolina Press, Columbus, S.C., 1994)

Antonia Handler Chayes is President of the Consensus Building Institute, and was the Under-Secretary of the Airforce in the Carter Administration. She is now on the Commission on Goals and Missions of the US Department of Defense.

Abram Chayes is Felix Frankfurter Professor of Law Emeritus at Harvard Law School, Cambridge, Massachussetts. He was Legal Adviser to the US Department of State from 1961 to 1964.

Joseph DiChiaro III is Senior Research Associate for the Conventional Arms Project at the Monterey Institute of International Studies. He was senior analyst on the International Missile Proliferation Project. In the spring of 1993 he served as an intern at the UN Office (now Centre) for Disarmament Affairs in New York, where his major responsibility was to develop the UN Register of Conventional Arms.

Colonel Andrew Duncan is the Assistant Director for Information at the International Institute for Strategic Studies where he is also the editor of *The Military Balance*. He served in the British Army for 34 years, where his posts included senior ground forces intelligence officer in British Forces Germany; as Defence Attaché in Israel; and in the Ministry of Defence supporting the MBFR and CSCE negotiations.

Holger Iburg is currently working as a freelance journalist covering scientific issues in Hamburg, Germany. He has written various articles on computer technology, U.S. nuclear strategy, and deterrence theory associated with the Hamburg based Forschungsstelle Rüstun, Kriege und Entwicklung.

Tim Mahon has worked in the area of providing information and consultancy services to the international defence community for thirteen years, eight of them with Jane's Information Group. He is currently Manager, Product Sales for Jane's US Western Region and US forces in the Pacific, based in the Los Angeles area.

Frederic S. Pearson is the Director of the Center for Peace and Conflict Studies and a Professor of Political Science at Wayne State University. He is the author of books on international relations, small countries in crisis and the international arms trade. He also has conducted numerous studies on international military interventions and has related these phenomena to changes in the distribution of arms.

Ravinder Pal Singh leads a SIPRI project on arms procurement decision making in selected countries. He combines military experience with advanced academic research at the Centre of Disarmament Studies, Jawahar Lal Nehru

University, New Delhi. As a Ford Fellow at the University of Maryland, he has worked on the US foreign policy processes in developing the MTCR. As a Senior Fellow at the Institute for Defence Studies & Analyses, New Delhi, he has been working on arms control issues.

Augusto Varas is Senior Researcher and Director of the International Relations and Security Studies Department at the Latin American Faculty of Social Sciences (FLACSO-Chile). He coordinates the "Peace and Security for the Americas Project", conjunction with The Woodrow Wilson Center for International Scholars (Washington, D.C.). He is also the editor of the Latin American quarterly *Armed Forces and Society* and the yearbook *Strategic Latin American Study*. His recent co-edited books are *Confidence Building Measures in Latin America* (FLACSO, Santiago, 1994) and *Security, Development and Democracy* (Pathfinder Publishers, New York, forthcoming).

Ambassador Hendrik Wagenmakers is a career officer of the Netherlands Foreign Service. Graduate of the Free University of Amsterdam and one-time visiting fellow of Oxford University (UK), he has served in a number of diplomatic posts, including Manila, Bangkok, Brussels and the Netherlands Mission to the European Community. His present post is as Head of the Netherlands delegation to the Geneva Conference on Disarmament, concurrently leader of the Netherlands delegation to the First Committee of the UN General Assembly, and Chairman of the 1994 Group of Governmental Experts on the UN Register of Conventional Arms.